**Information and Communication Technologies
for Development and Poverty Reduction**

**Other Books Published in Cooperation with
the International Food Policy Research Institute**

IFPRI

Agricultural Science Policy: Changing Global Agendas
Edited by Julian M. Alston, Philip G. Pardey, and Michael J. Taylor

*The Politics of Precaution: Genetically Modified Crops
in Developing Countries*
By Robert L. Paarlberg

*Land Tenure and Natural Resource Management:
A Comparative Study of Agrarian Communities in Asia and Africa*
Edited by Keijiro Otsuka and Frank Place

*Seeds of Contention: World Hunger and the Global Controversy
over GM Crops*
By Per Pinstrup-Andersen and Ebbe Schøler

*Innovation in Natural Resource Management: The Role of Property Rights
and Collective Action in Developing Countries*
Edited by Ruth Meinzen-Dick, Anna Knox, Frank Place, and Brent Swallow

Reforming Agricultural Markets in Africa
By Mylène Kherallah, Christopher Delgado, Eleni Gabre-Madhin,
Nicholas Minot, and Michael Johnson

The Triangle of Microfinance: Financial Sustainability, Outreach, and Impact
Edited by Manfred Zeller and Richard L. Meyer

Ending Hunger in Our Lifetime: Food Security and Globalization
By C. Ford Runge, Benjamin Senauer, Philip G. Pardey,
and Mark W. Rosegrant

*Household Decisions, Gender, and Development:
A Synthesis of Recent Research*
Edited by Agnes R. Quisumbing

*WTO, Agriculture, and Developing Countries:
Lessons from the Indian Experience*
By Ashok Gulati and Anwarul Hoda

Land and Schooling: Transferring Wealth across Generations
By Agnes R. Quisumbing, Jonna P. Estudillo, and Keijiro Otsuka

What's Economics Worth? Valuing Policy Research
Edited by Philip G. Pardey and Vincent H. Smith

Information and Communication Technologies for Development and Poverty Reduction

The Potential of Telecommunications

EDITED BY MAXIMO TORERO AND JOACHIM VON BRAUN

Published for the International Food Policy Research Institute

The Johns Hopkins University Press
Baltimore

© 2006 The International Food Policy Research Institute
All rights reserved. Published 2006
Printed in the United States of America on acid-free paper
9 8 7 6 5 4 3 2 1

The Johns Hopkins University Press
2715 North Charles Street
Baltimore, Maryland 21218-4363
www.press.jhu.edu

International Food Policy Research Institute
2033 K Street, NW
Washington, D.C. 20006
(202) 862-5600
www.ifpri.org

LIBRARY OF CONGRESS CATALOGING-IN-PUBLICATION DATA

Information and communication technologies for development and poverty reduction : the
potential of telecommunications / edited by Maximo Torero and Joachim von Braun
   p. cm.
  "Published for the International Food Policy Research Institute."
  Includes bibliographical references and index.
  ISBN 0-8018-8041-6 (alk. paper) — ISBN 0-8018-8226-5 (pbk.: alk. paper)
  1. Telecommunication—Developing countries—Case studies. 2. Economic development—
Case studies. I. Torero Cullen, Máximo. II. Von Braun, Joachim, 1950–
HE8635.I52   2006
384.09172′4—dc22   2005052796

A catalog record for this book is available from the British Library.

Contents

Figures

Tables

Foreword

The development and spread of information and communication technologies (ICT) to all areas of human activities is accelerating changes in economies and the societies worldwide. ICT has not only changed the mode of doing business, it has also changed the mode of all communications. The change is dramatic, both in speed and style. All indications tell us that it is going to be still more dramatic in the years to come.

Four things impress me very much about ICT: it connects everybody and everything at a very basic level, and it is borderless, timeless, and, best of all, almost costless. With all these attributes combined, ICT has enormous potential to create a new human society, and a new civilization. By itself ICT will not create or destroy anything. It will facilitate the rise of human capabilities to new heights. The creative design and innovative use of ICT will accomplish this. I have been urging, as passionately as I can, that we should not allow the future of mankind to be decided by the random needs, whims, and pleasures of individual users of ICT. Let there be a global vision, and a global commitment to translate this vision into reality through the use of ICT in the most creative ways. We must put the full power of ICT to use to accomplish the fond dreams of all ages: ending poverty and hunger, ensuring equality of all human beings, human rights for all, gender equality, equal opportunity to all, healthcare for all, education for all, good governance, peace among nations, and so on.

ICT can perform miracles in making human dreams come true faster than anything else, provided we devote our creativity and ingenuity in that direction. It must be a deliberate decision, carried out with nonstop efforts. Since we know very well that necessity is the mother of invention, we have to sit down and define our necessities and prioritize them. Every single effort for ending poverty in the world can become more effective with ICT than ever before. ICT has one great quality—we can use it for any purpose. It fits snugly into any need we want to use it for. If we want to solve the problem of hungry people finding food, ICT will help if we can come up with the right idea.

I even argue that ICT can become an "Aladdin's Lamp" in the hands of a poor woman. When she rubs the lamp, the digital genie will come out of the lamp and say, "What can I do for you, Ma'am?" And the genie will make sure she gets the best possible solution to her problem.

Presently ICT designers are not paying attention to exploring these issues. Overwhelmingly, ICT is now used for making life easier for people whose life already is easier than it is for most. Since ICT is being looked at as a tool to make businesses flourish, designers are busy filling business-to-business and business-to-consumer needs.

We at Grameen Bank have tried to bring ICT to the poor. We give loans to our borrowers to become telephone ladies. A borrower buys a cell phone and starts the business of providing telecommunications service to villagers. She achieves instant success. She does so well in this business that her family moves out of poverty in about two years. There are now 170,000 telephone ladies in this program. By next year we expect the number to reach 300,000. In each telephone lady's case, the telephone is not only a business, it is power in her hand—social, economic, political, and personal power.

Of course, ICT is much more than just making phone calls. We have a whole range of possibilities to empower each poor person and enable them to break out of poverty. Poverty is nothing but layers and layers of old ideas and economic and social relationships that keep the poor tightly wrapped, like a cocoon. Poor people need the power to cut themselves free from their cocoons and be liberated. ICT can play the most effective role in helping the poor cut through their cocoons.

This book makes an important contribution to our understanding of the potential that ICT has in making that happen. It does so by clarifying the conditions that are necessary for success. The book points out that in order to make it usable and useful to the poor, ICT must be conceptualized differently, with appropriate design of the gadgets and institutions. An upsurge of innovations is needed. Social business entrepreneurs have to step in in a big way, along with conventional businesses and government. It is my hope that the research reported in this book will help catalyze a big effort to widen poor people's access to ICT in ways that will make it easier and quicker for them to get out of poverty and go far beyond it.

Professor Muhammad Yunus
Founder, Managing Director
Grameen Bank, Bangladesh
November 8, 2005

Acknowledgments

The initial inspiration for this work came from the combination of global enthusiasm for the Okinawa Charter declaration, aimed at bridging the digital divide; the desire to enact the recommendations of G8's Digital Opportunity Task Force, an initiative in which we actively participated as members and discussants; and the success of the "village phone" concept, developed by the Grameen Bank with village-based microenterprises in Bangladesh. This led to the exploration of research opportunities for IFPRI on the important role of ICT for rural growth and poverty reduction, the results of which now constitute this book.

We are indebted to several knowledgeable researchers who attended one or more presentations of the material contained in the book, and to many individuals who contributed to the book's completion. We would also like to acknowledge the valuable suggestions of our colleagues at IFPRI, the Institute's Publication Review Committee, and the anonymous reviewers whose contributions improved the manuscript enormously.

The financial support of several institutions also enabled us to carry out this work. We acknowledge funding from the Center for Development Research (ZEF), the International Development Research Center (IDRC), the Tinker Foundation, and the KFW Development Bank; scholarships from the German Academic Exchange Service (DAAD); and the Georg Forster Research Fellowship from the Alexander von Humboldt Foundation, which supported Maximo Torero's initial research.

We are also pleased to acknowledge IFPRI's Communications Division, especially Uday Mohan, for support in the publication of the book, Mary Jane Banks for her superb editing of the manuscript, Vicky Lee and Joy Fabela for their secretarial support, and Jose Deustua for his research assistance in the final stages of manuscript preparation. Finally, we extend our appreciation to our families for their support and forbearance during the book's preparation, particularly over the many weekends spent finalizing it.

Abbreviations

2SLS	two-stage least squares
ADB	Asian Development Bank
ADP	accelerated development program (Ghana)
BRTA	Bangladesh Rural Telecom Authority
BSNL	Bharat Sanchar Nigam, Ltd. (India)
BTRC	Bangladesh Telecommunication Regulatory Commission
BTTB	Bangladesh Telegraph and Telephone Board
CAD	computer-aided design
CAGR	compound annual growth rate
CAM	computer-aided manufacture
CNC	computer numerical controlled
CPT	*Compañía Peruana de Teléfonos* [Peruvian Telecommunications Company]
CRS	contractual responsibility system (China)
CSC	China–Singapore Cable project (Laos)
CV	compensating variation
DLC	distance learning center
D-MAS	see DRCS
DMEOUs	domestic-market- and export-oriented units
DMOUs	domestic-market-oriented units
DOT Force	Digital Opportunity Task Force
DPT	diphtheria, tetanus, and pertussis vaccine
DRCS	digital radio concentrator system
ENTEL	*Empresa Nacional de Telecomunicaciones* [National Telecommunications Company] (Peru)
EOUs	export-oriented units
EPTL	*Entreprise d'Etat des Postes et Telecommunications Lao* [Laos Postal and Telecommunications Company]
ERP software	enterprise resource planning software
ETL	*Entreprise de Télécommunications Lao* [Laos Telecommunications Company]

FITEL	OSPITEL's Fund for Investment in Telecommunications (Peru)
GATS	General Agreement on Trade in Services
GDP	gross domestic product
GGT	Gerber garment technology
GMM	generalized method of moments
GMS	Greater Mekong Subregion
GNPC	Ghanaian Petroleum Company
GRADE	*Grupo de Análisis para el Desarrollo* [Group for the Analysis of Development] (Peru)
GSD system	general sewing data system
GSM	global system for mobile communication
GTC	Grameen Telecom (Bangladesh)
ICT	information and communication technologies
ILD	international long distance
IMF	International Monetary Fund
IMIS	integrated management information systems
ISDN	integrated services digital network
ISP(s)	Internet service provider(s)
IT	information technology
ITU	International Telecommunications Union
KFW	*Kreditanstalt für Wiederaufbau* [German Development Bank]
LAN	local area network
LDCs	least developed countries
LECS	Laos Expenditure and Consumption Survey
LSTC	Laos Shinawatra Telecommunications Company
LTC	Laos Telecommunications Company
MCTPC	Ministry of Construction, Transportation, Postal Services, and Communications (Laos)
MD	managing director
MIC	Millicom International Cellular
MMS	marker maker systems
MOPT	Ministry of Postal Services and Telecommunications (Bangladesh)
MPT	Ministry of Postal Services and Telecommunications (China)
MTC	Ministry of Transport and Communications (Ghana)
NCA	National Communications Authority (Ghana)
NEM	new economic mechanism (Laos)
NGO	nongovernmental organization
OECD	Organisation for Economic Co-operation and Development
OLS	ordinary least squares

OSIPTEL	*Oganísmo Supervisor de Inversión Privada en Telecomunicaciones* [Supervisory Agency for Private Investment in Telecommunications] (Peru)
PBTL	Pacific Bangladesh Telecom Limited (also known as City Cell)
PC(s)	personal computer(s)
PCO	public call office
PIM	perpetual inventory method
PPP	purchasing power parity
PSTN	public switched telephone network
PTO	postal and telecommunications operator
R&D	research and development
RTO	regional telecommunication operator (Kenya)
Rurtel	Rural Telecommunications (Laos)
SEL	socioeconomic level
SMEs	small- and medium-sized enterprises
SOC	social overhead capital
SOEs	state-owned enterprises
TCCL	Tanzania Telecommunications Company Ltd.
TFP	total factor productivity
UNDP	United Nations Development Programme
UNECA	United Nations Economic Commission for Africa
UNFCCC	United Nations Framework Convention on Climate Change
USAID	United States Agency for International Development
USO	universal service obligation
UUCPs	unix to unix copy
UUPC	unix-to-unix copy protocol
VOIP	voice over Internet protocol
VPP program	village payphone program (Bangladesh)
VSAT	very small aperture terminal
VSNL	Videsh Sanchar Nigam, Ltd. (India)
WDI	World Development Indicators
WSF	World Space Foundation
WTO	World Trade Organization
ZEF	*Zentrum fur Entwicklungsforschung* [Center for Development Research] (Germany)

**Information and Communication Technologies
for Development and Poverty Reduction**

1 Introduction and Overview

JOACHIM VON BRAUN AND MAXIMO TORERO

Scope and Approach

We live in the age of information. The development and proliferation of electronically communicated information has accelerated economic and social change across all areas of human activity worldwide, and it continues to do so at a rapid pace. While the use of information and communication technologies (ICT) largely remains concentrated in the developed world, ICT diffusion is reaching developing countries, bringing with it high hopes of positive development outcomes. Yet why is ICT—among so many modern technologies—assigned such importance in the development context? Certainly, through its inherent public-good characteristics, ICT is unique in having an impact beyond the individual user's welfare as a consumption good. Moreover, ICT infrastructure offers specific economies of scale that stimulate network building and network externalities (meaning that an existing ICT user may well benefit from the addition of new network users). But economic performance is determined not only by financial and human capital but also by social capital (Coleman 1988; Putnam 1993; Fukuyama 1995; Knack and Keefer 1998). Relationships form a network, and the network's size and diversity determine access to information. ICT enables interactive communication unhindered by distance, volume, medium, or time. This feature promotes greater inclusion of individuals within networks and, even more importantly, increases diversity of participation by overcoming the barriers of physical distance and social standing. The immediacy and reach of ICT also promote faster, more efficient, and ultimately better decisionmaking across all fields of endeavor. ICT has the potential to accelerate growth, create jobs, reduce migration pressure from rural to urban areas, increase agricultural and industrial productivity, increase services and access to them, facilitate the diffusion of innovations, increase public administration efficiency and the effectiveness of economic reforms, strengthen competitiveness in developing countries, and encourage greater public participation and democracy (G8 2000; DOT Force 2001; UNDP 2001). In short, ICT has

1

the potential to foster not only economic development and democracy but also sustainability in the process.

It must be noted, however, that some commentators are much more skeptical in their views of the benefits of ICT for development. They argue that access to ICT largely depends on education, income, and wealth, and that the so-called digital divide is only a part of a much broader development divide (Hewitt de Alcántara 2001; Sciadas-Orbicom 2002; Sciadas 2003). Limited education, inadequate language skills, or lack of resources could prevent disadvantaged segments of the population from accessing ICT, ultimately exacerbating information gaps and increasing income inequality between and within countries. The income gap would be widened further if ICT use raises the demand for skilled labor and—by its introduction into manufacturing and service industries—reduces the demand for unskilled labor, at least in the short term. It is often argued that developing countries have other, more pressing investment priorities, such as food, safe water, education, and public health, and that devoting limited resources to ICT must be justified on the basis of its opportunity costs relative to other development agendas (Heeks 1999). Finally, the spread of ICT has led several commentators to argue that it is creating a new "information economy" whereby information is becoming the critical resource and basis for competition, leaving developing countries with no choice but to invest in ICT in order to participate in the emerging global economy and avoid the tremendous costs of exclusion (Bedi 1999). On this basis, the goal may be not so much bridging the digital divide but rather ensuring that it does not expand.

Little conceptual and empirical research has been conducted to study the direct and indirect economic linkages between ICT and poverty reduction. The variety of views about ICT indicate that its role in development is unclear, especially without convincing evidence of its impact.[1] Although it may be true that the spread of ICT is a global trend that developing countries cannot afford to ignore, it is important to explore proactively the conditions that would be required for ICT to contribute positively to sustainable development and, consequently, to poverty reduction. This book attempts to shed light on how ICT affects economic development in low-income countries, how it affects poor people in these countries, and what policies and programs facilitate its potential to enhance development and the inclusion of poor constituents. Poverty is looked at from the perspective of "livelihood security," which comprises

---

1. Harris (2004), for example, describes how ICT is used to alleviate poverty. The authors provide several case studies, although they show significant variation in terms of impacts. Sciadas (2003) focuses on the macro-level in developing a framework to quantify and monitor the divide in order to compare data across countries and within countries over time. The authors found that the same kinds of ICT that create the digital divide (Internet use, cellular phones, and Internet networks) are also the ones that have the potential to overcome it.

income—determined by physical and human capital, labor, social networks, rights and powers, and access to public goods—and risk (or vulnerability), which is a function of local and international conditions, human behavior, and the probability of shocks affecting income such as illness, loss of employment, natural disasters, and so on.

Today ICT is generally understood to encompass both equipment and services that facilitate the electronic capture, processing, display, and transmission of information. In broad terms this includes the computing industry (hardware, software, networks, the Internet, and related services); electronic data processing and display (such as photocopiers, cash registers, calculators, and scanners, as well as a myriad of less well-known machines specifically tailored to production and manufacturing);[2] telecommunications and related services (such as fixed and cellular telephones, facsimile machines, instant messaging, teleconferencing, and so on); and audiovisual equipment and services (including television, radio, video, DVDs, digital cameras, compact disks, MP3 players, and so on). As previously mentioned, few studies have looked at the prospective relationship between ICT and development, especially from an economic perspective and with appropriate economic rigor. A significant inhibiting factor is the dearth of comprehensive statistical data—although efforts are currently under way to address this issue. In the interim, we need to rely on the information that is available. For this reason, and because telephony is the primary infrastructure that facilitates ICT access, this volume largely focuses on telephony as a proxy for ICT more generally. When it comes to a direct link to poor communities and poor people, the telephone still plays a key role. Although the telephone was invented more than a century ago, many people still have never made a phone call, and universal service provision in poor areas of low-income countries—in terms of neighborhoods, not necessarily households—has yet to be achieved. Realistically, for the foreseeable future, telephony is the ICT that will have the greatest penetration and impact when it comes to poor people. Telephony is important not only as a channel of improved access to information and communications but also as a prerequisite for the widespread use of more advanced technologies such as the Internet. Internet services have increasingly become important for the delivery of pro-poor public goods and community services—such as the use of very small aperture terminals (VSATs) for wireless Internet access in remote areas and voice recognition systems for illiterate users—especially as costs drop and as technologies advance to overcome

---

2. The case study on garment manufacturing enterprises in India presented in Chapter 4 of this volume provides a good example, whereby computer-aided design (CAD) is used in combination with scanners and plotters to create and modify patterns; determine fabric layouts that reduce fabric wastage; and transpose electronic patterns to paper, saving the time and labor that would otherwise be required to perform these functions manually.

difficulties in service provision. Nonetheless, Internet service penetration is still low, and the majority of Internet users are in developed countries and the more affluent segments of developing-country populations.

It is important also to keep in mind that access to information through ICT is a question not only of *connectivity* but also of *capability* to use the new tools. It is also dependent on *content,* in terms of relevant information provided in accessible and useful forms. While these three "Cs" are certainly critical, it is the first, connectivity, that matters most for poor people given that it is a pre-requisite for the others. This will be shown in some of the detailed micro-studies in the volume. ICT development, meaning improvement of the three "Cs" within a given country, depends on a set of supply-and-demand interactions between domestic and international public and private driving forces.

For poor people, the ability to use and to access information efficiently is critical in terms of resource allocation, be it labor, capital, or natural resources. On this basis, ICT can affect all the determinants of livelihood security mentioned earlier and, in doing so, reduce poverty. More specifically, ICT may contribute to poverty alleviation through the following avenues:

- *Making markets more accessible to both households and small enterprises.* For households, see, for example, Arunachalam (2002) and Bhatnagar and Schware (2000) on lessons drawn from experiences in 17 cases in applications of ICT in the delivery of services or products in rural areas in India; for small enterprises, see, for example, Duncombe and Heeks (2001) and Tanburn and Singh (2001).
- *Improving the quality of public goods provision, such as health services.* In developed nations, for example, the Internet is already being used as a key source of health information by individuals and practitioners (see, for example, Eysenback, Sa, and Diepgen 1999; Braa et al. 2001; Riegelman and Persily 2001; and Séror 2001). Similar trends in ICT access are found throughout the developing world, where a number of case studies world-wide show evidence of the potential for ICT to influence health outcomes in rural areas. For instance, doctors in rural Cambodia report benefiting from greater access to health information through mobile wi-fi (wireless) systems in rural schools (Brooke 2004). In Andhra Pradesh, India, a group of hospitals have established a center that offers medical advice via email to rural inhabitants with low-cost access to ICT. In Sub-Saharan Africa, the Internet has helped remote communities access health information, receive professional help for X-ray film evaluations, detect emerging epidemics, and facilitate vaccination campaigns (Harris 2002).
- *Improving the quality of human resources, primarily through education services.* A typical example is the African Virtual University, a network of universities that have joined with the World Bank in bringing courses in

computer science and business management to African students and professionals (www.avu.org).[3]

- *Allowing more effective utilization of existing social networks, or extending them.* For example, some forms of ICT have been used to design global telecommunications networks such as HealthNet,[4] which links healthcare workers around the world via email.
- *Creating new institutional arrangements to strengthen the rights and powers of poor people and communities.* For example, Fleming (2002) explores some of the potential and current reality of using ICT to strengthen democracy development in South Africa; the study concludes that access to information does play a crucial role in informing citizens about government activities, thus encouraging people to engage with decisionmakers on issues of governance.

Technological change in ICT reduces the unit price of goods and services and stimulates the development and adoption of new products. This is facilitated in part by foreign and domestic research and development (R&D) policies and by prevailing regulatory frameworks. Thus, low-income countries, and poor people in particular, have next to no impact—either directly or indirectly—in determining market expansion or development. And while they have an extremely marginal role when it comes to demand, they have even less influence on the forces that drive the supply of ICT. This reality is increasingly being recognized and has prompted international public action, or at least calls for action.[5] This is partly driven by the perception that there may be tremendous underinvestment in ICT for the poor and in related pro-poor public goods. Moreover,

---

3. For possible impacts on distance learning see Day, Raven, and Newman (1998) and Navarro and Shoemaker (2000).

4. HealthNet is provided by a nonprofit organization, SatelLife, with assistance from local and international partners. More than 10,000 members worldwide currently use the system, and many physicians rely on HealthNet as their sole source of information on HIV/AIDS and tropical diseases. For more information see www.healthnet.org.

5. The Digital Opportunity Task Force (DOT Force) sprang from the G8 summit held in Kyushu-Okinawa (Japan) in July 2000. At the summit, a charter on the global information society was adopted by leaders from G8 countries (Canada, France, Germany, Italy, Japan, Russia, the United Kingdom, and the United States). This, the Okinawa Charter, provided the mandate under section 18 for the establishment of DOT Force, which was subsequently formed during the fourth quarter of 2000 (see www.dotforce.org). Similarly, the United Nations ICT Task Force, which was launched in November 2001, aims to "provide overall leadership to the United Nations role in helping to formulate strategies for the development of information and communication technologies and putting those technologies at the service of development and, on the basis of consultations with all stakeholders and Member States, forging a strategic partnership between the United Nations system, private industry and financing trusts and foundations, donors, programme countries and other relevant stakeholders in accordance with relevant United Nations resolutions (www.unicttaskforce .org/about/planofaction.html).

the potential to include the poor and low-income countries via fast-tracking access to new ICT (also known as leapfrogging)[6] has raised additional expectations and hopes. As in discussions on the issues of ICT for development in general, much of the expected positive impact of ICT on poverty and low-income countries remains hypothetical. Equally hypothetical is the possibility that low-income countries and poor people in the services sector may be adversely affected by ICT because certain jobs related to information gathering, information, and communications may be taken over by new technologies. Overall, this volume aims to offer a conceptual clarification of the potential and emerging impacts of ICT on low-income and poor countries and how the direction of these impacts could be guided to benefit the poor. The available literature consists mostly of journalistic or short-term business studies rather than in-depth conceptual and empirical research on the impact of ICT at the household or community level, and on how the small and medium-sized enterprise (SME) sector in low-income countries has been or will be affected by ICT. Similarly, it is said that there is huge potential for ICT to deliver important pro-poor public goods, such as relevant types of health and education services, but there is little research on outcomes. Acknowledging that the majority of poor people live in rural areas, this book aims to reduce some of these deficits by presenting and synthesizing new research in this field and by providing theoretical and conceptual analyses to guide policy priorities, teaching, and further research. Thus, the objective is to explore the actual and potential linkages between ICT, economic growth, and development in low-income countries and the direct and indirect effects of ICT on poor people's livelihoods.

The book's broad conceptual framework examines the driving forces affecting the supply of and demand for ICT. It also identifies economic and social benefits in general and poverty outcomes in particular, as summarized in a simplified chart (Figure 1.1).

Figure 1.2 and Table 1.1 provide more detail on this conceptual framework to illustrate how ICT could promote economic and social benefits. The framework will be revisited in subsequent chapters as new material is presented. Essentially, the issues addressed are the high costs of acquiring information and how these costs may cause markedly different behavior than would have occurred if information had been more readily available.

Lack of information may reduce the extent of mutually beneficial exchanges and lead to economywide inefficiencies. Information constraints will also cause considerable market and event uncertainty surrounding economic and administrative decisions in least developed countries (LDCs). Such insecurity has implications for the efficiency, productivity, and welfare of various agents

---

6. Leapfrogging implies skipping many, if not most, of the rungs of the technology development "ladder" by directly adopting more advanced technologies.

FIGURE 1.1 ICT and development: A conceptual base

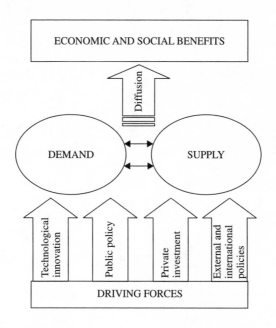

FIGURE 1.2 Conceptual framework: Driving forces and impacts of ICT

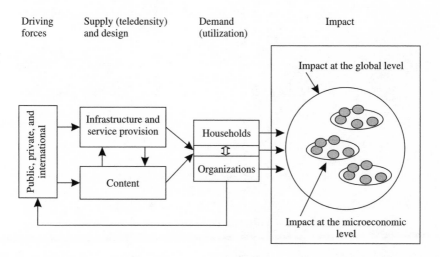

TABLE 1.1 Elements of conceptual framework

Driving forces	Supply	Demand	Impacts
Technical innovation	Supply of infrastructure	Service access	Economic benefits
Public policy	Availability of service	Intensity of use	Reduced transaction costs
External and international	Quality of service	Required investment	Increased efficiency
	Critical mass	Frequency of use	Market expansion
	Information	Motivation for use	Social benefits
	Supply of content		Improved social service provision
	Information		Emergency/disaster management
	Education, health, and so on		Decentralization/empowerment
			Strengthened informal social safety nets

in the economy, and, in this context, ICT can play a key role by facilitating the acquisition and processing of information. While the development of appropriate infrastructure will have direct and indirect effects for people and organizations, the economic effect will be reduced transaction costs, expanded markets, and increased efficiency. At the same time, ICT could help to provide better social services and strengthen informal social safety nets. Regardless, driving forces in the form of public, private, and international institutions are necessary preconditions for ICT growth.

The book describes empirical studies from a variety of developing countries (Figure 1.3), providing a view of the impact of ICT under different social, economic, and especially institutional conditions (Figure 1.4).

Hypotheses and Issues Addressed

Neither unduly enthusiastic nor untested negative positions are taken throughout the volume regarding the potential and limitations of ICT for poverty reduction. Five sets of critical hypotheses were formulated from a clearly skeptical perspective to challenge both the authors and the readers. These hypotheses form the basis of the book's five main chapters (Chapters 2 through 6):

1. *No clear link exists between ICT growth and economic growth; a key factor may be the lack of a critical mass.* Leapfrogging is not happening, and ICT in developing countries has not reached the critical mass necessary to capture network externalities; hence, gaps between high- and low-income countries are widening, and impacts are not reflected in economic growth. This is addressed in Chapter 2.
2. *Weak institutions block effective use of ICT.* The institutional setup in developing countries is insufficient to facilitate public and private investment in ICT infrastructure at a scale and scope to meet the specific needs of the economic structure and rural–urban settlement patterns. In other words, lack of institutional development hinders fundamental supply and demand interactions in ICT markets. This is addressed in Chapter 3.
3. *ICT has not been adapted to low-income countries and no impact is seen on SMEs or households.*
   a. *SME access to ICT remains constrained.* As ICT is basically developed by and marketed in high-income countries, lack of appropriate technologies and content persists. Adaptation and innovation are not occurring because institutional and market strength in low-income countries is lacking. This is addressed in Chapter 4.
   b. *Household access to ICT remains constrained.* ICT in low-income countries—implicitly or explicitly—excludes poor people, especially those in rural areas and urban ghettos, thereby accelerating their marginalization. In addition to the issues of price and availability, there

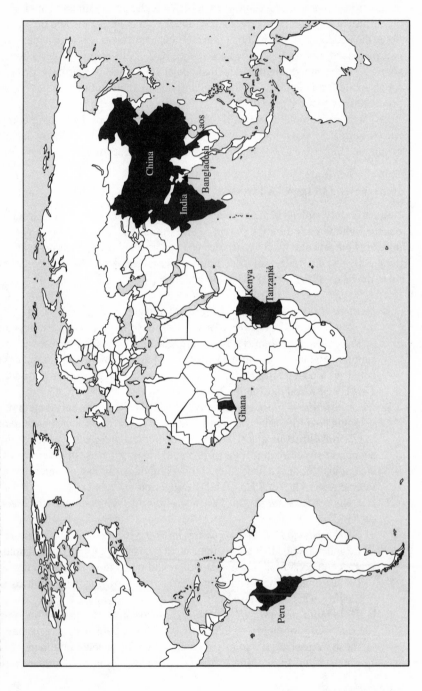

FIGURE 1.3 Countries included in the book

FIGURE 1.4　Numbers of fixed telephone lines and gross domestic product per capita, 2000

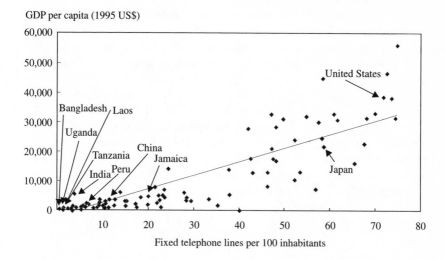

GDP per capita (1995 US$)

Fixed telephone lines per 100 inhabitants

SOURCE:　ITU (2002).
NOTE:　The figure includes data for 138 countries.

seem to be three principal types of barriers preventing the effectiveness of ICT in influencing household behavior, knowledge, and economic activity. These are barriers that prevent the use of ICT for purposes related to household economic activity; barriers resulting from lack of the skills needed to access online information; and barriers to the diffusion of online content. This is addressed in Chapter 5.

4. *ICT has yet to play a role in the provision of pro-poor public goods and services.* A number of potential barriers to the effectiveness of ICT exist in rural areas. Apart from the provision of facilities and technical support, sociocultural factors are likely to affect the success of ICT interventions related to health, education, and other public goods and services in terms of information diffusion generally and the impact of providing information via the Internet. This is addressed in Chapter 6.

Overview and Structure of the Book

An overview of the book is provided below, once again within the context of the five hypotheses introduced earlier. The hypotheses are also revisited, tested, and assessed throughout the book, particularly in the concluding chapter (Chapter 7).

Economic Growth and Pro-Poor Development

Because of the potentially important role of economic growth for pro-poor development (Dollar and Kraay 2002), Chapter 2 examines the linkage between economic growth and ICT through an empirical analysis of international and cross-country comparisons, focusing on the driving forces and broad development outcomes of ICT. As mentioned, inadequate communications facilities and high transmission costs reduce the use of existing information in developing countries and inhibit production of new information. Hence, the introduction of reliable and speedy ICT may have several effects. First, reduced transmission costs will lead to a rightward shift in the information supply curve—meaning a reduction in price and an increase in the quantity of information. Second, increased ICT will reduce the cost of producing and processing information, thereby increasing the amount of information, in turn further reducing the price. The use of ICT will also likely enhance the quality of available information as the technologies foster timely and reliable information delivery. This may lead to improved organizational procedures with respect to management and internal and external relationships, which would eventually bring about improvement in a country's overall economic performance.

One of the revolutionary aspects of ICT is the decoupling of information from property, which enables information to be immediately transmitted and shared by many people without the physical movement of information or people (Evans and Wurster 1997; Pohjola 1998). This nonrival use of information may generate large content-related externalities. The use of ICT networks is also nonrival in nature, and an increase in network size generates network externalities. Thus, the effects of ICT cannot be understood by looking at single enterprises or households only: changes in business networks and other social relationships must also be considered. ICT is not just a technological innovation; it also increases the knowledge content of products and services and brings about previously unknown products, jobs, and livelihoods.

On the other hand, there are several prerequisites to realizing the benefits of ICT, and as the technology becomes more sophisticated, more resources and skills are needed. Accessing information via ICT requires numerous resources, including telecommunications infrastructure to provide network access, electrical infrastructure to power ICT, skills to maintain the technologies, money to buy or access the technologies, skills to utilize the technologies, and literacy and language skills to understand the content (Heeks 1999). Recent empirical research across a large number of countries has shown that a broad range of social, economic, and political factors need to be in place for ICT development—and especially Internet development—to occur in a country. The presence of the technology is insufficient; it also depends on educational attainment, political freedom, a service-based economy, and technological infrastructure (Robinson and Crenshaw 1999).

In the presence of ICT externalities, and in the possible presence of a reverse causal relationship between ICT use and development (meaning that development could be causing ICT growth rather than the other way around), capturing the effects of increased ICT access is not an easy task. The effects of other factors such as trade liberalization and shifts in demand patterns because of changes in income make the task more complicated. The same is true for determining the relationship between ICT investments and growth. Whereas several authors find a positive correlation using a simple econometric framework, other estimates that take econometric problems such as omitted variables and endogeneity bias into account indicate that telecommunications density (teledensity for short)[7] has no impact on growth (Jimenez 1995; Bedi 1999). The positive associations between ICT and growth may be mutually reinforcing because countries experiencing high growth might have higher demand for and investment in these new technologies; the technologies may in turn provide the potential for future income growth.

Röller and Waverman (2001) present cross-country estimates of the effect of telecommunications on output based on a cross-section of 21 countries of the Organisation for Economic Co-operation and Development (OECD) over 20 years. The two-way relationships between growth and ICT require careful consideration in estimating real impacts. The authors account for these issues of endogeneity by estimating a four-equation model that enables them to capture the impact of telecommunications infrastructure. They also control for fixed effects (meaning additional unobserved variables that are fixed over time and can influence the results) within countries. Despite the drop in the magnitude of the elasticity on the telecommunication infrastructure, the growth effect attributed to telecommunications infrastructure is still quite large.

Chapter 2 adopts a framework and specification similar to those used by Röller and Waverman (2001), whereby telecommunications are endogenized by estimating a demand and supply model for telecommunication investments. A macroproduction function is simultaneously estimated. The empirical work is based on a data set that includes 113 countries and covers a time period from 1960 to 2000. The primary aim is to examine whether the idea of a critical mass is valid for a larger sample of nations and a longer time period, emphasizing an examination of this relationship for developing countries in particular.

Institutional Aspects and Public Policy Issues

From the 1960s and 1970s, advances in neoclassical economic theory investigated the causes and consequences of transaction costs, uncertainty, incomplete markets, and imperfect and asymmetric information, challenging the traditional

---

7. Teledensity (also referred to as penetration rate) is the number of telephone lines per 100 inhabitants.

assumptions of costless exchange at market clearing prices. This provided a new perspective—the "information-theoretic" approach to understanding development (Bedi 1999), which is illustrated by the costly nature of acquiring information, especially in the developing-country context (Geertz 1978). Difficulties involved in accessing and using information in developing countries have numerous implications for the poor. The high costs for acquiring information lead to less information input in decisionmaking processes and thus potentially suboptimal behavior. Eventually, lack of information may reduce mutually beneficial exchanges and lead to economywide Pareto inefficiencies (Greenwald and Stiglitz 1986; Arnott, Greenwald, and Stiglitz 1994). Thus, alleviating information constraints helps developing countries to reduce poverty and accelerate economic development. Consequently, the key role of ICT for development lies in its ability to handle and communicate information. Nonetheless, ICT is not a panacea and should not replace other urgent development agenda items. Hence, a basic issue is determining the optimal structure and levels of private and public investment in ICT or information services to achieve maximum benefit at the lowest cost.

Institutional aspects and public policy issues related to ICT are addressed conceptually and theoretically in Chapter 3. The role of government and appropriate regulation (or deregulation) measures are addressed with respect to their effects on the provision of information services at a national level, generally and for disadvantaged populations. The chapter begins with a discussion of the institutional factors needed for ICT to develop, and the kinds of interventions being used today. Essentially, the chapter focuses on how different forces —such as government, market, and individual users—are contributing to the development of ICT in general, and what measures are required to ensure broader and more equitable access to ICT services. Experiences from general development trends in ICT sectors are analyzed, and the cases of five developing and transition countries (Bangladesh, China, Ghana, Laos, and Peru) provide examples of different outcomes under different institutional frameworks.

Economic Effects at the Firm Level

In many developing countries, SMEs account for a significant share of employment; consequently they are linked with poverty reduction. Developing-country SMEs are especially challenged by globalization and the changing importance of various determinants of competitiveness. The basic question is whether the use of ICT can help SMEs increase their productivity and cope with these new challenges.

Business networks that could be strengthened through the availability of better information and communication channels may provide significant benefits to SMEs. They may not only reduce search and screening costs but also help produce economies of scale by efficiently sharing privately owned resources.

They can also form the basis for collective action aimed at the provision of public goods and the facilitation of flows of information about technological and organizational innovations and best practices (Barr 2000). These knowledge spillovers between enterprises can in turn facilitate economic growth (Romer 1993).

The rapid development of ICT might not only increase the performance of existing enterprises but also open up new sectors in which developing countries could gain a comparative advantage. The increased importance of trade in services could then increase the possibilities for developing countries to participate in e-commerce, and the increased use of ICT in enterprises could lead to a substitution of ICT equipment for other forms of capital and labor. In turn, this could generate substantial returns for enterprises that invest in ICT and restructure their organizations. However, this does not necessarily imply that the total factor productivity (TFP) in the whole economy will increase. In fact, though TFP itself has been found to increase with technical change in industrial countries, the overall growth of TFP associated with technical change has actually declined with the increased use of ICT in the past 10–20 years (Jorgenson and Stiroh 1999).

The diffusion of ICT may increase the demand for skilled labor, rendering some traditional skills and a variety of jobs redundant, especially jobs requiring unskilled labor. A large body of empirical literature has examined whether the recent increases in wage inequality in the United States and other developed countries are related to an ICT-induced increase in the relative demand for skilled labor. Consistent with the notion that skilled workers and advanced manufacturing technologies are complements, Doms, Dunne, and Troske (1997) find a positive correlation between the two variables for the United States. While these technologies may exacerbate wage inequality in some countries, the outcome will probably vary from one country or region to another and will be determined by the supply of labor and institutional features of the labor market (Bedi 1999). Furthermore, it is also possible that the diffusion of these technologies may spark an overall expansion in employment that may increase demand for all types of workers. The expansion of ICT may be expected to increase both TFP and the productivity of organizations. The increase in the marginal productivity of labor may lead to an increase in demand for all types of labor. Also, if ICT reduces uncertainty and enhances the efficiency of product and factor markets, its spread may be expected to bring about increases in the flow of capital and in output. The higher employment accompanying these increased investments and outputs may indeed have a positive effect on income distribution.

Chapter 4 moves the analysis to the firm level. It begins with a labor market perspective because the poor are largely labor dependent, asset poor, and essentially concentrated in SMEs. Once again, country case studies look at the role of ICT in the SME sectors in East Africa, India, and Laos. The existing literature deals mostly with phenomena in the developed world (OECD 2004), leaving the role of ICT for SMEs in developing countries largely unexplored. The empirical studies in Chapter 4 fill this gap in part.

Impacts on Low-Income Households

Research on the impact of ICT on households has been rare because households are considered consumptive users of ICT. Regardless of the way the technologies are used, the welfare effects they generate offer insights on the benefits associated with their diffusion to households. Another prevailing perception is that there is little demand for services in rural areas, or that where demand exists, returns to investment are too low to justify investment. Such perceptions are changing as evidence is accumulated on the tangible benefits of ICT to user households.

To look only at the economic impacts of access to ICT would leave important questions unexplored. As ICT is mainly a network technology, how social networks change with its increased use is of special interest. Whereas urban centers in many developing countries rapidly build their telecommunications infrastructure, rural areas still lack the most basic telecommunications services. This rural–urban divide may exacerbate the knowledge gap and continue to fuel trends of polarization. As previously discussed, it has been argued that access to ICT is a function of income and wealth distributions and accordingly that ICT access will be limited to a small segment of the population. With such limited access, information gaps and information inequality may be exacerbated, and information monopolies may be perpetuated. While this is a possibility, there is no reason to believe that access to ICT will be limited to a small segment of the population in every developing country. The latent demands may be there; the problem is whether poor people can afford access. This depends not only on the benefits they derive as consumers or producers but also on the costs determined by supply. Consequently, the distributional outcome in each country will likely differ and will depend on the prevailing policy environment and pattern of allocation of these technologies.

As social networks improve, the transmission and usage of ICT should have a significant impact on urban–rural information flows, bringing better trading opportunities, for example, or greater credit availability. To illustrate, Banerjee (1984) has shown that the level of urban–rural remittances depends on the strength of migrant family ties, especially in the case of married migrants. While there is an obvious need for an overall macro approach to this subject matter (ICT issues cannot be seen outside overall development efforts), the importance of this particular issue warrants micro-level analysis. Chapter 5 attempts to fill this research gap in several ways. Using a common conceptual framework, country case studies from Bangladesh, China, Ghana, Laos, and Peru are presented and synthesized. The analysis focuses on the regional and community context, accessing impacts at the household level in rural areas.

Effective and Pro-Poor Provision of Public Goods and Services

ICT can be of use in more effective provision of pro-poor public goods and services. ICT is expected to influence not only households and the private sector but also government and civil society. The effects on governance include lowering administrative costs as well as enhancing possibilities for social participation. ICT can also assist citizens in organizing their collective activities, thereby strengthening social capital. Chapter 6 assesses the impact of ICT on the provision of public goods and services, focusing on health services.

Electronic governance (e-governance) aims to provide citizens with better services via the latest advances in information technology (IT). E-governance has both social and economic impacts. It can be useful to a variety of stakeholders at various levels in the system: it provides decisionmaking support to the administrators for monitoring, planning, and improving citizen services; it promotes transparency; and it empowers citizens by giving them access to information. With lower administrative costs, smaller government agencies could become viable, and decisionmaking could be effectively decentralized. And because ICT improves monitoring systems, it can help to improve public goods provision, especially in rural areas in terms of basic needs such as access to health, education, and water.

Through better access to independent information and easier networking over long distances, people are able to voice their views and form nongovernmental organizations (NGOs) for support. NGOs could also serve as intermediaries to improve people's access to information. In this context, local Internet content plays an important role in ensuring that people find relevant information they can understand. Current evidence suggests that to achieve sustainability and success, Internet projects for rural and agricultural development must begin by assessing the needs of local community users. This requires an approach that catalyzes local participation; supports information and communication needs assessments; builds awareness of potential Internet uses; builds communities of users; and facilitates locally managed, self-supporting communication and information networks. Such assessment also requires attention to capacity building and institutional strengthening for the intermediary agencies that serve rural populations (that is, NGOs, extension services, healthcare agencies, various government bodies, and the private sector) so that they can make the most appropriate and creative use of Internet tools. In this way, the role of ICT in the provision of public services is evaluated, specifically as it relates to healthcare.

Policies for Digital Opportunities for the Poor
and Further Research Directions

Conclusions for development policy and research are drawn in Chapter 7, and the original five skeptical hypotheses are revisited. The chapter confirms that ICT is not a development panacea, but it does facilitate development. The use of information resources can open up new communication channels for rural households, communities, and support organizations. ICT affects economic indicators such as SME productivity and household welfare; it also fosters new alliances and interpersonal networks, together with lateral and cross-sectoral links between organizations. The latent demand for ICT by poor people is strong because they know very well that information is key to economic and social development. These findings have to be complemented by supply-side analyses. The comparison of countries and studies at different levels—in households and small enterprises, in labor markets, across various levels of income distribution—and of government issues such as administration and regulation are necessary to define where the best opportunities for the efficient use of ICT are, and what complementary measures or infrastructure are needed to realize such opportunities. Factors that influence the relationship between ICT use and outcomes, such as productivity, household performance, and welfare, provide valuable insights on the support needed for ICT projects and facilitate the design of efficient policies. Ultimately, key influences on the growth and diffusion of ICT—regulatory frameworks, choice of technologies, and public action related to ICT investment—can and should be made more broad based and pro-poor.

References

Arnott, R., B. Greenwald, and J. Stiglitz. 1994. Information and economic efficiency. *Information Economics and Policy* 6: 77–88.

Arunachalam, S. 2002. Reaching the unreached: How can we use ICTs to empower the rural poor in the developing world through enhanced access to relevant information?. World Summit on the Information Society (WSIS). <www.itu.int/wsis/docs/background/themes/development/mssrf2.pdf> (accessed February 2005).

Banerjee, B. 1984. The probability, size, and uses of remittances from urban to rural areas in India. *Journal of Development Economics* 16: 293–311.

Barr, D. 2000. Integrated rural development through telecommunications. Sustainable Development Department, FAO, Rome.

Bedi, A. S. 1999. The role of information and communication technologies in economic development: A partial survey. ZEF Discussion Papers on Development Policy 7. Bonn: Center for Development Research (ZEF).

Bhatnagar, S., and R. Schware. 2000. Information and communication technology in development: Cases from India. Thousand Oaks, Calif., USA: Sage.

Braa J., E. Macome, J. L. Da Costa, J. C. Mavimbe, J. L. Nhampossa, B. José, A. Manave, and A. V. Sitoe. 2001. A study of the actual and potential usage of information and communication technology at district and provincial levels in Mozambique with a focus in the health sector. *Electronic Journal on Information Systems in Developing Countries* 5 (1): 29. <www.is.cityu.edu.hk/ejisdc/vol5.htm> (accessed September 2001).

Brooke, J. 2004. Rural Cambodia, though far off the grid, is finding its way online. *New York Times,* January 26.

Coleman, J. 1988. Social capital in the creation of human capital. *American Journal of Sociology* 94: 95–120.

Day, T. M., M. R. Raven, and M. E. Newman. 1998. The effects of world wide web instruction and traditional instruction and learning styles on achievement and changes in student attitudes in a technical writing in agri-communication course. *Journal of Agricultural Education* 39 (4): 65–75.

Dollar, D., and A. Kraay. 2002. Growth is good for the poor. *Journal of Economic Growth* 7 (3): 195–225.

Doms, M., T. Dunne, and K. Troske. 1997. Workers, wages, and technology. *Quarterly Journal of Economics* 112 (1): 253–290.

DOT Force (Digital Opportunity Task Force). 2001. *Digital opportunities for all: Meeting the challenge.* <www.dotforce.org/reports/DOT_Force_Report_v5.0h.doc> (accessed February 2002).

Duncombe, R. A, and R. B. Heeks. 2001. *Information and communication technologies and small enterprise development in Africa: Lessons from Botswana.* Final report prepared for Department for International Development, United Kingdom. Institute for Development Policy and Management, University of Manchester, UK <www.man.ac.uk/idpm/ictsmefs.html> (accessed February 2005).

Evans, P., and T. Wurster. 1997. Strategy and the new economics of information. *Harvard Business Review* (September–October): 71–82.

Eysenbach, G., E. R. Sa, and T. L. Diepgen. 1999. Shopping around the Internet today and tomorrow: Towards the millennium of cybermedicine. *British Medical Journal* 319: 1294–1299.

Fleming, S. 2002. Information and communication technologies (ICTs) and democracy development in the South: Potential and current reality. *Electronic Journal on Information Systems in Developing Countries* 10.

Fukuyama, F. 1995. Social capital and the global economy. *Foreign Affairs* 74 (5): 89–97.

G8. 2000. *Okinawa charter on global information society* <www.dotforce.org/reports/it1.html> (accessed February 2002).

Geertz, C. 1978. The bazaar economy: Information and search in peasant marketing. *American Economic Review* 68: 28–32.

Greenwald, B., and J. E. Stiglitz. 1986. Externalities in economies with imperfect information and incomplete markets. *Quarterly Journal of Economics* 101: 229–264.

Harris, R. 2002. *A framework for poverty alleviation with ICTs.* Roger Harris Associates. <www.communities.org.ru/ci-text/harris.doc> (accessed February 2005).

———. 2004. *Information and communication technologies for poverty alleviation.* One of the e-primer series published by the United Nations Development Programme/ APDIP. <http://eprimers.apdip.net/series/info-economy/poverty-toc> (accessed March 2005).

Heeks, R. 1999. Information and communications technologies, poverty and development. Development Informatics Working Paper Series 5. Manchester, UK, June, Institute of Development Policy and Management, University of Manchester.

Hewitt de Alcántara, C. 2001. The development divide in a digital age: An issue paper. USRISD Programme Papers on Technology, Business and Society No. 4. Geneva: United Nations Research Institute for Social Development (USRISD).

ITU (International Telecommunications Union). 2002. Online database. <www.itu.int/home/index.html> (accessed February 2002).

Jimenez, E. 1995. Human and physical infrastructure: Investment and pricing policies in developing countries. In *Handbook of development economics,* vol. 3b, J. Behrman and T. N. Srinivasan, eds. Amsterdam: North Holland.

Jorgenson, D. W., and K. J. Stiroh. 1999. Information technology and growth. *American Economic Review* 89 (2): 109–115.

Knack, S., and P. Keefer. 1998. Does social capital have an economic payoff? A cross-country investigation. *Quarterly Journal of Economics* 112: 1251–1288.

Navarro, P., and J. Shoemaker. 2000. Performance and perceptions of distance learners in cyberspace. *American Journal of Distance Education* 14 (2): 15–36.

OECD (Organisation for Economic Co-operation and Development). 2004. *The economic impact of ICT: Measurement, evidence, and implications.* Paris: OECD. <www1.oecd.org/publications/e-book/9204051E.PDF> (accessed December 2004).

Pohjola, M. 1998. Information technology and economic development: An introduction to the research issues. WIDER Working Paper 153. Helsinki: World Institute for Development Economics Research, United Nations University.

Putnam, R. D. 1993. *Making democracy work: Civic traditions in modern Italy.* Princeton, N.J., USA: Princeton University Press.

Riegelman, R., and N. A. Persily. 2001. Health information systems and health communications: Narrowband and broadband technologies as core public health competencies. *American Journal of Public Health* 91 (8): 1179–1183.

Robinson, K. K., and E. M. Crenshaw. 1999. Cyber-space and post-industrial transformations: A cross-national analysis of Internet development. Working Paper, Department of Sociology, Ohio State University, December.

Röller, L., and L. Waverman. 2001. Telecommunications infrastructure and economic development. *American Economic Review* 91 (4): 909–923.

Romer, P. M. 1993. Idea gaps and object gaps in economic development. *Journal of Monetary Economics* 32: 543–573.

Sciadas, G. (in collaboration with the Orbicom network). 2002. *Monitoring the digital divide.* (presentation document). Montreal: Orbicom (Network of the UNESCO Chairs in Communications). English version <www.orbicom.uqam.ca/projects/ddi2002/ddi2002.pdf> (accessed December 2004).

Sciadas, G., ed. 2003. *Monitoring the digital divide . . . and beyond.* Montreal: Claude-Yves Charron in association with NRC Press, Canada Institute for Scientific and Technical Information. English version <www.orbicom.uqam.ca/projects/ddi2002/2003_dd_pdf_en.pdf> (accessed December 2004).

Séror, A. 2001. The Internet, global healthcare management systems and sustainable development: Future scenarios. *Electronic Journal on Information Systems in Developing Countries* 5.

Tanburn, J., and A. D. Singh. 2001. ICT and enterprises in developing countries: Hype or opportunity? International Labor Organization SEED Working Paper No. 17. Series on innovation and sustainability in business support services. <www.cefe.net/datenbank/files/4657/2/WP17-2001.pdf> (accessed February, 2005).

UNDP (United Nations Development Programme). 2001. *Human development report 2001: Making new technologies work for human development.* Oxford and New York: Oxford University Press for UNDP.

2 Telecommunications Infrastructure and Economic Growth: A Cross-Country Analysis

MAXIMO TORERO, SHYAMAL K. CHOWDHURY,
AND ARJUN S. BEDI

In recent years, the potential of information and communications technologies (ICT) to facilitate economic development, especially in low-income countries, has attracted considerable attention. Several commentators (Pohjola 2001, for example) have argued that development of these new technologies, in terms of proliferation and accessibility, should be integral to country-level development strategies and that ICT investments are essential in the process of enhancing living standards. Nevertheless, detractors also exist. They counter with the primary argument that developing countries have far more pressing investment priorities, and that investing scarce resources in ICT does not fulfill the needs of the poor (Roche and Blaine 1996; Saith 2002).

Whether additional investments in these technologies are justified and whether they have the potential to increase incomes and alleviate poverty can be determined only by empirical investigation. If these new technologies are to command the continued interest of the developing world and justify additional investments, a convincing demonstration of their effects on economic performance is required. On this basis, and given limited existing empirical evidence, this chapter examines the impact of terrestrial telecommunications infrastructure— by far the most prevalent communication technology in developing countries— on aggregate economic output. The conceptual framework that forms the basis of the book is once again presented in Figure 2.1, this time highlighting the area of analysis dealt with in this chapter.

For the purposes of the empirical investigation, a substantial data set covering 113 countries was assembled for the period 1980–2000. The empirical framework explicitly accounts for the two-way relationship between telecommunications infrastructure and economic output (meaning that the framework factors in issues of endogeneity). The four-equation framework used by Röller and Waverman (2001) was adopted and, in the first instance, replicated. However, the estimation methodology and empirical work in this study goes beyond Röller and Waverman's specification. In particular, this study examines the time-series properties of the data set used and corrects for the presence of unit-roots (an attribute of the time series within the statistical model).

21

FIGURE 2.1   Conceptual framework: Area of analysis dealt with in Chapter 2

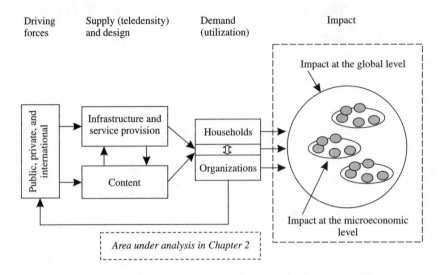

NOTE: Teledensity indicates the number of telephone lines per 100 inhabitants.

There are several ways that a country's ICT infrastructure can affect economic growth. Apart from making a direct contribution to gross domestic product (GDP), investments in these technologies are assumed to have pervasive
impacts throughout the economy—for example, by reducing transaction costs,
improving organizational functioning, and enhancing the spread and development of factor and product markets (along with many other potential effects that
have already been outlined by several authors, such as Saunders, Warford, and
Wellenius 1983; Leff 1984; and Norton 1992), and therefore are not elaborated
on further here. It is worth noting, however, that ICT is unlike other forms of
infrastructure in that its expansion generates benefits for both new and existing
users. This externality suggests that the effects of ICT on economic growth
may be subject to the attainment of a critical mass, meaning that, unless the said
infrastructure reaches a certain minimum level within a given country or region,
the growth effects may not be discernible. Put in simple economic terms, a nonlinear relationship may exist between telecommunications infrastructure and
economic growth. Thus, the empirical work in this chapter addresses two issues. First, does telecommunications infrastructure have an impact on economic
growth? Second, if a growth effect does exist, how does it vary with infrastructure and income levels across countries and regions?

This chapter presents a summary of the literature on infrastructure and
growth, a description of the data used (presenting correlations between GDP

and the availability of ICT), and conclusions. For those interested, the detailed econometric model and empirical results are included in appendix form at the end of the chapter.

A Review of Infrastructure Development and Growth

Overview

Early work on economic growth and development highlighted the necessity of adequate infrastructure. Defining the scope of social overhead capital (SOC), Hirschman (1958, 89) writes "SOC is usually defined as those services without which primary, secondary, and tertiary production activities cannot function." He goes on to write that in its wider sense SOC "includes all public services from law and order through education and public health to transportation, communications, power, and water supply." Although infrastructure implies a wide variety of services, such services have several traits in common. First, while these services yield direct benefits, it is often their indirect contribution—as intermediate inputs enhancing the productivity of all other inputs—that is often considered more important. Second, the development of these services is usually subject to increasing returns to scale. Third, while private-sector participation in the provision of infrastructure has increased, it is still largely funded and provided by the public sector. The rationale for public provision of these services is well known and is usually justified on the basis of a combination of externalities, nonrival consumption, and nonexcludable characteristics of such services.

The appropriate level and composition of public expenditure on different types of infrastructure services is an active area of debate, particularly because of their potential to spark growth and influence economic outcomes. For the purposes of assisting and informing public expenditure decisions, it is important to know the overall impact of infrastructure on economic output, as well as the relative effects of different types of infrastructure. The importance of this question for public policy has motivated a number of authors to examine the macroeconomic link between public capital and output. While there are micro-oriented studies of the infrastructure–growth output link, the economywide effects and potential externalities ascribed to such investments suggest the need for a macroeconomic approach.[1] The infrastructure–output literature consists of several branches; this study, however, reviews only the relevant portions of the existing evidence.

The discussion initially focuses on single countries, either over time or across regions, examining the effect of overall infrastructure capital on private

---

1. Micro-oriented studies lead to a deeper understanding of how infrastructure enhances output, but when the main goal is to establish the overall effect of infrastructure capital on output and productivity, a macroeconomic analysis is the more logical choice.

output. This is followed by a look at cross-country evidence of the impact of infrastructure capital on economic performance (meaning GDP growth over time). This review of the more general infrastructure literature is followed by a review of studies focusing on the links between telecommunications and output.

General Infrastructure Literature

Despite the existence of estimates of the link between infrastructure and output that predate Aschauer (1989), interest in the effects of public capital on output can be traced to this work. Aschauer used annual U.S. time-series data for the period 1949–85 and estimated that a 1 percent increase in the ratio of public to private capital stock was associated with a 0.39 percent increase in private-sector total factor productivity (TFP). A similar effect was reported by Munnell (1992). Such large effects—at a time when growth in productivity and in the stock of public infrastructure was declining—prompted Aschauer to propose that the declining growth of public infrastructure was an important determinant in the productivity slowdown. To examine whether these results could be extrapolated more generally, Ford and Poret (1991) used time-series data from several countries of the Organisation for Economic Co-operation and Development (OECD) to estimate production function relationships as similar as possible to those studied by Aschauer. Ford and Poret's estimates of the elasticity of output from infrastructure stock spanned a wide and implausible range (from 1.00 for Canada to –0.55 for Norway) and did not support the idea that a decline in infrastructure growth was responsible for the decline in TFP.

Despite this lack of support for the infrastructure–productivity link from studies based on other countries, support for Aschauer (1989) was provided by studies that relied on panel data to examine the effect of publicly provided inputs on the economic performance of U.S. states. Although his results were smaller in magnitude, Munnell (1992) reported that public capital was a statistically significant link in the determination of differences in productivity across U.S. states. Rather than focusing on public capital in its entirety, Garcia-Mila and McGuire (1992) used observations from the 48 contiguous states during 1969–83 to examine the effect of the stock of highway capital and educational expenditure on gross state product. While their results were smaller than the elasticities based on time-series data, they did show that these two variables played a substantial role in explaining statewide productivity differences.

The preceding studies focused exclusively on developed countries; the paucity of data makes it difficult to carry out single-country studies for developing countries. Clues to the link between infrastructure stock and economic development and growth in developing countries stem mainly from cross-country studies. Antle (1983) uses data from a sample of developing and developed countries to examine the extent to which intercountry differences in agricultural productivity can be explained by country-level investments in transportation and communications. For both developing and developed countries, Antle's analysis supports the conclusion that additional investments in infrastructure play a larger role than agricultural research and education in explaining inter-country differences in agricultural productivity.

The broad inference from the above studies is that the stock of public infrastructure plays a causal role in determining growth and productivity in both developing and developed countries. Policy implications drawn from such studies are fairly clear and support the argument for additional investments in physical infrastructure. Nevertheless, policy prescriptions based on the results of these studies have attracted strong criticism, primarily on the basis that they do not adequately account for the possibility of reverse causality and simultaneous determination of output and public capital—meaning that, while it is tempting to infer a causal relationship from public capital to output, it is equally likely that the direction of causality goes from output to public capital. In the context of time-series analysis, the estimated coefficient may reflect a spurious correlation between output and public capital stock that is driven by a common time-trend and not by any underlying relationship between the two variables. In short, the data may be what is economically termed "nonstationary" and inferences based on these data may be misleading. Another problem primarily afflicting panel-data studies stems from omitted variables. The first-generation panel-data studies usually ignore the possibility of unobserved state- or country-specific variables that may influence both output and the stock of public capital. Ignoring such fixed effects is quite likely to lead to an exaggeration of the effect of infrastructure on output.

The more recent literature in this area accounts for both of these problems —simultaneity bias and fixed effects—and presents a rather different picture. Holtz-Eakin (1994) uses panel data from the United States to estimate a variety of production functions in levels and in first differences. These estimates allow for fixed and random effects. Regardless of variations in the specifications, Holtz-Eakin finds no evidence that public capital is involved in productivity differences across states and concludes that the previous large positive findings "appear to be the artifact of an inappropriately restrictive framework" (Holtz-Eakin 1994, 20). In a reconsideration of some of their earlier studies, Garcia-Mila, McGuire, and Porter (1996) use a panel data set drawn from the United States to estimate the effect of public capital investments in highways, water and sewage systems, and all other infrastructure investments on private output. Their results confirm the conclusions reached by Holtz-Eakin (1994). From a cross-country perspective, Craig, Pardey, and Roseboom (1997) control for country-level fixed effects and conclude that, for developing countries, differences in road density are not responsible for differences in agricultural productivity.

Thus, in marked contrast to the first-generation studies, these second-generation studies find no evidence of high returns to investments in infrastructure. Despite these results, it would not be correct to argue that investments in infrastructure are not necessary. These studies show that within the context of a narrow production-function framework there are no indirect productivity effects associated with public capital. These results do not, however, detract from the large direct effects that investments in infrastructure services generate. Furthermore, any investment in public infrastructure calls for a project-specific cost–benefit analysis and should not be based on aggregate analysis.

Telecommunications Infrastructure Literature

Turning to studies more closely related to the topic of this chapter, Jipp (1963) and Hardy (1980) are some of the earliest that focus on the telecommunications–economic growth link.[2] Hardy (1980), for instance, uses data from 15 developed and 45 developing countries for the period 1960–73, regressing per capita GDP on lagged per capita GDP, lagged telephones per capita, and the number of radios. Hardy's results support the idea that the greater availability of telephones has a positive effect on GDP. By demonstrating the strong correlation between teledensity (the number of telephone lines per 100 inhabitants) and GDP, these early studies drew attention to the potential role of telecommunications in influencing growth. However, similar to the first-generation infrastructure literature, these early studies ignored the econometric issues outlined above.

A more sophisticated example of this genre is Norton (1992). Using data from a sample of 47 countries from the post–World War II period until 1977, Norton investigates the effects of telephone infrastructure on growth rates and also attempts to identify the channels through which the availability of this infrastructure leads to growth (that is, the effect of telephone infrastructure on the mean investment ratio, and consequently income growth). The empirical framework replicates Kormendi and Meguire (1985) but includes additional variables to capture telecommunications infrastructure. The inclusion of a more comprehensive set of macroeconomic regressors is designed to reduce the possibility of overestimating the effect of telecommunications infrastructure on growth. The two telecommunications infrastructure measures used are teledensity in 1957 and mean teledensity over the sample timeframe. The use of these two infrastructure variables is an attempt to address the endogenous nature of teledensity and growth. Norton argues that a measure of teledensity prevalent during the early years of the sample is less susceptible to endogeneity bias than a variable that captures the mean teledensity over the entire time period.

---

2. An emerging body of literature that examines the effect of the stock of computer hardware, software, and labor and other information technology-related measures in influencing economic growth and output. Since the main focus of this study is developing countries, where the stock of such capital is quite small, this body of evidence is not reviewed in detail here. Recent macroeconomic evidence on the United States is provided by Gordon (2000), Oliner and Sichel (2000), and Stiroh (2002). Results based on data from other countries and a cross-country analysis of the effect of information technology expenditure on economic growth are available in Pohjola (2001).

Norton's results show that the two measures of telecommunications infrastructure are statistically significant and exert positive effects on mean growth rates. For instance, increasing the 1957 teledensity by one standard deviation (9.909) leads to an increase in mean GDP growth of around 0.73 percent. The effect of the average density variable is greater but potentially more susceptible to reverse causality. The second set of estimates examines the effect of the telecommunications infrastructure variables on the mean investment–output ratio, and, similar to the earlier results, the impact is positive. Increasing teledensity by one standard deviation leads to an increase in the investment ratio of around 3.5–4.5 percent. While Norton controls for the endogeneity of telecommunications infrastructure and growth, the large effects reported in the study are reminiscent of the effects reported in early infrastructure literature. Norton does not control for country-level fixed effects, and it is likely that this omission is responsible for the large estimated effects of telecommunications infrastructure.

Madden and Savage (2000) follow the framework used by Mankiw, Romer, and Weil (1992) to estimate the effect of telecommunications on the level and growth of GDP for a cross-section of 43 countries (including 16 developing countries) for the period 1975–90. The authors present estimates based on ordinary least squares (OLS) and mention that they use instrumental variables estimation to control for the possible endogeneity between telecommunications capital and GDP. Their results are not sensitive to alterations in the estimation methodology, and they report large effects of telecommunications capital on the level of GDP. Once again their estimates may be upwardly biased because they do not control for country-level fixed effects.

As mentioned in Chapter 1, Röller and Waverman (2001) present cross-country estimates of the effect of telecommunications on output based on a cross-section of 21 OECD countries over a period of 20 years. They tackle the endogeneity problem by estimating a four-equation model that endogenizes telecommunications infrastructure, and they control for country-level fixed effects. Their results indicate that estimates allowing for fixed effects lead to a reduction in the teledensity elasticity from 0.15 to 0.045. Despite this drop, the growth effect attributed to telecommunications infrastructure is still quite large. The elasticity implies that about one-third of the economic growth in OECD countries between 1971 and 1990 may be attributed to growth in telecommunications infrastructure. An interesting element of Röller and Waverman's work is the investigation of whether a nonlinear relationship exists between teledensity and economic output. They found that teledensity begins to exert an influence on output only when it is universally available—more specifically, when a teledensity threshold or critical mass of about 40 percent is reached.

While the robustness and generality of the threshold effect may be questioned, these results do suggest that enhancements in telecommunications infrastructure may generate higher growth effects in developed countries than in developing countries. In addition, given low teledensity in developing countries (the 1995 average was around 4.0), it appears that marginal improvements in telecommunications infrastructure may not generate the desired growth effects. Thus, developing countries may require substantial investments in telecommunications infrastructure before they can benefit from the growth-generating effects of these technologies.

In this chapter we use a framework and a specification that is as similar as possible to Röller and Waverman (2001). We endogenize telecommunications by estimating a demand and supply model for telecommunication investments and simultaneously estimate a macro-production function. Our primary aim is to examine whether the idea of a critical mass is valid for a larger sample of nations and for a longer timeframe. Our analysis emphasizes an examination of this relationship for developing countries.

Data and Summary Statistics

To construct a comprehensive data set, the inclusion of a country was determined by the availability of time series data of long duration covering the variables required for the analysis. The countries included are presented in Appendix 2A, which also provides details of the income categories and the regional groupings used.[3]

The data set for this chapter is tailored to the needs of the empirical framework and contains information on economic variables such as output, labor force, capital stock, and budget deficit (surplus). The telecommunications-related variables are teledensity, revenue per fixed telephone line, and annual investment in telecommunications. In addition to these telecommunications-related variables, the data set also contains information on the availability of other ICT. Table 2.1 provides a list of the variables and their descriptive statistics, also indicating the sources of the variables.

With respect to variable sources, while most of the variables are readily available from publicly accessible databases, such as the World Development Indicators (WDI) and the International Telecommunications Union (ITU) database (World Bank 2002 and ITU 2002), some of the data—in particular telecommunications capital stock and total physical capital stock—required estimation. Construction of the telecommunications capital stock series is based on annual investment in telecommunications data available in WDI (World Bank

---

3. In terms of income categories, our data set consists of 36 low-income countries, 27 lower middle-income countries, 21 higher middle-income countries, 8 high-income non-OECD countries, and 21 OECD countries. We divided the countries across six geographic regions based on WDI classifications (World Bank 2002). The data set comprises 40 countries from Africa, 24 countries from the Asian/Middle Eastern region, 4 countries from the Australian region, 23 countries from the European region, 13 from the Central and North American region (including the Caribbean), and 9 countries from South America.

TABLE 2.1 Variables and summary statistics

Variable	N	Minimum	Maximum	Mean	SD
GDP (million 1995 U.S. dollars)	1,829	199.61	7,723,512.50	229,782.90	798,217.13
Total labor force in millions	1,829	0.02	979.67	33.75	113.90
Total physical capital stock (million 1995 U.S. dollars)	1,829	761.49	21,100,000.00	659,167.41	2,300,430.01
Annual investment in telecommunications (million 1995 U.S. dollars)	1,772	0.01	37,080.61	1,240.20	3,888.95
Land area (1,000 square kilometers)	1,819	0.32	9,326.41	838.60	1,891.43
Government budget surplus (deficit) (million 1995 U.S. dollars)	1,404	−309,010.96	84,042.30	−10,406.74	34,965.53
Fixed telephone lines per 100 inhabitants	1,828	0.09	70.69	15.83	18.29
Cellular subscribers per 100 inhabitants	1,791	0.00	47.47	1.17	4.02
Telephone service revenue per fixed line (1995 U.S. dollars)	1,369	58.21	1,314,365.28	3,499.36	51,340.28
Cellular service revenue per fixed line (1995 U.S. dollars)	393	0.00	17,532.79	1,141.04	1,387.06
Waiting list for fixed lines per 100 inhabitants	1,611	0.00	20.73	1.21	2.16
Internet users per 1,000 inhabitants	563	0.00	294.25	12.99	31.68
Internet hosts per 10,000 inhabitants	1,362	0.00	945.82	11.65	56.96
Personal computers per 1,000 inhabitants	689	0.01	406.87	57.65	81.09

SOURCES: Data on gross domestic product (GDP), total labor force, annual investment, land area, and government budget surplus (deficit) are from World Bank (2002); data on total physical capital stock and annual investment in telecommunications are from Nehru and Dhareshwar (1993) and authors' estimations based on World Bank (2002); data on fixed telephone lines, cellular telephones, the Internet, and personal computers are from ITU (2002).

NOTE: N indicates number of observations; SD, standard deviation.

FIGURE 2.2 Availability of ICT in various regions defined by income level, 2000

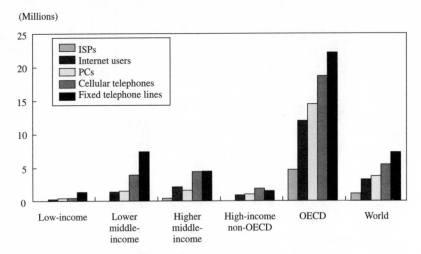

(Millions)

SOURCE: Calculated by authors from study data set.
NOTES: ISP indicates Internet service provider; OECD, Organisation for Economic Co-operation and Development; PCs, personal computers. For details of the countries within the income groupings, see Appendix 2A.

2002). The telecommunications capital stock is constructed using the perpetual inventory method (PIM). See Appendix 2B for details.

Figure 2.2 shows the availability of different types of ICT for five income groups. The availability of each technology is derived from the country average within each income group. Despite the explosive growth of modern ICT in the 1990s, on average, fixed telephony still predominates in low-income, lower middle-income, and OECD countries. However, cellular telephony has emerged as the second most important communications technology. In some cases, for instance in higher middle-income countries and high-income non-OECD countries, cellular telephony already outnumbers fixed telephony. With the exception of access to fixed telephony, the prevalence of modern ICT, such as Internet hosts and personal computers (PCs), remains very low in low-income countries.

Although countries in all income groups experienced sizable ICT growth in the 1990s (see Table 2.2), the total stock of ICT in low-income countries remained extremely low compared with other income groups. As of 2000, the average number of Internet hosts per low-income country was only 2,432— a mere 0.05 percent of the 4.7 million Internet hosts per OECD country on average. Although the stock in the case of fixed telephony was higher, it still represented only 5.8 percent of the OECD average. In fact, comparatively higher teledensity in certain countries inflated the fixed telephony average for low-income countries. For example, the total number of fixed telephone lines in India

TABLE 2.2 Compound annual growth rate of per capita gross domestic product and fixed telephone lines within income and regional groups

Income/regional group	GDP per capita 1980	GDP per capita 2000	CAGR (%) 1980–2000	Fixed lines per 100 inhabitants 1980	Fixed lines per 100 inhabitants 2000	CAGR (%) 1980–2000	Correlation between growth rates
Income group							
Low-income (36)	388	389	0.04	0.36	1.17	5.94	0.549**
Lower middle-income (27)	1,394	1,642	1.05	2.30	10.21	8.19	0.869**
Higher middle-income (21)	3,964	5,526	1.85	4.86	22.72	7.78	0.817**
High-income non-OECD (8)	13,466	17,147	1.81	16.67	47.84	5.24	0.146
High-income OECD (21)	19,155	29,624	2.11	32.06	58.24	3.12	0.518*
Regional group							
Africa (40)	943	1,150	0.22	0.83	3.61	6.02	0.644**
Asia (24)	6,139	8,104	2.11	6.85	19.17	8.29	0.539**
Australia (4)	8,209	11,193	0.84	18.25	28.02	2.78	−0.515
Europe (23)	14,376	22,712	2.11	23.76	51.82	4.74	0.203
North America (13)	5,225	7,279	1.03	10.08	28.11	6.97	0.404
South America (9)	3,152	3,490	0.31	3.95	14.11	6.12	0.819**
World, 113 countries	5,707	8,263	1.13	8.71	21.25	6.24	0.464**

SOURCE: Calculated by authors from study data set.

NOTES: CAGR indicates compound annual growth rate, where $CAGR = \left[\left(\dfrac{\text{Last Value}}{\text{First Value}} \right)^{1/N} - 1 \right] \times 100$.

The CAGR was calculated for each of the 113 countries. The number of countries within each income category is shown in parentheses. For details of the countries within the income and regional groupings, see Appendix 2A. Values are unweighted averages; *indicates significance at the 5 percent level; **indicates significance at the 1 percent level. OECD indicates Organisation for Economic Co-operation and Development.

FIGURE 2.3 Availability of ICT in various regions, 2000

(Millions)

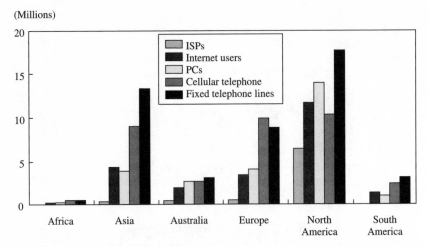

SOURCE: Calculated by authors from study data set.
NOTE: For details of the countries within the six regional groupings, see Appendix 2A. ISP indicates Internet service provider; PCs, personal computers.

in 2000 was 25 times the low-income country average, and the number of cellular telephones in Indonesia in 2000 was more than 12 times the low-income country average.

In addition to limited variety of ICT available in low-income countries, an imbalance also exists between the availability of fixed telephone lines and the availability of more recent technologies such as the Internet. While the ratio between fixed telephone lines and the Internet was 1.85 to 1 on average in OECD countries in 2000, it was 5 to 1 in low-income countries.

Figure 2.3 shows the availability of ICT across the six different regional categories for the year 2000, based on the country average per region. Like the income groups, there are regional differences in ICT levels. While countries in Africa have the lowest penetration rates on average, countries in the Central and North American region have the highest. For example, while the number of Internet hosts in Africa is 0.59 percent of the world average, the number in the Central and North American region is seven times the world average. In Europe, in contrast to other geographic regions, cellular telephony already outnumbers fixed telephony.

These averages mask individual differences within regions. Not surprisingly, the larger the country (or countries) within a region in terms of area or population, the larger the stock of ICT. In the case of Africa, for example, the number of Internet hosts in South Africa is 35 times the African average, and the number of fixed telephone lines in Egypt is 12 times the African average; in the case of Asia, the outliers are Japan and Korea for all types of ICT and India and China for fixed telephony. Differences in the other regions also follow income and country size (either by area or population). Table 2.2 shows compound annual growth rates (CAGR) of per capita GDP and fixed line teledensity for the period 1980–2000. Over this time, the 113 countries (representing "the world") reported positive growth in both per capita income and fixed telephony. While per capita income grew at 1.1 percent on average, the growth rate for fixed telephony per 100 inhabitants was 6.2 percent. The last column of the table indicates the correlation between the CAGRs for per capita GDP and fixed line teledensity (Table 2.2).

From 1980 to 2000, per capita income in low-income countries virtually stagnated, while all other income groups experienced substantial growth. All income groups achieved growth in fixed telephony per capita, but the growth rate was higher in low-income than in high-income countries. Despite this, the per capita number of fixed telephone lines in low-income countries was only 1.8 in 2000 compared with 58.2 in high-income countries. The growth rate of fixed telephone lines was higher in middle-income countries than in either low- or high-income countries, and per capita GDP growth was also higher for middle-income countries compared with low-income countries. Despite the differences in growth rates among the various income groups, for all groups—with the exception of high-income non-OECD countries—a positive and statistically significant correlation was demonstrated between telecommunications infrastructure and GDP growth (Table 2.2).

Some regional differences were evident. During 1980–2000, per capita GDP in the Asian and European regions grew at a higher rate than in the countries of other regions. African countries lagged behind, followed by the countries of South America. Asian countries displayed high per capita GDP growth, as well as attaining the highest per capita growth in the number of fixed telephone lines. African countries also achieved a high rate of growth in fixed telephony over the same period; nevertheless, in 2000, fixed line teledensity was only 3.6 in Africa compared with 19.2 in Asia. In South American countries the teledensity increased substantially over the 20-year period, reaching 14.1 in 2000. Although there are differences across regions, and with the exception of the Australian region, a high positive correlation exists between per capita GDP growth and per capita fixed telephony growth for all regions (Table 2.2).[4]

Figures 2.4a and 2.4b show the relationship between fixed line teledensity and per capita GDP for the years 1980 and 2000, respectively. In both figures,

---

4. When the four countries comprising the Australian region—two OECD countries (Australia and New Zealand) and two lower middle-income countries (Papua New Guinea and Fiji)—were separated into their income groups, the result produced a correlation coefficient that was positive, significant, and close to one.

FIGURE 2.4a Fixed telephone lines and per capita gross domestic product, 1980

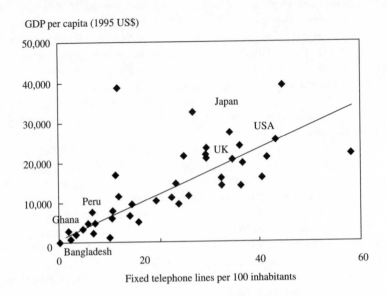

FIGURE 2.4b Fixed telephone lines and per capita gross domestic product, 2000

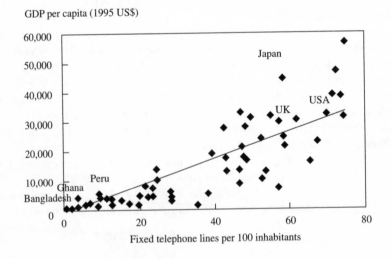

SOURCE: Calculated by authors from study data set.

per capita GDP expressed in constant 1995 U.S. dollars is the dependent variable, and fixed line teledensity is the independent variable. In 1980, there was a positive relationship between growth of fixed telephony and per capita GDP; a similar positive relationship was found to exist in 2000 as well. Although both per capita GDP and fixed line teledensity grew at different rates (1.1 percent per year and 6.2 percent per year, respectively), the relationship remained strong and positive over the period (Figures 2.4a and 2.4b).[5]

Because there are regional variations in the relative and absolute availability of ICT, as well as among income groups, additional figures detail regional subdivisions based on geographic and income classifications (see Appendix 2C). These supplementary figures show that the relationship between fixed line teledensity and per capita GDP has both regional and income characteristics. While the relationship is relatively weak for low-income countries, it is particularly strong for the lower middle-income and high-income non-OECD countries; in terms of regional groupings, the relationship is relatively high.[6]

As a means of assessing the relationship between the availability of modern forms of ICT and GDP, the relationship between per capita GDP and both PCs per 1,000 inhabitants and Internet users per 1,000 inhabitants was considered (Figures 2.5a and 2.5b). Given limited data availability, results are presented for the year 2000 only. The relationship between PCs per 1,000 inhabitants and per capita GDP is very strong and positive. A linear regression of per capita GDP on PCs per 1,000 inhabitants explains more than 85 percent variation in per capita GDP. Although weaker compared with the relationship to PCs, a positive relationship also exists between per capita GDP and the number of Internet users per 1,000 inhabitants. This regression explains about 73 percent of the variation in GDP.

Table 2.3 provides further evidence on the positive relationship between ICT availability and per capita GDP. In this instance, both traditional and modern forms of ICT are included (fixed and cellular telephones, the Internet, and PCs) for both income and regional groups. In addition, the bottom row of the table presents the combined relationships for the 113 sample countries. With the exception of fixed telephone lines, all the correlation coefficients are for the year 2000.

There is a positive relationship between teledensity and per capita GDP, and, with the exception of high-income non-OECD countries,[7] the correlation

---

5. A simple linear regression of per capita GDP on fixed line teledensity explains 75 percent of the variation in per capita GDP in 1980 and 78 percent of the variation in per capita GDP in 2000.

6. A linear regression of per capita GDP on fixed line teledensity explains at least 70 percent of the variation in per capita GDP.

7. Among the eight countries in this group, Kuwait and United Arab Emirates are oil-rich countries that suffered from the decline of oil prices. The exclusion of these two countries would result in a correlation coefficient of 0.9.

FIGURE 2.5a Personal computers and per capita gross domestic product, 2000

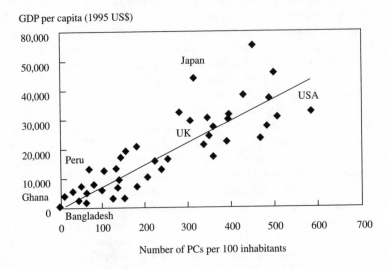

GDP per capita (1995 US$)

Number of PCs per 100 inhabitants

FIGURE 2.5b Internet users and per capita gross domestic product, 2000

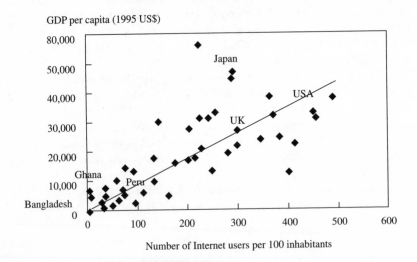

GDP per capita (1995 US$)

Number of Internet users per 100 inhabitants

SOURCE: Calculated by authors from study data set.

TABLE 2.3 Correlations between per capita gross domestic product and fixed telephone lines, cellular telephones, Internet hosts, and personal computers, 2000

	Fixed telephone lines per 1,000 inhabitants		Correlation coefficients between GDP per capita and			
Income/regional group	1980	2000	Cellular phones per 100 inhabitants	Internet users per 1,000 inhabitants	Internet hosts per 10,000 inhabitants	PCs per 1,000 inhabitants
Income group						
Low income (36)	0.34*	0.47**	0.52**	0.32	0.23	0.42*
Lower middle income (27)	0.35	0.22	0.15	0.52**	0.44*	0.57**
Higher middle income (21)	0.70**	0.56**	0.62**	0.66**	0.19	0.72**
High-income non-OECD (8)	−0.26	0.16	0.86**	0.89**	0.84**	0.87**
High-income OECD (21)	0.64**	0.66**	0.15	0.31	0.14	0.63**
Regional group						
Africa (40)	0.88**	0.86**	0.93**	0.86**	0.54**	0.87**
Asia (24)	0.71**	0.91**	0.84**	0.82**	0.90**	0.89**
Australia (4)	0.98**	0.98**	0.92	0.99**	0.96**	0.99**
Europe (23)	0.87**	0.83**	0.76**	0.73**	0.62**	0.91**
North America (13)	0.98**	0.87**	0.90**	0.96**	0.94**	0.97**
South America (9)	0.81**	0.84**	0.56	0.64	0.78**	0.76**
World, 113 countries	0.87**	0.89**	0.88**	0.86**	0.64**	0.93**

SOURCE: Calculated by authors from study data set.

NOTES: The number of countries within each category is shown in parentheses. For details of the countries within each category, see Appendix 2A. *Indicates significance at the 5 percent level; **indicates significance at the 1 percent level. GDP indicates gross domestic product; OECD, Organisation for Economic Co-operation and Development; PC, personal computer.

coefficients between fixed telephone lines and per capita GDP remained positive and significant for all income groups and for all geographic regions. In fact, for some income groups (such as the higher middle-income countries) and for all geographic regions, the correlation coefficient between fixed telephone lines and per capita GDP is very high, ranging from 0.56 to 0.98. Though there is a negative correlation between the CAGR of per capita GDP and the CAGR of fixed telephone lines for the Australian region, the correlation coefficient between per capita GDP and fixed line teledensity is as high as 0.98; it is also statistically significant both for 1980 and 2000. The correlation coefficient for all 113 countries is very high, at 0.87 in 1980 to 0.89 in 2000.

An important development in ICT in recent times is the tremendous surge in the penetration rate of cellular telephones. In fact, in the case of some low-income countries, the cellular penetration rate has surpassed that of fixed lines. Not surprisingly, a positive correlation exists between the growth rate of cellular telephones and per capita GDP. For low-income countries, the correlation is greater for cellular phones than for fixed line telephones; there is no observable pattern, however (that is, the correlation coefficient does not increase or decrease with the per capita GDP). In the case of regional groups, all regions show a strongly positive correlation between cellular phone penetration and per capita GDP—albeit at varying magnitudes. Similarly, a strongly positive correlation exists between cellular telephone penetration and per capita GDP for the world, represented by our 113-country sample.

Turning to more modern ICT, a similar pattern emerges. Similar to the relationship between fixed and cellular teledensity and per capita GDP, the availability of modern ICT—specifically, the Internet and personal computers—shows a strong correlation with per capita GDP. With the exception of the OECD countries, there is a correlation between GDP and Internet users and PCs, although the trend is stronger for high-income than for low-income countries. For the geographic regions, however, there is no observable trend. Among the different types of ICT, the strongest relationship exists between per capita GDP and the PC penetration rate. The correlation coefficients are significant for all income groups and all geographic regions; for Australia, the European and Central/North American regions, and the 113-country sample as a whole, the correlation coefficient is higher than 0.9.

Econometric Model and Empirical Results

To identify the effect of telecommunications on economic growth, we chose to adopt the model used by Röller and Waverman (2001), with two major differences. The first main difference is that we extend their database to include developing countries and not only 21 OECD counties, and second we correct our estimates for the presence of unit roots by estimating the model in first differences following the two-step Arrellano and Bond (1991, 1998) generalized method of moments (GMM) estimator. Appendix 2D provides further details on the model and the econometric techniques used.

Empirical Results

As discussed above, differencing the data and using Arellano and Bond's (1991, 1998) instrumentalization technique is the preferred estimation methodology, first because it may increase the efficiency of the parameters in terms of ordinary least squares (OLS) or GMM in levels, but most importantly because it tackles the problem of unit roots. Table 2.4 shows the results of the Phillips–Perron test for unit roots for GDP, capital, and the real investment in telecommunications infrastructure (TTI). The results clearly show the presence of unit roots in practically all the series for all the countries. It also shows how this problem is significantly reduced when differences are used instead of levels, and when the Hodrick–Prescott filter is applied to the series. From this result it is clear that OLS or even GMM estimates in levels (such as the ones carried out by Röller and Waverman 2001) may lead to spurious results.

Table 2.5 presents estimates of the output equation (1′) using different estimation methods. Equations (2′)–(4′) have been used to instrumentalize this equation (see Appendix 2D for details on the equations). Models (1)–(3) present the results for different estimation methods using the variables in levels, while models (4) and (5) present the results following Arrellano and Bond's (1991, 1998) dynamic panel data estimation. The presence of unit root problems results in an overestimation of the impact of the penetration rate on aggregate output. For example, if we use model 3, a 1 percent increase in the penetration rate is associated with a 0.11 percent increase in output. On the other hand, if we correct for the unit root problem using GMM with the data in first differences, the impact of the penetration rate on economic output is substantially smaller. In this sense, models (4) and (5) show that a 1 percent increase in the penetration increases economic output by 0.03 percent, which is clearly a more realistic coefficient.

Tables 2.6 through 2.9 show the results using Arrellano and Bond (1991, 1998) dynamic GMM techniques for each of the four equations outlined above. A regression for each income group is presented in each table. It should be emphasized that the focus of the empirical analysis is not the estimation of demand and supply relationships in the telecommunications industry but rather the impact of telecommunications infrastructure on economic development, and the best way to estimate this impact. In this respect, the results of the demand, supply, and production equations are inputs for the output equation.

From Table 2.6, it is clear that, although telecommunications penetration has a significant impact on output growth when we include all the countries in our sample, there are differences across regions. Consistent with the results of our simple regression analysis, the impact of telecommunications is statistically significant for lower and higher middle-income countries only, while it is

TABLE 2.4 Phillips–Perron test for unit roots by country

Country	Level GDP	Level TTI	Level KNT	Differenced GDP	Differenced TTI	Differenced KNT	Filtered[a] GDP	Filtered[a] TTI	Filtered[a] KNT
1. Argentina	0.707	0.000	0.591	0.004	0.000	0.503	0.006	0.000	1.000
2. Australia	0.741	0.251	0.872	0.001	0.001	0.070	0.104	0.007	0.026
3. Austria	0.287	0.625	0.106	0.001	0.082	0.088	0.318	0.002	0.019
4. Bahrain	0.154	0.246	0.999	0.004	0.001	0.593	0.000	0.000	0.008
5. Bangladesh	0.430	0.167	0.844	0.000	0.000	0.333	0.039	0.000	0.865
6. Barbados	0.404	0.000	0.637	0.040	0.000	0.228	0.076	0.000	0.006
7. Belgium	0.395	0.451	0.570	0.000	0.000	0.182	0.142	0.000	0.113
8. Belize	0.571	0.000	0.945	0.103	0.000	0.660	0.102	0.000	1.000
9. Bolivia	0.965	0.688	1.000	0.035	0.149	1.000	0.053	1.000	1.000
10. Botswana	0.987	0.264	0.985	0.039	0.000	0.567	0.030	0.000	0.000
11. Bulgaria	0.637	0.811	0.998	0.509	0.003	0.582	0.004	0.000	0.000
12. Burkina Faso	0.004	0.093	0.495	0.000	0.002	0.743	0.000	0.000	0.000
13. Burundi	0.937	0.103	0.990	0.007	0.000	0.402	0.001	1.000	0.000
14. Cameroon	0.775	0.998	0.000	0.023	0.010	0.113	0.000	0.179	0.000
15. Chile	0.854	0.174	0.784	0.071	0.001	0.530	0.078	0.000	0.115
16. China	0.024	0.533	0.469	0.036	0.001	0.047	0.073	0.000	0.085
17. Colombia	0.602	0.225	0.659	0.140	0.000	0.541	0.024	0.000	0.000
18. Costa Rica	0.916	0.974	0.213	0.001	0.000	0.630	0.087	0.000	0.026
19. Côte d'Ivoire	0.416	0.413	0.998	0.025	0.000	0.591	0.003	0.000	1.000
20. Cyprus	0.846	0.339	0.967	0.000	0.000	0.043	0.000	0.004	0.000
21. Denmark	0.391	0.725	0.455	0.002	0.048	0.003	0.005	0.103	0.000
22. Ecuador	0.289	0.048	0.000	0.000	0.000	0.180	0.001	0.000	0.000
23. Egypt	0.001	0.284	0.012	0.004	0.069	0.000	0.001	0.000	0.000
24. Ethiopia	0.693	0.765	0.432	0.005	0.157	0.000	0.000	0.000	0.000
25. Fiji	0.037	0.048	0.000	0.000	0.000	0.016	0.000	0.015	0.000
26. Finland	0.765	0.405	0.002	0.344	0.042	0.000	0.319	0.057	0.000
27. France	0.233	0.507	0.707	0.077	0.167	0.094	0.565	0.133	0.003
28. Gabon	0.434	0.000	0.728	0.000		0.006	0.042	1.000	1.000
29. Gambia	0.070	0.006	0.822	0.000	0.000	0.072	0.051	0.000	0.000
30. Ghana	0.746	0.005	0.000	0.038	0.003	0.000	0.040	1.000	1.000
31. Greece	0.155	0.648	0.653	0.050	0.074	0.008	0.179	0.025	0.017
32. Hungary	0.625	0.621	0.011	0.144	0.003	0.454	0.248	0.000	0.000
33. India	0.222	0.214	0.969	0.000	0.003	0.001	0.008	0.033	0.077
34. Indonesia	0.967	0.580	0.986	0.015	0.000	0.014	0.004	0.002	0.002
35. Iran (Islamic Rep. of)	0.915	0.151	0.951	0.003	0.000	0.623	0.023	0.000	0.212
36. Ireland	0.999	0.465	0.562	0.067	0.202	0.347	0.979	0.008	0.175
37. Israel	0.436	0.073	0.280	0.070	0.000	0.000	0.041	0.001	0.002
38. Italy	0.118	0.581	0.998	0.047	0.160	0.217	0.032	0.004	0.000
39. Japan	0.969	0.624	0.940	0.013	0.034	0.444	0.023	0.008	0.001
40. Jordan	0.109	0.000	0.278	0.004	0.074	0.870	0.001	0.000	0.283
41. Kenya	0.908	0.374	0.003	0.064	0.000	0.018	0.006	0.000	0.000
42. Korea (Rep. of)	0.762	0.002	0.976	0.007	0.000	0.061	0.074	0.000	0.008
43. Kuwait	0.888	0.014	0.987	0.359	0.000	0.033	0.002	0.000	1.000
44. Lesotho	0.465	0.020	0.729	0.118	0.000	0.337	0.030	0.000	0.239

TABLE 2.4 *Continued*

Country	Level			Differenced			Filtered[a]		
	GDP	TTI	KNT	GDP	TTI	KNT	GDP	TTI	KNT
45. Luxembourg	0.913	0.691	0.431	0.003	0.001	0.000	0.571	0.003	0.001
46. Madagascar	0.843	0.768	0.875	0.001	0.005	0.406	0.011	1.000	1.000
47. Malawi	0.039	0.758	0.463	0.000	0.348	0.251	0.000	0.000	0.000
48. Malaysia	0.510	0.675	0.680	0.013	0.044	0.283	0.057	0.024	0.248
49. Mali	0.824	0.552	0.974	0.000	0.167	0.379	0.001	1.000	1.000
50. Malta	0.257	0.124	0.934	0.669	0.006	0.090	0.823	0.039	0.011
51. Mauritania	0.986	0.846	0.998	0.000	0.431	0.471	0.000	1.000	0.130
52. Mauritius	0.335	0.287	0.569	0.000	0.000	0.065	0.001	0.000	0.000
53. Mexico	0.602	0.690	0.568	0.000	0.000	0.494	0.000	0.004	0.004
54. Mongolia	0.562	0.000	0.008	0.608	0.000	0.671	0.001	0.000	0.000
55. Morocco	0.011	0.309	0.873	0.000	0.000	0.174	0.000	0.000	0.000
56. Nepal	0.575	0.443	1.000	0.000	0.060	0.625	0.000	0.000	0.146
57. Netherlands	0.987	0.824	0.223	0.014	0.103	0.012	0.668	0.123	0.058
58. New Zealand	0.468	0.854	0.770	0.008	0.205	0.541	0.048	0.003	0.005
59. Niger	0.440	0.164	0.858	0.011	0.000	0.070	0.012	1.000	1.000
60. Norway	0.223	0.839	0.419	0.078	0.000	0.000	0.127	0.000	0.010
61. Oman	0.741	0.002	0.528	0.087	0.000	0.630	0.044	0.000	1.000
62. Pakistan	0.999	0.922	0.918	0.000	0.282	0.002	0.000	0.000	1.000
63. Panama	0.560	0.611	0.618	0.033	0.124	0.558	0.012	0.001	0.016
64. Papua New Guinea	0.602	0.118	0.843	0.050	0.000	0.500	0.019	0.000	0.000
65. Paraguay	0.478	0.242	0.105	0.227	0.049	0.199	0.064	0.060	0.000
66. Peru	0.481	0.108	0.712	0.034	0.000	0.000	0.028	0.000	0.000
67. Philippines	0.327	0.564	0.971	0.219	0.044	0.080	0.139	0.000	0.087
68. Poland	0.493	0.954	1.000	0.149	0.000	1.000	0.000	0.000	1.000
69. Portugal	0.281	0.274	0.562	0.144	0.000	0.018	0.319	0.000	0.032
70. Romania	0.286	0.636	0.204	0.277	0.000	0.575	0.018	0.000	0.000
71. Rwanda	0.313	1.000	0.843	0.000		0.802	0.000	1.000	1.000
72. Senegal	0.600	0.225	0.869	0.000	0.001	0.000	0.000	0.000	0.000
73. Seychelles	0.231	0.000	0.891	0.000	0.000	0.103	0.000	1.000	1.000
74. Sierra Leone	0.837	0.000	0.000	0.000		0.000	0.000	1.000	1.000
75. Singapore	0.535	0.159	0.256	0.095	0.000	0.039	0.244	0.002	0.000
76. South Africa	0.399	0.620	0.276	0.011	0.014	0.129	0.008	0.004	0.000
77. Spain	0.902	0.752	0.419	0.105	0.282	0.577	0.799	0.043	0.027
78. Sri Lanka	0.779	0.027	0.000	0.012	0.000	0.944	0.710	0.000	0.000
79. Swaziland	0.499	0.613	0.093	0.137	0.000	0.142	0.002	0.025	0.004
80. Switzerland	0.594	0.515	0.673	0.031	0.001	0.009	0.100	0.003	0.002
81. Syria	0.692	0.875	0.008	0.000	0.002	0.627	0.001	0.001	0.000
82. Thailand	0.967	0.453	0.437	0.472	0.000	0.536	0.093	0.000	0.000
83. Togo	0.151	0.552	0.446	0.000	0.406	0.783	0.001	0.061	0.000
84. Trinidad and Tobago	0.262	0.700	0.100	0.001	0.160	0.838	0.000	0.000	0.514
85. Tunisia	0.160	0.496	0.562	0.000	0.000	0.120	0.065	0.000	0.061
86. Turkey	0.290	0.540	0.778	0.000	0.002	0.000	0.001	0.013	0.001
87. Uganda	0.580	0.191	0.004	0.230	0.248	0.000	0.000	1.000	1.000

(continued)

TABLE 2.4 *Continued*

Country	Level			Differenced			Filtered[a]		
	GDP	TTI	KNT	GDP	TTI	KNT	GDP	TTI	KNT
88. United Arab Emirates	0.383	0.539	0.000	0.074	0.000	0.163	0.001	0.000	0.000
89. United Kingdom	0.583	0.221	0.853	0.221	0.215	0.476	0.363	0.011	0.030
90. United States	0.907	0.352	0.914	0.040	0.069	0.001	0.465	0.079	0.238
91. Uruguay	0.747	0.007	0.569	0.167	0.000	0.745	0.115	0.000	0.314
92. Venezuela	0.517	0.572	0.324	0.002	0.092	0.000	0.002	0.000	0.000
93. Yemen	0.956	0.437	1.000	0.000	0.999	0.013	1.000	1.000	1.000
94. Zambia	0.084	0.000	0.149	0.000	0.136	0.000	0.001	0.000	0.000
95. Zimbabwe	0.342	0.523	0.858	0.066	0.021	0.038	0.030	0.799	0.000

SOURCE: Compiled and calculated by authors from study data set.

NOTES: The figures report MacKinnon approximated p-values to test for the presence of unit roots in the Phillips–Perron test. The null hypothesis indicates that the variable contains a unit root; the alternative is that the variable was generated by a stationary process. P-values larger than 0.1 mean that the Phillips–Perron test lies inside the acceptance region at 1, 5, and 10 percent; hence we cannot reject the presence of unit roots. GDP indicates gross domestic product; KNT, stock of capital net telecommunication; TTI, telecommunications infrastructure.

[a] Hodrick–Prescott filter.

not significant for OECD and high-income non-OECD countries or for low-income countries.

This result is consistent with the idea that high-income countries have reached a critical mass of telecommunications infrastructure, so marginal increases in telecommunications infrastructure have limited impact on output. In direct contrast, telecommunications infrastructure is expanding in lower and higher middle-income countries, and this has a positive effect on aggregate output. Finally, for low-income countries, our results indicated no impact on aggregate output from telecommunications infrastructure. On a technical note, Sargan's test of overidentifying restrictions does not reject the validity of instruments when we subdivide the countries by income groups.

This differentiated result across income groups could be reflecting the characteristic of network externalities. As mentioned in several studies, an implication of network externalities is that the impact of telecommunications infrastructure on growth may not be linear. The piecewise linear regressions presented here show that in poor countries lacking a critical mass of telecommunications infrastructure (the mean penetration rates for this group of countries is 0.58 percent), marginal increases in the penetration rate do not spark economic growth. On the other hand, in lower and higher middle-income countries, where mean penetration rates range from 5 to 11 percent, telecommunications infrastructure has a positive and statistically significant impact on aggregate output. In OECD and other high-income countries, where penetration rates are about 40 percent (which may be considered universal coverage), the effect is muted. These results are contradictory to the results reported in

TABLE 2.5 Output equation

Dependent variable: $\log(\text{GDP})_{it}$	Two-stage least squares (1)	Three-stage least squares (2)	Generalized method of moments-IV (3)	A-bond dynamic panel data[a] (4)	(5)
$\log(\text{GDP})_{i(t-1)}$	—	—	—	0.793 (38.11)**	0.959 (27.87)**
$\log(\text{GDP})_{i(t-2)}$	—	—	—	—	-0.188 (7.20)**
$\log(\text{PEN})_{it}$	0.113 (9.87)**	0.173 (18.78)**	0.113 (9.57)**	0.033 (3.33)**	0.033 (2.96)**
$\log(\text{KNT})_{it}$	0.468 (29.41)**	0.370 (27.51)**	0.468 (28.52)**	0.028 (1.96)*	0.057 (3.68)**
$\log(\text{TLF})_{it}$	0.061 (2.89)**	0.114 (6.43)**	0.061 (2.81)**	-0.004 (0.41)	-0.009 (0.73)
Trend	0.008 (9.58)**	0.009 (13.76)**	0.008 (9.29)**	—	—
Constant	5.188 (10.66)**	6.769 (16.55)**	4.135 (8.69)**	0.003 (6.36)**	0.003 (5.68)**
Number of observations	1,655	1,655	1,655	1,639	1,596
Number of countries	95	95	95	95	95
R^2	0.9983	0.9982	0.9669		
Sargan test	88.818**			816.70**	687.57**

SOURCE: Compiled and calculated by authors from study data set.

NOTES: Absolute values of z statistics are shown in parentheses. All models include fixed effects. *Indicates significance at the 5 percent level; **indicates significance at the 1 percent level. GDP indicates gross domestic product; KNT, stock of capital net telecommunication; PEN, penetration rate; TLF, total labor force.

[a] Generalized method of moments estimates, all variables in first differences. The estimations underlying the results in columns (4) and (5) differ slightly in the variables used.

Röller and Waverman (2001), who find a strong causal link between telecommunications infrastructure and economic output in OECD countries. It is possible that their results were driven by the presence of unit roots in the GDP, the investment in telecommunications infrastructure, and the nonresidential capital stock net of telecommunications capital.

Turning to the demand, supply, and production equations, all of which are used as instruments for the output equation, most of the estimated coefficients display the expected indications and are statistically significant. For the demand equation shown in Table 2.7, the effective demand is inversely related to telephone price for the full sample. There are differences in this effect across income groups, but for the three lowest income groups the price effect is negative.

TABLE 2.6 Output equation—generalized method of moments estimates (all variables in first differences)

Dependent variable: log(GDP)$_{it}$	All countries	OECD	OECD and high non-OECD	Higher middle-income	Lower middle-income	Low-income
log(GDP)$_{i(t-1)}$	0.959	1.34	1.24	1.054	1.046	0.952
	(27.87)**	(29.37)**	(29.11)**	(19.90)**	(19.06)**	(18.41)**
log(GDP)$_{i(t-2)}$	–0.188	–0.382	–0.39	–0.24	–0.339	–0.115
	(7.20)**	(7.96)**	(8.85)**	(4.69)**	(6.46)**	(2.29)**
log(PEN)$_{it}$	0.033	0.012	0.015	0.064	0.032	0.017
	(2.96)**	(1.16)	(0.91)	(3.98)**	(2.36)*	(1.24)
log(KNT)$_{it}$	0.057	–0.033	0.074	0.016	0.073	0.031
	(3.68)**	(1.53)	(2.62)**	(0.82)	(6.07)**	(1.41)
log(TLF)$_{it}$	–0.009	–0.045	–0.008	0.211	0.211	–0.018
	(0.73)	(1.07)	(0.27)	(4.49)**	(4.46)**	(1.50)
Constant	0.003	0.002	0.002	–0.004	–0.005	0.003
	(5.68)**	(2.69)**	(2.45)*	(2.79)**	(3.35)**	(2.67)**
Number of observations	1,596	395	518	321	372	385
Number of countries	95	19	26	20	21	28
Sargan test	687.57**	326.81	400.31	363.27	365.54	371.98

SOURCE: Compiled and calculated by authors from study data set.

NOTES: Absolute values of z statistics are shown in parentheses. In all models, PEN is instrumentalized according to models of equations (2′)–(4′). *Indicates significance at the 5 percent level; **indicates significance at the 1 percent level. GDP indicates gross domestic product; KNT, stock of capital net telecommunications; OECD, Organisation for Economic Co-operation and Development; PEN, penetration rate; TLF, total labor force.

Moreover, the elasticity is less than one, implying inelastic demand for telecommunications. This result is consistent with many other studies, such as those of Doherty (1984), Zona and Jacob (1990), Duncan and Perry (1994), Levy (1996), Gatto, Kelejian, and Stephan (1988), Gatto et al. (1988), and Pascó-Font, Gallardo, and Fry (1999).[8]

Demand for telecommunications infrastructure is positively correlated with income, and income elasticity is considerably higher than the price elasticity.

With respect to the supply equation, neither geographic area nor government surplus (deficit) is significant in explaining telecommunications investment. Although government surplus has the expected positive indication—implying that telecommunications infrastructure investment would be positively

8. These studies found elasticities ranging from –0.21 to –0.475. See Pascó-Font, Gallardo, and Fry (1999) for further details.

TABLE 2.7 Demand equation—generalized method of moments estimates, all variables in first differences

Dependent variable: log(PEN+WL)$_{it}$	All countries	OECD	OECD and high-income non-OECD	Higher middle-income	Lower middle-income	Low-income
log(PEN+WL)$_{i(t-1)}$	0.729	0.944	0.925	0.820	0.695	0.649
	(37.76)**	(160.60)**	(139.07)**	(31.18)**	(20.23)**	(20.12)**
log(GDP/POP)$_{it}$	0.636	0.021	0.017	0.123	0.618	0.234
	(14.99)**	(10.78)**	(5.75)**	(3.33)**	(9.60)**	(3.20)**
log(TELP)$_{it}$	−0.035	0.425	2.048	−0.035	−0.030	−0.080
	(3.07)**	(0.13)	(0.32)	(2.20)*	(1.31)	(3.28)**
Constant	0.001	0.000	0.001	0.007	0.013	0.020
	(0.51)	(0.01)	(3.18)**	(3.39)**	(5.44)**	(6.56)**
Number of observations	1,366	451	597	266	288	346
Number of countries	95	19	26	20	21	28
Sargan test	882.82**	862.11**	663.75**	435.86	519.01	507.75

SOURCE: Compiled and calculated by authors from study data set.

NOTES: Absolute values of z statistics are shown in parentheses. *Indicates significance at the 5 percent level; **indicates significance at the 1 percent level. GDP indicates gross domestic product; OECD, Organisation for Economic Co-operation and Development; PEN, penetration rate; POP, population; TELP, total labor force in millions; WL, waiting list for fixed lines per capita.

affected by a government surplus—this result is not significant in any of the regressions. As expected, the waiting list for fixed lines (per capita) is positively related to the supply of telecommunications infrastructure, suggesting that countries with excess demand tend to invest more in telecommunications infrastructure. Finally, price is positively correlated with investment in telecommunications infrastructure.

The last table reported, Table 2.9, showed the production function, relating investment to penetration rates. As expected, the relationship is positive and significant for the panel of all countries and across all income groups, with the exception of low-income countries. The elasticity is about 0.024, indicating that a one-time 10 percent increase in investment would result in about a 0.2 percent increase in the penetration rate. This is consistent with observations in historic series. Although the geographic area is not significant, this could be because the lagged penetration rate could already be incorporating this effect.

Conclusion

While the empirical approach presented in this chapter mirrors the work of Röller and Waverman (2001), some notable differences exist. Unlike those

TABLE 2.8 Supply equation—generalized method of moments estimates, all variables in first differences

Dependent variable: $\log(TTI)_{it}$	All countries	OECD	OECD and high-income non-OECD	Higher middle-income	Lower middle-income	Low-income
$\log(TTI)_{i(t-1)}$	0.261	0.635	0.626	0.152	0.344	0.394
	(6.82)**	(19.30)**	(17.86)**	(2.50)*	(6.30)**	(5.35)**
WL_{it}	0.104	0.024	−0.005	0.094	0.110	0.076
	(3.56)**	(2.20)*	(0.43)	(2.35)*	(3.55)**	(0.27)
$\log(GA)_{it}$	−238.924	−96.720	31.892	—	—	—
	(0.48)	(0.99)	(0.22)	—	—	—
GD_{it}	0.000	0.000	0.000	0.000	0.000	0.000
	(0.11)	(0.44)	(0.39)	(1.44)	(1.23)	(0.52)
$\log(TELP)_{it}$	0.116	0.477	0.075	0.654	−0.062	0.115
	(2.21)*	(7.58)**	(3.64)**	(3.77)**	(0.47)	(0.62)
Constant	0.047	0.000	0.018	0.053	0.062	0.023
	(9.90)**	(0.00)	(6.19)**	(5.65)**	(5.30)**	(1.99)*
Number of observations	889	290	365	200	189	135
Number of countries	83	19	24	19	20	20
Sargan test	495.63	383.14	421.97	205.16	272.86	154.96

SOURCE: Compiled and calculated by authors from study data set.

NOTES: Absolute values of z statistics are shown in parentheses. *Indicates significance at the 5 percent level; **indicates significance at the 1 percent level. GA indicates geographic area in thousands of square kilometers; GD, goverment surplus (deficit) in billions of U.S. dollars; OECD, Organisation for Economic Co-operation and Development; TELP, total labor force in millions; TTI, telecommunications infrastructure; WL, waiting list for fixed lines per capita.

of Röller and Waverman (2001), our estimates are corrected for the presence of unit roots. Estimates based on the entire set of countries indicated a positive causal relationship between telecommunications infrastructure and GDP. These estimates suggested that a 1 percent increase in the telecommunications penetration rate could be expected to lead to a 0.03 percent increase in GDP. Piecewise regression models for different country groups revealed a nonlinear effect of telecommunications infrastructure on economic output. The impact was particularly pronounced for lower and higher middle-income countries and was muted for other country groups. These results imply that telecommunications networks need to reach a critical mass, or threshold level, of connectivity before impact on economic output is discernible. Of note, growth effects were strongest for telecommunications penetration rates of between 5 and 15 percent. Outside this range, growth effects were limited.

TABLE 2.9 Production equation—generalized method of moments estimates, all variables in first differences

Dependent variable: log(PEN)$_{it}$	All countries	OECD	OECD and high-income non-OECD	Higher middle-income	Lower middle-income	Low-income
log(PEN)$_{i(t-1)}$	0.941	0.944	0.883	0.916	0.971	0.885
	(119.56)**	(160.60)**	(61.59)**	(81.08)**	(87.08)**	(47.38)**
log(TTI)$_{it}$	0.024	0.021	0.013	0.038	0.046	0.005
	(7.27)**	(10.78)**	(3.02)**	(9.95)**	(10.33)**	(1.10)
log(GA)$_{it}$	−1.91	0.425	—	−294.542	0.000	0.000
	(0.13)	(0.13)		(0.56)		
Constant	0.002	0.000	0.010	0.003	0.002	0.011
	(3.64)**	(0.01)	(8.39)**	(3.20)**	(2.14)*	(6.99)**
Number of observations	1,671	451	724	350	379	345
Number of countries	95	19	49	20	21	28
Sargan test	984.73**	862.11**	648.38**	483.67	485.22	482.14

SOURCE: Compiled and calculated by authors from study data set.

NOTES: Absolute values of z statistics are shown in parentheses. *Indicates significance at the 5 percent level; **indicates significance at the 1 percent level. GA indicates geographic area in thousands of square kilometers; OECD, Organisation for Economic Co-operation and Development; PEN, penetration rate; TTI, telecommunications infrastructure.

While there are some similarities between the results presented here and those of Röller and Waverman (2001), some differences also exist. Röller and Waverman (2001) report a similar positive relationship, but their estimate of the impact of telecommunications infrastructure on economic output is about 50 percent larger than our estimate (0.045 versus 0.03). They also report a critical mass for telecommunications infrastructure, estimating the level to be close to a universal penetration rate of about 40 percent, and suggest that growth effects are strongest in OECD countries. While we also detect a critical mass, our results suggest that this threshold is reached at a much lower penetration level and that growth effects are strongest for countries in the low- and middle-income categories.

Notwithstanding these differences, considering that the average telecommunications penetration rate in low-income countries is below 1, our estimates imply that developing countries need continued investment in their telecommunications networks if they are to reap positive growth effects. Marginal improvements in telecommunications infrastructure are unlikely to yield discernible growth effects. Moreover, given the even lower penetration level of other forms of ICT, growth effects will remain elusive without widespread increases in access to these technologies in low-income countries.

Appendix 2A: Additional Data Set Details

See tables on pages 49–53.

Appendix 2B: Construction of Physical Capital Stock and Telecommunications Capital Stock

The telecommunications capital stock is constructed using PIM, which may be represented by the following equation:

$$K_t = (1 - \delta)^t K(0) + \sum_{i=0}^{t-1} I_{t-i}(1 - \delta)^i. \tag{1}$$

In this equation, K_t is the stock of capital at time t, δ is the rate of depreciation, $K(0)$ is the initial stock of capital in period 0, and I_{t-i} is investment. Since we did not know the initial stock of telecommunications capital, we estimated the initial stock using

$$K_{t-1} = I_t / (g + \delta), \tag{2}$$

where g is the growth rate of fixed telephone lines. For the stock of telecommunications capital, we used the growth rate of fixed telephone lines. Following Röller and Waverman (2001) we used a three-year average for investments in telecommunications and growth in fixed telephone lines and adopted a 10 percent rate of depreciation for capital. Given the high depreciation rate for telecommunications capital, the initial stock plays only a minor role in the 1990s.

To construct the physical capital stock series, we built on the work by Nehru and Dhareshwar (1993), who provide a data set on physical capital stock for a group of 92 developing and industrial countries covering the period 1960–90. Following their methodology, and using data on gross domestic fixed investment from the World Bank (2002), we extended the physical capital stock series to cover, as far as possible, the period 1980–2000 and the 113 countries in our data set. We employed the same measure for constructing the initial stock of physical capital for the countries for which data on output growth and gross domestic fixed investment were available. For construction of the stock of physical capital we used PIM and adopted a rate of depreciation of 4 percent for all countries. To avoid short-term variations in growth in aggregate output and investment, we used a three-year average for investment and output following Harberger (1978).

TABLE 2A.1 Countries included in the study

Country income group	Regional groupings[a]					
	African region	Asian region	Australian region	European region	Central and North American region, including Caribbean	South America
Low-income	Benin	Bangladesh			Nicaragua	
	Burkina Faso	India				
	Burundi	Indonesia				
	Cameroon	Mongolia				
	Central African Republic	Nepal				
	Comoros	Pakistan				
	Congo	Yemen				
	Côte d'Ivoire					
	Ethiopia					
	Gambia					
	Ghana					
	Kenya					
	Lesotho					
	Madagascar					
	Malawi					

(continued)

TABLE 2A.1 *Continued*

Country income group	Regional groupings[a]					
	African region	Asian region	Australian region	European region	Central and North American region, including Caribbean	South America
	Mali Mauritania Mozambique Niger Nigeria Rwanda Senegal Sierra Leone Tanzania Togo Uganda Zambia Zimbabwe					
Lower middle-income	Algeria Cape Verde Egypt Morocco Namibia Swaziland Tunisia	China Iran Jordan Philippines Sri Lanka Syria Thailand	Fiji Papua New Guinea	Bulgaria Romania	Belize El Salvador Honduras Jamaica	Bolivia Colombia Ecuador Paraguay Peru

Higher middle-income	Botswana Gabon Mauritius Seychelles South Africa		Hungary Poland Turkey	Costa Rica Mexico Panama Saint Kits Trinidad Barbados	Argentina Chile Uruguay Venezuela

High-income non-OECD	Bahrain
	Korea,
	  Republic of
	Malaysia
	Oman
	Hong Kong
	Israel
	Kuwait
	Singapore
	United Arab
	  Emirates
			Cyprus
			Malta		

OECD (high-income)	Japan	Australia New Zealand	Austria Belgium Denmark Finland France Greece Ireland Italy Luxembourg Netherlands Norway Portugal Spain Sweden Switzerland United Kingdom	Canada United States	

NOTE: OECD indicates Organisation for Economic Co-operation and Development.

[a]Regional groupings are based on world development indicators categories (World Bank 2002).

TABLE 2A.2 Variables and summary statistics for different income groups

Variable	Low-income	Lower middle-income	Income groups Higher middle-income	High-income non-OECD	OECD
GDP (million 1995 U.S. dollars)	15,755.73	35,727.42	68,404.39	33,132.12	752,551.27
	(49,554.76)	(92,365.61)	(101,965.25)	(35,844.59)	(1,445,354.68)
Total labor force (millions)	38.19	27.18	6.30	1.21	26.25
	(123.06)	(112.88)	(8.41)	(0.99)	(34.05)
Total physical capital stock	41,855.14	94,706.70	183,438.61	89,215.31	2,180,765.34
(million 1995 U.S. dollars)	(121,767.55)	(203,262.88)	(247,650.52)	(94,773.50)	(4,064,327.04)
Annual investment in telecommunications	2,166.63	2,798.31	6,028.50	2,131.78	67,653.58
(million 1995 U.S. dollars)	(5,857.52)	(9,199.73)	(9,978.45)	(2,672.64)	(134,908.30)
Land area	559.85	815.71	500.43	16.70	1,430.49
(1,000 square kilometers)	(619.05)	(1,765.74)	(697.60)	(26.48)	(2,992.91)
Government budget surplus (deficit)	−985.72	−781.10	−1,833.62	135.19	−25,797.30
(million 1995 U.S. dollars)	(3,313.11)	(1,909.74)	(4,852.64)	(3,967.68)	(53,174.59)
Fixed telephone lines per 100 inhabitants	0.58	4.70	10.87	28.47	41.75
	(0.67)	(5.21)	(9.34)	(14.88)	(14.90)

Cellular phone subscribers per 100 inhabitants	0.11 (0.51)	0.78 (2.56)	2.63 (7.55)	8.05 (17.15)	9.57 (19.37)
Telephone service revenue per fixed line (1995 U.S. dollars)	995.48 (642.18)	667.79 (516.73)	791.89 (632.76)	28,335.73 (162540.96)	648.76 (216.80)
Telephone service revenue per cellular line (1995 U.S. dollars)	701.33 (1,957.44)	609.23 (487.91)	977.35 (976.53)	1,172.61 (1,188.79)	1,079.01 (1,174.86)
Waiting list for fixed lines per 100 inhabitants	0.28 (0.41)	1.98 (3.01)	1.58 (1.71)	1.52 (2.20)	0.63 (1.63)
Internet users per 1,000 inhabitants	1.28 (2.66)	8.42 (15.97)	31.17 (61.41)	85.59 (112.47)	112.25 (138.20)
Internet hosts per 10,000 inhabitants	0.06 (0.27)	0.86 (3.15)	8.57 (24.23)	41.25 (95.79)	208.38 (403.95)
Personal computers per 1,000 inhabitants	3.31 (3.67)	17.63 (19.89)	44.12 (45.69)	126.05 (106.70)	184.81 (138.17)

SOURCES: Data on 1995 GDP, total labor force, annual investment, land area, and government budget surplus (deficit) are from World Bank (2002); data on total physical capital stock and annual investment in telecommunications are from Nehru and Dhareshwar (1993) and authors' estimations based on World Bank (2002); data on fixed telephone lines, cellular telephones, the Internet, and personal computers are from ITU (2002).

NOTES: Standard deviations are shown in parentheses. GDP indicates gross domestic product; OECD, Organisation for Economic Co-operation and Development.

Appendix 2C: Supplementary Figures

FIGURE 2C.1 Fixed telephone lines and gross domestic product in low-income countries, 1980

GDP per capita (1995 US$)

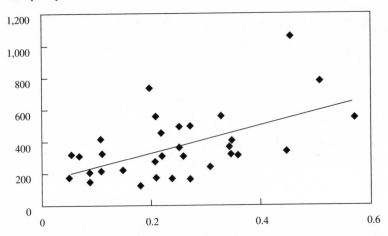

Fixed telephone lines per 100 inhabitants

SOURCE: Calculated by authors from the study data set.

FIGURE 2C.2 Fixed telephone lines and gross domestic product in lower middle-income countries, 1980

GDP per capita (1995 US$)

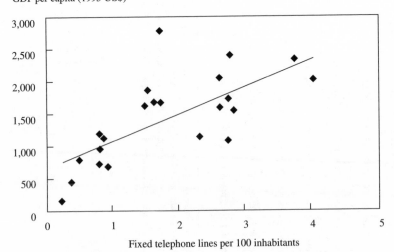

Fixed telephone lines per 100 inhabitants

SOURCE: Calculated by authors from the study data set.

FIGURE 2C.3 Fixed telephone lines and gross domestic product in higher middle-income countries, 1980

GDP per capita (1995 US$)

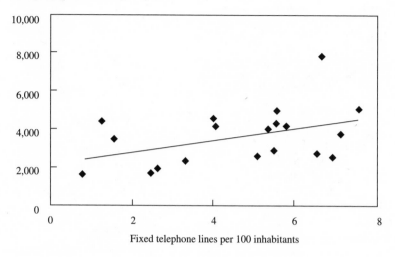

Fixed telephone lines per 100 inhabitants

SOURCE: Calculated by authors from the study data set.

FIGURE 2C.4 Fixed telephone lines and gross domestic product in non–Organisation for Economic Co-operation and Development countries, 1980

GDP per capita (1995 US$)

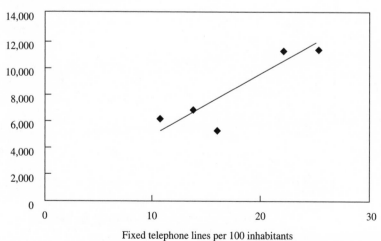

Fixed telephone lines per 100 inhabitants

SOURCE: Calculated by authors from the study data set.

FIGURE 2C.5 Fixed telephone lines and gross domestic product in Africa, 1980

GDP per capita (1995 US$)

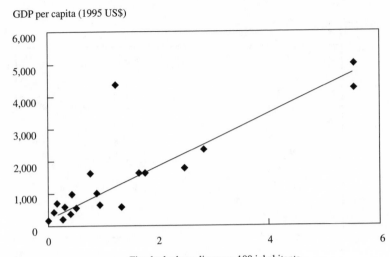

Fixed telephone lines per 100 inhabitants

SOURCE: Calculated by authors from the study data set.

FIGURE 2C.6 Fixed telephone lines and gross domestic product in the Asian region, 1980

GDP per capita (1995 US$)

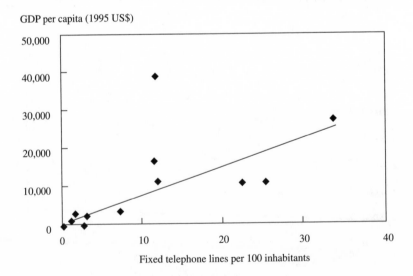

Fixed telephone lines per 100 inhabitants

SOURCE: Calculated by authors from the study data set.

FIGURE 2C.7 Fixed telephone lines and gross domestic product in the Australian region, 1980

GDP per capita (1995 US$)

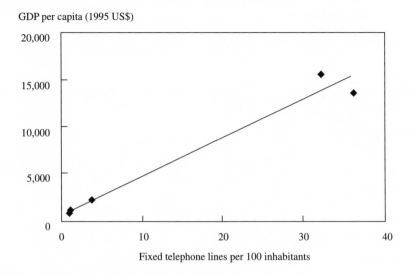

Fixed telephone lines per 100 inhabitants

SOURCE: Calculated by authors from the study data set.

FIGURE 2C.8 Fixed telephone lines and gross domestic product in the European region, 1980

GDP per capita (1995 US$)

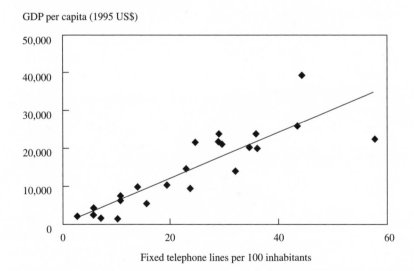

Fixed telephone lines per 100 inhabitants

SOURCE: Calculated by authors from the study data set.

FIGURE 2C.9 Fixed telephone lines and gross domestic product in the Central and North American region, including the Caribbean, 1980

GDP per capita (1995 US$)

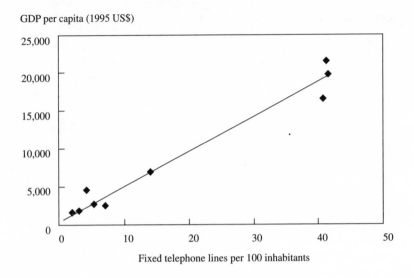

Fixed telephone lines per 100 inhabitants

SOURCE: Calculated by authors from the study data set.

FIGURE 2C.10 Fixed telephone lines and gross domestic product in South America, 1980

GDP per capita (1995 US$)

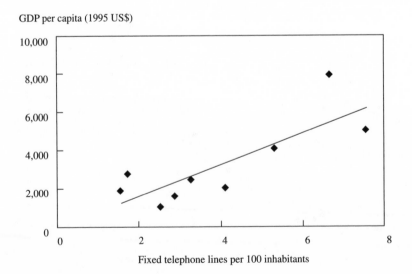

Fixed telephone lines per 100 inhabitants

SOURCE: Calculated by authors from the study data set.

Appendix 2D: Econometric Model and Empirical Results

Econometric Model

The Röller and Waverman (2001) four-equation system consists of an aggregate production function equation in which the coefficient on *TELECOM* estimates the one-way causal relationship between the stock of telecommunications, measured through the penetration rate, and economic output:

$$GDP_{it} = f(K_{it}, HK_{it}, TELECOM_{it}, t). \tag{1}$$

This equation is empirically estimated as follows:

$$\log(GDP_{it}) = a_{0i} + a_1 \log(K_{it}) + a_2 \log(TLF_{it}) + a_3 \log(PEN_{it}) + a_4 t + u_{it}^1, \tag{1'}$$

where *GDP* is the real gross domestic product, *K* is a measure of the real capital stock net of telecommunication capital as mentioned in the data section. *TLF* is the total labor force, which is a proxy for human capital, and *t* is a linear time trend. The variable *PEN,* that is, the penetration rate, is defined by the number of fixed lines per hundred inhabitants. This variable is a proxy for the stock of telecommunications infrastructure (*TELECOM*).

The demand for telecommunications infrastructure is treated as a function of per capita GDP and the price of telephone service:

$$TELECOM_{it} = h(GDP_{it}/POP_{it}, TELP_{it}). \tag{2}$$

Given that the objective is to measure the demand for telecommunications, in this equation *TELECOM* is approximated by the sum of the penetration rate and the waiting list per hundred habitants (*WL*). The price for telephone service is approximated by the total service revenue per fixed line (*TELP*) and per capita GDP measures income. The empirical counterpart of (2) is given by

$$\log(PEN_{it} + WL_{it}) = b_0 + b_1 \log(GDP_{it}/POP_{it}) + b_2 \log(TELP_{it}) + u_{it}^2. \tag{2'}$$

The third equation corresponds to the supply of telecommunications investment. It is treated as a function of the price of telephone service (*TELP*) and other variables specific to the country:

$$TTI_{it} = g(TELP_{it}, Z_{it}). \tag{3}$$

The empirical counterpart of this equation is given as:

$$\log(TTI_{it}) = c_0 + c_1 \log(GA_{it}) + c_2 GD_{it} + \log(TELP)_{it} + u_{it}^3, \tag{3'}$$

where (as in the demand equation) service revenue per fixed line is used as a proxy for price. The scale of the country and the economic well-being of the country is measured by the geographic area in thousands of square kilometers (*GA*) and the government surplus (deficit) in billions of 1985 U.S. dollars (*GD*), respectively.

Finally the telecommunications infrastructure production function measures the relationship between investment in telecommunications infrastructure and the change in the stock of telecommunications infrastructure:

$$TELECOM_{it} - TELECOM_{i,t-1} = (TTI_{it}, R_{it}). \tag{4}$$

To empirically estimate this equation, the change in the stock of telecommunications is approximated by the change in penetration as a function of investment in telecommunications infrastructure and the geographic area:

$$\log(PEN_{it}/PEN_{t,t-1}) = d_0 + d_1 \log(TTI_{it}) + d_2 \log(GA_{it}) + u_{it}^4. \tag{4'}$$

Since Equations (2)–(4) involve the demand for and supply of telecommunications infrastructure, they endogenize telecommunications infrastructure. All four equations may be estimated as a system or using a two-step estimation procedure.

Röller and Waverman (2001) estimate the empirical model outlined above using variables in levels, and with and without country-level fixed effects. An issue that Röller and Waverman do not take into account is that variables such as GDP and capital may follow a random walk. If these variables do follow a random walk, then a regression of one on the other may lead to spurious results. De-trending the variables before running the regression may not help because the de-trended series may still be nonstationary. It is likely that only first-differencing will yield stationary series.

We attempt to solve this problem by estimating equations in first differences, and in our empirical work we assume that the error terms in the four equations follow an error component model,

$$u_{it} = \mu_i + v_{it}, \tag{5}$$

where $\mu \sim IID(0, \sigma^2\mu)$ and $v_{it} \sim IID(0, \sigma^2 v)$ are independent of each other and represent unmeasured time-invariant country and country/year effects, respectively. Given this error structure, lagged values of the dependent variable (let's call the generic dependent variable Y[9]) will be correlated with the error terms in equations (1)–(4). Even though the first difference transformation mitigates this correlation problem by eliminating the individual effect, μ_i, OLS estimation of the differenced model would also be inconsistent because now ΔY_{it-1} and Δv_{it} are correlated (given that Y_{it-1} and u_{it-1} are correlated). Anderson and Hsiao (1981) observed that as long as u_{it} is not serially correlated, ΔY_{it-2} (which depends on the second and further lags of u_{it}) is clearly correlated with ΔY_{it-1} but not with Δv_{it} (which only depends on v_{it} and v_{it-1}). Therefore, ΔY_{it-2} is a valid instrument for ΔY_{it-1} and may be used to estimate the model consistently.

---

9. Y represents the four dependent variables in the four equations: $\log(GDP)$, $\log(PEN + WL)$, $\log(TTI)$ and $\log(PEN_t/PEN_{t-1})$.

Arellano and Bond (1991) observed that, when the number of periods is small and the number of groups in the panel is large, in order to gain efficiency, the number of valid instruments grows with the number of available periods. For example, for $t = 3$ the only valid instrument is Y_{it-1}, but for $t = 4$ both Y_{it-1} and Y_{it-2} are valid instruments. Consequently, for any given period T, the set of valid instruments becomes $(Y_{i1}, Y_{i1t-1}, \ldots, Y_{iT-2})$. Because the exogenous variables (called x_{it} for simplicity, though they actually include the model's other explanatory variables such as capital and labor force) may be predetermined and correlated with μ_I, the valid set of instruments is $[x_{i1'}, x_{i2'}, \ldots, x_{i(s-1)'}]$, given that $E(x_{it} v_{is}) \neq 0$ for $s < t$ and otherwise equals zero.

With the instruments obtained from the lagged Y and the lagged explanatory variables, a matrix of instruments W[10] can be obtained, so that $E(W_i' \Delta v_i) = 0$. Using generalized method of moments (GMM), the one-step estimators of α and δ would be

$$\begin{pmatrix} \hat{\alpha}_1 \\ \hat{\delta}_1 \end{pmatrix} = ([\Delta Y_{-1} \Delta X]'WV_N^{-1}W'[\Delta Y_{-1}\Delta X])^{-1}([\Delta Y_{-1}\Delta X]'WV_N^{-1}W'\Delta Y), \quad (6)$$

where

$$V_N = \sum_{i=1}^{N} W_i'(\Delta v_i)(\Delta v_i)'W_i. \quad (7)$$

This GMM estimator does not require any knowledge of the initial conditions or distributions of v_i and μ_i. However, to correct for the presence of unobserved firm heteroskedasticity, we operationalize this procedure by replacing Δv with differenced residuals obtained from the preliminary consistent estimator δ_1. This yields the more efficient, two-step GMM estimator (Arellano and Bond 1991, 1998) used in our study. This second-step estimation provides robust standard errors. In the absence of such standard errors, test statistics could be highly misleading, especially in long panel data sets such as the ones with which we are working.[11]

References

Anderson, T. W., and C. Hsiao. 1981. Estimation of dynamic models with error components. *Journal of the American Statistical Association* 76 (375): 598–606.

Antle, J. M. 1983. Infrastructure and aggregate agricultural productivity: International evidence. *Economic Development and Cultural Change* 31 (4): 609–619.

---

10. The transformed W_i are deviations from individual means.

11. For the hypothesis that there is no second-order serial correlation for the disturbances of the first-differenced equation, we follow the test by Arellano and Bond (1991, 282), which assumes the consistency of the GMM estimation because it relies on the following: $E[\Delta v_{it} \Delta v_{i,t-2}] = 0$. Finally, we performed Sargan's (1958) test of overidentifying restrictions, suggested by Arellano and Bond (1991).

Arellano, M., and S. Bond. 1991. Some tests of specification for panel data: Monte Carlo evidence and an application to employment equations. *Review of Economic Studies* 58 (2): 277–297.

———. 1998. Dynamic panel data estimation using DPD98 for Gauss. Working Paper No. 88/15, Institute for Fiscal Studies, London.

Aschauer, D. A. 1989. Is public expenditure productive? *Journal of Monetary Economics* 23 (2): 177–200.

Craig, B. J., P. G. Pardey, and J. Roseboom. 1997. International productivity patterns: Accounting for input quality, infrastructure, and research. *American Journal of Agricultural Economics* 79 (4): 1064–1076.

Doherty, A. 1984. Empirical estimates of demand and cost elasticities of local telephone service. In *Changing patterns in regulated markets and technology: The effect of public utility pricing.* East Lansing, Mich., U.S.A.: Michigan State University Institute of Public Utility Pricing, Institute of Public Utilities.

Duncan, G., and D. Perry. 1994. IntalLATA toll demand modelling a dynamic analysis of revenue and usage data. *Information Economics and Policy* 6: 163–178.

Ford, R., and P. Poret. 1991. Infrastructure and private-sector productivity. *OECD Economic Studies* 17 (Autumn): 63–89.

Garcia-Mila, T., and T. J. McGuire. 1992. The contribution of publicly provided inputs to states' economies. *Regional Science and Urban Economics* 22 (2): 229–241.

Garcia-Mila, T., T. J. McGuire, and R. H. Porter. 1996. The effect of public capital in state-level production functions reconsidered. *Review of Economics and Statistics* 78 (1): 177–180.

Gatto, J. J., H. Kelejian, and S. Stephan. 1988. Stochastic generalizations of demand systems with an application to telecommunications. *Information Economics and Policy* 3 (4): 283–309.

Gatto, J. J., L. Hooper, P. Robinson, and H. Tyan. 1988. Interstate switched access demand analysis. *Information Economics and Policy* 3 (4): 333–358.

Gordon, R. J. 2000. Does the new economy measure up to the great inventions of the past? *Journal of Economic Perspective* 14 (4): 49–74.

Harberger, A. 1978. Perspectives on capital and technology in less developed countries. In *Contemporary Economic Analysis,* M. J. Artis and A. R. Nobay, eds. London: Croom Helm.

Hardy, A. 1980. The role of the telephone in economic development. *Telecommunications Policy* 4 (4): 278–286.

Hirschmann, A. O. 1958. *The strategy of economic development.* New Haven, Conn., USA: Yale University Press.

Holtz-Eakin, D. 1994. Public-sector capital and the productivity puzzle. *Review of Economics and Statistics* 76 (1): 12–21.

ITU (International Telecommunications Union). 2002. Online database. <www.itu.int/home/index.html> (accessed February 2002).

Jipp, A. 1963. Wealth of nations and telephone density. *Telecommunications Journal* 20: 199–201.

Kormendi, R., and P. Meguire. 1985. Macro-economic determinants of growth: Cross-country evidence. *Journal of Monetary Economics* 16: 141–163.

Leff, N. H. 1984. Externalities, information costs, and social benefit–cost analysis for economic development: An example from telecommunications. *Economic Development and Cultural Change* 32 (2): 255–276.

Levy, A. 1996. Semi parametric estimation of telecommunications demand. Ph.D. dissertation, University of California–Berkeley, Berkeley, Calif., USA.

Madden, G., and S. J. Savage. 2000. Telecommunications and economic growth. *International Journal of Social Economics* 27 (7–10): 893–906.

Mankiw, N. G., D. Romer, and D. N. Weil. 1992. A contribution to the empirics of growth. *Quarterly Journal of Economics* 107: 407–437.

Munnell, A. H. 1992. Policy watch: Infrastructure investment and economic growth. *Journal of Economic Perspectives* 6 (4): 189–198.

Nehru, V., and A. Dhareshwar. 1993. A new database on physical capital stock: Sources, methodology and results. *Revista de Análisis Económico* 8 (1): 37–59.

Norton, S. W. 1992. Transaction costs, telecommunications and the microeconomics of macroeconomic growth. *Economic Development and Cultural Change* 41 (1): 175–196.

Oliner, S. D., and D. E. Sichel. 2000. The resurgence of growth in the late 1990s: Is information technology the story? *Journal of Economic Perspectives* 14 (4): 3–22.

Pascó-Font, A., J. Gallardo, and V. Fry. 1999. La demanda residencial de telefonía básica en el Perú. In *Estudio en Telecomunicac*iones No. 4. Lima: Organismo Supervisor de la Inversión Privada en Telecomunicaciones (OSIPTEL).

Panzar, J. C. 2000. A methodology for measuring the costs of universal service obligations. *Information Economics and Policy* 12 (3): 211–220.

Pohjola, M., ed. 2001. *Information technology, productivity and economic growth: International evidence and implications for economic development.* World Institute for Development Economics Research, United Nations University, Studies in Development Economics. Oxford and New York: Oxford University Press.

Roche, E. M., and M. J. Blaine. 1996. *Information technology, development and policy.* Avebury, UK: Aldershot.

Röller, L.-H., and L. Waverman. 2001. Telecommunications infrastructure and economic growth: A simultaneous approach. *American Economic Review* 91 (4): 909–923.

Saith, A. 2002. ICT: Hope or hype. Paper presented at ICTs and Indian Development, held in Bangalore, India, December.

Saunders, R. J., J. J. Warford, and B. Wellenius. 1983. *Telecommunications and economic development.* Baltimore: Johns Hopkins University Press.

Stiroh, K. J. 2002. Are ICT spillovers driving the new economy. *Review of Income and Wealth* 48 (1): 33–57.

Torero, M., S. Chowdhury, and V. Galdo. 2003. Willingness to pay for the rural telephone service in Bangladesh and Peru. *Information Economics and Policy* 15 (3): 327–361.

World Bank. 2002. *World development indicators.* Online database <www.worldbank.org/data/countrydata/countrydata.html> (accessed February 2002).

Zona, J. D., and R. Jacob. 1990. The total bill concept: Defining and testing alternative views. Presented at the Bellcore/Bell Canada Industry Forum, "Telecommunications Demand Analysis with Dynamic Regulation," held in Hilton Head, S.C., in April 1990. Cambridge, Mass., USA: National Economic Research Associates.

3 Institutional and Public Policy Aspects of ICT Infrastructure Provision

MAXIMO TORERO AND JOACHIM VON BRAUN

The growing demand for information and communication technologies (ICT)[1] in developing countries is evident from long waiting lists for telephone connection, growing demand for cellular telephony, and rapidly expanding numbers of Internet users. For this reason, consideration of ICT is increasingly being integrated into national development agendas. In fact, a virtual "phone frenzy" occurred in the 1990s in the developing world, requiring some US$200 billion in investments. This was intended to be achieved through a massive influx of foreign capital, encouraged by the deregulation of developing-country markets to open them to equipment manufacturers and service providers. A rapidly increasing number of developing countries have either begun the process of privatizing their telephone companies or have plans to do so. According to the International Telecommunications Union (ITU), the percentage of Asian and Latin American countries with privatized telecommunications systems increased to almost 50 percent between 1997 and 2003 (in Latin America and the Caribbean, examples of such countries include Argentina, Bolivia, Brazil, Chile, Guatemala, Honduras, Mexico, Nicaragua, Panama, Paraguay, Peru, Trinidad and Tobago, and Venezuela; and in Asia examples include India, Indonesia, Pakistan, Sri Lanka, and Thailand). In Africa, as of 2003, 14 of 42 African ITU member states had privatized their operations and another 8 had plans to do so (examples of these countries include Cape Verde, Côte d'Ivoire, Ghana, Guinea, Uganda, and Zambia).

---

1. The discussion in this chapter focuses on the benefits of increased information made available by ICT rather than on the technologies themselves. Nevertheless, the term "ICT" encompasses both information and the technologies that facilitate its exchange. As discussed in Chapter 1, telephony is used throughout this book as a proxy for ICT more generally because of the dearth of statistical data on ICT in developing countries (which is in the process of being addressed) and—most importantly for the issues under consideration here—the reality that, for the foreseeable future, telephony is the ICT that will have the greatest penetration and impact for poor people.

The privatization of state-owned telecommunications systems has had an important impact on the quality of infrastructure. It has also had the effect of releasing state resources for more pressing social needs. Importantly, telephone coverage in countries that have undergone reform has increased substantially, reducing the large service gap in most of them, and the introduction of market mechanisms and incentives has enabled private investment to reach users more quickly and efficiently than under former regulations. A large gap still remains in most countries, however, especially in rural areas, where costs, lack of information, or risk associated with installing the infrastructure prevent private initiatives from doing so. This is a universal problem. Several initiatives have been implemented worldwide in attempts to address this gap in access to basic infrastructure both for the rural poor and marginalized inhabitants of urban areas. Although there is little doubt that information and knowledge can affect poverty reduction, verified data are still lacking for the identification of solutions with the greatest impact (Accascina 2001). In addition, little research has been done to determine the critical mass of technologies necessary to maximize their potential benefits.

This chapter examines the institutional factors necessary to facilitate the development of ICT as well as the kinds of interventions in use today, following the conceptual framework established for this volume (see Figure 3.1). The questions asked include the following:

- Are these interventions necessary?
- Are poor people directly affected by the introduction of ICT or do they receive benefits only indirectly via a "trickle down" effect?
- Where should interventions be targeted most effectively: at the village or district level, or at nation or global levels?
- Are there current examples of institutional frameworks and government interventions under which ICT is helping to reduce poverty?
- Are there other factors that should be considered when utilizing ICT as a poverty reduction tool?

This chapter continues with an analysis of the benefits of ICT, including specific characteristics that make some government intervention necessary. Case studies are then presented that outline different experiences under various institutional frameworks in Bangladesh, China, Ghana, Laos, and Peru.

Theoretical Issues and the Political ICT Economy

Information technologies can be defined as technologies that facilitate the production, gathering, distribution, consumption, and storage of information. The

FIGURE 3.1 Conceptual framework: Area of analysis dealt with in Chapter 3

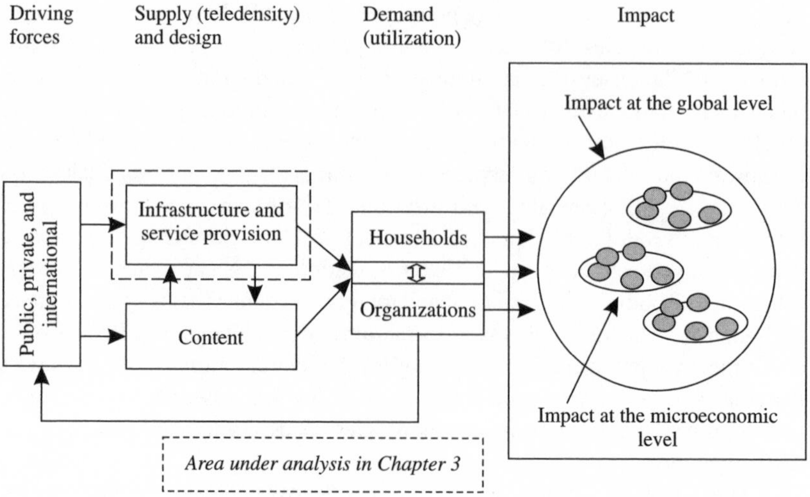

most prevalent of these technologies are fixed telephone lines[2] and cellular telephones, the Internet, and email. Markets for these technologies have characteristics that distinguish them from markets for products. These include significant
scales of production; compatibility of standards; switching and "lock-in" costs,
meaning that once you are committed to certain technologies it is expensive and
inconvenient to change to others; and consumption or network externalities,
meaning that an existing ICT user may well benefit from the addition of new
network users (Shapiro and Varian 1999; Shy 2001).

ICT-Specific Characteristics

As Shapiro and Varian (1999) explain, information is costly to produce but
cheap to reproduce. The cost of producing the first copy of information goods
may be substantial, but the cost of reproducing additional copies is negligible
(that is, high fixed costs and low marginal costs). This cost structure leads to
substantial economies of scale. Moreover, the fixed costs are predominantly
"sunk costs" (meaning that they are not recoverable), while the marginal costs
of additional units tend not to increase as with other commodities.

---

2. Throughout this book, fixed telephone lines are defined as lines that connect a customer's
equipment (telephone set, facsimile machine, computer) to the public switched telephone network
(PSTN) and that have a dedicated port on a telephone exchange. In most countries, fixed (main) lines
also include public payphones.

On the other hand, complementarities are often a crucial factor in information markets. If consumers want to access the Internet, they need a computer, a telephone line, and an Internet provider. In this sense, and unlike simple consumables like bread, ICT must often be consumed together with other products. In some cases, new technologies are linked with lock-in effects as mentioned above. While lock-in effects are not as extreme as new technologies, which actually displace old technologies, they can affect a firm's business strategy, the options available to it, and its ability to compete.[3] Another feature of many ICT-related products is that they tend to exhibit network externalities. Communication technologies are a prime example: telephones, email, Internet access, fax machines, and modems, all exhibit network externalities. Would someone subscribe to a telephone service knowing nobody else subscribed? Would people use email if nobody else did? These examples demonstrate, as mentioned by Shy (2001), that the number of other people using similar or compatible products affects the utility derived from consumption of these goods.

The presence of these standard-adoption effects can profoundly affect the market behavior of firms and consumers. The precise nature of the market outcome depends on how consumers form expectations on the size of the network. The reliance on joint-consumer expectations generates multiple equilibriums, whereby in one equilibrium all consumers adopt the new technologies, and in the other no one adopts them (Shy 2001). Both equilibriums are "rational" from the consumers' viewpoint because they reflect the best response to the decisions made by all other consumers in the market. Therefore, these kinds of technologies tend to be introduced with long lead times followed by explosive growth. The pattern results from positive feedback: as the installed base of users grows, more and more users find adoption worthwhile. The key challenge is to obtain a critical mass so that the market can build.[4]

---

3. The extreme historical example of a lock-in problem is the case of the layout of a computer keyboard in the so-called QWERTY arrangement. Why is this slower arrangement still in use, even though others—such as the Dvorak (1932) system—appear to be more efficient? The problem stems from the obstacle to any one individual changing systems, given that the benefit to any one person depends on which system everyone else is using. Hence, the problem ceases to be simply a question of QWERTY or Dvorak in a vacuum. This divergence between individual costs and social gains occurs whenever a system of production or organizational form exhibits externalities such that the cost or benefit of individual adoption depends on the volume of other individuals adopting that same system. Therefore the costs of adoption may be reduced by the number of existing adopters (Shy 2001).

4. A nice example of critical mass is the advent of the facsimile machine. The basic technology was patented in 1843, and AT&T introduced it in the United States in 1925. However, fax machines remained a niche product until the mid-1980s, when the demand for and supply of machines exploded over a five-year period. Before 1982, virtually no one had a fax machine, but after 1987 the majority of businesses had one or more. The Internet follows the same pattern. The first email message was sent in 1969, but up until the mid-1980s email was used only by "techies." Internet technology was developed in the early 1970s but didn't really take off until the late 1980s. When

From the previous discussion it is clear that competitive equilibriums do not exist in markets for network products and services, as is the case with ICT (Shy 2001); the markets involved cannot function competitively. Even if a competitive equilibrium existed, consumption and production externalities would make the "first welfare theorem" inapplicable.[5] Therefore, market failures may occur in these markets.

Natural Monopolies Versus Access Pricing

Most of the economic literature from the 1950s to the early 1980s suggests that network industries like telephony are subject to strong economies of scale, due to the significant initial investment needed to establish operations, and should therefore be termed "natural monopolies" (see Figure 3.2).[6] Put simply, it is socially wasteful for competing telephone companies to establish separate networks so that customers can choose between carriers.

With this view in mind, most governments license telecommunications service to a single company within a given region, and in many cases for the entire country. To avoid excessive monopoly charges, governments assigned regulating authorities to determine prices based on product costs. In the 1970s, governments began identifying two major problems with the operation of these regulated natural monopolies: the service was relatively poor, and it was not improving at the same rate as technological advances in these industries. In addition, regulators failed to control prices and other charges levied on consumers. Owing to asymmetric information, the regulators failed to observe the true production costs that service providers were facing, so firms tended to inflate their reported production costs as a means of lobbying for higher prices. As a consequence, governments began realizing that despite the significant economies of scale in production, competition could actually improve social welfare, or at least consumer welfare, which tends to gain significantly from improved service and reduced prices.

Nonetheless, under a natural monopoly framework it is argued that a multi-firm industry is inefficient due to a less than optimal scale of production. Hence

---

Internet traffic finally began increasing, however, it doubled each year from 1989 until 1995. When the Internet was privatized in April 1995, it began to grow even faster (Shapiro and Varian 1999).

5. The first welfare theorem says that, given consumer preferences are well behaved, trading in perfectly competitive markets implements a Pareto-optimal allocation of the economy's endowment.

6. An industry is said to be a natural monopoly when the fixed costs of establishing it are indivisible (as is the case in establishing the physical infrastructure for a telecommunications network). Once the establishing costs are incurred, however, output can be produced in unlimited amounts at a constant marginal cost within a certain range. Under these circumstances, marginal cost pricing is socially efficient but private firms find it difficult to enter the market because they cannot afford the establishment costs. Hence competition in such an industry is infeasible.

FIGURE 3.2 Natural monopoly

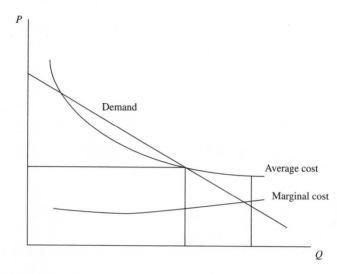

NOTE: *P* indicates price; *Q*, quantity.

the major question is how to solve this inefficiency under a natural monopoly framework. "Access pricing" turned out to be the answer: all firms share use of the existing infrastructure, paying access charges to the firm that owns and maintains it. As a result access pricing is now practiced in most network industries.[7] In fact, this introduction of competition combined with the demand from regulators that existing infrastructure be made available to all competitors at a reasonable access charge has led to even more efficient use of infrastructure.

To be able to institute access pricing, however, the initial infrastructure is needed. This can be a substantial hurdle in poor countries with very low penetration rates (approximate number of telephones per 100 households), where firms will be willing to commit the initial investment only under a natural monopoly. To understand this process Noam (2001) looks at a network as a cost-sharing arrangement among several users. Since fixed costs are high and marginal costs are low, a new participant helps network users to lower their costs. Also, the new user adds to the utility of the existing users by increasing network externalities. The benefit of joining a network rises, though at a declining rate. In the range, below a "critical mass" (point n_1), the development of a network

---

7. In recent years there have been a variety of practices concerning access pricing; see Laffont and Tirole (1996) and Mitchell and Vogelsang (1991).

FIGURE 3.3 Model of network expansion and breakdown

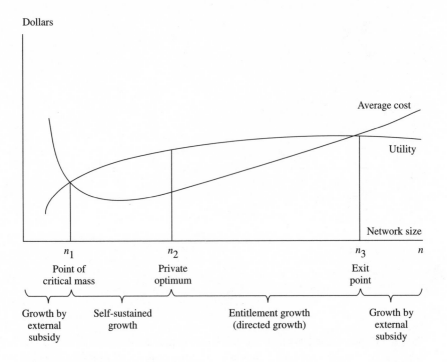

SOURCE: Noam (2001).

will be infeasible unless supported by external sources. Such sources might be subsidies from the government or from other parts of the network organization, as was the case with early cellular networks, or they could be provided by regulatory means, such as assigned monopolies or advantageous terms of interconnection with other networks (Noam 2001; see Figure 3.3).

Beyond the point of critical mass (n_1), a network's growth is self-sustaining. But when growth reaches the private optimum (n_2), marginal net benefits are zero. Left to themselves, existing network subscribers would not accept new members, but from a societal viewpoint, the optimal network size diverges from the private optimum because social welfare increases beyond n_2. The political process, therefore, tends to expand the size of the network beyond the private optimum, to the exit point (n_3), through policies of "universal service connectivity." Beyond that point, the pro-expansion policy creates incentives to form alternative networks: the greater the success of the network policy in achieving universal service connectivity and affordable rates, the greater the pressure of network fracture. In the case of telecommunications, ironically, the breakdown of the network is not caused by the failure of the system but rather by its success (Noam 2001). The traditional fear is that loss of cost-sharing and externalities resulting from the second network reduce social welfare. Where mutual interconnection is assured, however, the externality benefits remain (or even increase).

As may already be assumed, most poor countries and certain rural areas fall into the region before n_1 so government interventions are still necessary to shift their networks further along in the competitive process.

Government Interventions

As discussed above, networks need to reach a critical mass before achieving self-sustained growth; in addition, to achieve universal access, a certain level of government intervention is needed (Shy 2001 and Table 3.4). In less developed countries, and specifically poor areas, the primary objective of universal service is addressing the isolation for communities and households in rural and remote areas. A notionally similar—but more applicable—concept for developing countries is universal access. In contrast to industrialized countries where access to telecommunications is defined at the household level, the notion of universal access seeks to ensure access at a "reasonable level," such as at the community level. While the maintenance of universal service in telecommunications is a cornerstone of public policy in industrialized countries, its minimum achievement has remained the key public policy in developing countries.

At this stage of the discussion it will be helpful to define the kinds of information transmitted via ICT and how they are beneficial. At the local level (meaning in villages, districts, and in some cases urban areas) ICT provides citizens with information about market prices and social services like health and education; at the national level, more complex ICT systems carry information about employment, investment opportunities, and goods and services; and finally, at the broadest level, systems connect nations to the global information infrastructure (though higher levels usually overlap lower levels to some degree).

In terms of interventions, there are those that directly benefit poor people, usually at the local level. A typical example is farmers using technology to obtain daily market prices, allowing them to reduce their costs and increase their profits by eliminating the middleman. Even though the technology may only be available at a nearby district center and data have to be conveyed to villages in hard copy or by word of mouth, farmers directly benefit. If we employ a broader definition of poverty to include the right to participate more widely in society, there are many more ways that poor people directly benefit from ICT. These include improved provision and quality of public goods, more effective use of existing social networks, and new institutional arrangements that strengthen the rights and powers of poor people and communities. The indirect benefits of ICT "trickle down" through the economy, such as when a child from a very poor family manages to go to school, get a good job in the capital city involving the use of technology, and then provide financial support to his or her family in the village. The third type of intervention is the use of ICT in support of poverty reduction mechanisms and development policies and programs. Cross-cutting areas in poverty management can be greatly aided by technology (for example, the use of information systems to manage conditional cash transfer programs through decentralized offices that manage information on program compliance). A common example is the use of databases to organize, monitor, and evaluate the progress of poverty alleviation projects.

Universal Service versus Universal Access

Universal service obligation (USO) is commonly aspired to as a communication policy, the goal being for all the inhabitants of a particular country to have access to a telephone line, regardless of the cost of providing it. Both political and economic rationales underlie USO, which has been enforced by regulatory authorities through service providers worldwide. As mentioned in Crémer (2000) and summarized in Chowdhury (2002a), justifications for the need for USO in the context of ICT include (a) its potential to improve income distribution; (b) its value as a "merit good"; (c) its primary characteristic of creating network externalities; and (d) its potential in decentralizing regional policies (see Crémer 2000).[8]

In terms of income distribution, by providing the same service at the same price to every client (known as "uniform price restriction"), USO ensures price equality between high-cost and low-cost areas. By subsidizing the "basic package" or "connection charge" through higher price for other services, USO can be used to favor low-income groups who would not otherwise subscribe to the network. Such a policy can ensure redistribution toward high-cost areas and low-income groups, while also increasing network externalities. In this way, USO is useful as a distributive mechanism that can simultaneously foster economic development. In fact, some economists think this is the most compelling justification for imposing it (see Cremer et al. 1998, 6, for example). In situations where standard distributive instruments suffer from information asymmetry and are politically costly to implement, USO is a useful way to implement distributive mechanisms.

Maintaining universal service in telecommunications is a cornerstone of public policy in industrialized countries. Yet its minimum achievement has remained a key public policy concern in developing countries. Clearly, the system of sole state-owned providers, which was successfully used in developed countries to meet USO, failed in developing countries. Historically, monopolistic state-owned telecommunications operators have not met consumer demand for services. This was true even in urban areas where the marginal cost of ex-

---

8. Note that (a) and (c) are the most widely cited in economic literature (see Panzar 2000).

tending the network was relatively low. Political interference with tariffs introduced severe distortions in the price structure, and as a result most developing countries had large waiting lists for connection and even wealthy consumers were unable to get fixed lines. Most telecommunications services needed investment resources and drastic technological upgrades. Deregulation and growth of liberalization and competition has only made it more difficult to finance USO.

This raises the question of whether USO is a reasonable goal in developing countries, given their limited resources. A similar but more applicable concept in the context of developing countries is universal access, which—in contrast to the household-level definition of access prevalent in industrialized countries—seeks to ensure access at a "reasonable" level, such as at the community level. Thus, the primary objective of universal service in terms of telecommunications in developing countries is to "break the isolation of communities and households living in rural and remote areas" by giving them access to a basic communications network. The primary benefit of universal access is to reduce the cost of communications for communities and groups, to facilitate increased commercial activity, and to reduce the delivery costs of other public services such as education and health. With few exceptions, state-owned telecommunications enterprises in developing countries have provided low coverage, deficient quality, and low productivity, and they have generally exhibited a deficient management record, largely because of political interventions. This has resulted in severely limited telecommunications access in those countries.

A wave of reforms has been instituted in developing countries in recent years with the aim of achieving, among other goals, universal access. Countries with transition economies have been at the forefront here, and particularly countries in Latin America. As mentioned above, reforms included privatization, the introduction of regulatory authorities, and the fostering of competition where possible. Results have been impressive on the supply side of the market (see Table 3.1 for some best practices). Coverage has also increased substantially with privatization and liberalization. Old equipment has been renewed with digital switches and fiber optics, and the price of new lines has decreased substantially. Although there are complaints about post-reform tariff levels, there is no doubt that privatization has substantially improved telecommunications access for vast numbers of the population, especially in those countries that imposed specific coverage goals for poor marginal areas.

The lesson seems to be clear: the first step in increasing universal service is to promote private investment and competition in the market to close the existing gap—that is, to provide telecommunications services to the thousands of consumers that fell outside the network because of inefficient business practices. This is no easy task. In order for privatization to work, a sound legal and institutional framework is needed, and interconnection rules among different operators must be clear and transparent. However, strong, autonomous, and

TABLE 3.1 Best practices in rural telecommunications

Country	Project	Property	Concession	Funding	Institutional structure	Market structure of resulting service
Bangladesh	Grameen Telecom–village (cellular) payphone	Public–private partnership	—	Grameen Bank microcredit Initial subscriber deposits Investor contribution Private self-sustainability	Grameen Bank (lease-financing program) Grameen Telecom (receives the payment of the airtime charges) Bangladesh Telegraph and Telephone Board (state-owned telecommunications company) Grameen Phone Ltd. (operator of the cellular network) Village phone operator (a Grameen Bank member who purchased the phone)	The rural telephone market is licensed to two operators, in addition to Grameen Telecom, with exclusive rights for 25 years (Sheba Telecom and Bangladesh Rural Telecom Authority).

Country		Type				
China	Implementation of poverty alleviation measures and well-being attainment through the introduction of information	Public	China Agriculture Bank, City of Zhangjiakou	—	Overall planning and program coordination provided by the government; main implementation undertaken by the Ministry of Electronic Industry; the Ministry of Broadcasting, Film, and Television; the *Economic Daily*; Beijing Municipality; and the State Education Commission.	Network of stations in Zhangjiakau City, China, and 13 other counties established in 1995 for the collection and dissemination of economic information and trade opportunities. Links with newspapers used in information dissemination.
Chile	*Fondo de Desarrollo de las Telecomunicaciones*	Private	Internal public funding External credit	—	*Fondo de Desarrollo de las Telecomunicaciones* (under the oversight of the Ministry of Transport and Telecommunications) *Consejo de Desarrollo de las Telecomunicaciones* (fund administration)	Competition

(continued)

TABLE 3.1 *Continued*

Country	Project	Property	Concession	Funding	Institutional structure	Market structure of resulting service
Peru	*Fondo de Inversión en Telecomunicaciones* (FITEL)	Public–private partnership	—	One percent of public service operator revenues	Fund administration and project selection by OSIPTEL (*Oganismo Supervisor de Inversión Privada en Telecomunicacione*); project approval by Ministry of Transport and Communications	Open entry for unserved areas, and competition since 1998, but incumbent operator actually has a monopoly inside the concession area.
Senegal	Telecenters	Private	—	Private self-sustainability	SONATEL (national telecommunications provider); operator in rural areas (a tenant or owner of the telecenter whose installations fulfill standards set by SONATEL)	Local monopoly
South Africa	Gaseleka Telecenter	Owned by the local branch of South African National Civic Organization (SANCO), the major community-based group allied to the African National Congress	—	South African Universal Service Agency Universal Service Fund External funding	South African Universal Service Agency SANCO	Local monopoly

Uganda	Nakaseke Multi-purpose Community Telecenter	Owned by the Nakaseke Subcounty Council	—	Budget support from international partners and the Ugandan government

Local community fund | The organization is composed of a management committee, local steering committee, and core user group

Support by United Nations Educational, Scientific and Cultural Organization (UNESCO); International Development Research Centre (IDRC); International Telecommunications Union (ITU); and Danida | Multiple ICT products and associated telecommunications monopoly |
| Bangladesh | Grameen Bank group provides the financing and Grameen Telecom (part of the bank group) provides, promotes, and selects the village phone operators. | The village operator purchases the basic village phone package determined by Grameen Telecom. A state-owned monopoly exists for interconnection services. | No | Determined by Grameen Telecom; same tariff structure as the Bangladesh Telegraph and Telephone Board (BTTB). For calls between the Bangladesh Rural Telecom Authority (BRTA) and BTTB, the sender bares the international outgoing charges. | Global system for mobile communications (GSM) cellular phone network | 950 village phones; consumer surplus = US$1.17 per call (Bayes 2001); very high revenues per rural line (village phones bring in three times the revenue of urban phones—US$100 per month compared with US$30 per month). |

(continued)

TABLE 3.1 *Continued*

Country	Project	Property	Concession	Funding	Institutional structure	Market structure of resulting service
				For incoming calls, BTTB splits 70/30 with BRTA after settlement of third party charges.		
China			No		Satellite-based electronic networking	Supply of agricultural product meets demand far more quickly; trade has been expanded and access to investment increased; as of April 1996, 60 counties were actively using the network; profit realized in the first year was estimated to be million US$0.3–0.35.

| Chile | Multiple projects; freedom of business and technology choice | Regulated interconnection charges | Lowest subsidy request; single transfer of resources to the provider who wins the bid | Rural operators are free to set prices for all their services, with the exception of pay-phone charges within the primary calling area (fixed for 10 years in the license) and interconnection charges (fixed for 5 years in a separate tariff decree). | Satellite and other networks; provider is free to choose the technology used. | Coverage increased to 6,093 rural locations with about 2.2 million inhabitants. |

(continued)

TABLE 3.1 *Continued*

Country	Project	Property	Concession	Funding	Institutional structure	Market structure of resulting service
Peru	Multiple projects under the FITEL program; private investors able to provide telecommunications services or equipment individually or as a consortium	Determined by the winner of the concession; monopoly on interconnection services held by the winner of the concession	20-year concession awarded to the service provider with the lowest subsidy request.	Regulated, with price caps		0.66 public telephones per 500 households; service provided to villages with populations of 400 to 3,000 people, or main districts without telephone service.
Senegal	The installation of a telecenter is given by mutual agreement between SONATEL and the operator.	SONATEL	No	Provided by SONATEL	GSM cellular phone network	Not measured

			Discretionary		
South Africa	Two managers and two supervisors, a full-time computer trainer, and the general secretary of SANCO	Mobile Telephone Network (MTN), Vodacom, Cell C, Telkom South Africa	No	Fixed line telephone network owned by the national telecommunications operator, Telkom South Africa	Not measured
Uganda	The Ministry of Transport and Communications (MTC) has a staff of four (manager, assistant manager, information officer, and assistant information officer).	Uganda Telecom	No	"Pseudo tele-shadow" of Mobile Telephone Network (MTN)	Provides Internet, telephone, and fax services to the school community (7,000 children), community workers, and medical officers. Community access to telecommunications services (42 villages and 3,000 households).

NOTE: A concession is a service contract assigned to telecommunications service providers by the government, usually through a competitive process.

capable regulatory agencies are hard to build, especially because local expertise in this area is lacking. Professionals need to be trained in every aspect.

Nevertheless, even in countries where telecommunications systems have been successfully reformed, the private infrastructure investment needed to extend coverage is limited, and it is unlikely that private investors will engage in risky or unprofitable ventures without suitable compensation. Traditionally, lack of universal access is correlated with insufficient rural funding to allow poor constituents to afford the service. In response to this problem, a number of subsidy mechanisms have been implemented in attempts to ensure that poor people pay no more than their wealthier urban counterparts for access to telecommunications. The economic rationale for subsidies is based on the existence of consumption and production externalities, network externalities, and scale economies. Also, in a modern society, affordable access to these services is considered essential to equitable and effective participation by all members of the population.

The main problem with such schemes, however, is sustainability, although in some cases (as is reviewed in the case studies later in this chapter) rural inhabitants are actually willing to pay much more than urban consumers for telecommunications services, overcoming this problem, and invalidating lack of resources as an argument against the subsidy schemes. Several authors have challenged the unprofitability of providing rural telecommunications services, blaming regulatory agencies for incorrectly estimating rural inhabitants' willingness to pay (see Richardson 2002). This partially corresponds with the lower than anticipated subsidy requirements set by private rural operators in the tender process. While this is a valuable discussion, justifying the need for private operator subsidies is beyond the scope of this chapter. Our focus is merely to describe mechanisms that have been successful in closing the gap in access to telecommunications services in rural areas and access the sustainability of such mechanisms.

Interventions have varied across countries. Regardless of the subsidy issue, public funds are needed if universal access is to be achieved. How these funds can be used most effectively—that is, to increase the coverage at the lowest possible cost—is a key question. Once again evidence supports the success of mechanisms that use private-sector ingenuity; solutions, however, also depend on the degree of institutional sophistication achieved. Because of the difficulty in implementing the reforms, no single path can be recommended to work for every country. Some potential best practices implemented after reform in countries like Chile or Peru have proven to be efficient; a key factor in these instances was a public bidding process to assign funds to the private operator that made the largest coverage offer at a fixed tariff level. Nevertheless, as already discussed, such strategies are only appropriate in the presence of telecommunications sectors that have undergone reform and have strong and efficient regulatory agencies in place. Such approaches would not work in countries where the reform process or related institutions are weak. Thus, the next logical question is whether measures could be implemented in parallel, enabling reform to occur in tandem with the development of infrastructure. Despite some restrictions, cases in Africa and Bangladesh seem to support the possibility of simultaneous paths.

Country Studies of Different Experiences

Of the five countries that form the focus of the case studies in this chapter—Bangladesh, China, Ghana, Laos, and Peru—three of them have per capita GDP below the low-income country average of US$484, and more than one-third of the population in four of five countries (China being the exception) is under the national poverty line. Combining the overall picture of poverty with a substantial rural population in each country (more than 60 percent), a picture of high rural poverty emerges.[9] In terms of telecommunications service provision, three countries had teledensity rates lower than the low-income country average of 2.83 in 2002. Penetration rates are generally low countrywide, but they are especially low in rural areas. Once again China is the exception, having undergone tremendous growth in recent years (for example, a growth rate of 25 percent between 1998 and 2002).[10] While narrowing the gap with developed countries is an urgent goal, narrowing the gap between urban and rural areas is an equally high priority from the perspective of pro-poor rural development. See Table 3.2 for a general overview of the five countries.

The focus of the case studies is the impact of both fixed line and cellular telephony on the rural population and particularly poor people.[11] Reflecting the lack of service provision in rural areas, the studies deal with telephone service through publicly accessible facilities, with the exception of the case on China, which looks at subscribed users.

Overview of the Reform Process

Public monopoly and unregulated private enterprise are polar-opposite systems of ICT provision. Many other possibilities also exist between these two extremes, such as partial privatization, whereby both public and private enterprises provide services; privatization of the public monopoly to a private

---

9. Peru has a relatively low rural population, but they are very much dispersed, making delivery of social services more difficult.

10. These figures overestimate rural teledensity because they cover all areas of the country except the largest city; rates would be much lower if rural areas were considered on their own.

11. As previously discussed, telephony is used throughout this book as a proxy for ICT more generally because of the dearth of statistical data on ICT in developing countries and the reality that, for the foreseeable future, telephony is the ICT that will have the greatest penetration and impact for poor people.

TABLE 3.2 Overview of the five case study countries, 2002

Indicator	Peru	Bangladesh	China	Ghana	Laos
Per capita GDP (constant 1995 US$)	2,380	396	944	429	477
Share of population under national poverty line (percent)[a]	49.0	49.8	4.6	39.5	38.6
Share of rural population (percent)	26.5	73.9	62.4	63.3	79.8
Teledensity (fixed telephone lines per 100 inhabitants)	6.6	0.5	16.7	1.3	1.1
Share of fixed telephone lines in rural areas	na	8.5[b]	36.6	8.7[b]	na
Share of fixed telephone lines in areas excluding the largest city (percent)[b]	32.6[c]	39.5[b]	95.1[b]	31.5[b]	42.7

SOURCES: World Bank (2004), ITU (2004), and OSIPTEL (2004).
NOTE: na indicates that data were unavailable.
[a]Latest single year between 1996 and 2002 (World Bank 2004).
[b]2001 data.
[c]2003 data.

regulated monopoly; and provision under a regulated competitive market structure. Until the 1980s, government ownership of telecommunications services—
paid for, as needed, by tax revenues—was a common telecommunications strategy in both developed and developing countries. In reality, services under state
monopolies were inadequate in terms of coverage and service quality. Consequently, by the 1990s, the idea of a natural monopoly of telecommunications
infrastructure fell out of favor, and the trend shifted toward liberalization and
competition.

Under state monopoly, the extent of network development remained very
low in all five countries prior to reform: fixed line teledensity (the number of
fixed telephone lines per 100 inhabitants) numbered 0.17 in Bangladesh in
1988, 0.26 in China in 1985, 0.36 in Ghana in 1995, 0.35 in Laos in 1995, and
2.97 in Peru in 1993. And these countries are not the only examples of poor
telecommunications service under state monopoly in developing countries. In
terms of the distributive goal of the state monopoly to provide access to the
poor and to households that live in rural and remote areas, no substantial improvement was seen among the case study countries; the extremely low coverage of telecommunications networks remained predominantly urban based. In the
late 1980s and early 1990s, many developing as well as industrialized countries
made the decision to privatize their telecommunications sectors, shifting to regulated private monopolies with the goal of improving the service quality and
coverage. Under such regulations, prices were maintained below the profit-
maximizing level, just covering the average costs. The telecommunications

regulator was expected to ensure this price, and the private monopoly was expected to attract private capital to the sector to facilitate the expansion of the network. In some cases, such as in Peru, privatization of state monopolies resulted in a windfall for the government and improvement in overall consumer welfare, whereby consumers benefited from increased service coverage and waiting lists for telephones were virtually eliminated.

Further moves toward introducing competitive telecommunications markets in developing countries have occurred since the 1990s. Yet complications have led economists and regulators to question the value of regulated private monopolies. Consequently, the trend in recent years has been to move away from regulation toward deregulation and competition. Regulating a telecommunications monopoly is complex because of the different cost conditions and lines of business involved. Further, technological progress has changed the cost structure, making competition possible. This has led to the recent trend of deregulation and competition.[12]

In the case of these five countries, Bangladesh is the only one to have maintained a state monopoly in urban fixed telephony until very recently (2004). Bangladesh has now privatized its rural telecommunications market, introducing two private providers in two parts of the country. In Peru, the government privatized two state monopolies in 1994 that later merged to become a regulated private monopoly; as of 1998, the regulated private monopoly era ended, and competition was introduced in all market segments. In Laos, the government allowed the state monopoly to form a joint venture with a foreign company in 1996; competition was introduced in 2002. In China, the government separated its postal and telecommunications services in the 1990s and introduced limited competition among state-owned telecommunications enterprises. The overseeing authority is now considering breaking up the market leader, China Telecom. In Ghana, liberalization began in 1995 with the formation of Ghana Telecom, along with a subsequent joint venture that allowed foreign capital. A duopoly market structure was maintained in fixed telephony until 2002, when Ghana opened its market for competition.

A summary of changes in institutional arrangements within the telecommunications sectors of these five countries is provided in Table 3.3. The specific case studies follow thereafter.

---

12. Technological progress has made the natural monopoly argument less relevant. The Bell monopoly in the United States offers a classic example of technological progress and change in market structure through the unbundling of long-distance telephone services. This separation of services became even more important in the past decade with the prevalence of cellular and other wireless systems that are increasingly substituting fix networks. Note that deregulation does not imply the elimination of regulations but rather significant cut backs in their scope. At minimum, private providers gain more freedom in setting prices, while in most cases they are no longer protected from competition.

TABLE 3.3 Overview of reform in the five case study countries, 1990–2003

Telecommunications indicators	Peru	Laos	Bangladesh	China	Ghana
			Case study countries		
Overview	Fixed telephone service; privatized in 1994	Partial privatization in 1994; joint venture between government and private sector	State monopoly in fixed lines	State pluralistic competition between telephone services	Started an accelerated development program in 1994 with the objective to increase the quality and quantity of telecommunications services
	Private monopoly in fixed service, 1994–98	Monopoly in fixed, cellular, and Internet services in 1996 and 2001	State monopoly in cellular market until 1990	State monopoly in cellular market until 1990	Introduction of a new fixed operator in 1996 and partial privatization of state fixed telephone operator in 1997
	Competitive but regulated fixed market since 1999	Since 2002 there have been three enterprises: a state-owned enterprise and two mixed (private and state-owned) enterprises	Private monopoly in cellular market, 1990–96	Private monopoly in cellular market, 1990–96	Opened fixed market in 2002
	Competitive cellular and Internet market since 1994	Competitive cellular and Internet market since 1994	Opened cellular market in 1996		Opened cellular market in 1995
			Opened Internet market in 1996		Opened Internet market in 1996

2003 indicators

Per capita GDP, 2002 (PPP in current international dollars)	5,010	1,720	1,700	4,580	2,130
Per capita GDP, 2002 (constant 1995 US$)	2,380	477	396	944	429
Total (fixed line and cellular) teledensity, 1990	2.6	0.2	0.2	0.6	0.3
Total (fixed line and cellular) teledensity, 2003	17.3	3.2	1.6	42.4	4.9
Revenue (million US$)	1,395[a]	31	524[b]	55,527	128[b]
Share of digital fixed lines (percent)	96	100	94.7	100	100[b]
Waiting list for fixed lines (number of customers)	33,000[a]	5,921[c]	153,100	na	154,782[a]
Fixed line teledensity, 1990	2.6	0.2	0.2	0.6	0.3
Fixed line teledensity, 2003	6.7	1.2	0.5	20.9	1.3
Cellular teledensity, 1990	0	0	0	0	0
Cellular teledensity, 2003	10.6	2.0	1.0	21.5	3.6
Internet density, 1990	0	0	0	0	0
Internet density, 2003	10.4	0.3[b]	0.2	6.3	0.8[b]
Number of Internet hosts, 2003	65,868	937	1	160,421	389

(continued)

TABLE 3.3 *Continued*

Telecommunications indicators	Case study countries				
	Peru	Laos	Bangladesh	China	Ghana
Rural telephony Details of programs	The FITEL program subsidized auctions to install public payphones in rural cities Shared risk between private and state counterparts 6,556 rural public payphones were installed	Rurtel provided basic telecommunications services (voice telephony and text transmission) based on a digital radio concentrator system Aid funding was provided by the German Devel-	Market opened to geographic duopoly in rural fixed telephone service in 1990 Village payphone program undertaken to provide cellular phones to rural households, allocated through the Grameen Bank	National program comprising the "golden card," "golden bridge," and "golden gate" projects (ongoing) State-owned and subsidized projects undertaken to promote telephone and	Build–operate–transfer privatization to provide rural fixed lines, only 500 new lines generated Rural cellular telephone services have been driven by private initiatives resulting in

covering 6,460 rural towns and benefiting 3.9 million inhabitants (2003)	opment Bank The goal was to achieve coverage of 73 percent of rural districts	to selected borrowers Reached over 45,000 subscribers covering 68,000 villages and 60 million inhabitants	Internet service in rural areas. Educational programs to learn how to use ICT Provision of information services by the private sector allowed	coverage in all 10 regional capitals, predominantly in urban areas.

Share of fixed lines in urban
areas (percent)

	na	na	92[a]	65	91[a]

SOURCES: Data on indicators are from ITU (2004) and World Bank (2004).

NOTES: Teledensity/density is the number of units (fixed line or cellular phone or Internet users as indicated) per 100 inhabitants. Data are for 2003 unless otherwise indicated. PPP indicates purchasing power parity, an index used to reflect the purchasing power of currencies by comparing prices among a broader range of goods and services than conventional exchange rates; na indicates that data were not available.

[a]2001 data.
[b]2002 data.
[c]2000 data.

Telecommunications Privatization: The Case of Peru
Maximo Torero

Peru's telecommunications market has undergone a period of fundamental change since the mid-1990s. Principal forces behind these changes include market liberalization, privatization, technical progress, and changes in consumer demand. These forces have had direct, long-term effects on both consumers and providers. It is essential, therefore, to evaluate these processes and gain a greater scientific knowledge of the effects of these changes.

To do this, it is first necessary to briefly review the industry conditions prior to privatization. Surprisingly, during the time of state ownership, Peru's telecommunications sector was unable to meet the high demand for access to basic telephone services. Lack of investment and prevailing price control policies were responsible for much of this imbalance. As of 1993, penetration rate (number of telephones per 100 households) was only 2.0. Based on the degree of development at the time, the rate should have been closer to 6.0. In addition, the distribution of telephone lines was concentrated in Lima and in wealthy households.

Another prominent characteristic of the telecommunications sector in Peru prior to privatization was the presence of distorted tariffs. In fact, while the charges for installation were quite high, compared with the international average (close to US$1,000 per residential telephone line in 1993), the flat monthly charge was relatively low. In contrast, the tariffs for long-distance and additional local calls were quite high. As in other countries, the idea that only rich (inelastic) consumers used international long-distance service prevailed, so the company cross-subsidized local service with its long-distance service. With privatization, the government decided to establish a five-year plan to "re-balance" tariffs to reflect the marginal costs of providing the service. The alternative—adjusting the tariffs immediately—was considered to be too harsh a measure for consumers (indeed, the monthly charge would have increased from US$1 to US$17). With the five-year plan, the cross subsidies were reduced incrementally over time. As of 2004, about 10 years after privatization, the balance remained unclear. Although more people—mainly at the lower socioeconomic levels—have telephone access, many do not take advantage of this option because they cannot afford the flat monthly fee.

This case study concentrates on one of the most significant changes to affect Peru's telecommunications industry during the reform years, the privatization of *Compañía Peruana de Teléfonos* (CPT) and *Empresa Nacional de Telecomunicaciones* (ENTEL), which were purchased by *Telefónica de España* in 1994. The primary objectives are to estimate the impacts of the changes in telephone services arising from privatization in terms of consumer welfare at different socioeconomic levels, focusing on the period of limited competition, 1994–98. Specifically, the benefits to consumers of greater access to telephones are compared with the costs of increased monthly access tariffs. In addition, the new policies implemented to improve telephone access in rural areas are assessed.

Before and After Privatization

The record of the telecommunication sector under state management was extremely poor. By 1993 Peru had unusually low telephony coverage, with lines concentrated in the capital city, Lima, and in wealthy households. By comparison with international standards, and based on per capita GDP, Peru should have had a teledensity of 11.0. However, Peru's teledensity was only 2.6 in 1992, one of the lowest in the region. Waiting time for a new line in 1993 was 118 months, while customers in Colombia were waiting 17 months, and those in Mexico were waiting 11 months. Service quality was below international standards. In 1992, only 40 percent of all phone calls were actually completed, partly due to the small network and obsolete technology in use, which easily became congested. Inadequate maintenance also affected communications quality. Telephone cables generally have a 15-year life, yet by 1993 some cables in use in Peru were over 60 years old. In addition, only 33 percent of the network was digital. Exacerbating this situation, CPT and ENTEL had excessive employee numbers, resulting in low productivity indicators and a distorted structure of operating costs. Another distinctive feature, as mentioned, was the distorted tariff structure.

Privatization was designed to increase coverage, boost efficiency, and encourage a competitive market in the medium term. The privatization contract set specific investment goals to address the existing supply constraint, the five-year rebalancing plan was intended to foster competition. By 1998, improvements were impressive. The number of lines increased by 167 percent during 1993–98. Thus, *Telefónica de España* amply met the concession contract's coverage goals. By 1998, the entire market for basic telephony was covered, and the waiting list was eliminated. Service quality also improved substantially. By 1998, 90 percent of the network had been digitized and 99 percent of local and international long-distance calls were completed. By 1998, rates had been rebalanced and the sector was open to free competition several months ahead of schedule (Figure 3.4).

Finally, fixed lines in service per employee increased from 87 in 1994 to 275 in 1998, and waiting time for new lines fell from 33 months in 1993 to 1.5 months in 1998. Accordingly, net profits increased from 5 percent in 1993 to almost 25 percent in 1997, and total profits increased from US$35.5 million in 1993 to US$400 million by 1997. Table 3.4 presents data on the sector's performance at three time intervals: at the end of public monopoly (1993), the end of limited competition (1998), and five years after competence was reached in the fixed and long-distance market (2003).

Peru has also seen explosive growth in the use of cellular and public telephones. While in December 1993, only 36,000 cellular telephones were in use,

FIGURE 3.4 Number of fixed telephone lines installed in Peru five years after privatization, 1993 and 1999

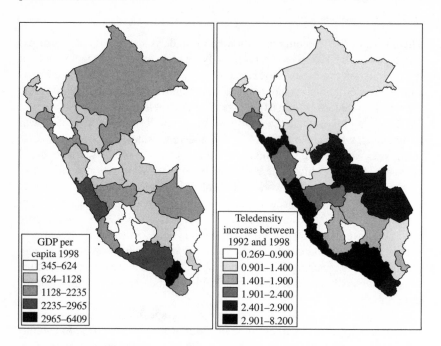

SOURCE: OSIPTEL (2004).
NOTE: Fixed line teledensity is the number of fixed telephone lines per 100 inhabitants.

by December 2003, that number had increased to 2,900,000. The 2003 figure for cellular telephone subscribers outnumbers fixed telephone lines by nearly 600,000. Another point of note concerning cellular telephone use in Peru is that only 22 percent is in metropolitan Lima. The prevailing billing regime is "Calling Party Pays." Table 3.4 presents data for cellular phones and other non-regulated sectors, all of which increased penetration significantly, at the same time establishing the necessary infrastructure for a future development of other ICT.

Similarly, public telephone availability grew from 8,000 in 1993 to 1,230,000 in December 2003, an increase of 1,400 percent. Like cellular telephone distribution, the majority of public telephone growth occurred outside Lima, although the story in rural areas was different. According to the Population and Housing Census of 1993, Peru has over 70,000 rural settlements of fewer than 3,000 inhabitants. The majority of these—30 percent of the national population according to the census—represent the poorest zones of the country, which lack basic services like electricity, water, and sewage. Given the adverse conditions in these rural regions, the Fund for Investments in Telecommunications (FITEL) was created under OSIPTEL to promote private investment in these poor areas by telecommunication companies, ultimately promoting universal service access across most of rural Peru. Funds are generated through a 1 percent levy on the gross revenues of all telecommunication firms (excluding cable and Internet companies), and then the funds are awarded through a competitive bidding process. Collection of funds began in 1994, and the first project was awarded in 1998. *Telefónica del Perú,* being the incumbent service provider, is not eligible to bid for any of the subsidy projects managed by FITEL.

The main objective of FITEL, however, is not only to promote access to telephones but also to promote social and economic development by including

TABLE 3.4 Performance of the telecommunications sector in Peru, 1993, 1998, and 2003

Performance indicator	1993	1998	2003
Installed fixed telephone lines	670,400	2,012,141	2,249,508
Waiting time for installation of a fixed telephone line	118 months	45 days	5 days
Installation charge per fixed telephone line	US$1,500	US$170	US$143
Fixed line teledensity	0.27	0.61	0.67
Number of locations with telephones	1,450	3,000	4,941[a]
Number of public telephones	8,000	49,399	123,002
Digitalization of the network (percentage)	33	90	96
Fiber-optic cable (kilometers)	200	3,000	8,173
Direct sector employment	13,000	7,773	9,986

SOURCES: OSIPTEL (2004), ITU (2004), and BCRP (2004).

NOTE: Fixed line teledensity is the number of fixed telephone lines per 100 inhabitants.

[a]Data are from 2002.

TABLE 3.5 Unregulated sectors in Peru, 1993, 1998, and 2003

Indicator	1993	1998	2003
Cellular telephone subscribers	36,000	736,294	2,930,343
Cities with cellular telephone access	7	117	120
Cable television subscribers	725	305,200	339,739
Number of cable television firms	6	39	122[a]
Internet users	na	100,000[b]	2,850,000

SOURCES: OSIPTEL (2004) and ITU (2004).

NOTE: Internet user data for 2003 have been estimated; na indicates that data were not available.

[a]2002 data.

[b]2001 data.

these lower socioeconomic areas in the information society through appropriate access to communication networks (including the Internet). As of 2003, FITEL had assigned six projects of rural telephony benefiting 6,460 rural cities, covering approximately 3.9 million rural inhabitants and translating as 6,556 rural telephones installed.

Although it is clear from these results that privatization had a significant positive impact in terms of supply, the increased costs of monthly tariffs need to be included in the analysis in terms of the types of households that bore the greater burden or enjoyed the greater benefits (classified by their observable characteristics). This involves measuring changes in consumer welfare to determine whether the gains (higher number of people with telephone access) counterbalance the higher resulting tariffs. The intention of this study, however, is not to obtain an aggregate indictor of consumer welfare including all groups affected by the privatization of the telecommunications sector in Peru, but rather to simply measure the net effects to consumers before and after privatization. Although we follow many ideas suggested by Galal et al. (1994) and Martin and Parker (1997), we use a different model to value consumer welfare. See Appendix 3A for details of the model and empirical estimations.

Measuring Consumer Welfare of Urban Consumers

Since privatization in 1994, an absolute gain in total consumer surplus by service and by socioeconomic level is evident and the growth rate has only marginally contracted since 1997 (Tables 3.6 and 3.7).

However, in analyzing per capita consumer surplus, the story is not the same across the different socioeconomic levels (SELs). There is a clear gain in welfare for the high and medium SELs (A and B); but for the low and very low SELs (C and D), consumer welfare began decreasing in 1996, and fell below pre-privatization levels for SEL D (Table 3.7). This result provides insight into

TABLE 3.6 Total consumer surplus by service type in Peru, 1993–98

	Total net benefits to consumers (US$ millions)					
Type of service	1993	1994	1995	1996	1997	1998
Local fixed line telephone service	5.8	8.7	11.1	14.1	17.5	17.9
Domestic long-distance telephone service	0.9	1.0	1.3	1.8	2.2	3.2
International long-distance telephone service	0.7	0.9	1.1	1.4	1.8	2.2
Total	6.3	10.5	13.5	17.4	21.5	23.2
Total less fixed rental fees	6.2	7.7	9.7	11.2	12.9	12.7
Growth rate (percent)	—	24.0	26.0	15.0	15.0	–2.0

SOURCE: Authors' estimations.

why public opinion about privatization worsened over time, especially considering that the low SEL formed the majority in opinion polls. The primary reason for the fall in consumer surplus was the increase in the price of the permanent monthly tariff (Figure 3.5). Not surprisingly, its impact is stronger for lower socioeconomic levels because a greater proportion of their spending goes to pay the flat monthly charge. There is also a secondary price impact with local calls because of the proportionately larger reduction of long-distance tariffs, which led to substitution of local calls with long-distance calls.

To make things worse, in 1997 the regulator changed the unit of measure of local calls from three-minute blocks to one-minute units and expanded the definition of the geographic area; these measures translated as an increase in the price of local calls, which explains the reduction in the growth of the total

TABLE 3.7 Per capita consumer surplus by socioeconomic level in Peru, 1993–98

Socioeconomic level	1993	1994	1995	1996	1997	1998
High (SEL A)	44.5	54.7	58.5	63.4	67.4	62.7
Medium (SEL B)	18.6	19.8	23.8	23.5	26.6	23.8
Low (SEL C)	7.6	6.8	6.6	9.0	8.2	8.2
Very low (SEL D)	6.0	4.5	0.5	1.3	0.9	1.3

SOURCE: Authors' estimations.

NOTE: SEL indicates socioeconomic level.

FIGURE 3.5 Index of the basic local tariff in Peru, 1990–2003
(August 1990 = 100)

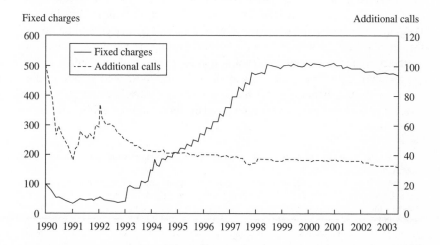

SOURCE: OSIPTEL (2004).

NOTE: Fixed line teledensity is the number of fixed telephone lines per 100 inhabitants.

consumer surplus after 1997. In fact, comparing the Peruvian price structure (in terms of the price of local calls and the fixed monthly fee) with fee structures in Argentina and Chile—countries that have also been through a privatization process—it is clear that there is still room for tariff reduction in Peru.

Impact on Rural Consumers

The FITEL strategy has been quite successful. Results began with a pilot project in the northern border area of Peru (Table 3.8). First, the process generates enough competition. Six contenders participated in the pilot tender (four or more in the subsequent schemes). The subsidies requested were much lower than originally estimated, at 41 percent below the amount estimated by OSIPTEL and 74 percent below the amount requested by the incumbent operator to provide the service. By December 2000, a year after the concession (tender) was granted in the pilot area, the project reduced the distance to a payphone by 90 percent on average for the 144,500 inhabitants.[13] This dramatically increased telephone access. For example, in Amazonas, thanks to the project, 90 percent of the population had access to a phone compared with only 10 percent prior to the project. Payphones were located in local grocery stores and other businesses, with the host business receiving a share of the revenues. The coverage goals were met by the deadline, and traffic was higher than expected by OSIPTEL—by 7 percent in the first six months and by 32 percent in the second six months.

Although there were minor problems with access to prepaid phone cards and service reliability in the first six months, penalties and corresponding subsidy payment delays encouraged the operator to quickly solve these problems. According to service surveys, satisfaction grew from 57 percent the first six months to 75 percent in the following semester, and access to payphone cards increased from 35 to 50 percent over the same period. After the success of the pilot project, FITEL initiated the *Programa de Proyectos Rurales* (Rural Projects Program [PPR]) with the objective of providing universal access to the rest of the country. PPR comprised six subprojects covering six Peruvian regions (the northern, southern, central east, central north, central south, and northern jungle regions),[14] for which subsidies totaling slightly more than US$38 million were committed, benefiting 1.7 million inhabitants directly and 2.2 million indirectly. These six rural projects involved the installation of public telephones

---

13. This figure includes inhabitants residing within a 5-kilometer radius of each of the respective towns.

14. Gilat to Home is in charge of five of these subprojects: the northern region project (Amazonas, Cajamarca, and Piura), the central east region project (Huanuco, Junin, Urna, Pasco, and Ucayali), the central south region project (Apurimac, Ayacucho, Cusco, Huancavelica, Ica, and Madre de Dios), the northern jungle region project (Loreto and San Martin), and the southern region project (Arequipa, Moquegua, Puno, and Tacna). Rural Telecom S.A.C. has the concession for the sixth region (the central north: Ancash, La Libertad, and Lambayeque). The central south, northern jungle, and southern regional projects are also referred to as FITEL II; the remaining three regional projects are referred to as FITEL III.

TABLE 3.8 Pilot project in the northern border area of Peru, 1998–2000

Indicator	Amazonas	Cajamarca	Piura	Tumbes	Total
Rural towns served	57	54	54	28	193
Direct beneficiaries (inhabitants of the towns served)	14,769	20,605	15,660	7,838	58,872
Indirect beneficiaries (inhabitants living within 5 kilometers of the towns served)	24,317	24,754	30,710	5,869	85,650
Total beneficiaries	39,086	45,359	46,370	13,707	144,522
Distance to the nearest phone (kilometers)					
Without the project	251.4	26.1	26.1	9.0	—
With the project	6.2	4.9	4.2	3.0	—
Penetration rate (number of fixed lines per 100 households)					
Without the project (percent)[a]	10	20	16	91	48
With the project (percent)[a]	90	85	71	99	89

SOURCE: Authors' estimations.

NOTE: SEL indicates socioeconomic level.

[a] Share of populations in the project area with telephone access.

in 4,227 rural towns. As of 2003, the projects had installed approximately 4,693 rural telephones in 4,618 rural towns (Table 3.9).

In addition, in December 2001, a complementary project (FITEL IV) was initiated focusing on increasing the number of public telephones in rural towns with teledensities below 0.002. FITEL IV comprised six components (following the regional divisions described above). A total of US$11.4 million was awarded as a concession for the installation of an additional public telephone in the 1,616 rural towns selected.[15]

FITEL amassed private investments of US$22 per inhabitant through a subsidy of US$11 per inhabitant, excluding start-up costs of US$1.7 million and administrative costs of around 2 percent of disbursements, making it quite efficient. One of the major problems, however, was that despite the project's 1994 establishment and the accumulation of sufficient funds by 1996, the first concession was not granted until 1998 because of bureaucratic issues in obtaining the necessary approval from the Vice Ministry of Communications. Similarly, the remaining concessions were not granted until 2000. The need to build sufficient resources over time is clearly a limitation of this scheme, although realistically it is probably the only option for cash poor governments in developing countries. Lack of political will is also a factor in many countries.

---

15. The subsidies were awarded to the same enterprises as the FITEL II and FITEL III projects following the same regional distribution.

TABLE 3.9 Rural Projects Program, Peru, 1998–2003

Indicator	South	Central south	Northern jungle	Central north	Central east	North	Total[a]
Rural towns served	534	1,029	374	582	770	938	4,227
Capitals of district included	60	156	20	64	100	91	491
Direct beneficiaries (inhabitants of the towns served)	135,917	303,260	141,621	317,648	258,140	519,957	1,676,543
Indirect beneficiaries (inhabitants living within 5 kilometers of the towns served)	249,468	528,734	187,424	363,682	342,181	499,114	2,170,603
Total beneficiaries	385,385	831,994	329,045	681,330	600,321	1,019,071	3,847,146
Distance to the nearest phone (kilometers)							
Without the project	36.1	48.2	97.0	19.3	25.8	24.5	36.3
With the project	11.3	6.1	7.0	3.7	4.9	4.2	5.6
Penetration rate (number of fixed lines per 100 households)							
Without the project (percent)[b]	68.6	53.5	62.6	57.3	64.3	34.8	53.2
With the project (percent)[b]	85.0	82.0	89.1	80.4	86.3	79.3	82.6

SOURCE: OSIPTEL (2003).

[a] Weighted averages.

[b] Share of populations in the project area with telephone access.

It seems that the process ignores some potential economies of scale that have recently emerged because one company has acquired concessions from other companies, with the result that it is now responsible for virtually all of the bidding areas. Although tariffs are regulated, there could be risk for monopolistic practices under these conditions. The fact that local tariff limits are the same as the tariffs for urban payphones and hence relatively low. It could very well be that higher tariffs could have expedited the process and introduced more competition among rural operators in a first phase. No willingness to pay studies were conducted in rural areas prior to granting the concessions, which would have been preferable than setting tariffs by guesswork. In fact there was a risk of setting tariffs below their long-term incremental cost, making the whole process unsustainable. Further, tariffs set below the costs of provision discourage operators from providing the service or from increasing traffic. In this case, the subsidies need to promote not just access (number of connections) but traffic as well (intensity of use in terms of minutes per public phone). The current system of subsidies favors access, but consumers primarily benefit from usage. This reality needs to be incorporated into the concession contract so that the service provider is encouraged to comply with standards for both connection and usage. Generating such an incentive system, however, would probably increase the complexity of supervision.

There has been some over-regulation of the process in its initial stages. OSIPTEL could have limited its supervision to a check of some key indicators instead of overseeing the private business practices. On the other hand, benchmarks and performance indicators of the process are too inflexible. Such methods are more appropriate for a mature network rather than for a start-up operation (Table 3.9). As in Chile, FITEL should be focusing on the smaller, poorer populations and on other services; it should also be considering fast track mechanisms for small towns to expedite telephone access and usage.

Conclusion

By the early 1990s, the Peruvian telecommunication sector, largely as a result of poor state management, was characterized by low coverage, long waiting times, outdated technology, poor service, and distorted prices. With privatization, the situation was certainly turned around. In terms of service coverage, service quality, and technology, there has been a dramatic improvement. By 1998, *Telefónica del Perú* amply met the goals set in its concession contract, by which time it virtually covered the market for basic telephony. Further, relative to other utility sectors that have undergone privatization in Peru, telephony as a sector is the most improved. Despite these positive results, the Peruvian population is still quite unhappy with the privatization process.

The main conclusion of this case study is that, on aggregate, telecommunications privatization improved total consumer welfare in Peru, mainly by increasing consumer access to the service. However, the correction of tariff distortions to reflect their long-term marginal cost—primarily by increasing the fixed monthly payment and the cost of local calls—negatively affected some consumers, particularly those of low- and very low-income households. After 1996, and after three periods of constant growth, the growth rate of the per capita consumer surplus fell. Consequently, clients who had a telephone prior to privatization but had low usage experienced welfare reductions. In addition, changes in the timing from three-minute increments to one-minute increments, as well as changes in the local area boundaries also caused local tariffs to increase.

This problem could have been avoided if consumer plans had been introduced to take socioeconomic differences among consumer groups into account. Households in the lowest income brackets mostly use their telephones to receive calls; hence the fixed monthly rental is a major burden. In this case, a calling plan with a low fixed monthly tariff and higher charges for local calls would improve welfare. The opposite is the case for rich households, where the primary welfare gain is through the intensive use of the telephone and hence their welfare increases when local and long-distance tariffs are reduced and the fixed monthly tariff is increased. In either case, the central objective is to maintain tariff equilibrium to avoid the entrance of inefficient competitors into the market.

By the time limited competition ended in Peru, there was insufficient competition in the sector. The price of long-distance calls was higher in Peru than in other South American countries. It was clear that, contrary to expectations, there was no substantial increase in consumer gains from the use of domestic or international long-distance. The situation was even worse for local calls. Lack of adequate interconnection fees continues to prevent other companies from using the incumbent operator's infrastructure to compete in the local market. For consumer welfare to improve, this needs to change.

Finally, with respect to rural areas, despite the success of the pilot subsidy projects carried out under FITEL, results were severely delayed pending the approval of concession contracts between FITEL and the Vice Ministry of Communications. Despite initial positive indicators, insufficient information is available to date to definitively evaluate the impact of these mechanisms on consumers, or their sustainability over time.

Public–Private Partnership Initiated by Aid: The Case of Laos
Gi-Soon Song

Laos is a low-income, mountainous landlocked country, located in Southeast Asia. In 2000, per capita annual income averaged about US$330 (World Bank 2004).[16] Since 1975 the country has been governed by the Laos People's Revo-

---

16. Data and information presented in this case study were drawn from two projects conducted by the ICT research team at the Center for Development Research in Bonn (ZEF); the projects are "the Rural Telecommunication Assessment Project," for the German Development Bank

lutionary Party, under which the economy is managed on the basis of ongoing five-year plans (the first of which was launched in 1981). Disappointing results from the first five-year plan led to the 1986 adoption of a "new economic mechanism" (NEM) in efforts to spark growth during the second five years. The mechanism was designed to reduce centralized bureaucratic decisionmaking and increase the focus on business considerations. Although understated, the aim was clearly to move to a more market-oriented system. Changes under NEM appear to have promoted growth in Laos, evidenced by average annual growth rates of around 7 percent during 1988–98. Despite this growth, however, skilled labor shortages and lack of transport and communications infrastructure remained major obstacles to sustained economic growth.

As early as 1983, the Government of Laos considered transport and communications to be primary drivers of economic development; this was reflected in the second five-year plan. Telecommunications in Laos at that time were founded on analogue exchanges and shortwave transmission links that had been installed in the 1950s, so the need for modern infrastructure—both to link remote regions with the rest of the country and the country to the rest of the world —was recognized as a priority. Several projects were subsequently implemented with multilateral and bilateral donor support,[17] and marked improvements in the country's telecommunications infrastructure resulted. Fixed line teledensity increased from 0.21 in 1992 to 1.1 in 2002. Despite these improvements, however, teledensity remained far below the 2002 low-income country average of 2.83 (ITU 2004). Further, the distribution of telecommunications access was marked by considerable regional imbalance; teledensity was 4.5 in the largest city, about 1.3 in other urban areas, and only 0.02 in rural areas.

This case study reviews the implications of the evolution of the policy and market structure for telecommunications service provision in rural areas of Laos. After an overview of the country's telecommunications sector compared with other LDCs of similar levels of economic development, a review of market structure and related regulatory issues is provided. The Rural Telecommunications Project, a major initiative to provide the disadvantaged with telecommunications services, is introduced and evaluated in terms of its implications for sectoral development and institutional arrangements for providing telecommunications services in rural areas where market failure persists.

Laos Telecommunications Sector: Status and Perspectives

Despite reform of state-owned enterprises (SOEs), the government continued to predominate in many sectors as the regulator and owner-operator. The

---

(KFW) in 2000, and "ICT for Development: German Contributions," for the German Agency for Technical Cooperation (GTZ) in 2001.

17. See Appendix 3B for details of major telecommunications projects supported by bilateral and multilateral aid.

TABLE 3.10 Performance of the telecommunications sector in Laos, 1991, 1998, and 2003

Indicator	1991	1998	2003
Installed fixed telephone lines	7,266	28,472	69,710
Cellular telephone subscriptions	0	6,453	112,275
Total	7,266	34,925	181,985
Waiting time to install a fixed line	na	2.1 years	0.7 years[a]
Installation charge (US$)	100	90.95	33.11
Average cost of a three-minute local call (US$)	0.28	0.02	0.06
Fixed line teledensity (number of fixed lines per 100 inhabitants)	0.16	0.57	1.23
Locations with telephones	na	44	69[b]
		(137)	(141)
Public telephones	7	230	374
Digitization of the network (percentage)	12	99	100
Fiber-optic cable (kilometers)	0	0	423[c]
Employment by the sector	620	1,075	1,400

SOURCE: ITU (2004).

NOTE: The number of districts is shown in parentheses; na indicates that data were not available.

[a]2002 data.

[b]2001 data.

[c]2000 data.

telecommunications sector was no exception, with the government playing a central role in financial, technical, and institutional support of donor organizations. To secure much-needed investment for network expansion, the government introduced commercialization and partial privatization from the mid-1980s. With the end of the monopoly of the incumbent operator, Laos Telecommunications Company (LTC), in November 2001, Laos's telecommunications market became competitive, despite these movements toward liberalization.

Given several development projects, there has been a remarkable improvement in the telecommunications infrastructure (Table 3.10). By December 2003, the total exchange capacity amounted to 69,710 fixed lines, representing a growth rate of 21 percent per year since 1991. As a result, fixed line teledensity increased from 0.16 in 1991 to 1.23 in 2003. Including the rapidly growing cellular subscription, which increased by 1,640 percent between 1998 and 2003, the total (fixed line and cellular) teledensity was 3.2. Laos benefited from the introduction of digital technology, which replaced analogue technology across 100 percent of the network by 2003 (ITU 2004).

Despite rapid growth relative to other sectors, telecommunications sector development in Laos is still below the average for low-income countries (ITU 2004). For example, as of December 2002, total (fixed line and cellular) tele-density in Laos was far below the low-income country average, at 4.59. In addition to low network coverage, service quality was also below comparable international standards. As of September 2000, the average annual fault level (meaning the number of times a line fails) for the network per 100 lines was over 85. This is very high compared with the international standard of 30–40 faults per 100 lines. The successful call rate—another quality indicator—was around 70 percent in 2000. Though this rate is within the world average (65–75 percent), it had fallen from 90 percent in prior years. This was apparently caused by bottlenecks because the network was not expanding in line with traffic and demand growth. With restructuring of the network, productivity (measured as the number of subscribers per employee) improved from 12 in 1991 to 85 in 2002; however, the country's telecommunications operator remained less productive compared with telecommunications carriers in other developing countries, where rates averaged 113 subscribers per employee staff at that time (ITU 2003).

The slow growth in the telecommunications sector in Laos is due to supply constraints rather than weak demand. Telecommunications development in Laos has not kept pace with the rapidly growing demand accompanying economic development and openness to the world. As a result, there remains substantial unmet demand. According to the World Telecommunication Development Report (ITU 2003) there are 5,900 applications for fixed telephone line connections that have had to be held over through lack of network availability. This includes both switches and transmission capacity. In order to meet the increasing demand, major breakthroughs in network development are necessary.

Lack of supply is a prominent problem in rural areas. As of 2003 the capital, Vientiane, had 57 percent of the country's fixed telephone lines, despite representing only 8 percent of the population. The need to extend the network to both rural and remote areas remains a priority. The need for a cheap and reliable telecommunications network as a prerequisite for Internet use only increases the importance of network capacity and coverage. While regional telecommunications infrastructure initiatives and the introduction of competition into the market are expected to improve the network in the years to come,[18] rural areas will be continuously underserved or unserved as a result of several problems. These include the disadvantages of transition economies (weak

---

18. There have been two development plans for regional fiber-optic networks. The first was intraregional, the China–Singapore Cable (CSC) project, which was completed in 2001; the second is the Greater Mekong Subregion (GMS) telecommunication network project led by the Asian Development Bank (ADB) and regional governments.

market institutions and underdeveloped private sector), lack of public financial resources, low-income levels in rural areas, the absence of universal access criteria (see the section on Universal Service versus Universal Access, above), weak regulatory frameworks, possible negative impacts of competition, and technological advances.

Telecommunications Sector Issues

The Legal and Regulatory Structure. Entreprise d'Etat des Postes et Télécommunications Lao (EPTL) was established under NEM as a public enterprise to provide postal and telecommunications services in 1986. It marked commercialization of the country's telecommunications sector, as well as separation of the regulator from the network operator (EPTL provided the service, while the Ministry of Construction, Transportation, Postal Services, and Communications [MCTPC] adopted the role of regulator). As a result, the opportunities for private-sector participation were expanded. In 1995, EPTL's postal and telecommunications functions were separated with the creation of *Entreprise des Télécommunications Lao* (ETL) and *Entreprise des Postes Lao* (EPL), both as state-owned enterprises. In 1996, the Laos Shinawatra Telecommunications Company (LSTC) was created under a joint venture between Shinawatra-Thailand (49 percent) and the Government of Laos through ETL (51 percent). A vice minister of MCTPC was allocated to each operator's board in support of their competing interests. In turn, MCTPC was influenced both by the government and by the operators.[19] LSTC was structured on the basis of the 25-year build–operate–transfer agreement, which expires in 2021.[20] As mentioned in the preceding section, LTC held a monopoly in the telecommunications market until November 2001.

In August 2000, the government effectively established a second telecommunications operator by separating ETL, as a state-owned enterprise, from LTC.[21] The new ETL took control of donor-funded assets, including the Fujitsu switches that constituted the national backbone, the main satellite earth station,

---

19. A government official from the MCTPC described the relationship between the telecommunications operators and the ministry as "a family."

20. LTC had registered capital of US$91 million, of which Shinawatra contributed US$45 million, and the government US46.84 million in the form of state-owned assets. Under the agreement, LTC committed to investing US$100 million in the first 5 years, $100 million in the subsequent 5 years, and US$200 million in the remaining 15 years.

21. Prior to the separation, ETL was embedded within LTC, and LTC was often called ETL without differentiation. The background to the separation of ETL is complex. The government was disappointed with LTC's investment commitment, which was delayed as a result of the financial crisis. In addition, donor agencies were reluctant to leave the assets they funded under the control of commercial interests. With little domestic resources to mobilize telecommunications infrastructure development, the government seemingly complied with donor pressure.

the China–Singapore Cable project (CSC) cable, and several local switches. LTC and ETL were left to negotiate leasing charges for LTC's use of ETL assets. ETL initially received income from leasing and interconnection fees, but in April 2002, they started fixed line, cellular, and VOIP services. Apparently, ETL have the right to launch any kind of service and will become the sole competitor to LTC in all services including the Internet in the near future.

The government signed a memorandum of understanding with Millicom International Cellular (MIC) in 1998, which set the stage for the introduction of a second Global System for Mobile Communications (GSM) provider. Although this ran counter to LTC's period of exclusivity, it signaled the government's intention to open the market at the earliest possible date. In mid-2000, MIC gained approval-in-principle from the government to provide nationwide cellular telephony, eventually entering into a joint agreement to establish cellular service (Laos PDR 2002).

With the introduction of competition, a stronger regulatory body was needed, leading to the ratification of a new telecommunications law by the National Assembly in April 2001. The law outlines the rights and responsibilities of MCTPC in areas related to communications (Laos PDR 2001). While MCTPC is autonomous in overseeing telecommunications service and network and resource management, the central government maintains a strong influence, first in terms of policy through its approval of larger development projects and foreign investments, and, second, in terms of licenses and permissions for telecommunications service provision and the approval of telecommunications tariffs and charges, given that telecommunications sector revenues—through taxes, charges, and dividends—are an important source of government funding. These two factors may, in fact, negatively influence regulatory activities and hinder sector development more generally (ADB 1997). Though the new telecommunications law stipulated the creation of a telecommunications development fund, fundraising mechanisms and expenditure allocation have yet to be determined. Moreover, universal access criteria were not explicitly included, leaving it unknown as to whether the fund will focus on the areas of greatest need.

In addition to government interests, MCTPC's role as regulator includes ensuring affordable telecommunications services to the people. To date it has kept tariffs low by cross-subsidizing local service with international service (as was seen in the previous case study in this chapter on Peru). An MCTPC vice minister sits on each of the LTC and ETL boards, supporting MCTPC's interests. In this way, MCTPC mediates between the government and the service operators. Apparently there are plans to restructure MCTPC, but details are not yet known.

The new telecommunications law also stipulates that both national and international investors be encouraged to participate in investment in the telecommunications sector. There remain many obstacles to fair competition, however (a dispute between LTC and ETL regarding interconnection fees is one example). Competition can be allowed in the market through deregulation, but the proper promotion of competition through effective oversight is still lacking.

The Market Structure. Of the three telecommunications operators in Laos as of 2002, LTC has an advantage as the former monopolist and established incumbent carrier in the market. However, LTC's failure to meet growing demand and mobilize promised investment for telecommunications development offer opportunities for the new operators to substantially erode its market share.

The government introduced partial privatization with the formation of LSTC (later LTC), against the recommendations of ITU. According to the initial joint agreement, the Government of Laos held a 30 percent of the share of the company, while Shinawatra held 70 percent. With the evolution of LTC, the agreement was amended, increasing the government's share to 51 percent on the basis of the 25-year "build–operate–transfer" agreement until 2021. LTC was also granted monopoly status for five years (until November 2001), during which time it offered fixed and cellular telephone service, paging (Lao Link), Internet service (Lao Internet), text transmission (telex, fax), and shortwave radio communication services.

With its introduction as a separate entity, ETL retained its aid-funded assets, including Fujitsu switches that constituted the backbone of the sector, the main satellite earth station, China–Singapore cable, and several local switches. As of 2002, LTC and ETL were negotiating leasing charges for LTC's use of ETL's infrastructure,[22] and ETL was planning to commence its own fixed line and cellular service. To maintain its services, LTC should pay leasing fees for the network components, such as international gateways, as well as interconnection fees. Competition with ETL presents challenges to LTC, especially if ETL can provide cheaper and better quality services to subscribers while charging LTC high interconnection charges. This could decrease LTC's profit margin and discourage it from investing in rural areas. In addition, a recent surge in voice over Internet protocol (VOIP) services among small illegal service sellers has squeezed fixed line revenue, especially from international calls. This may affect the ability and willingness of the operators to invest in network expansion, but as of 2002 no action had been taken to enforce related laws.[23]

---

22. Of 60 switches, including those planned as of 2001/02, 24 belong to LTC, though most are in rural areas installed through the Rural Telecommunications (Rurtel) project (discussed below). Regardless, traffic from LTC switches needs to be routed through the main and secondary level switches owned by ETL.

23. While new technologies may greatly benefit users by providing better service, they may also hinder healthy development of the sector as opposed to allowing leapfrogging (shared learning) in the absence of clear understanding of technologies and their impact, well-defined laws, and measures to enforce the laws. According to the new telecommunications law, any activities related to communications require MCPTC approval, but as of October 2001 no measures had been taken to enforce this requirement.

Initiative to Connect the Disadvantaged: Rural Telecommunications Project

Given its status as a transition economy, Laos does not have fully developed market institutions and its private sector is not strong enough to invest in the development of the network to the degree necessary. While foreign investment played an important role in privatization and the introduction of competition, Laos's telecommunications sector could be considered less attractive to foreign investors compared with other developing countries because of its generally weak economy, small market, and the danger of government expropriation. Lack of investment results in market failure, especially in rural areas. As in other developing countries, a large proportion of the rural population is poor and served with rudimentary infrastructure only. In addition, mountainous topography and thinly distributed population make it very costly to provide services to rural areas. Hence, as in other developing countries, public-sector intervention is necessary in the provision of basic services to the rural population.

To mitigate the regional imbalance in access to telecommunications services and to assist the rural livelihoods, the German Development Bank (KFW) began providing the Government of Laos with funding in 1992. As of 1994, KFW had provided DEM 44.6 million (approximately US$8.9 million) in aid to LTC as a non-interest-bearing loan for 30 years in support of the Rural Telecommunications (Rurtel) project. From the perspective of the donor and the government (based on profit before tax), the financial internal rate of return (FIRR) was 5.62 percent. The fund was given to LTC as an interest-free loan of 12 years' duration, including a two-year grace period. The loan must be repaid in the local currency (kip) in equal annual installments at the official exchange rate of the date of signing the agreement. This is advantageous to LTC because the kip has been depreciated many times and capital goods have to be imported in U.S. dollar prices.

The Rurtel project has provided basic telecommunications services, such as voice telephony and text transmission using a digital radio concentrator system (DRCS or D-MAS) that connects different levels of stations via radio waves. As of October 2001, phase 4 of the project was in the implementation stage, and 53 percent of 128 rural districts had been connected to service through Rurtel. The systems are installed in rural district capitals that serve as administrative, social, and economic centers. Each station receives a system of 24 to 48 fixed telephone lines, which are distributed among administrative, business, and private users leaving one or two lines for public use.[24] Phase 5 was to be completed by 2004, by which time 73 percent of rural districts were to be connected, although to date, results are still unavailable.

---

24. Until Phase III, 11 percent of the installed telephones were public payphones and the remainder were allocated to businesses (61 percent), "government" (25 percent), and private subscribers (3 percent).

BOX 3.1 Incentives for private-sector participation in rural areas

There are several ways of creating incentives for private-sector participation (including foreign investment) in the provision of telecommunications services in rural areas. Offering subsidies through competitive bidding has been successful in Chile, Peru, and Thailand. Active NGO involvement can reduce the risk to the operator, which worked as a great incentive for Grameen Phone in Bangladesh. In a situation where the government does not have resources to provide a subsidy and the NGO option is not available, rationalizing the tariff structure for rural telecommunications service may provide incentives. Currently, the tariff is regulated by the government, which is concerned about exclusion effect of higher tariffs in the telecommunication market. Cross-subsidizing domestic service with international service has also been used to keep the domestic tariff at quite low levels.

Service providers require government approval to raise tariffs, and any tariff increase should be introduced gradually over several months. As shown in other studies, rural residents and poor people are willing to pay more than the prevailing service charges of urban areas (Chowdhury 2002a). A study on rural telecommunications in Laos also revealed that rural residents are willing to pay much higher rates than the actual service charge (Song 2003). Hence, allowing service providers to charge rates that reflect the cost of service provision, thereby profiting, would actually encourage private participation in expanding rural markets at affordable prices.

As of 2001, the installed facilities had been used extensively and revenues were twice as high as projected. From the supply side, this high revenue per telephone line indicates cost-effective operation of the system; from the demand side, it suggests that demand for telecommunications service is much higher than was expected. According to an impact assessment study of the Rurtel project conducted by the Center for Development Research (ZEF) in Bonn in 2000 (see Chapters 4 and 5 of this volume), access to telecommunications service has positive and tangible benefits for users. In addition, not only has the Rurtel project been profitable for LTC, it has contributed to other aspects of telecommunications development in rural areas. The presence of rural telephony has triggered further demand for telephone service. According to the ZEF survey, in communities without telephone service, only 29 percent of interviewees wanted a telephone, while in communities with telephone service, 54 percent of interviewees wanted a phone. Higher-capacity switches were planned to be installed in some project areas to replace existing systems, so the older systems were to be relocated to districts without service. In this way, the Rurtel project was encouraging local demand and helping ICT to appraise the rural demand for service.

Conclusion

As a developing country, Laos has a broad development agenda and limited resources. While public-sector intervention is inevitable to serve the rural population, raising the necessary funds for the development of infrastructure is a widespread challenge, as discussed elsewhere in this volume. Laos has a relatively short telecommunications history. Like comparable sectors in other developing countries, telecommunications has developed quickly in Laos and it has been difficult to establish and maintain the appropriate regulatory and legal frameworks for further development. At the same time, lack of a strong private sector, low levels of sector-specific foreign investment, and problems in service deployment led to market failures in rural areas.

Laos began moving toward privatizing its telecommunications sector in the mid-1980s, opening the market to competition in 2001. It has, however, maintained strong interest in the sector through joint ventures with all three of the existing operators—the first being state owned (ETL), the second being 51 percent state owned (LTC), and the third (Millicom) being privately owned but operating through a joint venture with the Government of Laos since January 2002. The government also acts as the regulating body through MCTPC (the relevant ministry), although to date there has been a lack of enforcement of stipulated regulations.

The Rurtel project, funded by the German Development Bank, is a successful example of a public–private partnership for the provision of rural telecommunications services. Not only has the Rurtel project enabled a semi-private operator to undertake much needed expansion of service into rural areas, where private operations would likely be unprofitable and highly risky, the introduction of telecommunications services has actually encouraged demand, increasing the profitability and attractiveness of the rural market to private enterprises. The Rurtel project also contributed to institutional development in Laos, given that the recipient of the project funding, LTC, is a semi-private, semi-public entity.

Anticipating future sector development, the Government of Laos included provision for a telecommunications development fund within its recently enacted telecommunications law, though how such funds will be raised and how they might be allocated has yet to be determined. The success of the Rurtel project may offer valuable insights in this regard.

As reflected in market trend of liberalization, government intervention should be removed in the longer term with the development of private-sector involvement and effective regulation. Less attractive telecommunications markets, however, will continue to depend on government intervention, and in the absence of appropriate incentives for private-sector input, foreign aid will continue to be crucial.

Leadership from Nongovernmental Organizations:
The Case of Bangladesh
Shyamal K. Chowdhury and Abdul Bayes

This case study reviews the state of ICT in Bangladesh, focusing on access, availability, and the evolution of the sector. Rather than looking at total service access, the study reviews both rural and urban household access, emphasizing service provision for poor constituents. With the worldwide expansion of ICT infrastructure in the 1990s, it is appropriate to first compare the ICT situation in Bangladesh with the situations in comparable developing countries and regions. We also review the institutional arrangements and market and regulatory structure prevalent in Bangladesh as a means of gaining insight into the current state of ICT development.

In terms of rural household access, the study reviews the village payphone (VPP) program undertaken by the Grameen Bank in cooperation with Grameen Phone. Since the prevalence of poverty in Bangladesh is predominantly a rural phenomenon, the review of the VPP project offers insights into the potential benefits to poor households of access to and the use of ICT.

ICT Development in Bangladesh to Date

Given the dependence on data availability, the indicators reviewed in this section include fixed and cellular telephony, Internet hosts and users, and ownership of personal computers (PCs). Table 3.11 provides some basic indicators for the fixed telecommunications sector in Bangladesh. Four years, 1990, 1996, 1999, and 2003, were chosen to illustrate the state of telecommunications under different market regimes: pure state monopoly, market intervention in the rural market, and liberalization of cellular telephony. It should be noted, however, that despite these interventions, fixed telephony in Bangladesh has remained primarily state owned under a monopoly market structure.

The level of network development in the fixed telephony in Bangladesh has remained very low. In 1990, there was only one telephone for every 454 inhabitants (teledensity of 0.22, Table 3.11). Despite changes in the sector, the situation had improved only marginally by 2003, with fixed line teledensity at a mere 0.55. As in other developing countries, these low levels are not the result of lack of effective demand. Despite a high connection charge—which has always remained higher than the per capita GDP—the waiting list for fixed telephone lines increased over time and, as of 2003, was around 21 percent of the existing supply (that is, the fixed lines in operation).

TABLE 3.11 Basic indicators of fixed telephony in Bangladesh, 1990, 1996, 1999, and 2003

Indicators	State monopoly 1990	Rural sector liberalization 1996	Cellular telephone liberalization 1999	2003
Fixed line teledensity (fixed lines per 100 inhabitants)	0.22	0.26	0.34	0.55
Fixed line penetration (approximate number of fixed lines per 100 households)	1.29	1.47	1.8	na
Waiting list for fixed telephone lines	113,656	145,854	172,096	153,100
Cost of a three-minute local call (US$)	0.04	0.04	0.03	0.03
Residential telephone connection charge (US$)	298	246	375	171.97
Business telephone connection charge (US$)	298	246	375	171.97
Residential monthly telephone subscription (US$)	4.33	3.58	3.05	2.58
Business telephone monthly subscription (US$)	4.33	3.58	3.05	2.58
Digitization of the fixed line network (percentage)	11	40	62	95
Telephone faults per 100 fixed lines	91.08	na	17.32	na

SOURCES: ITU (2004); BTTB (2004).

NOTE: na indicates that data were not available.

Bangladesh entered into the era of cellular telecommunications in 1989 with the private monopoly operator Pacific Bangladesh Telecom Limited (PBTL or "City Cell"). The sector opened to competition in 1996 when the regulatory authority allocated nationwide cellular service licenses to three new operators. After seven years of competition, cellular penetration (approximate number of cellular telephone subscribers per 100 households) grew from 0.002 in 1995 to 1.01 in 2003 (Table 3.12); despite this explosive growth, however, the new network remained biased toward urban areas. With the exception of Grameen Phone, which expanded its coverage from 61 to 64 districts and 320 to 470 up-azillas (subdistricts), plans to quickly expand coverage across the entire country were in place as of 2003 (Table 3.12).

Table 3.13 shows the basic indicators of the information sector for the period 1997–2003. The availability of off-line email access to limited users in Bangladesh's capital city began in 1993. On-line service users, however, had to wait until 1996, when the state monopoly operator, the Bangladesh Telegraph and Telephone Board (BTTB), commissioned the installation of a very small

TABLE 3.12 Development of cellular telephony under different regulatory structures in Bangladesh, 1995, 1999, and 2003

Indicators	Private monopoly 1995	Competition 1999	2003
Connection charge (US$)	868.96	30.55	9.89
Monthly subscription (US$)	49.65	10.19	0.00
Cost of a three-minute peak local call (US$)	0.52	0.32	0.31
Cellular penetration rate (approximate number of cellular phone subscribers per 100 households)	0.002	0.12	1.01

SOURCES: Compiled by authors from ITU (2004) and additional data from various cellular telecommunications providers.

aperture terminal (VSAT)[25] enabling two private providers to commence VSAT-based Internet services. Prior to this, dial-up links were used to communicate with an overseas email server, requiring international phone calls and uploading/downloading of email messages through unix to unix copy protocols (UUCPs). With the introduction of VSAT, the ease of access to the Internet increased exponentially on the basis of direct transmission. In 1997, the Internet penetration rate was a miniscule 0.0008—one Internet user for every 125,000 inhabitants; by 2003, this rate had increased to 0.1798, or one Internet user for every 556 inhabitants. Despite this surge in use, however, low PC numbers inhibit the potential growth of Internet use to less than 4 percent of the population.

Looking at ICT development in Bangladesh within the context of the Asian region—analyzed in terms of telephony, Internet use, and PC ownership—Bangladesh fares poorly. While there is a high correlation between a country's per capita GDP and its teledensity (in both U.S. dollars and purchasing power parity [PPP]), compared with five neighboring countries of similar development levels, as of 2002/03, Bangladesh had fallen behind. The country should have had a minimum 2002 fixed line teledensity of 2.2,[26] whereas in reality it was only 0.6 (Table 3.14). The picture is similar for Internet and PC availability in 2003 (Table 3.15). While the availability of these technologies is low in all six countries by world standards, it is lowest in Bangladesh.

Given the statistics presented above, it should not be surprising that Bangladesh falls behind world averages in ICT development. By way of perspective, more than 75 percent of the world's Internet users live in the high-income countries of the Organisation for Economic Co-operation and Development (OECD), which represent less than 25 percent of the world's population (see

---

25. VSAT is a small station designed to carry voice, data, and video communication.
26. Regional average derived from the relationship between fixed lines and per capita GDP.

UNDP 2001, 40, for more details). Table 3.16 presents data on the ICT availability, comparing data for Bangladesh with averages for low- and high-income countries, as defined by the World Bank, and for the world.

The Legal and Regulatory Framework

It would appear from the above data that a country's income level is not the only factor affecting the development, and ultimately the stock, of ICT. This section reviews the legal and regulatory framework underpinning Bangladesh's telecommunications sector in an effort to shed light on other factors hindering development.

TABLE 3.13 Information technology indicators in Bangladesh, 1997–2003

Indicators	1997	1998	1999	2003
Estimated number of Internet users	1,000	5,000	50,000	243,000
Number of PCs	30,000	120,000	130,000	1,050,000
Internet penetration rate (number of Internet users per 100 households)	0.0008	0.004	0.04	0.18
PC penetration rates (approximate number of PCs per 100 households)	0.12	0.52	0.54	4.03

SOURCES: Compiled by authors from ITU (2004) and additional data from various cellular telecommunications providers.

NOTE: PC indicates personal computer.

TABLE 3.14 Access to fixed line telephony in Bangladesh and five other Asian countries, 2002

Country	Fixed line teledensity	Cost of a three-minute local call (US$)	Cost of a three-minute local call (PPP)	per capita GDP (US$)	per capita GDP (PPP)
Bangladesh	0.51	0.03	0.14	352	1,700
Bhutan	2.84	0.02	na	734	na
India	3.98	0.02	0.11	494	2,670
Nepal	1.41	0.01	0.06	237	1,370
Pakistan	2.50	0.02	0.09	428	1,940
Sri Lanka	4.66	0.03	0.13	863	3,570

SOURCES: ITU (2004) and World Bank (2004).

NOTES: Teledensity is the number of fixed lines per 100 inhabitants; GDP indicates gross domestic product; na indicates that data were unavailable. PPP indicates purchasing power parity, an index used to reflect the purchasing power of currencies by comparing prices among a broader range of goods and services than conventional exchange rates.

Legal and Regulatory Structure. The ICT sector in Bangladesh is regulated by the Ministry of Postal Services and Telecommunications (MOPT). The primary legislation that governs the sector is the Telegraph Act of 1885, which confers exclusive power over the provision of telecommunications services and products to the national government. The Bangladesh Telegraph and Telephone Board Ordinance of 1979 provides BTTB with monopoly rights and powers to issue licenses for telecommunications and wireless services, though some of BTTB's rights—including exclusivity in providing telegraph service and in granting licenses—were cut back by a 1995 amendment, which also transferred the regulatory authority from BTTB to MOPT.

Despite this one amendment, laws regulating the ICT sector in Bangladesh have not been appropriately amended with introduction of modern technology

TABLE 3.15 Access to fixed line telephony, the Internet, and personal computers in Bangladesh and five other Asian countries, 2003

Country	Fixed line teledensity	Number of Internet hosts per 10,000 inhabitants	PC density
Bangladesh	0.55	0.0	0.34
Bhutan	3.43	13.4	1.45
India	4.63	0.8	0.72
Nepal	1.57	0.4	0.37
Pakistan	2.66	1.0	0.42
Sri Lanka	4.90	1.0	1.32

SOURCE: ITU (2004).

NOTE: Teledensity/density is the number of units (fixed lines or personal computers as indicated) per 100 inhabitants. Data on PCs (personal computers) are for 2002.

TABLE 3.16 ICT levels in Bangladesh compared with low- and high-income country averages and world averages, 2003

Indicators	Low-income countries[a]	High-income countries[a]	World	Bangladesh
Fixed line teledensity	2.83	58.54	17.90	0.51
Cellular teledensity	1.75	66.39	19.07	0.81
Internet density	1.33	44.53	10.22	0.15
PC density	0.72	46.68	9.91	0.34

SOURCES: ITU (2004) and World Bank (2004).

NOTE: Teledensity/density is the number of units (fixed telephone lines, cellular phone subscribers, Internet users, or personal computers [PCs] as indicated) per 100 inhabitants.

[a]Based on the World Bank's definition.

TABLE 3.17 Summary of the ICT market in Bangladesh, 2003

Services	Market structure	Number of licensed operators	Ownership
Fixed line telephony			
Urban	Monopoly	1	State
Rural	Partially liberalized[a]	2	Private
Payphones			
Urban	Monopoly	1	State
Rural	Duopoly	2	Private
Cellular telephony	Oligopoly	4	Private
Internet access	Open competition	50	State and private
International PSTN	Monopoly	1	State
Radio paging	Monopoly	1	Private
Telegraph	Monopoly	1	State

SOURCE: BTTB (2004).

NOTE: PSTN, Public switched telephone network.

[a]Two licenses had been granted by the government as of 2003, one for the southern region and one for the northern region.

over time, leaving many regulations redundant and many new facets of the sector overlooked.

New legislation was finally introduced in the form of the Bangladesh Telecommunication Act of 2001, leading to the establishment of the Bangladesh Telecommunication Regulatory Commission (BTRC). The BRTC promptly recommended that BTTB be made a semi-autonomous (though still state owned) corporation to increase both the transparency and accountability of its operations (though as of 2003 this had not been acted on). The commission has reportedly also initiated rationalization of cellular telephone pricing on services provided by four companies. Another move by the BTRC is to examine proposals to legalize VOIP and Internet telephony as a means of increasing service and revenues.

Limited Market Structure. The telecommunications sector has only undergone partial liberalization (Table 3.17). The urban fixed telephony market—by far the largest—remains under state ownership. In contrast to fixed telephony, the cellular telephony sector was liberalized in 1998, enabling a total of 4 private operators to enter the market, based on the number of concessions granted by the government. Open competition in the provision of Internet services was introduced in 2002; consequently the sector has by far the largest number of private operators (at 30).

Under state ownership, the telecommunications sector had remained at only 0.3 percent of GDP; after partial liberalization of the rural telecommunications sector in 1989 the sector rose to 0.6 percent of GDP in 1990, and after

FIGURE 3.6 Development of the telecommunications sector in Bangladesh, 1983–2002

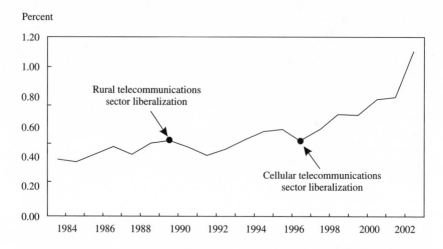

SOURCE: ITU (2004).

the introduction of cellular service in 1996 the sector represented 0.9 percent of GDP. Although it should not be overlooked that a GDP share of under 1 percent is still extremely small, little improvement had been achieved by 2002 (Figure 3.6).

In addition to the limited supply of fixed telephony in Bangladesh, under state ownership a highly distorted tariff structure exists and remains, despite partial liberalization. BTTB's local tariff is heavily subsidized; while local calls cost BTTB US$0.032 (Tk 1.59) per minute, it charges US$0.03 (Tk 1.7) per call irrespective of call duration (Grameen Phone 1999). In terms of quality, the fixed telephony network has undergone some improvement since 1990—for example the percentage of digital lines reached to 95 percent in 2003, up from 11 percent in 1990—but problems remain. The fault rate was still very high, at 465 faults per 100 main lines per year (JBIC 2002), complaints totaled more than 50 per 100 lines (World Bank and BCAS 1998), and the percentage of unsuccessful local calls was around 70 percent (JBIC 2002).

With liberalization of the cellular telephony market and the introduction of competition, foreign private investment in the sector became possible, resulting in rapid network expansion, reduced tariffs and charges, and improved service quality. In 1992 there were only 250 cellular telephone subscribers; numbers reached 1,365,000 by the end of 2003, representing growth of more than 500,000 percent. This unprecedented growth was matched by an equal drop in connection charges. Under the private monopoly, the connection fee for cellular service was US$869; this charge had been cut to US$9.89 by 2003 under the competitive market, a drop of 96 percent. This was accompanied by the abolition of monthly subscription charges and a more than 40 percent reduction in local call tariffs over the same period. The explosive growth of cellular telephony was understandably fueled by the scarcity of fixed telephony, market liberalization, and competition. But because the need for interconnection between the cellular and fixed networks remains, limitations in the growth of fixed telephony ultimately limit the growth of cellular telephony as well. In fact, difficulties with fixed telephony interconnection have led to the creation of parallel fixed and cellular networks.

In terms of Internet access, the market was opened to competition in 1996, as already mentioned. As of 2003, there were about 30 private Internet service providers (ISPs), although about 80 percent of them were located in Dhaka. Only three were operating in Sylhet, three in Chittagong, and one each in Rajshahi, Khulna, and Bogra. Apart from private ISPs, BTTB also operates an Internet service, primarily for government entities (see Management Consulting Group 2001).

The poor levels of ICT development prevailing in Bangladesh are primarily a result of government's regulatory policy and the associated market structure in place. While countries of similar income levels have introduced privatization, allowing competition and private foreign investment, Bangladesh has maintained a protectionist approach to the sector. It is evident that liberalization and competition in both cellular telephony and Internet service provision have provided tangible benefits to consumers by increasing the availability and quality of services and by lowering the prices of such services. Liberalization also benefited the government by attracting foreign investment in the sector and by increasing the tax revenues it generates.

Rural Telecommunications and the Village Payphone Program. Unlike the urban fixed telephony market, rural fixed telephony was partially liberalized as early as 1989. The authorities divided into northern and southern regions and granted licenses to two private operators for monopolistic operations. Of 464 *upazillas*—the smallest (village-level) administrative unit in Bangladesh—Bangladesh Rural Telecom Authority (BRTA) was granted a 25-year license to operate in 200 *upazillas* in the northern region, and Sheba Telecom was granted a comparable license to operate in the 199 *upazillas* of the southern region. BTTB continued to operate in the remaining 65 *upazillas*. Table 3.18 shows the state of rural telephony under public monopoly and limited competition. With this partial privatization, rural telecommunications remained underprovided in terms of both relative share and absolute performance. In 1980, rural fixed teledensity was 0.015. Eight years later, that number had only increased to 0.039—one telephone per 2,546 rural inhabitants. Over the same period, 1980–98, urban fixed teledensity had risen from 0.68 to 1.735—still low, but significantly higher than the rural levels. So despite privatization, the rural share of fixed lines still

TABLE 3.18 Rural telecommunications in Bangladesh before and after liberalization, 1980 and 1998

Indicators	Public monopoly 1980	Oligopoly 1998
Total number of rural fixed telephone lines	26,683	38,534
Rural share of fixed telephone lines	10.50	8.90
Rural fixed teledensity	0.03	0.04

SOURCE: Personal communications with telecommunications firm.

NOTE: Rural fixed teledensity is the number of fixed telephone lines per 100 rural inhabitants.

declined over this time. In addition, within the rural areas, coverage was biased toward (urbanized) town centers. Rural settlements, particularly villages, are still effectively without telecommunications service.

In a country averaging approximately US$300 in per capita income, a US$375 connection fee for a fixed private telephone limits customers largely to wealthy, usually urban inhabitants. Under such conditions, public telephones are extremely important for the rest of the population. Contrary to the expectation, however, the total number of public telephones in 1991 was 1,812, increasing to only 2,064 by 1999. In relative terms, astonishingly, this translates as fewer than one public telephone per 60,000 inhabitants. To address the extreme lack of access to telecommunications in rural areas, the Grameen Bank and Grameen Phone initiated a joint project: the village payphone (VPP) program. Under the project—which is managed by the Grameen Bank through its wholly owned subsidiary, Grameen Telecom (GTC)—Grameen Phone offers discounted access to the network. In addition, the bank allows female borrowers in its credit program to become the owner-operators of cellular phones. GTC provides the phones to these borrowers, who purchase phones under a lease program and then make them available to other villagers. In this way, each owner-operator under the program acts like a public call office (PCO), reselling phone calls, providing message services, and allowing others to receive incoming calls. Between its inception in 1998 and December 2003, the program had drawn more than 45,000 subscribers (owner/operators) to the telecommunications network, from over 68,000 of Bangladesh's villages. As of 2004, GTC had plans to introduce other products/services, such as facsimile and email services to the VPP program.

The VPP program is considered a best practice in rural telecommunications provision. The project ensures positive producer surplus for the providers (the VPP operators, the Grameen Bank, and Grameen Phone), and the program also complies with the country's universal service restrictions (although it is required to). First, there is no price discrimination between urban and rural users;

second, the program is eventually expected to connect all of the country's rural settlements; and third, the program maintains—at least to a certain extent—comparable service quality among rural and urban users. In addition, the project does not distort the market, nor does it require any explicit government subsidy or cross-subsidy between urban and rural operations.[27]

It has been found in the case of Bangladesh that the availability of a public telephone in a settlement increases a household's telephone use, and the difference in a household's telephone use between a settlement with and one without a public telephone is significant. (See Chowdhury 2002a for empirical evidence.) To examine whether the availability of public telephones in villages through the VPP program had increased telephone use among poor rural households, user households under the program were divided into two income groups based on caloric intake per day. Households with a per capita caloric intake equal to or below 2,122 calories per day were classified as poor, while those with a per capita intake higher than 2,122 calories per day were classified as nonpoor. On this basis, 15 percent of the VPP user households fell into the poor category, and the remaining 85 percent fell into the nonpoor category. In terms of the numbers of phone call made, however, the poor category was responsible for 21.5 percent of all calls made (Bayes, von Braun, and Akhter 1999). The use of VPP by rural households ensures consumer surplus to the users because it saves both direct costs, such as the cost of traditional alternatives to the telephone, and indirect costs, such as the travel expenses and the opportunity cost of the traveling time (Table 3.19). In 1998, participants of the VPP program received net benefits equivalent to US$1.17 per call. Further, the benefits to poor users (US$1.66 per call) were higher than the benefits to nonpoor users (US$1.08 per call). By 2001, although benefits had decreased, the magnitude of change was virtually negligible, indicating that rural telephony remained a cheaper means of communication for the rural households.

In terms of saving, the net benefits to VPP user household represent 2.3 percent of the rural household expenditure, and as much as 3.4–4.5 percent of the poor rural household expenditure. These benefits represent an absolute welfare gain and an improvement in the relative welfare of poor versus nonpoor households.

Conclusion

The most telling outcome of this study is Bangladesh's low level of ICT development as indicated by fixed and cellular telephony, Internet access, and PC ownership. As in other developing countries, ICT provision is particularly

---

27. See Chowdhury (2002b) for details of the incentive and operating mechanisms employed under the VPP program.

TABLE 3.19 Consumer surplus to user households per call under the village payphone program, Bangladesh, 2001

	Consumer surplus per cellular phone call (US$)	
Economic category	1998	2001
Poor (15 percent of the sample)	1.66	1.43
Nonpoor (85 percent of the sample)	1.08	1.10
Sample total	1.17	1.16

SOURCES: Primary surveys, 1998 (see Bayes 2001) and 2001 (see Bayes, von Braun, and Akhter 1999).

NOTE: Survey households were further divided according to whether or not their village had a village payphone (VPP) program phone. Though all households benefit by using phones provided through the program, those from villages without VPP service receive higher benefits per call. This apparent contradiction may arise because villages participating in the VPP program offer more alternatives to telephone use than villages without VPP service; similarly, villages without VPP service may be located in more remote rural areas, making the costs of alternatives to telephone use comparatively more expensive.

inadequate in rural areas. Recent positive developments, however, include competition in the cellular telephony and Internet markets, resulting in growth of cellular phone and Internet use, and success of an innovative rural program to increase the accessibility of telephones in rural areas.

Bangladesh is one of the few countries to maintain a state monopoly in urban fixed telephony (ongoing as of 2003). As a result, both teledensity and telephone penetration have remained at much lower levels than in neighboring countries, such that in 2002/03, Bangladesh had the lowest stock of ICT (in the form of the four indicators used in this study) relative to five comparable Asian neighbors. Further, Bangladesh's network of fixed telephony did not compare well with other countries in terms of service quality, as indicated by the percentage of digitalization and the call completion rate. As a result of limited sector reform, pricing was also high in terms of connection charges, and the tariff structure remained distorted.

Competition in the provision of cellular telephony and Internet services has facilitated rationalization of tariff structure, improved service quality, and expanded the network. Ongoing dependence on interconnection between the state-owned fixed network and privately owned cellular network has constrained growth in cellular telephony, however, and promoted the development of two parallel networks. In terms of the Internet, given fixed telephony is a prerequisite to access, Internet expansion has also been hindered.

While competition has facilitated growth in cellular telephony, a competitive market structure is not conducive to service provision in rural areas, as has

TABLE 3.20 Consumer surplus to user households of the village payphone program, villages with and without program access, Bangladesh, 2001

				With VPP access			Without VPP access		
Indicator	Total	Poor	Nonpoor	Total	Poor	Nonpoor	Total	Poor	Nonpoor
Net benefits per call	1.16	1.43	1.10	0.97	1.33	0.83	1.41	1.79	1.37
Net benefits per month	2.83	1.90	3.07	2.46	1.93	2.68	3.3	1.79	3.45
Net benefits as a percentage of expenditure	2.3	4.3	1.9	2.6	4.5	1.8	2.0	3.4	1.9

SOURCES: Primary surveys, 1998 (see Bayes 2001) and 2001 (see Bayes, von Braun, and Akhter 1999).

NOTE: VPP indicates village payphone.

been discussed elsewhere in this chapter. To this end, and in the absence of government intervention, the VPP program, initiated by the Grameen Bank and Grameen Phone, has offered an innovative alternative in the rural areas of Bangladesh since 1998. The program offers a win–win–win solution for the bank, program subscribers (female participants of the bank's credit program who lease cellular phones and onsell services to within their villages), and VPP users who gain access to telephone services at rates that are cheaper than the alternative existing form of communication. In this way, the VPP program ensures an absolute welfare gain as well as an improved relative welfare gain to poor households in the rural areas of Bangladesh.

Competition without Privatization: The Case of China
Wensheng Wang

Economic reform in the telecommunication sector compared with other sectors in China is unique. Not surprisingly, despite worldwide trends toward privatization and competition, China's telecommunications sector remains state owned; competition does exist, however, in major service areas. Despite the reported shortcomings of state-owned monopolies (such as were described in the previous case study on Bangladesh), China's telecommunication sector grew during 1990–2003 at annual rates of 30–50 percent.[28] By December 2003, China's total teledensity had reached 42.0 (Figure 3.7). In fact, China now has the largest fixed line, public, and cellular telephone market in the world.

Internet access has grown even faster than telephone penetration. The Chinese government invested heavily in a number of backbone networks and in the PC-manufacturing industry for about 10 years, with the result that networked computer and Internet applications have spread at an unprecedented pace nationwide. By December 2003, the number of Internet subscribers and users reached 68 and 80 million respectively (ITU 2004), placing China as the second-largest Internet user in the world (behind the United States), although if the trend continues, China could become the largest user nation by 2010.

The fast development of China's telecommunications sector is in large part the result of a unique reform process, dubbed "competition without privatization." Changes were deeply rooted in an integrated strategy of national economic reform, best explained as a socialist market economy—meaning the use of market forces to improve the production efficiency, while retaining a managed, predominantly state-owned economy with authoritarian control over political activity. The intention of the Chinese government was to achieve "an economic system that integrates the basic system of socialism with the market

---

28. The population growth rate over this time averaged about 1 percent, and the GDP growth rate averaged about 11 percent (World Bank 2004).

FIGURE 3.7 The development of fixed line and cellular telephony in China, 1990–2003

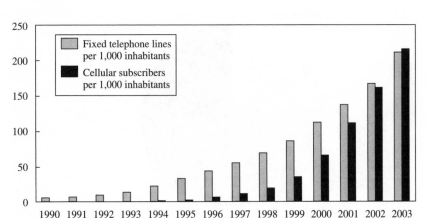

SOURCE: ITU (2004).

economy in an organic way whereby, under macro-regulation and control by the state, the market mechanism plays a fundamental role in the disposition of resources and a high degree of balance between efficiency and fairness" (Mueller 1997, 1).

This case study introduces the current state of China's telecommunication sector, focusing on the difficult and complex reform process and highlighting China's DOT force policy, which is an attempt to address, and ultimately bridge, the digital divide.

The Current Development of China's Telecommunications

The Digital Divide among Nations. As the largest developing country in the world, China faces the daunting challenges of the technological imbalance between the developed and the developing world known as the digital divide. Even with the progress in ICT development that China has achieved, the statistics are remarkable. By 2002, the United States had 190 million computers, representing an average availability ratio of one computer to fewer than two people. With 35.6 million computers in 2002, Germany had an average computer availability ratio of one computer to fewer than 3 people. In contrast, China has 35.5 million computer, 1 for every 37 inhabitants (ITU 2004).

The Digital Divide across Regions. Biases also exist in the development of ICT across China. Traditionally, regional divisions have stemmed from topography—marked by the plains of the east, the hills of the central region, and the mountains of the west; population density—which is highest in the east

FIGURE 3.8 The distribution of Internet users in China across regions, 2002

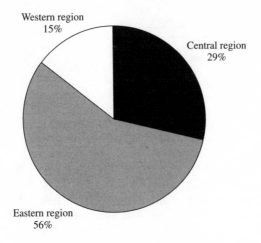

SOURCE: CNNIC (2004).

and lowest in the west; and economic development—which mirrors population density. Internet access is a good example of how ICT development follows regional divisions (Figures 3.8 and 3.9). There is also unequal distribution within regions, with the majority of Internet users located in the southern and seashore provinces. Further, as in other developing countries, Internet access in China is largely concentrated in urban areas. Statistics show that Beijing's Internet users represent 5 percent of the nation's total, while Shanghai accounts for 5.4 percent, Tibet for 0.1 percent, and Qinghai Province (in the northwest) for 0.3 percent (CNNIC 2004).

The Urban–Rural Bias. ICT development is comparatively very expensive in rural areas (as has been discussed earlier in this chapter) because of factors like low population density and geographic obstacles. By the end of 1998, the rural areas of China represented about 70 percent of the population but only 20 percent of its telephony. Urban teledensity was 27.7, while rural teledensity was only 2.85—nearly 10 times lower. Some improvement had occurred as of the end of 2002, though the gap was still present; urban teledensity was still three times higher than rural teledensity (28.2 compared with 9.8).

The urban–rural gap in Internet use is far more pronounced, with a mere 1 percent of Internet users living in rural areas (CNNIC 2004), and the urban network dissemination ratio is 740 times that of rural areas. In fact, while commercial Internet access is now available in over 200 metropolitan cities covering every province, most rural areas have yet to be networked (Press, Foster, and

FIGURE 3.9 The distribution of Internet users in China across provinces, 2002

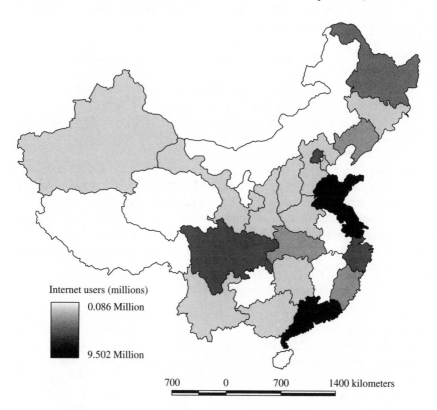

Internet users (millions)

0.086 Million

9.502 Million

700   0   700   1400 kilometers

SOURCE: CNNIC (2004).

Goodman 2002). Even when Internet access is available in rural areas, connection speeds are lower than in urban areas because the technology in use is older (a problem that will be exacerbated when broadband technologies are introduced in rural areas). Nevertheless, despite these imbalances, ICT development in rural China has been gradually improving as a result of general economic development and an influx of rural ICT investment. In 2002, the number of fixed telephone subscribers in rural areas reached 78.478 million, a 338 percent increase from 1997. The rural growth rate is also 34 percent higher than the urban growth rate.

The Threat of Inequality. According to the United Nations Development Programme (UNDP), the digital divide is a reflection of broader socioeconomic inequalities. The risk is that the divide will further marginalize underdeveloped regions and societal groups that can afford neither the cost of the initial ICT infrastructure nor the cost of learning how to utilize the technologies effectively. The following issues are of concern:

- The gap in ICT availability is much larger than income disparities for some regions.
- The gap increases as the technologies become more advanced (meaning, for example, that it is greater for Internet access than for telephone access).
- The gap is greatest in rural and remote regions, increasing the risk that inhabitants of such regions will become even further isolated and forced further into poverty.
- The gap among the social groups only aggravates social and economic inequalities, a problem that will increase as government and social-service providers increasingly use ICT to communicate and disseminate information. In light of these realities, governments need to form telecommunications policies that seize the opportunities of ICT development, address the challenges of ensuring rural and remote access, and ultimately avert the significant threats posed by the digital divide.

China's Telecommunication Reform and Dot Force Policy

The Ministry of Postal Services and Telecommunications (MPT) maintained sole monopoly powers over telecommunications in China for over four decades. Recognizing the inherent challenges of this system in the presence of an enormous market and increasing demand, the Chinese government undertook telecommunications reform aimed at introducing competition. As expected, however, a unique reform model was required for China, to attract investment, improve efficiency, and stimulate development but avoid reduction in the government's control of information flows. Hence, the Chinese government carefully managed the introduction of market forces, balancing development goals with its need to maintain control. Initially this meant a shift from a state-owned monopoly to a state-owned duopoly; plans are in place, however, to introduce pluralistic competition.

Telecommunication Reform. Prior to 1978, the Chinese telecommunications sector formed a natural monopoly[29] operated by MPT, and the sector was seen purely as a tool for administrative needs. Telecommunications expenses were classified as nonproductive and were often the subject of cut in hard times. By 1978, China had a telephone switching capacity of 1.75 million sets, and a teledensity of only 0.18 percent (Lu 1999). In fact, China's telecommunications sector presented one of the worst bottlenecks in the economy by the time economic reform was launched.

---

29. See the section on natural monopolies at the beginning of this chapter.

Telecommunications reform began in 1978 with decentralization of some of the decisionmaking and some of the profits through the contractual responsibility system (CRS), supplemented in 1985 by a nationwide accounting system. Under CRS, telecommunications enterprises were given greater management autonomy as well as incentives for business expansion. Further reforms separating postal and telecommunications functions were implemented in 1988–91. In the 1990s, the Chinese government undertook a series of measures, first to establish the service operators as separate entities apart from government, second to reorganize industry subsectors, and third to introduce competition in all service sectors, including basic and value-added telecommunications and information services. In 1994, China Unicom was formed and supported in building and operating a nationwide cellular network. A new round of reform was launched in 1998 to promote a fair market by breaking up China Telecom and strengthening China Unicom through market restructuring. China Telecom Hong Kong, China Mobile Group, Jitong, and China Net Communication were formed (Gao and Lyytinen 2000). In addition, paging services were separated from China Telecom and Guoxin Paging Ltd. was formed.

Competition created changes in the market dynamic and hastened sector growth. Some crucial problems remained, however. First, MPT's role was rather ambiguous; it was both a competitor (in the form of China Telecom) and a regulator. To completely separate the functions of the government and the telecommunications enterprises, the Ministry of Information Industry (MII) was established as a neutral body, taking over MPT's regulatory functions in 1998. Separate MII departments were given responsibility for policymaking, administration, market regulation, and internal affairs.

From 2000, competition in the domestic telecommunications market intensified, with each of the seven telecommunications companies offering particular advantages:

- China Telecom had a customer base in telephony of over 100 million, held a 99.9 percent market share, and owned 70–80 percent of the country's long-distance telephone network. The network had links to more than 2,000 counties and cities and control of the urban Internet domain network.
- China Mobile held an 80 percent share of the cellular telephone market, cementing its market position.
- China Unicom and IP (Internet Protocol) Telephone developed in tandem with a long-distance fiber-optic communications network covering 250 counties and cities, plus an additional 100 cities via a leased long-distance network.
- With broadband as its core business, China Netcom offered a broadband telecommunication network, and gained recognition for its up-to-date technologies.

- China Railcom relied on its existing customer base of one million fixed line telephone users.
- Jitong Telecommunications specialized in Internet protocol telephones.
- China Guangdian specialized in a cable television network.

In addition, as of 2000, the State Power Corporation was preparing to enter the telecommunications market under the name China Powercom. It is important to emphasize, however, that competition in China's telecommunications market remains still limited because all of the service providers are state-owned enterprises with separate and restricted licenses that limit their service scope; China Telecom, for example, is not licensed to provide cellular telephone service.

Despite initial progress, China Telecom still maintained a national monopoly in fixed telephony (with 99.9 percent of the market share) until the Chinese government settled on a solution in 2001 that involved subdividing operations along regional boundaries and creating decentralized branches. In addition, ChinaSat—a subsidiary established in 1985—was restructured as a government-owned independent operator regulated by MII and renamed ChinaSat Communications Group.[30] In the north, the branches of China Telecom, China Netcom, and Jitong were combined to form the China Netcom Corporation, while in the south, 21 branches were grouped under the China Telecommunications Corporation. These two reorganized corporations maintained the former activities of China Telecom as well as establishing new local telephone networks and offering reciprocal (and equitable) fixed line services in each other's service areas. The southern and northern regions share a 70 percent–30 percent split of the national base network in addition to maintaining 100 percent of the local networks in their respective service areas. As a result of the reorganization, a new competition pattern arose known as "5+1," comprising China Telecom, China Mobile, China Netcom, China Unicom, and China Railcom as the main operators, plus ChinaSat.[31] Under this new pattern of competition, China Mobile became the market leader in terms of revenues, followed by China Telecom and China Netcom. Figure 3.10 illustrates that shift in the revenue shares of the main telecommunication operators as a result of the subdivision of China Telecom.

---

30. In addition to its own operations, ChinaSat also comprises China Orient Satellite, another satellite operator with which it merged in 2001; ChinaSat (Hong Kong); Spacecom, a satellite service reseller; and Spacenet Information, which provides a broadcast data service. ChinaSat has 5.2 billion yuan (US$626 million) in assets.

31. ChinaSat does not offer any direct residential services; most of its customers are telecommunications operators, banks, securities brokerages, insurance, television companies, and the military. ChinaSat predominantly leases space to telecommunications operators, private networks, and public broadcasters and provides a gateway and VSAT for fixed and cellular service, such as voice and data (including Internet) access, television relay or direct broadcasting, and overflow routing or emergency communications.

FIGURE 3.10 Revenue shares in China's telecommunications sector before and after restructuring

Revenue shares before restructuring, 2002

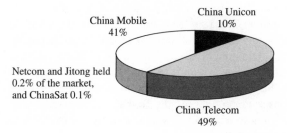

China Mobile
41%

China Unicon
10%

Netcom and Jitong held
0.2% of the market,
and ChinaSat 0.1%

China Telecom
49%

Revenue shares after restructuring, 2002

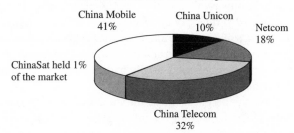

China Mobile
41%

China Unicon
10%

Netcom
18%

ChinaSat held 1%
of the market

China Telecom
32%

SOURCE: MII (2002).

In parallel with structural reform, financial stimuli also promoted the development of China's telecommunications sector. Traditionally, MPT controlled the pricing of most services, including monthly rental fees. The tariff structure was lower for local services and higher for domestic long-distance and international services. At the end of 1990, the ministry set a price cap based on the local telephone companies' average costs plus a profit mark-up. Local telecommunications companies could set their own local rates up to but not exceeding the cap, subject to the approval of local government's price control authorities (Lu 1999). During this time, the Chinese government also prioritized legislative reform and oversight of the sector. In 2000, a centralized regulatory body was created; "Telecommunications Regulations of the People's Republic of China" and "Administrative Methods for Internet Services" were established and disseminated; and telecommunications-related laws were updated.

WTO and Privatization, International Competition. China's accession to the World Trade Organization (WTO) is generally recognized as an external driving force in the strengthening and acceleration of the telecommunications reform, given the domestic telecommunications market will gradually open to foreign investors and competitors. According to the WTO agreement, China must eliminate import restrictions on pagers and cellular phones, as well as regional restrictions on fixed telephones by 2007. By 2005, China is required to allow foreign investors to own between 49 and 51 percent of telecommunications companies depending on the service. The emergence of multiple markets will no doubt fuel competition in China's telecommunications sector, which in turn will improve quality, lower prices, and stimulate demand. It should also go a long way toward bridging the digital divide.

DOT Force Strategy and Actions. China's telecommunications sector has taken steps to prepare for the "real" competition that international investment in their telecommunications sector could provide. To that end, in parallel with the structural reform, the Chinese government was guided by the DOT Force strategy[32] in its development of ICT.

Initially, this involved a national information strategy. To promptly embrace the opportunities of the new digital technologies, the Chinese government formulated further policy to promote construction, modernization, and optimization within the relevant industries. This included a series of important information projects called Golden Card, Golden Bridge, and Golden Gate, which were implemented sequentially beginning in 1993 specifically to promote the development of infrastructure.

Next, the government initiated an Internet program in the mid-1990s with a view to creating an online government presence to facilitate information access for all citizens. Under the program, goals were set to build this governmental Internet presence to 30 percent by 1998, 60 percent by 1999, and 80 percent by 2000. In addition, 100 large conglomerates, 10,000 midsize firms, and 1,000,000 small firms were to be connected during the year 2000. By 2002, more than 220 million government departments were offering electronic services according to Xie Lijuan, member of the Ninth National Committee of the Chinese People's Political Consultative Conference (*People's Daily* 2002). By 2002, the Chinese government was represented by 5,864 ".gov.cn" domain names, including national ministries and provincial and municipal governments across the country; this number rose to 7,796 in 2003. Approximately 4.3 percent of all Web sites under the ".cn" domain have ".gov" suffixes (Xiang Zhou 2004).

Third, the government committed specific expenditure to address issues relating to the digital divide. This enabled significant investment in the creation of telecommunications infrastructure in urban regions as well as in rural and remote areas. To reduce the widening gap in Internet access between urban and

---

32. In July 2000, the G8 committed to creating a Digital Opportunity Task Force (DOT Force), based on the Okinawa Charter on Global Information Society, to investigate the digital divide in the developing world.

rural areas, the government launched two state-owned or subsidized projects, "Every Village has a Phone" and "Gold Farm Engineering," which promote rural telephone and Internet access. As of 2000, 5,000 networked telephones had been installed and over 200 agricultural Web sites had been created through these projects (Xinhua News Agency 2000). In particular, significant efforts were made to accelerate the construction and improvement of infrastructure to satisfy the socioeconomic needs of the western regions of the country. To this end, the Chinese government prepared a series of key policies to encourage both domestic and foreign investors to develop telecommunications infrastructure and service in the region, and efforts have been made to cultivate a number of promising IT enterprises in the area.

Education and gender issues are also being explored in relation to the digital divide. The Chinese government encourages and supports colleges and universities in educating students on ICT and the benefits of their application. After networking almost all the country's universities and important institutes, the Chinese government shifted focus to the provision of long-distance education facilities in less-developed regions. For example, with support from the Government of Australia and the World Bank, the Government of the Ningxia Hui Autonomous Region launched a distance learning center (DLC). The center helped to promote development and poverty reduction in this western province by introducing ICT use and thereby promoting distance learning and information and knowledge dissemination. Using state-of-the-art distance learning technology, DLC allows participants from across China and other East Asian countries (and even other continents) to learn and share information without leaving their hometowns (GDLN 2001).

Finally, the Chinese government has allowed the private sector to provide information services without sensitive political content. This policy significantly facilitates dissemination of information via the Internet. Despite strong arguments as to whether private Internet cafes are harmful to the political regime and society more generally, the number of cafes has grown rapidly. The resulting private competition for Internet service provision counterbalances the state monopoly and reduces the cost of Internet use to affordable levels for large segments of the society.

Conclusion

The unique reform of China's telecommunications sector has been marked by the need to maximize competition within the framework of the broader government agenda. As a result, China's telecommunications sector has become more market oriented despite state ownership. Still, competition is limited by licenses that restrict operations and lack of essential legal and regulatory safeguards that would ensure fair competition. China's accession to WTO is a driving factor in the reform process. The domestic telecommunication market will gradually open to both domestic enterprises and foreign investors, which will herald the introduction of "real" competition, ultimately improving service quality, lower prices, and stimulating demand.

Institutional Trends and Infrastructural Developments in Telecommunications in Sub-Saharan Africa: The Case of Ghana
Romeo Bertolini

With the revelation of the "missing link"[33] (Independent Commission for World Wide Telecommunication Development 1984), interest in strengthening telecommunications infrastructure of low-income countries began to grow. This was due in part to the realization that well-managed telecommunications entities can generate large financial surpluses. More importantly, telecommunications networks were acknowledged as a potential driving force for macroeconomic growth through a variety of direct and indirect effects (as was discussed in Chapter 1). The explosive growth of ICT made reliable and cheap telecommunications networks more important than ever as the foundation for wide deployment of technologies like the Internet. And while low-income countries generally lag behind other countries in basic telecommunications (and consequently in ICT development), the situation is of particular concern in Sub-Saharan Africa, where regional teledensity is among the lowest in the world, and most rural areas have no access to services at all.[34]

This case study provides an overview of Sub-Saharan African telecommunications sectors focusing on institutional evolution in the 1990s. Patterns of institutional and organizational change in Africa were not significantly different than those in developed countries; most reform programs tended to be modeled after continental European precedents (Mustafa, Laidlow, and Brand 1997). Nevertheless, Sub-Saharan African countries exhibited some peculiarities in the transformation process, which are analyzed in this case study in terms of sector reform in Ghana—a country strongly committed to trade and market liberalization, and one that, together with a few other countries, was widely regarded as a best practice case for the region (ITU 1998; World Bank 1998).

General Trends in Telecommunication Sector Reform

Until the end of the 1980s, "telecommunications used to be regarded as a natural monopoly[35] and a relatively straightforward public utility. Economies of

---

33. A report of the Independent Commission for World Wide Telecommunications Development on the disparity in the distribution of telecommunications services around the world.

34. In 1999, low-income countries had an average teledensity of 2.9 and about 0.62 Internet users per 100 inhabitants. Sub-Saharan African countries, excluding South Africa, had a teledensity of 0.6 and fewer than two subscribed Internet users in 1998. In South Africa, about 46 percent of urban households have telephones compared with only 8 percent of rural households.

35. See the discussion of natural monopolies at the beginning of this chapter.

scale, political and military sensitivities, and large externalities made tele-communications a typical public service" (Saunders, Warford, and Wellenius 1994, 305). Consequently, the services were mostly provided by monopolists,[36] either as government departments or state-owned enterprises (as was seen in the preceding case studies on Bangladesh and China). In the early stages of telecommunications development, industrialized countries profitably operated infrastructures and succeeded in providing near universal access to telephones. Developing countries, however, began at a different level. Their telecommunications services were initially run by foreign private companies and colonial government agencies. They provided an infrastructure that was primarily de-signed to meet the needs of the colonial administration rather than the population. During the 1960s and 1970s, most monopolistic telecommunications service operators were taken over by the public sectors of newly independent national governments. These monopolies fell short of meeting the demand for telephone services, which resulted in long waiting lists, congested call traffic, poor service reliability, and limited network coverage. This was due not only to the scarcity of capital but also to the inefficient management of existing resources, as well as limited motivation to meet the existing demand (Mustafa, Laidlow, and Brand 1997; Saunders, Warford, and Wellenius 1994).

Despite the poor market performance, Mustafa, Laidlow, and Brand (1997, viii) observe that "there is evidence of substantial ability and willingness by customers to pay for services which were [simply] not available." Revenues per line are high by world standards, and consequently telecommunications sectors of Sub-Saharan African countries have the potential to be profitable. These pos-itive perspectives and the increasing discussion on ICT as a catalyst for more efficient economic performance and increased global integration made sector reform a widely discussed issue. In the North, this was mainly because the old monopolistic structures could not meet the challenges imposed by the emer-gence of new technologies and services, and the huge demand for new ser-vices. In the South, where the need for greater penetration of basic services was urgent, obtaining access to so-called leapfrogging technologies was par-ticularly challenging. For both hemispheres, telecommunications sector reforms were designed along similar patterns. Although some low-income countries—especially in Sub-Saharan Africa—remained hesitant to adapt reform measures, some governments overcame their reluctance and joined ICT-related programs and initiatives established by international organizations such as the United Na-tions Economic Commission for Africa (UNECA), UNDP, ITU, and the United States Agency for International Development (USAID). Substantial parts of these programs and initiatives address financial and managerial challenges related to

---

36. Major exceptions in this respect were Canada, Finland, and the United States (Saunders, Warford, and Wellenius 1994).

sector reform. Thus, they help to attract private investment and accelerate the expansion of the infrastructure and services (ITU 1998; Jensen 1998).

Some Sub-Saharan African countries that became involved in such programs —Côte d'Ivoire, Ghana, Mauritius, Senegal, and South Africa—eventually embarked on international agreements and restructured their telecommunications sectors to comply with the WTO agreement on basic telecommunications services and the General Agreement on Trade in Services (GATS, ITU 1998, 8). From a global perspective, and with regard to telecommunications, this agreement was introduced to meet the need for a new international system of governance for telecommunications generated by economic globalization and technological convergence (Tarjanne 1999). The agreement was signed early in 1997 by countries that account for more than 90 percent of the world's telecommunications service revenues. The most important principles to be introduced under the umbrella of GATS and to promote the aforementioned acceleration of infrastructure and service provision for these countries are outlined below (ITU 1998; Männistö, Kelly, Petrazzini 1998; Saunders, Warford, and Wellenius 1994; Tarjanne 1999):

- separating the former monopolist, the national postal and telecommunications operator (PTO), into telecommunications and postal service providers;
- fostering the privatization of the former incumbent telecommunications service provider and promoting of foreign investment;
- liberalizing markets (that is, introducing competition within the sector); and
- establishing a legal framework that efficiently regulates sector developments.

The respective governments progressively followed these structural undertakings with the assistance of the ITU. Although there are differences among individual countries, the elements discussed below appear to be the institutional "best practice" (ITU 1998, 1999a).

Separation, Privatization, and Liberalization

The separation of the telecommunications operator from postal services and the establishment of both entities as corporate bodies is the first step toward sector reform (as was seen in the case studies on Bangladesh and China earlier in this chapter). Next, the telecommunications operator must be reorganized following commercial principles: "There is widespread agreement that regardless of who owns them, telecommunications operating entities perform best when they are run as profit-driven businesses" (Saunders, Warford, and Wellenius 1994, 310). A number of Sub-Saharan African countries have separated their postal and telecommunications operations, given them a corporate structure, and privatized the resulting entities (see Figure 3.11 and Appendix 3C, Table 3A.1).

FIGURE 3.11 Regulatory reform in Sub-Saharan Africa in the 1990s

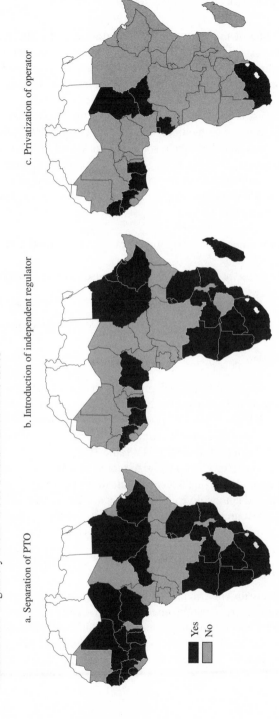

a. Separation of PTO b. Introduction of independent regulator c. Privatization of operator

Yes

No

SOURCES: BMI-T (1998); ITU (1998).

NOTE: PTO indicates postal and telecommunications operator.

As stated, one of the purposes of separating and privatizing the telecommunications service provider is to attract financial investment. ITU points out that, especially for Sub-Saharan African countries, there is an increasing desire to attract foreign investment into the telecommunication sector (ITU 1998). The most common strategy in low-income countries is to offer a share of the new company to a strategic foreign investor as a partner. This is often regarded as the only way to generate the necessary investment for development of the network in view of scarce domestic resources (One World 1997). This strategy also allows the investor to inject managerial and technical expertise on which the operator can build. Whatever the process of privatization (share-offering, joint ventures, or full privatization), the anticipated positive effects are as follows (ITU 1998; Tarjanne 1999):

- enhanced efficiency in management, production, and the provision of services;
- financial benefits for governments, freeing resources for other public sector needs or reducing foreign or internal debt;
- reduced hidden and open subsidies;
- expanded infrastructure in underserved areas and increased network quality; and
- reduced tariffs.

Although most African countries took measures to increase private-sector participation, investment inflows in the telecommunications sector actually fell from US$5 to US$4.7 billion in 1994/95 (One World 1997). There were, however, large differences across countries in terms of their commitment to telecommunications sector reform (see Appendix 3C, Table 3C.2).

Competition is perceived as integral to sector reform. There are two mainstream strategies for liberalizing telecommunications markets: complementary entrance policies and competitive entrance policies. Both aim to attract capital and management resources for the telecommunications sector, mainly through mechanisms that involve licensing obligations or create competition among service providers.

Regulatory Framework

Regulation naturally differs with market structure—whether government ownership, corporatization, privatization, or competition—and a regulatory body can take the form of a government department, a public corporation, or an intermediate version "in which the operating entity has the status of a government department but can act as a commercial agency" (Mustafa, Laidlow, and Brand 1997, 56). Details of regulations under the various market structures are provided below:

- With a state monopoly, regulations mainly concern business issues such as the market scope, external financial resources, and the form of management (ITU 1998).
- With corporatization, the regulatory framework should include statutes limiting the influence of government officials over the corporation (ITU 1998) and company law (Mustafa, Laidlow, and Brand 1997). In addition, regulations should be established that limit the monopoly status of the operator.
- Privatization is often subject to licensing or concession contracts; regulations should consider future sector policies, such as tariff rules, the degree of liberalization, liabilities, exit options, and commitments to universal access and service obligations (ITU 1999a; Saunders, Warford, and Wellenius 1994).
- Competition involves opening the market to new operators and introducing new services. To facilitate competition, the regulatory body should develop an appropriate licensing regime. Regulation of interconnection between multiple operators is of particular importance to guarantee fair competition after the entry stage.[37]

From an organizational perspective, regulatory bodies are quasi-autonomous, having limited powers. Often, the ministry responsible retains the authority to issue directives to the regulator to control the funding and the board of the entity. The degree of regulator autonomy depends on the way the body was established, that is, whether by comprehensive law or ministerial decree (ITU 1999a; Scherer 1994). It is argued, however, that only complete independence of the regulatory authority can provide sufficient assurance that ad hoc government interventions will not occur. Mustafa, Laidlow, and Brand (1997) indicate that of the developing countries that had undergone privatization by 1997, none had an effectively independent regulator.

Ghana's Telecommunications Sector Policy and Infrastructure

In 1982, the Republic of Ghana was undergoing its deepest economic crisis since gaining independence in 1957. Toward the end of that year the government began economic restructuring primarily following the patterns of structural adjustment proposed by the International Monetary Fund (IMF) and the World Bank. IMF loans were a necessary precondition for regaining credibility with the donor community and acquiring the necessary financial resources to facilitate economic recovery (Schmidt-Kallert 1994). Since that time, the country has carried out a couple of "the most thorough structural adjustment programs in

---

37. For a detailed discussion of regulatory issues, see Bertolini (2002).

Africa" (Chibber and Fischer 1991, 7) and also been committed to GATS. Important steps taken at that time are outlined below (IMF 2000; SAPRIN 2000):

- privatizing state-owned enterprises;
- reducing public-sector expenditures;
- fostering deregulation policies;
- enhancing macroeconomic stabilization through adequate monetary and fiscal policies; and
- liberalizing imports and the promotion of exports.

These elements were included in the 1999 Structural Adjustment Facility Policy Framework, which was extended until 2001 (IMF 2000) and paved the way for telecommunication sector reform.

The State of the Ghanaian Telecommunications Sector

The Ghanaian government first restructured its Ministry of Transport to form the Ministry of Transport and Communications (MTC). With the assistance of various international organizations, such as the ITU, the ministry then formulated a national strategy for broad information and communications sector reform. The fundamentals of this reform were then formalized within the telecommunications policy for an accelerated development program (ADP) that was launched in 1994 (MTC 1999). Details are discussed below.

Sector Policy: Aims and Measures. The strategy for the telecommunications sector targeted the following issues. First, a tariff policy was suggested to allow operators to recover the full cost of service provision. Second, it was established in the ADP that customers should be able to access services at competitive and affordable prices. This included the intention to foster public accessibility in urban and rural areas through the implementation of payphone facilities. Universal public access was also planned for the longer term through the installation of "payphone facilities to every village of a minimum of 250 inhabitants" (IICD 1999, 5). The government had a long-term objective of increasing Ghana's international competitive advantage and of becoming the Gateway to West Africa (Frempong and Atubra 2001). So the establishment of high-quality communications services for the business community was a priority in addition to universal public access.

The primary means of achieving these ambitious goals was the establishment of Ghana Telecom in June 1995. Ghana Telecom took over the telecommunications division of the Ghanaian PTO, which had been established as an SOE as early as 1974. This corporatization did not, however, have positive effects on either the profitability of the company or its supply of services (Ghana Telecom 2000) (Figure 3.12).

To attract financial investment in the newly established—but heavily indebted—telecommunications operator, a 30 percent share of Ghana Telecom was sold

FIGURE 3.12 Fixed line teledensity, 1970–79, and Ghanaian postal and telecommunications operator revenues, 1977–79

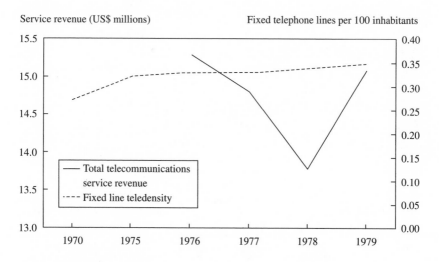

SOURCE: ITU (2004).
NOTE: Teledensity is the number of fixed telephone lines per 100 inhabitants.

to a consortium (led by a strategic foreign investor, Telecom Malaysia Berhad) for US$38 million (BMI-T 1998). In December 1996, a second operator, ACG Telesystems Ghana, was licensed to build a national fixed network. Other value-added services, such as cellular telephone services, data transmission, paging, and payphones were soon added. Reform also enabled large corporate users to develop their own private networks.

The National Communications Authority (NCA) was established as the sector's regulatory body in 1996 to oversee the implementation of the reform measures, promote fair competition, and protect consumers and operators. Further, NCA was to supervise the fulfillment of the preconditions linked to the license agreements that were established to ensure universal access (MTC 1999).

Market Participants and Infrastructural Developments. The political and institutional framework induced a number of developments. Although Ghana Telecom maintained control of the vast majority of the market, additional agents were introduced, as mentioned, beginning with ACG Telesystems Ghana as the second national network operator in the fixed line market. ACG is jointly owned by the Ghanaian Petroleum Company (GNPC), Western Wireless (United States), and ACG Telesystems (United States) and operates under the trade name Westel (BMI-T 1998). Westel and Ghana Telecom were the only fixed line operators in Ghana, although the market was opened to competition in 2002. This agreement was based on the condition that Westel would install 100 payphones

FIGURE 3.13 Participants in the Ghanaian telecommunications sector

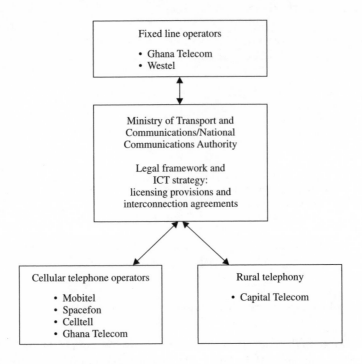

SOURCE: Frempong and Atubra (2001).

and 50,000 fixed lines between 1998 and 2001 investing US$30 million (Figure 3.13).

Westel was effectively crippled by problems with the NCA over its inability to meet licensing conditions relating to subscriber targets in the first year of its operations. It was subsequently fined a penalty of approximately US$25 million, which grew, with interest, to more than US$35 million because of Westel's inability to pay. Consequently, Westel is no longer a viable market competitor; it continues to serve a small number of subscribers, who—despite the difficulties—report that Westel's services are excellent (Ghanaweb 2004). Westel's competitiveness was further compromised because the wireless technology that underpins its network required a prohibitive initial investment in hardware, necessitating a subscription fee of US$260 per line.

Capital Telecom, which is wholly Ghanaian-owned, commenced operations in 1997, primarily to serve southern rural areas. Originally conceived as a "build–operate–transfer" provider of a rural telecommunications network (meaning build, operate, and eventually transfer ownership to the government), it later became a "build–operate–own" provider under the privatization process. The company provides rural communications using a multi-access radio system with a potential capacity of 1,000 subscribers per hub (as of 2001, three hubs were in operation). Capital Telecom also had serious problems, primarily in attracting customers. By 2004, the total number of lines in operation was still only about 500. Being a rural service provider, Capital Telecom faces the difficulty of serving a low density, low-income rural customer base (the difficulties of which have already been discussed elsewhere in this volume). In addition, Capital Telecom's tariffs are two to three times higher than those of Ghana Telecom, making effective competition virtually impossible in areas served by both operators, such that potential Capital Telecom customers are generally only found in very remote areas beyond the Ghana Telecom grid. According to Capital Telecom, the reason for the high tariffs is the company's interconnection agreement with Ghana Telecom, under which it is require to pay Ghana Telecom 75 percent of all revenues earned through calls that originate or terminate in the Ghana Telecom network (Morten Falch 2003).

By the end of 1997, the cellular services market was fully liberalized. It covered the major cities in the south of the country and served approximately 20,000 subscribers (BMI-T 1998). Despite comparatively high charges, this figure grew to approximately 40,000 by May 1999 (Ghanaweb 1999; Frempong and Atubra 2001), and 800,000 by December 2003 given an enormous demand for telecommunication services and a substantial wait for fixed lines.[38] Moreover, ongoing changes are expected to promote the cellular sector even further. The influx of cellular receivers from the United States and Europe and the introduction of a prepaid system are significantly lowering entrance costs for end users. Also, decreased costs are expected to increase competition, which should in turn further decrease costs.

Infrastructural Developments. According to Frempong and Atubra (2001, 205), NCA is "grappling with the thorny problem of putting critical structures in place to regulate and manage the sector efficiently." The authors argue that the organization was not able to provide comprehensive regulation and was therefore weakening its hold on the sector's operators. Despite these problems, however, the changing framework seems to have enhanced the access to telecommunication services for the country's population. The overall number of fixed telephone lines tripled during 1990–2003 (Figure 3.14). From what was mentioned beforehand, this is due more to market liberalization and the new market players than the network expansion by the former incumbent. The latter's motivation to expand its infrastructure is due to the aim of ensuring the companies'

---

38. In 2002, fixed line telephones cost US$1.26 in monthly subscription charges and US$0.03 per local (peak rate) three-minute call; cellular service cost US$7.42 in monthly subscription charges (in 2001), and US$0.95 per local (peak rate) three-minute call (ITU 2004).

FIGURE 3.14 Development of fixed lines, cellular subscribers, and teledensity in Ghana, 1990–2003

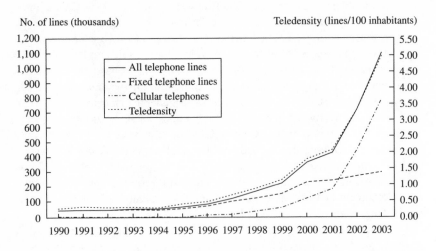

No. of lines (thousands)   Teledensity (lines/100 inhabitants)

SOURCE: ITU (2004).
NOTE: Total teledensity is the number of fixed lines and cellular telephone subscribers per 100 inhabitants.

hold on the market but also due to an important regulatory agreement. Ghana Telecom was required to provide around 225,000 fixed telephone lines over a five-year period and invest more than US$80 million (Frempong and Atubra 2001).

The overall increase of telephones is based on the rapid development of the cellular market (Figure 3.14). Growth of the cellular market share indicates that cellular services are not just a complement to the fixed line market but rather an alternative, compensating for long waiting periods for fixed lines (Ghanaweb 1999). One negative factor resulting from the rapid growth of the cellular market is that Ghana Telecom's switching capacity did not expand relative to market growth. It therefore fell far short of demand, which "appears to have affected the ability of the company to give more capacity to other competitors as well as keeping to its mandatory obligations" (Frempong and Atubra 2001, 205). Consequently, calling a cellular subscriber via Ghana Telecom's network can be a difficult if not an impossible task, particularly during the day times. Frempong and Atubra (2001) use this example to emphasize problems with the NCA, even suggesting a trade war between the new cellular network operators and the former monopolist. Spacefone (the leading cellular operator) has engaged in a war of words with Ghana Telecom over lack of interconnect between their networks; Celltell, Mobitel, and One Touch have not reported having this problem (Ghanaweb 2004).

Telecommunication Infrastructure at the Regional and District Levels. While the greater Accra region accounts for nearly 93 percent of the country's fixed telephone lines, the other nine regions each account for only 0.3– 8.6 percent of all lines (see Appendix 3C, Table 3C.3 for more details). Unsurprisingly, teledensity follows the same spatial pattern; it is highest in Accra (4.9), decreasing rapidly to 0.4 in Ashanti, and to less than 0.1 in the northern, upper eastern, and upper west regions. All in all, the country's major economic centers—Accra–Tema, Kumasi, Cape Coast, and Sekondi-Takoradi—account for nearly 90 percent of all Ghanaian telephone lines. Additionally, the regional capitals account for between 48 percent and 100 percent of all fixed lines within their respective regions. Although no detailed data are available to show the current spatial pattern of the cellular service infrastructure, network coverage is restricted to urban centers in all regions (Ghanaweb 2004) (Figure 3.15 and Appendix 3C, Table 3C.3).

Analysis of district-level infrastructure shows that only 49 of the 110 district capitals were connected to the national telecommunication network as of 1998 (Ghana Telecom 1998). Other areas within districts did have access, however. Unlike the regional distribution of telephony, district-level telephone access is not correlated with urban development (Figure 3.16). It is likely that strategic interests (border towns, for example) and the presence of other physical infrastructure (such as roads and electricity) may be more important factors in determining telecommunications development, highlighting service diffusion is not primary linked with the market mechanisms involved and, once again, indicating market failure within the telecommunications sector.

Conclusion

Ghana's telecommunications sector expanded rapidly in line with government objectives to gain market power and develop the sector in line with world trends toward privatization and liberalization. The vast majority of gains in infrastructure, however, have remained limited to urban areas, and conditions actually enabled the former monopolist to strengthen its position in the fixed line market. Insufficient switching (meaning interconnection) capacity and lack of a level competitive playing field—exacerbated by the inadequacy of the regulator— significantly hindered overall sector performance and customer satisfaction (Frempong and Atubra 2001).

While universal access to services at competitive and affordable prices was a stated objective in the reform process, it has certainly not been achieved. This is largely because of lack of effective regulation, which in the first instance, needs to (a) foster real competition in areas that, while outside the more lucrative urban centers, are nonetheless economically viable; and (b) devise mechanisms to motivate/enable operators to provide service in economically infeasible regions. In this second case, subsidies should be allocated via competitive bidding to determine which operators can provide services at the least cost, and hence what degree of subsidy is actually needed.

FIGURE 3.15 Teledensity in administrative regions in Ghana and disparities in urban–rural access, 2000

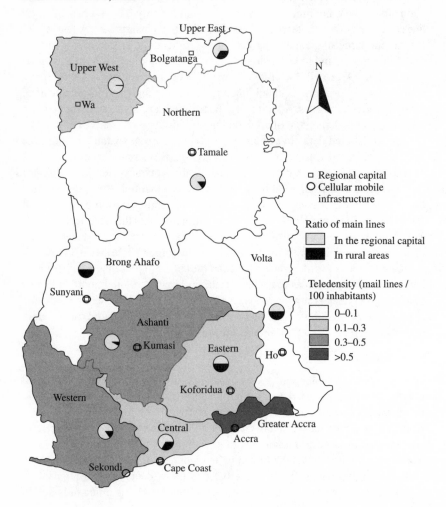

SOURCE: Ghana Telecom (2000).

FIGURE 3.16 Districts with at least one community connected to Ghana Telecom's fixed line network, 2000

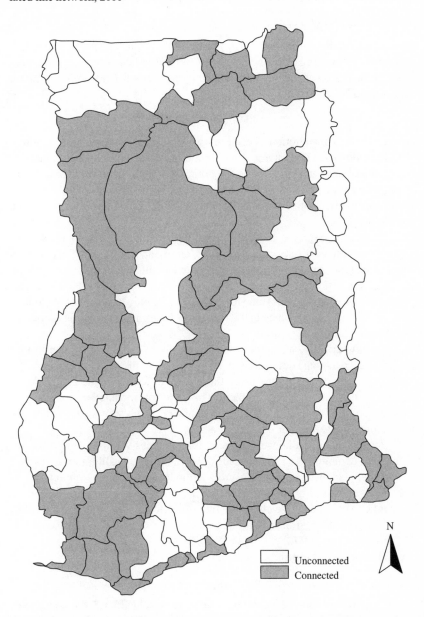

Unconnected
Connected

N

SOURCE: Ghana Telecom (2000).

Appendix 3A: Econometric Model, Empirical Estimations, and Estimated Telephone Use Demand: The Case of Peru

Econometric Model

First we model the market for each product in both the pre- and post-privatization scenarios, identifying changes in access to and use of each service, then measuring consumer surplus changes at each stage. Household preferences are represented by a utility function:

$$u = u(x_{local}, x_{ldn}, x_{ldi}, z), \tag{1}$$

where x_I is the consumption of each service available to a residential customer (local and domestic and international long-distance calls), and z is a consumption index of other goods. Solving the optimization problem, we derive the indirect utility function, $V(p,y)$, where y is the income of each household and p is a vector with prices of the three basic services and a general price index for the remaining goods.

To access the service, a household compares the value of using the service $V(p,y)$, with the cost of access. Having a telephone line allows customers to make three types of calls (local and domestic and international long-distance). On the panel, among the households for which we were able to obtain a telephone bill, we observed that some households make only local calls while others make local and long-distance calls. Hence we can order households according to their consumption decisions.

Econometrically, we model the demand for specific telecommunication services as a two-stage decision rule. First, we model the decision to access the network using a probit model. From this equation, we obtain the Inverse Mills ratio to correct for the access problem. This ratio was included in demand estimations to obtain price elasticities and consumer surpluses for the three services under study, correcting for the lack of access bias.

Because we use a household panel that includes variations in prices, income, and demographic characteristics, we can directly calibrate the position of each curve in different points of time without additional assumptions in unobserved variables. Furthermore, it is not necessary to assume linearity for the demand curves. In fact, we chose the functional form of the demand curves in order to obtain the best fit rather than for algebraic simplicity (see Pascó-Font, Gallardo, and Fry 1999).

The functional form that yields the best fit was:

$$q_{it}^n = \exp(x_{it}\beta^n + p_{it}\alpha^n + \varepsilon_{it}), \tag{2}$$

where superscript font indicates socioeconomic level (SEL); i, the household; and t, time. The relevant prices are p_{it}, so the elasticities are recovered from the parameters, α, for each SEL. Finally, q_{it} is the measured traffic for each of the three services considered in this study.

After calibrating the demand functions, we measure consumer welfare five years before and five years after privatization. The combined effect of increasing the number of installed lines and reducing the charges for access increased consumer welfare over pre-privatization levels. Our welfare measure will be the difference between the consumer surplus of making a certain number of calls and the fixed amount paid for accessing the line (the value of the flat installation charge is converted to an annuity). So, for a given SEL we define:

$$S_{it}^j(p_{it},.) = \int_{p_t}^{P_{max}} q_{it}^j(p,.)dp, \ \forall j \in \{\text{Local, DLD, ILD}\} \tag{3}$$

as the consumer surplus for using the line for any of the three services, and r_{it} as the annual installment made on the flat installation charge. Hence,

$$\tilde{S}_{it}(p_{it}, r_{it}) = \sum_j S_{it}^j(p_t) - r_{it} \tag{4}$$

measures the total net surplus of all services. Replacing the functional form given in (2), and solving the equation, we obtain the surplus as

$$\tilde{S}_{it}(p_{it}, r_{it}) = -\frac{1}{\alpha^j} \exp(x_{it}\beta^n + p_{it}\alpha^n + \varepsilon_{it})|_{p_{it}}^{P_{max}} - r_{it}$$

$$\tilde{S}_{it}(p_{it}, r_{it}) = -\frac{1}{\alpha^j} \exp(x_{it}\beta^n + p'\alpha^n + \varepsilon_{it}) - r_{it},$$

$$\tag{5}$$

where α^j is the elasticity of the price itself.

Empirical Estimations

We use data from a household panel specially surveyed for this study in 1997 regarding access and monthly consumption of telecommunications services over the previous year (for details on the survey see Pascó-Font et al. 1999; OSIPTEL 1995; and Torero and Pascó-Font 2000).

This section reports demand estimates for basic telephony services and computes households welfare changes for SEL A to D, D being the poorest. We also use results from Torero, Chowdhury, and Galdo (2003) for households on SEL A and SEL B for provinces out of Lima. The demand estimation corrects for the selection bias resulting from whether or not consumers have a telephone, and also for the selection bias caused by households for which telephone billing information could not be obtained. We also included a dummy variable identifying whether or not the household has any cellular phones, which is a crucial factor, especially since 1997 when the intensity of cellular phones increase substantially. Cellular teledensity rose sharply from 0.002 in 1993 to 0.03 in 1998, although cellular phones are a complement to fixed line phones rather than a substitute.

The econometric estimations exhibit the expected signs and coefficients (see details of the regressions in Tables 3A.1 and 3A.2). Furthermore, the price of international long-distance service is significant (and positive) in explaining the use of both local and domestic long-distance service, indicating some degree of substitution between the two products. Education and income levels of households are also significant, exhibiting the expected signs. We also included fixed district effects, which were significant as a whole according to the F statistical test (see Torero and Pascó-Font 2000 for details on other controls used and on econometric estimations).

Demand for local and domestic long-distance services is inelastic in all cases. The price elasticities where -0.49, -0.478, and -1.095 for local, domestic long-distance, and international long-distance calling, respectively.[39] This result is consistent with many other studies, including Doherty (1984); Gatto et al. (1988); Gatto, Kelejian, and Stephan (1988); Zona and Jacob (1990); Duncan and Perry (1994); Levy (1996); and Pascó-Font, Gallardo, and Fry (1999).

Using the demand elasticities thus obtained, we measure the welfare effects of tariff readjustments for all three services, as well as for the increases in flat monthly charges (see Equations 3–5). We must note that, given the functional form of our estimated demand functions, similar percentage tariff changes induce equal percentage changes in household welfare—that is, welfare does not depend on total consumption but on the parameters of the demand function. However, the consumer surplus varies from household to household because the flat monthly service charged represents a different proportion of each household's expenditure on telephony service. This variance is naturally less important within each socioeconomic level that comprises households with similar spending patterns.

Estimated Demand for Telephone Use

See tables on pages 149–151.

Appendix 3B: Supplementary Table, the Case in Laos

See table on page 152.

Appendix 3C: Supplementary Tables, the Case of Ghana

See tables on pages 153–160.

---

39. The price elasticities for provinces outside Lima were -0.69, -0.55, and -1.59 for local, national long-distance, and international long-distance calling, respectively.

TABLE 3A.1 Estimated demand for telephone use in Lima

Variables	Local calls			National long-distance			International long-distance		
	Model 1	Model 2	Model 3	Model 1	Model 2	Model 3	Model 1	Model 2	Model 3
Local rate	-2.50**	-2.44**	-2.70**	-3.62	-3.45	-3.61	3.28	3.27	3.63*
	(1.08)	(1.065)	(1.145)	(2.388)	(2.366)	(2.386)	(2.069)	(2.067)	(2.017)
International long-distance rate	0.47***	0.47***	0.57**	0.23**	0.22**	0.23**	-0.30**	-0.30**	-0.30**
	(0.145)	(0.145)	(0.229)	(0.101)	(0.1)	(0.101)	(0.133)	(0.133)	(0.129)
Domestic long-distance rate	-0.03	-0.03	-0.07	-0.76**	-0.77**	-0.76**	0.47**	0.47**	0.17
	(0.026)	(0.026)	(0.069)	(0.375)	(0.375)	(0.375)	(0.257)	(0.258)	(0.312)
Penetration rate in Lima (network externality)	1.55***	1.50**	1.68***						
	(0.481)	(0.479)	(0.478)						
Relatives in provinces				0.80***	0.80***	0.80***			
				(0.101)	(0.101)	(0.101)			
Relatives abroad							0.42***	0.42***	0.44***
							(0.08)	(0.079)	(0.08)
Household owns cellular phone			0.25*			-0.06			0.82***
			(0.13)			(0.203)			(0.212)
Constant	4.33***	4.27***	4.41***	0.33	0.46	0.33	-0.31	-0.21	-0.25
	(0.378)	(0.37)	(0.447)	(0.729)	(0.715)	(0.73)	(0.697)	(0.691)	(0.687)
Mills inverse ratio (reported bill)	-0.35***		-0.36***	-0.16		-0.16	0.16*		0.15*
	(0.075)		(0.075)	(0.115)		(0.115)	(0.091)		(0.091)
Mills inverse ratio (has a telephone)		-0.48***			-0.34**			0.16	
		(0.102)			(0.156)			(0.126)	
Number of observations	2,021	2,021	2,021	1,993	1,993	1,993	1,940	1,940	1,940
F-test	39.18	39.27	37.71	14.94	14.89	14.47	8.63	8.61	8.72
Prob > F	0.0000	0.0000	0.0000	0.000	0.000	0.000	0.000	0.000	0.000
R^2	0.4472	0.4471	0.4489	0.1802	0.1813	0.1802	0.107	0.106	0.129

SOURCE: Authors.

NOTES: *Indicates significance at the 90 percent level; **indicates significance at the 95 percent level; ***indicates significance at the 99 percent level. The first three regressions correspond to the demand for local calls (minutes); the second three, to the demand for national long-distance calls; and the last three, to the demand for international long-distance calls. Three models are presented within each dependent variable. The first model corrects both for the selection bias resulting from whether or not consumers have a telephone and that caused by households for which telephone billing information was unobtainable; the second model only corrects for the selection bias for consumers having a telephone; the third model includes a dummy variable identifying whether or not the household owns cellular phones. Standard errors are shown in parentheses. Robust standard errors account for sample clustering and stratification. Demographic controls include household income, household income squared, percentage of 13- to 24-year-olds in the household, percentage of 13- to 24-year-old females in the household, household size, and education degree level of household head. All regressions included district-level fixed effects; the F-test was significant with $p < 0.001$.

TABLE 3A.2 Estimated demand for telephone use in the rest of Peru

Variables	Model 1	Model 2	Model 3	Model 1	Model 2	Model 3	Model 1	Model 2	Model 3
Local rate	-2.52**	-2.50**	-2.74**	-4.12***	-4.12***	-4.44***	-0.02	-0.02	-0.07
	(1.09)	(1.086)	(1.026)	(1.613)	(1.612)	(1.469)	(.393)	(.395)	(.406)
International long-distance rate	0.13	0.14	0.09	-0.13	-0.12	-0.17	-0.43**	-0.43**	-0.43**
	(0.174)	(0.175)	(0.174)	(0.155)	(0.155)	(.162)	(.197)	(.195)	(.194)
Domestic long-distance rate	-0.17**	-0.16**	-0.20**	-0.89***	-0.88***	-0.93***	0.04	0.04	0.03
	(0.085)	(0.083)	(0.08)	(0.267)	(0.267)	(.266)	(.147)	(.145)	(.148)
Relatives in provinces				0.65***	0.65***	0.61**			
				(0.248)	(0.248)	(.246)			
Relatives abroad							0.23***	0.22***	0.22***
							(.032)	(.032)	(.033)
Household owns cellular phone			0.49***			0.67***			0.13
			(0.105)			(0.191)			(0.138)
Constant	5.03***	4.99***	5.33***	2.72***	2.51**	3.05***	1.49**	1.68**	1.55**
	(0.605)	(0.513)	(0.594)	(0.98)	(0.885)	(0.987)	(0.762)	(0.738)	(0.753)

	(1)	(2)	(3)	(4)	(5)	(6)	(7)	(8)	(9)
Mills inverse ratio (reported bill)	-0.22* (0.126)		-0.23* (0.125)	-0.11 (0.197)		-0.11 (0.197)	-0.06 (0.101)		-0.06 (0.102)
Mills inverse ratio (has telephone)		-0.48*** (0.153)			-0.06 (0.264)			-0.30 (0.119)	
Number of observations	1,367	1,367	1,367	1,348	1,348	1,348	1,356	1,356	1,356
F-test	18.84	19.99	20.70	9.04	8.89	9.31	5.56	5.7	5.25
Prob > F	0.000	0.000	0.000	0.000	0.000	0.000	0.000	0.000	0.000
R^2	0.143	0.147	0.154	0.094	0.094	0.103	0.094	0.098	0.096

source: Authors.

notes: *Indicates significance at the 90 percent level; **indicates significance at the 95 percent level; ***indicates significance at the 99 percent level. The first three regressions correspond to the demand for local calls (minutes); the second three, to the demand for national long-distance calls; and the last three, to the demand for international long-distance calls. Three models are presented within each dependent variable. The first model corrects both for the selection bias resulting from whether or not consumers have a telephone and that caused by households for which telephone billing information was unobtainable; the second model only corrects for the selection bias for consumers having a telephone; the third model includes a dummy variable identifying whether or not the household owns cellular phones. Standard errors are shown in parentheses. Robust standard errors account for sample clustering and stratification. Demographic controls include household income, household income squared, percentage of 13- to 24-year-olds in the household, percentage of 13- to 24-year-old females in the household, household size, and education degree level of household head. All regressions included district-level fixed effects; the F-test was significant with $p < 0.001$.

TABLE 3B.1 Major communications development projects in Laos, 1986–96

Project	Objective and involved foreign organizations	Achievements
The Primary Telecommunications Network Development, 1986–90	Improving existing facilities Training personnel Funds from the International Development Association (IDA)	Failure to achieve objectives because of deteriorated and unrestorable equipment
Telecommunications Development Plan, 1990	Developing a long-term plan for the telecommunications sector Involvement of the International Telecommunications Union (ITU) and the United Nations Development Programme (UNDP)	A master plan for 1991–2010 determined
Telecom I and Telecom II, 1992–95	Telecommunications network development Involvement of IDA and UNDP Bilateral funding from the governments of Australia, Germany, France, and Japan	A digital network was established including: Digital switching systems for the country's capital and five provincial capitals (total 17,200 line units) International links South–north trunk route by microwave transmission Rural telephones (208 fixed telephone lines in 11 district capitals)
Telecom III, 1994–97	Expanding the network by 20,000 lines by 1995 Involvement of ITU and DETECON IDA funding and national resources	A total of 12,000 fixed lines were added Full implementation was not achieved
Telecom 2000, 1996–2000	Network expansion by 30,000 lines and investment of US$40 million before 2000 Involvement of ITU as planner	Project was delayed because of the Asian economic crisis and organizational problems on the part of the operator

SOURCE: Compiled by authors from personal contact with ITU, UNDP, International Development Association (IDA), and Detecon International.

TABLE 3C.1 Telecommunication regulations in Sub-Saharan Africa, 1985–98

Country	Separation of postal and telecommunications activities (1)	Independent regulator (2)	Operator privatized (3)	National carrier's international partners (4)	Cellular competition (5)
Angola	Angola Telecom (1985)				
Benin	—				
Botswana	Botswana Telecommunications Corporation (1980)	Botswana Telecommunications Authority (1996)			1998
Burkina Faso	Onatel (1994)				
Burundi	Onatel (1979)	Telecommunications Regulatory and Supervisory Agency (1997)			
Cameroon	—				
Cape Verde	Cabo Verde Telecom (1995)	Direccion General de Comercio (1992)	1996		
Central African Republic	Socatel (1982)		1990 40 percent[a]	*FranceCables et Radio*	
Chad			1976 48 percent[b]	*FranceCables et Radio* 43 percent Alcatel 5 percent Telspace	
Comoros	—				
Congo	—				

(continued)

TABLE 3C.1 *Continued*

Country	Separation of postal and telecommunications activities (1)	Independent regulator (2)	Operator privatized (3)	National carrier's international partners (4)	Cellular competition (5)
Côte d'Ivoire	CI-Telecom (1995)	Agence des Télécommunications de Côte d'Ivoire (AT-CI) (1996)	1997 51 percent	*FranceCables et Radio*	1996
DR Congo	—				
Djibouti			1977 25 percent[b]	na	
Equatorial Guinea			40 percent[b]	na	
Eritrea	Telecommunications Service of Eritrea (1993)	Communications Department (1996)			
Ethiopia	Ethiopian Telecommunications Corporation (1967)	Ethiopian Telecommunications Agency (1996)			
Gabon			39 percent[b]	na	
Gambia	Gamtel (1984)				
Ghana	Ghana Telecom (1995)	National Communications Authority (1997)	1996 30 percent	Telecom Malaysia Bd.	1995
Guinea	Sotelgui (1992)	Direction Nationale des Postes et des Télécommunications (1996)	1995 60 percent	Telecom Malaysia Bd.	1995

Guinea-Bissau	Guiné-Telecom		1989	51 percent	na	
Kenya	—					
Lesotho	Laos Telecommunications Company (1980)				na	
Liberia	—					
Madagascar	Telma (1994)	*Office Malgache des Etudes et de Régulation des Télécommunications* (1997)	1995	34 percent[a]	na	1998
Malawi	—					
Mali	Sotelma (1989)					
Mauritania	—					
Mauritius	Mauritius Telecom (1988)	Telecommunications Authority (1988)				1996
Mozambique	*Telecomunicações de Moçambique* (1981)	*L'Institut national des communications du Mozambique* (1992)				
Namibia	Telecom Namibia (1992)	*Namibische Kommission für Kommunikation* (1995)				
Niger	Sonitel					
Nigeria	Nitel (1985)	Nigerian Communications Commission (1993)				

(continued)

TABLE 3C.1 *Continued*

Country	Separation of postal and telecommunications activities (1)	Independent regulator (2)	Operator privatized (3)	National carrier's international partners (4)	Cellular competition (5)
Rwanda	Rwandatel (1992)				
São Tomé	*Companhia Santomense de Telecomunicações* (1982)		1989 51 percent		
Senegal	SONATEL (1985)		1997 61 percent	*FranceCables et Radio*	
Seychelles			100 percent	na	
Sierra Leone	Cable and Wireless Sierra Leone National Telecommunications Company (SLNTC) (1995)				
Somalia	—				
South Africa	Telkom (1991)	South African Telecommunications Regulatory Authority (1997)	1997 30 percent	SBC Communications Int., Telecom Malaysia Bd.	1994
Sudan	Sudatel (1994)	National Commission of Telecommunications (1996)			
Swaziland	—				

Tanzania	Tanzania Telecom (1992)	Tanzania Communications Regulatory Authority (1994)	1996
Togo	Togo Telecom (1996)		
Uganda		Uganda Communications Commission (1997)	
Zambia	Zamtel (1994)	Communications Authority (1994)	1997
Zimbabwe	Postal and Telecommunications Corporation (1998)		1998

SOURCES: ITU (1998) and BMI-T (1998).

NOTES: Column 1 indicates whether postal and telecommunications activities have been separated: if so, the name of the principal telecommunication operator and the year of separation are shown. The name may have changed since postal and telecommunications services were separated. Column 2 indicates whether an independent telecommunications regulatory agency has been established; if so, the name of the agency and year it was created are shown. Column 3 indicates whether the telecommunications operator has been privatized; if so, the date and percentage sold are shown. Column 5 indicates whether there is more than one network operator providing cellular service. na indicates that data were not available.

[a]Refers to privatization through the fusion of the partly private international operator and the state-owned national operator.

[b]Refers to the international operator.

TABLE 3C.2 Tariffs and charges, Ghana Telecom and Capital Telecom, 1998

Operator/cost category	Fixed cost (cedis)	6 a.m.–6 p.m.	Tariff rate (cedis) 6 p.m.–6 a.m.
Ghana Telecom			
Connection charge	300,000		
Monthly line rental	2,500		
Local tariff		200 per 4 minutes	200 per 5 minutes
National tariff			
Less than 32 kilometers		200 per 2.5 minutes	200 per 4 minutes
32–80 kilometers		200 per 1.5 minutes	200 per 2 minutes
More than 80 kilometers		200 per minute	200 per 1.5 minutes
Cellular tariff		800 per minute	800 per minute
Deposit for international direct dial	300,000		
International tariff plans			
Plan 1		2,600 per minute	2,600 per minute
Plan 2		3,000 per minute	3,000 per minute
Plan 3		2,600 per minute	2,600 per minute

Capital Telecom		7 a.m.–4 p.m.	4 p.m.–10 p.m.	10 p.m.–7 a.m.
Connection charge	900,000[a]			
Monthly line rental	10,000[a]			
Monthly equipment rental	20,000[a]			
Tariff within hub		500 per minute	400 per minute	120 per minute
National deposit	30,000			
National tariff		600 per minute	500 per minute	400 per minute
Cellular tariff		900 per minute	900 per minute	900 per minute
Deposit for international direct dial	300,000			
International tariff plans				
Plan 1		2,600 per minute	2,600 per minute	2,600 per minute
Plan 2		3,200 per minute	3,200 per minute	3,200 per minute
Plan 3		3,600 per minute	3,600 per minute	3,600 per minute
Plan 4		4,000 per minute	4,000 per minute	4,000 per minute
Plan 5		4,600 per minute	4,600 per minute	4,600 per minute

SOURCES: Ghana Telecom (1998) and Capital Telecom (1999).
[a]Values are approximate.

TABLE 3C.3 Regional telecommunications infrastructure in Ghana, 1998

Region	Regional capital	Number of fixed telephone lines in regional capital[a]	Regional capital lines as share of total regional lines (percent)	Number of connected fixed telephone lines within region	Fixed line teledensity within region
Greater Accra	Accra	115,300	92.8	124,230	4.27
Upper East	Bolgatanga	560	62.2	900	0.10
Central	Cape Coast	2,500	67.8	3,690	0.23
Volta	Ho	710	48.8	1,455	0.09
East	Koforidua	2,300	47.9	4,797	0.23
Ashanti	Kumasi	15,000	95.0	15,790	0.50
West	Sekondi	5,800	88.5	6,555	0.36
Brong Ahafo	Sunyani	850	49.4	1,720	0.09
North	Tamale	1,450	86.3	1,681	0.09
Upper West	Wa	830	100	830	0.14

SOURCE: Ghana Telecom (1998).

NOTE: Teledensity is the number of fixed telephone lines per 100 inhabitants.

[a]Values are approximate.

References

Accascina, G. 2001. *Information technology and poverty alleviation*. New York: United Nations Development Programme, Asia Pacific Development Information Programme.

ADB (Asian Development Bank). 1997. *Subregional telecommunications sector study: Greater Mekong subregion*. Manila.

Bayes, A. 2001. Infrastructure and rural development: Insights from a Grameen Bank village phone initiative in Bangladesh. *Agricultural Economics* 25: 261–272.

Bayes, A., J. von Braun, and R. Akhter. 1999. *Village pay phones and poverty reduction: Insights from a Grameen Bank initiative in Bangladesh*. ZEF Discussion Paper No 8. Bonn: Center for Development Research, University of Bonn.

BCRP (Banco Central de Reserva del Peru). 2004. Statistical Information. <www.bcrp .gob.pe> (accessed December 2004).

Bertolini, R. 2002. *Telecommunication services in Sub-Saharan Africa: An analysis of access and use in the southern Volta region in Ghana*. Development Economics and Policy 26. Frankfurt: Peter Lang.

BMI-TechKnowledge Group, ed. 1998. *Communication technology handbook 1998*. Johannesburg.

———. 2004. <www.bttb.net> (accessed December 2004).

Capital Telecom. 1999. Information collected directly from the company.

Chibber, A., and S. Fischer, eds. 1992. *Economic reform in Sub-Saharan Africa*. A World Bank Symposium. Washington, D.C.: World Bank.

Chowdhury, S. 2002a. *Institutional and welfare aspects of the provision and use of information and communication technologies in rural areas of Bangladesh and Peru*. Frankfurt: Peter Lang.

———. 2002b. *Attaining universal access: Public–private partnership and business–NGO partnership*. ZEF Discussion Papers on Development Policy No. 48. Bonn: Center for Development Research, University of Bonn.

CNNIC (China Internet Network Information Center). 2004. <www.china.org.cn/english/ index.htm> (accessed December 2004).

Doherty, A. 1984. Empirical estimates of demand and cost elasticities of local telephone service. In *Changing patterns in regulated markets and technology: The effect of public utility pricing*. East Lansing, Mich., U.S.A., Institute of Public Utilities, Michigan State University.

Duncan, G., and D. Perry. 1994. IntaLATA toll demand modeling a dynamic analysis of revenue and usage data. *Information Economics and Policy* 6: 163–178.

Frempong, G. K., and W. H. Atubra. 2001. Liberalization of telecoms: The Ghanaian experience. *Telecommunications Policy* 25: 197–210.

Galal, A., L. Jones, P. Tango, and I. Vogelsang. 1994. Welfare consequences of selling public enterprises: An empirical analysis. Oxford and New York: Oxford University Press.

Gao, P., and K. Lyytinen. 2000. Transformation of China's telecommunications sector: A macro-perspective. *Telecommunications Policy* 24 (8–9): 719–730.

Gatto, J., J. Langin-Hooper, P. Robinson, and H. Tyan. 1988. Interstate switched access demand analysis. *Information Economics and Policy* 3: 333–358.

Gatto, J., H. Kelejian, and S. Stephan. 1988. Stochastic generalizations of demand systems with an application to telecommunications. *Information Economics and Policy* 3: 283–310.

GDLN (Global Development Learning Network). 2001. News archive. <www.gdln.org> (accessed October 31, 2001).

Ghana Telecom. 1998. *Telephone directory 1998*. Accra.

———. 2000. The company: Basic facts. <www.ghanatel.net> (accessed October 2000).

Ghanaweb. 1999. WESTEL hooks up with MOBITEL. <www.ghanaweb.com> (accessed March 1999).

———. 2004. News archive. <www.ghanaweb.com/GhanaHomePage/NewsArchive/dossier.php?ID=11> (accessed December 2004).

Grameen Phone. 1999. *Annual report 1998*. Dhaka.

IICD (International Institute for Communications and Development). 1999. Draft communications policy discussion paper. Accra, Ghana: Ministry of Communications. <www.iicd.org> (accessed March 1999).

IMF (International Monetary Fund). 2000. *Ghana enhanced structural adjustment facility policy framework paper, 1999–2001.* <www.imf.org/external/NP/PFP/1999/Ghana> (accessed November 2000).

Independent Commission for World-Wide Telecommunication Development. 1984. The missing link: Report of the Independent Commission for World-Wide Telecommunication Development. Geneva: International Telecommunications Union.

ITU (International Telecommunications Union). 1998. *African telecommunication indicators (ATI) 1998.* Geneva.

———. 1999a. Trends in telecommunication reform: Convergence and regulation. Geneva.

———. 1999b. World telecommunication indicators, 1998/99. Geneva.

———. 2003. World telecommunication development report 2003: Access indicators for the information society. 7th ed., World Summit on the Information Society, Geneva 2003–Tunis 2005.

———. 2004. *World telecommunication indicators database*. Geneva.

JBIC (Japan Bank for International Cooperation) 2002. *Greater Dhaka Telecommunications Network Improvement Project.* Ex-Post Evaluation Report on Official Development Assistance (ODA) Loan Projects. <www.jbic.go.jp/english/oec/post/2002/pdf/103_full.pdf>.

Jensen, M. 1998. The current status of the internet and related developments in Africa. In *BMI-T, communication technologies handbook 1998.* Johannesburg: BMI-TechKnowledge Group (Pty) Ltd.

Laffont, J.-J., and J. Tirole. 1996. Creating competition through interconnection: Theory and practice. *Journal of Regulatory Economics* 10: 227–256.

Laos PDR (Laos People's Democratic Republic). 2001. Law on telecommunication. Vientiane, Laos: National Assembly.

———. 2002. New mobile player enters telecom sector. <www.laoembassy.com/news/JanFeb02.htm#14> (accessed December 2004).

Levy, A. 1996. Semiparametric estimation of telecommunications demand. Ph.D. dissertation. Berkeley, Calif., USA: University of California at Berkeley.

Lu, D. 1999. China's telecommunications infrastructure buildup: On its own way. In *Deregulation and interdependence in the Asia–Pacific region,* Takatoshi Ito and Anne O. Krueger, eds. National Bureau of Economic Research, East Asia Seminar on Economics, vol. 8. Chicago and London: University of Chicago Press.

Management Consulting Group. 2001. *Survey on ICTs.* Dhaka.

Männistö, L., T. Kelly, and B. Petrazzini. 1998. Internet and global information infrastructure in Africa. International Telecommunication Union. Geneva: International Telecommunications Union.

Martin, S., and D. Parker. 1997. *The impact of privatization. Ownership and performance in the UK.* London: Routledge.

Matambalya, F., and S. Wolf. 2003. Information and communication technologies (ICT) for Africa's economic development. In *African economic development,* E. Nnadozie, ed. Boston: Academic Press.

MII (Ministry of Information Industry). 2002. Information provided by the ministry.

Mitchell, B., and I. Vogelsang. 1991. *Telecommunication pricing: Theory and practice.* New York: Cambridge University Press

Morten, F. 2003. The way to Real Competition. CTI, News Letter No. 22, Center for Tele Information, Technical University of Denmark, Lyngby, June.

MTC (Ministry of Transport and Communications). 1999. Telecommunications policy for an accelerated development programme 1994–2000. <www.communication .gov.gh> (accessed March 1999 and October 2000).

Mueller, M. 1997. China's telecommunication sector and the WTO: Can China conform to the telecom regulatory principles? Presented at the Cato Institute and Fudan University conference "China as a Global Economic Power: Market Reforms in the New Millennium," held in Shanghai, June 15–18, 1997.

Mustafa, M. A., B. Laidlow, and M. Brand. 1997. Telecommunication policies for Sub-Saharan Africa. World Bank Discussion Paper No. 353. Washington, D.C.: World Bank.

Noam, E. 2001. *Interconnecting the network of networks.* Cambridge, Mass., USA: MIT Press.

One World. 1997. Telecommunications development and the market: The promises and the problems. Panos Media Briefing No. 23. <www.oneworld.org/panos/briefing/ telecoms.htm> (accessed July 1977).

OSIPTEL (Oganísmo Supervisor de Inversión Privada en Telecomunicaciones). 1995. *La transformación de las telecomunicaciones: Memoria 1994.* Lima: OSIPTEL.

———. 2002. <www.osiptel.gob.pe> (accessed December 2002)

———. 2003. <www.osiptel.gob.pe> (accessed December 2003).

———. 2004. *Compendio de Estadísticas del Sector de Telecomunicaciones en Perú 1994–2003.* Estudios en Telecomunicaciones No. 17. Lima: Osiptel.

Panzar, J. C. 2000. A methodology for measuring the costs of universal service obligations. *Information Economics and Policy* 12: 211–220.

Pascó-Font, A., J. Gallardo, and V. Fry. 1999. La Demanda Residencial de Telefonía Básica en el Perú. *Estudio en Telecomunicaciones* 4 (all volume). Lima: OSIPTEL.

People's Daily. 2002. CPPCC member proposes expansion of e-government. March 8. <http://english.peopledaily.com.cn/other/archive.html> (accessed December 2002).

Press, L., W. A. Foster, and S. E. Goodman. 2002. The Internet in India and China. *First Monday* 7 (10). <firstmonday.org/issues/issue7_10/press/index.html> (accessed December 2002).

SAPRIN (Structural Adjustment Participatory Review International Network). 2000. Draft SAPRI Methodological Framework. <www.saprin.org/> (accessed November 2000).

Saunders, R. J., J. J. Warford, and B. Wellenius. 1994. *Telecommunications and economic development.* Baltimore: Johns Hopkins University Press.

Scherer, P. B. 1994. Telecommunications reform in developing countries: Importance and strategy in the context of structural change. In *Implementing reforms in the telecommunications sector,* B. Wellenius and P. A. Stern, eds. World Bank Regional and Sectoral Studies. Washington, D.C.: World Bank.

Schmidt-Kallert, E. 1994. Ghana. Perthes Länderprofile. Gotha, mimeo.

Shapiro, C., and H. Varian. 1999. Information rules: A strategic guide to the network economy. Cambridge, Mass., U.S.A.: Harvard Business School.

Shy, O. 2001. *The economics of network industries.* Cambridge, Mass., USA: Cambridge University Press.

Song, G. 2003. *The impact of information and communication technologies (ICTs) on rural households: A holistic approach applied to the case of Laos People's Democratic Republic.* Frankfurt: Peter Lang.

Tarjanne, P. 1999. Preparing for the next revolution in telecommunications: Implementing the WTO Agreement. *Telecommunications Policy* 23: 51–63.

Torero, M., S. Chowdhury, and V. Galdo. 2003. Willingness to pay for the rural telephone service in Bangladesh and Peru. *Information Economics and Policy* 15 (3): 327–361.

Torero, M., and A. Pascó-Font. 2000. The social impact of privatization and regulation of utilities in urban Peru. Helsinki: World Institute for Development Economics Research, United Nations University.

UNDP (United Nations Development Programme). 2001. *Human development report 2001.* Geneva.

World Bank. 1998. *World development report 1998/99: Knowledge for Development.* Washington, D.C.

———. 2004. *World development indicators.* <https://publications.worldbank.org/register/WDI?return%5furl=%2fextop%2fsubscriptions%2fWDI%2f> (accessed December 2004).

World Bank/BCAS (Bangladesh Center for Advanced Studies). 1998. Bangladesh 2020: A long-run perspective study. <worldbank-bangladesh.org> (accessed December 1998).

———. 2002. Information and communication technologies for development: Present situation, perspectives, and potential areas for German Technical Cooperation in Peru, Laos PDR, Vietnam, Tanzania, and Uganda. Eschborn, Germany: German Agency for Technical Cooperation (GTZ).

Xiang Z. 2004. E-government in China: A content analysis of national and provincial web sites. *Journal of Computer-Mediated Communication* (JCMC) 9 (4) (July 2004) (electronic journal).

Xinhua News Agency. 2000. November 15, 2000, and November 28, 2000.

Zona, J., and R. Jacob. 1990. The total bill concept: Defining and testing alternative views. Bell Communication Research/Bell Canada Conference on Telecommunications Demand Analysis with Dynamic Regulation, Hilton Head, South Carolina, 22–25 April 1990.

4 The Economic Effects of ICT at Firm-Levels

GI-SOON SONG AND DIETRICH MUELLER-FALCKE

Conceptual Issues

Promoting growth of small- and medium-sized enterprises (SMEs)[1] is fundamental to building a vibrant socioeconomic environment—regardless of the country in question, or its level of development. SMEs are of particular importance in developing countries because they comprise such a large share of the economy. In addition, SMEs have specific beneficial qualities for developing economies; they create jobs, improve welfare, alleviate poverty, enhance technical and entrepreneurial capacity, and foster key elements of civil society (IFC 2000, 2001). Nonetheless, SMEs have not been successful in realizing these potentials in many developing countries. Resource and institutional constraints hinder SMEs in these regions, and rapid globalization poses challenges in the form of international competition, and opportunities in terms of access to new markets and resources.

Information and communication technologies (ICT) could help developing-country SMEs to overcome resource constraints by making valuable knowledge and information available and by improving business-related communications. On the other hand, if developing-country SMEs are unable to fully exploit the benefits of ICT, they will be less able to compete with large firms. It is therefore difficult to predict the net effects of ICT on SMEs. This chapter discusses these issues and explores them empirically through a number of case studies, following the conceptual framework of this volume as shown in Figure 4.1. (See appendix 4A for an overview of the methodologies used in the analysis for this chapter.)

SMEs in Developing Countries: Pro-Poor Engine of Growth?

Collectively, SMEs are perceived as an engine of growth in developing countries. As mentioned, they represent a large share of economic productivity, and

---

1. For the purposes of this chapter, SMEs are defined as businesses with up to 250 employees.

FIGURE 4.1 Conceptual framework: Area of analysis dealt with in Chapter 4

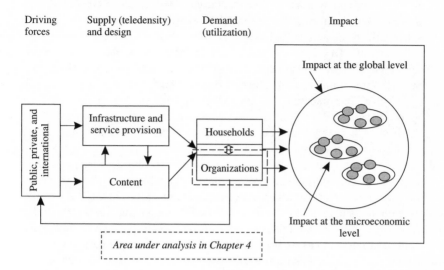

although their share declines as the economy develops, they continue to constitute a substantial share of developing-country employment.[2] In Ecuador in 1980 for example, small firms—defined as those with 50 or fewer employees—accounted for 99 percent of enterprises and 55 percent of employment. In Bangladesh in 1986, 99 percent of firms were SMEs with fewer than 100 employees, representing 58 percent of employment (Hallberg 2000). Gillis et al. (1996) also reported that, in the early 1980s, in countries with average per capita incomes of US$500–1,000, 63 percent of employment in the manufacturing sector was generated by registered firms with fewer than 100 employees. Considering that a substantial number of microenterprises and small firms actually operate in the informal sector, these figures no doubt significantly underestimate the contribution of SMEs in developing economies.

SMEs can play a particularly crucial role in reducing poverty by creating jobs. Microenterprises—which are generally unregistered firms with fewer than 10 employees—offer nonfarm employment opportunities in least developed

---

2. The share of SMEs declines as per capita income increases, but even in countries where annual incomes average more than US$5,000, SMEs contribute around 30 percent of total employment (based on industrial data from 34 countries in the 1960s and 1970s; Snodgrass and Biggs 1996).

countries (LCDs); informal jobs as a first step toward entering the formal market in small-scale enterprises in middle-income countries; employment for individuals who lose their formal-sector jobs in times of economic downturn in more industrialized economies; and an alternative to structural joblessness in transition economies (IFC 2000). In addition, SMEs make important contributions to the public good by paying taxes, providing social services, building capital,[3] and facilitating more equitable income distribution.[4]

With all this potential, why have SMEs in developing economies not lived up to expectations? Small firms create far more jobs than large firms, but they also have higher rates of loss than their larger counterparts (Haltiwanger 1999). To illustrate, start-up and closure rates are as much as three times higher in developing countries than they are in industrialized countries (Mead and Liedholm 1998). This leaves many SME workers vulnerable given all the economic pressures that threaten the survival of SMEs. Hence, jobs in the SME market are insecure, and they can also involve unsafe working conditions (IFC 2001). Tybout (1998) cites several obstacles to private-sector growth in developing countries: product markets are small, access to manufactured inputs is limited, human capital is scarce, infrastructure is poor, financial markets are thin, macroeconomic environments are volatile, the legal system functions poorly, and corruption and property crimes are relatively common. For SMEs, these disadvantages only aggravate constraints on financial, physical, and human resources (Mueller-Falcke 2002). In LDCs, especially in African countries, microenterprises in the informal sector have little opportunity to grow and transition to the formal sector because of the aforementioned obstacles. Romijn (1998) described this combination of large numbers of informal microenterprises and a few large firms as the "missing middle."

The Role of ICT for SMEs

SME development requires several prerequisites including an appropriate legal framework, sound macroeconomic policy, innovative thinking, infrastructure, privatization and deregulation, and sustainable economic expansion (IFC 2000). Along with these challenges, developing-country SMEs face another formidable

---

3. Formal-sector firms contribute to government revenues, and thereby to the provision of essential social services, such as health and education. In addition, when public provision is not available, private firms can often supply social services directly to their employees. The private sector also plays an important and unique role in enabling the mobilization and saving of capital (IFC 2000). Although these roles are not limited to SMEs, their considerable share of the private sector in developing countries increases the significance of their contribution.

4. Hallberg (2000) suggested that more equitable income distribution through SMEs is unlikely because SME workers do not usually belong to the poorest segment of the population in developing countries.

task—surviving and competing in a global market. As one of the driving forces of globalization, ICT may deliver unprecedented opportunities.

ICT offers potential advantages to SMEs in several ways, primarily relating to obtaining and using knowledge and information, improving internal and external communications, improving decisionmaking and thereby responsiveness and efficiency, and improving overall flexibility. Finally, ICT has the potential to facilitate improvements to productivity. These points are discussed in turn below.

Knowledge and Information. Knowledge and information are crucial to the development process (World Bank 1998) and key to achieving a competitive advantage (Porter and Millar 1985). By lowering the costs of gathering, processing, and disseminating information, ICT increases the amount of available information, and that information becomes more up-to-date, more complete, and more reliable. This leads to the conversion of uncertainty to predictable risk, ultimately improving decisionmaking (Bedi 1999). Lybaert (1998) also found that SMEs using more information performed better and were more optimistic about the future.

Communication. ICT permits interactive communication at lower costs, thereby facilitating negotiations and transactions. Further, by improving external communication, ICT can reduce the costs of initiating, negotiating, and enforcing contracts. This is particularly important for SMEs because external transaction costs are high compared with internal transaction costs (Mueller-Falcke 2002).

Flexibility. Defined as the capacity to adapt promptly to changing environments, flexibility can create significant competitive advantages (Piore and Sabel 1984). ICT can increase a firm's flexibility by providing information, hastening the internal decisionmaking process, expanding and diversifying a firm's trading partners, and even expanding and diversifying its customer and product base.

Productivity. The potential for ICT to improve productivity is a hotly debated topic. Empirical studies from the early 1990s on the causal relationship between ICT investment and productivity showed no impact and, in some cases, even negative impact (Brynjolfsson and Yang 1996). Suggested causes of the so-called productivity paradox are unmeasured quality improvements, time-lags in the manifestation of effects, additional variables that affect organizational change, and other specific firm differences (Brynjolfsson and Hitt 1995, 2000b; Dos Santos and Sussman 2000).

These recent studies reported a positive causal relationship between ICT investment and productivity or between ICT use and productivity using data sets for U.S. firms over longer periods of time. While causality was statistically established, the possibility of reverse causality cannot be denied—meaning that rather than ICT enhancing firm productivity, more productive firms actually need and use more ICT (Brynjolfsson and Hitt 2000b). Using a data set of 500 large U.S. enterprises, Hitt (1999) found a tendency toward decreased optimal scale with rising ICT investment—meaning the more you invest in ICT, the smaller the optimal size of the firm. Outsourcing of the noncore business activities, such as customer relations and data processing, is an example.

Globalization. The increasing participation of several developing-country SMEs in the global market is an indicator that the high transaction costs of participating in foreign markets have been reduced by ICT. Web sites such as Novica.com help artisans in developing countries find buyers from all over the world, and many countries are developing national or regional e-commerce portals to promote their products.

Concerns and Opportunities

In addition to the general constraints on ICT adoption in developing countries such as poor infrastructure and lack of skills, SMEs face several challenges in adopting and using ICT. Blili and Raymond (1993) argue that the specific characteristics of SMEs influence the impact of ICT. First, SMEs operate within a more uncertain environment, which reduces their options and makes them more dependent on large customers and suppliers. Second, SMEs do not have the resources to develop their own information systems so they are forced to rely on third parties. This reduces their control and increases risk. Third, because of a lack of cognitive resources SMEs often have a short life span. Fourth, decisions about ICT are often limited by the knowledge and training of the firm's owner/manager. Relatedly, information systems in SMEs are generally quite simple, with applications limited to accounting and inventory management as opposed to functions that enhance strategic competence. Thus ICT is often underutilized in SMEs.

In addition to these concerns, the prevalence of ICT in large enterprises may affect the competitiveness of SMEs in developing countries. ICT enables a more complex division of activities that add value to products and services, and facilitate new forms of production and organization in response to rapidly changing markets. With the importance of information flows in the global economy, taking advantage of ICT is fundamental to market competition, and large enterprises are in a much stronger position to reap the benefits. Nevertheless, this reality does not preclude SMEs from partaking of these benefits. Changes in the supply chain are a prime example. In the past it was difficult to source goods and services in developing economies. ICT now facilitates real-time information sharing regardless of location, so it has become possible to extend the supply chain to developing countries. Indian software engineers, for example, provide high-quality, cost-effective labor, enabling major U.S. firms to develop software around the clock. Because ICT influences the optimal size of firms (Mueller-Falcke 2002), noncore business activities are commonly outsourced by large enterprises. Outsourcing customer service functions offshore illustrates the role of ICT in relocating labor-intensive business to areas with low labor costs.[5] This is not to say that SMEs in developing countries can attract foreign partners on the basis of cheap labor alone. A cheap and reliable communications system is needed, along with a well-trained, relatively cheap labor force (with appropriate language skills), a supportive institutional environment, and the necessary infrastructure. For example, the call center industry has increasingly been outsourced in recent years, with India being one of the major winners (Ascutia 2002).

On the supply side, SMEs can also take advantage of ICT through umbrella organizations, such as cooperatives or associations, that provide information services, training, and organized activities to meet the needs of SMEs. While costs make it difficult for individual small firms to utilize e-business solutions, umbrella organizations generate sufficient demand to provide this service. In this way, SMEs and umbrella organizations come to operate as an integrated larger entity, and—once again—ICT makes this innovative small business solution possible.

Despite the obstacles to adopting and using ICT in developing countries, these small firms cannot avoid the reality of the new ICT-driven economy. Adapting to change will be the only way to survive, let alone thrive.

Country Studies of Different Experiences

Most studies on the impact of ICT on businesses have been done with data from developed countries, in particular from the United States, where ICT led the prolonged economic prosperity of the 1990s. Evidence of the role of ICT for SMEs in developing-countries is rare and mostly anecdotal (Tam 1998; Bedi 1999). Comprehensive studies are few. Tam (1998), for example, explored the impact of ICT investment on performance indicators, such as returns on equity, returns on assets, and turnover rates, reporting mixed ICT impact. However, the countries included in the study—Hong Kong, Singapore, Malaysia, and Taiwan —belong to a group of newly industrialized countries in which the export-oriented private sector is quite strong. Studies on LCDs focus on the difficulties of adopting and using rather than on its effects.

The empirical studies compiled for this chapter are intended to fill gaps in the literature by providing evidence of the impact of ICT on SMEs in low-income countries. The studies offer cutting-edge empirical evidence in terms of approaches and geographic coverage. The studies focus on India (two cases),

---

5. A U.S. company can save 20–40 percent of the operating costs associated with customer contacts when they outsource to India, the Philippines, and South Africa because of the lower wages and reduced staff turnover (Read 2002). GE Capital and HSBC subcontracted their customer service call centers to Indian firms, resulting in employment for 300–800 people in 2000 (Bhatttacharjee and Bhattacharya 2000).

TABLE 4.1 Basic economic indicators for case study countries, 2000

Indicator	India	Kenya	Tanzania	Peru	Laos
GDP per capita (constant 1995 US$)	493	322	207	2,380	477
GDP, 1999 (current US$ billion)	510.2	12.3	9.4	56.5	1.7
Manufacturing value-added as a share of GDP (percent)	15.6	13.0	7.6	15.8	17.7[a]
Manufacturing value-added per capita (current US$)	69	45	19	305	57.3[a]
Teledensity (fixed lines per 100 inhabitants)	4.0	1.0	0.5	6.6	1.1

SOURCES: World Bank (2004), ITU (2001), and UNDP (2002).

NOTE: GDP indicates grosss domestic product.

[a]2001 data.

Laos, Peru, and two countries of East Africa—Kenya and Tanzania. See Table 4.1 for some basic economic indicators for these countries. As of 2000, per capita GDP in India, Kenya, Laos, and Tanzania was lower than US$500, and manufacturing value-added represented a relatively low share of GDP in all five countries (less than 18 percent, which was the 2001 world average), reflecting small manufacturing sectors.

In the first case on India, the impact of ICT on small enterprises is explored in terms of market reach, productivity, profitability, and labor demand. Using survey data on 295 small-scale industrial enterprises and nonparametric ranking, the study examines the differences in enterprise performance between ICT users and non-users, early and late adopters, and user groups at different levels of adoption. While a strong correlation is found to exist with labor productivity, turnover, and the growth of turnover, the possibility of reverse causality is acknowledged, as is the role of ICT within best practice guidelines for small enterprises in developing countries.

The East African study examines the effect of ICT on SMEs in terms of total factor productivity (TFP) from varied Cobb–Douglas production function specifications applied to a data set of 300 SMEs in Kenya and Tanzania. The study attempts to capture the overall impact of ICT on TFP by analyzing investments in ICT, the types of ICT used, and their contributions (each technology is assumed to have different degrees of impact). Findings reveal that, while investment in ICT has minimal impact on output, specific ICT—particularly the facsimile machine (henceforth fax machine)—appears to have a significant positive impact on output. Interestingly, Kenyan SMEs are less productive than their Tanzanian counterparts, contrary to the expectation that a more stable, developed economy would be more productive.

While most of the studies deal with SMEs in the formal sector in relatively urbanized areas, the Laos case study focuses on rural firms, including unregistered microenterprises within households. The study focuses on a very basic form of ICT—telephony—applying a conventional production function model and matching method to survey data on 121 businesses to determine the effect of telephone access on economic performance. Despite a high adoption and usage pattern and willingness to pay for telephone subscription among unsubscribed user businesses, formal analysis does not indicate a positive correlation between access to telephone services and economic performance.

The final case study in this chapter shifts the focus from the communicative aspect of ICT to its impact on production processes, such as integrated management information systems (IMIS) and computer-aided design (CAD). Using a data set of 74 garment manufacturing firms in Okhla, India, the study explores the impact of adoption intensity, quality of raw materials, unskilled labor, and entrepreneurial capacity on export performance. The results indicate a significant impact.

Synthesis

The case studies in this chapter present a general picture of ICT in developing countries that is consistent with existing literature. The finding of little or no impact on firm performance from ICT investment, as in the East Africa and Laos case studies, echoes early research on the productivity paradox. Considering that ICT has only been used by SMEs in the case countries for a relatively short time, time-lags in the appearance of impact may be a factor. Low penetration rates in developing countries, below the reported minimum threshold level, may also be responsible (Röller and Waverman 2001). In addition, and perhaps more importantly, the lack of complementary infrastructure may reduce the opportunities for firms adopting ICT to perform better, as in the Laos case. The concentration on quantitative performance indicators may also have negated notable improvement in the qualitative performance of the firms.

Nevertheless, all the cases indicate that ICT adoption is positively linked to firm performance. Wide use of the available technologies shows that ICT adoption is perceived to be a key element in remaining competitive. The relationship between intense ICT use and export performance, in the second Indian case study in particular, illustrates the global trend toward a changing value chain, especially in terms of the supply chain when it comes to developing-country producers. The Indian garment industry also sheds light on possible opportunities to advance labor-intensive industries through the use of ICT, enabling them to remain competitive in international markets while continuing to offer significant job opportunities. This should be a priority because SMEs fill an important role in developing countries in terms of income distribution and poverty reduction. This is especially so given impending changes to the international trade regime will eliminate the preferred status of developing countries in the world export market.

The case studies suggest several issues for future research. The issue of the causal link between firm performance and ICT use needs further exploration, specifically in the context of developing countries. Primary processing and labor-intensive manufacturing are areas of particular interest because (a) the majority of developing countries depend heavily on primary products and (b) job creation is extremely important for poverty alleviation. The effects of ICT adoption on demand for skilled and unskilled labor is also an important issue. The lack of conclusive results as to the impact of ICT points to a need to consider other adoption indicators than just ICT investment. The case of Indian garment-manufacturing firms implies that the level of usage may well be a better indicator, such that ICT investment should be correlated with intensity. The East African case also shows that a single technology (that is, the fax machine) can show impact, while overall investment in ICT does not—although the question of the necessary investment threshold to capture ICT's network externalities remains. New panel data need to be explored and tested, combining ICT indicators with firm characteristics so as to capture the extent of adoption. Further research is also required into the impact of ICT on larger firms, and the resulting implications for the SMEs in developing countries. In-depth studies on best practice among businesses with respect to SME adoption could also help to identify optimal ways to promote ICT access in small firms where resources for investment are scarce.

Because the biggest obstacles to ICT adoption by SMEs are its high costs and lack of associated skills, creative solutions need to be explored. These include external resources, such as market research, database development, and intranet and Internet sites to facilitate information sharing, sales, purchasing, training, and so on. Some governments already encourage SMEs to use ICT by providing public email and Internet access (as in the Indian cases in this chapter). Similarly, business organizations (such as associations and networking groups) could provide more targeted, business-oriented services relevant to SMEs.

The Impact of ICT on Small Enterprises:
The Case of Small-Scale Industry in India
Dietrich Mueller-Falcke

This case study aims to explore the impact of ICT on small enterprises in developing countries by examining small-scale industry in India. India has a long history of protecting its economy. These inward-looking policies hindered development in the 1980s, prompting the government to follow the world trend toward liberalization and privatization in the 1990s. The telecommunications market, however, was founded on an unfavorable institutional framework, frequent policy changes, and outright incompetence. By 2000, a public quasi-monopoly was in place, operated by Bharat Sanchar Nigam Ltd. (BSNL), the fixed telephony incumbent. Fixed teledensity (the number of fixed telephone lines per 100 inhabitants) increased about sixfold in the 1990s, although by 2000 it still remained at only about 3.0, leaving more than 200,000 villages without telephone service (Government of India 2001). In addition, the prevailing licensing regime left the cellular telephone market highly fragmented. Its growth was further hindered by the government's refusal to approve the "calling party pays" principle. Consequently, the number of cellular subscribers was just over 3 million by the end of 2000.

Internet development was more successful, although a number of problems arose, including attempts by public-interest groups to obstruct private-sector participation. Commercial Internet services commenced comparatively late (in 1995) by Videsh Sanchar Nigam Ltd. (VSNL), the monopolistic public international carrier. Private Internet service providers (ISPs) were only allowed to enter the market at the end of 1998, by which time VSNL had about 140,000 subscribers. The rapid arrival of real competition led to a significant fall in Internet service prices and a rapid expansion of subscriber numbers to about 1.8 million by the end of 2000—with user numbers estimated at around 5.5 million (NASSCOM 2001). Since the onset of liberalization, international as well as national bandwidth has increased rapidly. Indian content on the World Wide Web has increased dramatically, much of it in regional languages.

The development in the Indian ICT environment is important for small-scale industry, especially as the Indian economy becomes more open. Traditionally the small-scale industry in India has been well protected against outside influences and internal competition from large enterprises. In India, small-scale manufacturing enterprises—classified as those with a capital investment of less than about US$230,000—are important to the economy. In financial year 1999/2000, these enterprises produced over 3.2 million units and had a combined turnover of US$133 billion, offering employment to nearly 18 million people. Exports from these enterprises accounted for about one-third of Indian exports that year (Government of India 2001). To a large extent, the importance of the small manufacturing enterprises stems from a wide range of protective measures that have developed over recent decades, such as sole production of particular products by small enterprises or preferred supplier status with government agencies. Although recent policy has focused on promotional measures, bureaucracy still constrains the overall performance of small manufacturing businesses (Bala Subrahmanya 1998). Decades of protection shielded these enterprises from the need to upgrade their technologies; however, with the introduction of liberal trade and industrial policies they have become increasingly exposed to both internal and external competition. Thus, many small entrepreneurs now acknowledge the need to upgrade their technologies, as well as their organizational systems.

Methods for Measuring the Impact of ICT on Small Enterprises

Measuring the impact of ICT on enterprises is difficult—as the longstanding debate about the productivity paradox clearly shows (Solow 1987; Brynjolfsson 1993; Brynjolfsson and Hitt 1996). For small businesses, the measurement problem is even more severe. First, data requirements for quantitative analysis are particularly high. Most studies on ICT and productivity, for example, have been conducted for large corporations with publicly available, standardized business and accounting data. For small-scale enterprises, especially in developing countries, comprehensive data sets are virtually nonexistent. The smaller the enterprise, the less likely it is that written records are kept, and where such records do exist, the time span covered is insufficient. Enterprises may have kept some records themselves, but the reliability and comparability of self-reported data are questionable. Second, investment in ICT by small-scale enterprises is generally sporadic, requiring nontrivial sums of capital. Hence investment in a personal computer (PC), for example, may only occur every couple of years. This problem is manageable with comprehensive time series data, but such data are difficult to obtain from small-scale enterprises. Third, it is difficult to assign a specific share of labor to IT services in small-scale enterprises, given the enterprises are too small to warrant separate IT professionals or departments. This function is either undertaken by the owner/operator or by one or more employees in combination with other activities. Assigning a quantifiable share of their workload to IT introduces a high degree of uncertainty in the valuation. Fourth, the impact of ICT on enterprises is multidimensional. Avgerou (2000) for example, stresses that the impact will be of a non-straightforward economic nature, that is, covering issues of organizational structure and strategic gains and losses. Other authors claim that the potential benefits of ICT can only be realized when their adoption is accompanied by organizational adaptations (for example, Brynjolfsson and Hitt 2000a,b; Porter and Millar 1985). Being qualitative, these changes are difficult to classify and quantify.

With these difficulties in mind, this case study utilizes easily observable indicators from survey data in an attempt to measure the relationship between ICT adoption and small enterprise performance. The indicators used are listed below:

- turnover (as an indicator of market reach);
- labor productivity (as an indicator of productivity);
- profit margin (as an indicator of profitability); and
- wages and educational attainment in administration and management (as an indicator of labor demand).

There are different ways to account for ICT use, so three methods are proposed and tested in relation to the proposed performance indicators. The first and most simple method is to check for differences between the samples of current users and non-users for each single technology. However there may be a considerable time-lag before ICT adoption produces measurable effects, as many studies have pointed out (see, for example, Lefebvre and Lefebvre 1996 and Brynjolfsson and Hitt 2000a,b). Karshenas and Stoneman (1993) introduce "order effects," explaining that returns from technology adoption depend on when the technology is adopted in relation to its availability. Rogers (1995) categorizes entrepreneurs as "innovators," "early adopters," "the early majority," "the late majority," and "laggards," according to their position in the adoption distribution.[6] Taking this categorization as a rough guide, enterprises can be grouped according to the time of adoption and statistical tests can be applied to identify whether there are differences among the subgroups.

Looking at single technologies, as in these two proposed methods, may not be sufficient because the impact of any one technology depends on the overall technological level of the enterprise as well. In a third method, adoption patterns for ICT can be examined and levels of ICT use can be identified, so that enterprises belonging to one level can be compared with those belonging to the other levels.

The Data

During May and June 1999, 295 small-scale enterprises in the Ambattur industrial estate of Chennai were interviewed about their use of ICT.[7] The enterprises were generally well established (most had been operating for over a decade), and all were in the manufacturing sector (the majority involved in metal processing and engineering). The average annual 1998/99 turnover was about US$265,000, 6.6 times higher than the average for small industrial enterprises in India. Averaging 27.6 staff, the sample enterprises employed five times as many workers as the national average of 5.5, and average labor productivity in the interviewed enterprises was 30 percent higher than the Indian average for small manufacturing firms. Average wages were about US$90 per month in 1998 for management and administrative functions and US$60 per month for production functions. Despite economic downturn at the time the survey was conducted, the vast majority of interviewed enterprises claimed to be profitable and about 20 percent reported that they exported some of their output. (For details of the key variables, see Appendix 4B, Table 4B.1).

The enterprises were interviewed about their use of telephones, fax machines, pagers, cellular telephones, computers, the Internet, and email (Table 4.2).

---

6. Assuming a normal distribution of adoption over time, "innovators" would be the first 2.5 percent of adopters; "early adopters," the next 13.5 percent; "the early majority," the next 34 percent; "the late majority," the next 34 percent; and "the laggards," the final 16 percent (Rogers 1995).

7. The results presented in this section are part of a comprehensive survey examining the adoption, use, and impact of ICT within small-scale industry in India; see Mueller-Falcke (2002).

TABLE 4.2 Types of ICT used by the sample enterprises

Type of ICT	Percentage of enterprises using specified technology	Average number of devices used per enterprise
Fixed line telephone	100	2.3 (lines)
Facsimile machine	55	1.1
Pager	35	2.1
Cellular phone	37	1.4
Computer	64	2.7
Email	34	—
World Wide Web	19	—
Own Web site	4.4	—

SOURCE: Compiled by author from primary survey data (1999).

Unexpectedly, a large number of enterprises used email. By the time of the survey, when Indian Internet subscribers totaled only about 300,000, one-third of the enterprises had email access.[8] This was much more than expected, even by the business operators themselves.

The intensity of ICT use tends to increase in small enterprises with adoption, so these firms—while not pioneers—are an important user category for service providers. On average, the interviewed enterprises spent about US$110 per month on fixed telephony. Where fax machines were owned, 25 percent of the monthly phone bill stemmed from fax use. Cellular telephone subscribers spent about US$52 per month on average. Only email use was relatively low, mainly because of poor telecommunications infrastructure. These data indicate that the regular costs incurred from ICT can be significant for small manufacturing enterprises.

At the time the survey was done, all the relevant technologies were well established with penetration rates of at least one-third. Non-users generally indicated a cost–benefit rationale for delaying adoption (in almost all cases, perceived lack of benefits or high costs were of prime importance (see Mueller-Falcke 2002 for details). Looking at the time the individual technologies were adopted, the enterprises were roughly grouped according to when technologies were adopted (using the categories presented above, Table 4.3).[9]

---

8. International Data Corporation (IDC) India (1999) reports that, as of July 31, 1999, there were 311,720 Internet subscribers in India; 41.7 percent of these subscribers were within small- and medium-sized organizations; 31.0 percent were within large organizations; 7.9 percent were within government, research, and education agencies; and 19.4 percent were home users. Small business and home users were the fastest growing segments at that time.

9. In the case of fax machines and pagers, the adoption growth rate began declining as of 1998. The peak years for new users were 1995–97 for fax machines and 1997 for pagers. Assuming that the mid-point of the time period indicates 50 percent of the number of final adopters, final

TABLE 4.3 Categorizing ICT users according to adoption time

Category	Facsimile machine		Pager		Cellular phone		Email	
	Period	Number	Period	Number	Period	Number	Period	Number
Innovators	Until 1992	31	1994–95	21	1995–96	26	1995–96	13
Early adopters	1993–96	81	1996–97	59	1997	29	1997	21
Early majority	1997–99	45	1998–99	27	1998–99	56	1998–99	61
Late majority	—	133	—	181	—	179	—	196
Non-adopters								

SOURCE: Compiled by author from primary survey data (1999); adoption categories follow Rogers (1995).

TABLE 4.4 Categorizing levels of ICT use

		Computer used			
		No		Yes	
		Email used		Email used	
		No	Yes	No	Yes
Fax usage	No fax used	52	1	14	9
	Fax office	22		15	5
	Fax machine owned	25	3	67	82

SOURCE: Compiled by author from primary survey data (1999).

NOTE: The five shaded categories reflect different levels of ICT use from "only telephone used" to "telephone, fax machine, computer, and email used," accounting for 84 percent of all cases.

Usage patterns for the different office automation technologies are interesting (Table 4.4). The five shaded categories—reflecting different levels of ICT use from "only telephone used" to "telephone, fax machine, computer, and email used"—account for 84 percent of all cases. This may indicate a step-by-step approach to technology adoption beginning with the use of public fax offices, moving to buying a fax machine, then buying a computer, and eventually adding email access.

Results

Tests were conducted for differences in enterprise performance, first between the user and non-user groups, then between user groups—that is, between early and late users—and finally between different usage categories as previously defined. This section presents an analysis of the relationship between ICT use and the proposed performance indicators. Labor productivity, turnover, profit margin, and growth variables were included in the analysis to consider the dynamics over time (see Appendix 4B, Table 4B.1, for details). Since normal distribution could not be assumed for most variables, nonparametric tests were applied to determine distribution ranks. Mean differences are also reported to clarify differences (see Appendix 4B, Table 4B.2, for the results, and Appendix 4B, Tables 4B.3 through 4B.5, for details of the test variables).

Labor productivity in 1998/99 is significantly higher in the user versus the non-user enterprises for each of the technologies examined. No signs of enhanced labor productivity growth were found during 1997/98–1998/99, how-

---

user rates were estimated at about 200 for fax machines and 125 for pagers. Category borders were set according to these numbers. For cellular phones and email, no slowdown in growth was observable. A final user rate of 100 percent was assumed to set the limit of the borders.

ever. Differences in the mean labor productivity between user and non-user enterprises ranged from about US$3,100 per year for fax ownership to about US$5,700 for cellular phone subscription. Labor productivity and labor productivity growth were consistent between early and late user enterprises for all technologies except email. Pre-1998 email adopters were, on average, more productive than late adopters. In addition, labor productivity was shown to be significantly correlated with the level of technology used by firms. In comparing the means across the different categories, on average, labor in enterprises using more technologies was more productive than labor in enterprises only using the telephone or the telephone and the fax machine. Once again, however, labor productivity growth was not shown to be correlated with technology use.

These results reflect the general difficulty of measuring the impact of ICT on productivity. Literature reports considerable time-lags from the time of investment to the point of productivity growth (for example, Brynjolffson and Hitt 2000a,b); for this study, the time-lags exceeded two years. Lack of proof of a relationship between ICT use and productivity growth puts the causality between productivity level and ICT use into question. Of the sample firms, well managed and productive enterprises appeared to adopt new technologies faster than enterprises that performed less well, and ICT did not seem to have any general effect on profitability. Profit during 1996/97–1998/99 was growing faster in enterprises using cellular telephones and pagers, but no clear relationship was observed based on the time of adoption or general level of ICT use.

This result is consistent with most of the literature. Hitt and Brynjolfsson (1996) examine the relationship between IT investment and profitability parameters, finding no relationship based on time spans of a single year; when data are pooled over several years, results actually indicate negative effects for returns on assets and total returns. At best, the impact of IT on profitability is very small. Hitt and Brynjolfsson suggest that enterprises use the "correct" amount of IT, so improvements are not achieved by raising or lowering IT investment; they conclude that IT investments are necessary to maintain a competitive position, but they do not generate competitive advantages. A similar result is derived for enterprises in Hong Kong, Malaysia, Singapore, and Taiwan by Tam (1998), who tests the effect of capital investments in computers on returns of equity, returns on assets, total shareholder returns, and returns on sales. Evidence is mixed, and even with lagged specifications, no significant positive impact on total shareholder returns and returns on sales was found. Tam concludes that these relationships are affected by institutional and cultural factors.

Only Stoneman and Kwon (1996) find a significant relationship between technology adoption and profitability. Based on a sophisticated adoption model and an empirical test of the diffusion of Computer Numerical Controlled (CNC) machines, computers, microprocessors, and carbide tools in British manufacturing enterprises, the authors conclude that enterprises classified as early adopters are more profitable than those termed non-adopters.

The use of ICT also appeared to have no general effect on labor, other than the fact that managerial and administrative employees were paid significantly higher wages in cellular phone and email using enterprises (the mean wage was about 10 percent higher than the average). The number of business administration and management graduates was not a related factor.

Notably, no relationship was found to exist between computer use and wages and skills, despite indications in survey responses that employees using computers received higher wages. More than 75 percent of respondents indicated the high importance of computer skills for new administrative staff, and over 50 percent reported wage surcharges of over 10 percent for computer skills. Thus, evidence should show an upward bias in wage structure with computerization. Literature on employment effects also states that increased use of IT is accompanied by increased demand for higher skilled labor. Comprehensive research on the wage effects of computer use in U.S. enterprises indicates that workers earned about 10–15 percent more in the 1980s as a result of their computer skills (Krueger 1993). A number of other studies, however, question whether these wage differentials reflect other attributes that in fact cause the higher computer usage. "The results are consistent with the conclusion that firms with more highly skilled workers are more likely to adopt new technologies. However, subsequent to adoption, these technologies do not have much impact on wages" (Bedi 1999, 31). Other studies conclude that the demand for skilled workers rises with increased diffusion of computers. Lal (1996) examines the relationship between IT use and a number of conduct and performance parameters in 59 Indian electronics and electrical goods enterprises. He found that enterprises using IT employ more qualified managers and highly skilled workers. Wage rates, however, were not significant, as is the case in this study.

Market reach, approximated by 1998/99 turnover, was shown to be highly correlated with technology use. The mean ranks in turnover for user and non-user enterprises differed by at least 48 ranks. User enterprises had at least twice the turnover, on average, of non-user enterprises. The turnover of user enterprises also grew faster during 1996/97–1998/99 than that of non-user enterprises for all technologies except email. In terms of labor productivity, however, the time of adoption generally had no effect. Only enterprises that adopted email before 1998 had a significantly higher turnover than other enterprises. The technology level became important in terms of the size of the turnover. Looking at the mean ranks, there was a continuous increase in turnover as more advanced technologies were used. For turnover growth, the only relevant difference was whether or not the enterprise owned a fax machine. Enterprises that used a telephone only, or a telephone and an external fax service, exhibited lower growth than enterprises that, at minimum, owned their own fax machine.

Unsurprisingly, ICT use is more prevalent in small manufacturing firms that have wider market reach. In these instances, ICT can lower the costs and increase the speed of communication, offering a distinct advantage. The relative importance of ICT becomes particularly clear for exporting enterprises. There is ample evidence that export performance is related to ICT adoption. Mueller-Falcke (2002) shows that operating in foreign markets is a determinant of cellular phone, computer, and email use. Lal (1999b) shows in a survey of Indian garment manufacturers that the degree of IT adoption is positively correlated with the export intensity of these enterprises (see the second case study on India in this chapter). Nassimbeni (2001) examines the relationship between exports and technology, using Italian small manufacturing firms. He concludes, however, that the success of the business depends not only on the technologies used but also on the application of intangible resources and competencies that make the technologies work.

Conclusion

It appears that ICT use and labor productivity are positively correlated. On average, labor in enterprises using ICT is more productive, and with increased use of ICT, productivity also increases. No direct effect is observed, however, for labor productivity growth. Given that productivity and productivity growth do not depend on the time of adoption, evidence is lacking to confirm that ICT use causes increased productivity.

ICT adoption is strongly related to turnover. Empirical evidence shows that there is a relationship between ICT use and market reach, as well as turnover growth. On average, ICT-using enterprises are larger and grow faster than their non-using counterparts. This holds for nearly all the technologies studied. Again, the level of adoption is the relevant factor rather than the time of adoption. The move to owning a fax machine constitutes a growth threshold. In the case of turnover and turnover growth, causality is questionable, although the positive relationship between ICT use and growth may indicate that the growth is caused by ICT use. Again, however, enterprises with wide market reach have higher information requirements and can benefit more from the adoption of ICT; they are therefore expected to adopt faster than their smaller, locally operating peers. A simultaneous process, as it is proposed by other authors, such as Nassimbeni (2001) for export performance, is most likely.

The other examined performance indicators were not generally related to ICT use. Profit margins were not significantly related, although enterprises that use pagers and cellular telephones appeared, on average, to have higher margins of growth than their peers. Thus, it can be assumed that profit margins depend first on market position and the structure of relationships with customers and suppliers. A wage surcharge was only observed for enterprises that used email and cellular phones. Surprisingly, no significant surcharge was observed for enterprises using computers, although a majority of entrepreneurs stated that computer skills would attract higher wages. There was a tendency, however, for computer-using enterprises to employ more graduates. The lack of indication of better performance for early adopters over late adopters may stem from a categorization problem, although it is more likely that these effects do not exist, or are not very strong. Karshenas and Stoneman (1993), for example, find no evidence of advantages from early adoption. Mueller-Falcke (2002) shows that adoption depends very much on the relative advantages and potential benefits of lowering costs and increasing the speed of information flows. These properties would have a much stronger impact than the actual benefits of ICT use.

As pointed out earlier, the results presented in this study do not support causality in the relationship between enterprise performance and ICT use. Nevertheless, a definite relationship exists, in that successful enterprises use more ICT. Thus, applying and using ICT is an indisputable component of best practice for small enterprises even in developing countries. Entrepreneurs that aim to develop their businesses should take due consideration of the potential advantages of ICT and the pressure toward adoption from partners at the different levels of the production chain. In realizing the relative advantages of new technologies, small enterprises can react much faster to technological change. The high proportion of email-adopting enterprises in our survey illustrates this point.[10] Considering these dynamics, telecommunications, IT policy, and the related regulations in developing countries need to be designed to facilitate easy access to the latest technological developments even for small enterprises. As described above, telecommunications policy clearly failed to meet this goal in the 1990s. Limited competition within the telecommunications and IT sectors kept prices high and service levels low, constraining mass deployment of new technologies. This affected not only the telecommunications industry but also other important areas of the economy, such as small-scale industry. Policies and regulations that ensure early availability and fast rollout of ICT at low prices are key to enabling small enterprises to adopt beneficial technologies early, even with their limited resources. ICT enables small enterprises to keep pace with industry developments, allowing them to stay competitive and defend their position in national and international markets.

Does the Use of ICT Improve the Productivity of SMEs in East Africa? The Case of Kenya and Tanzania
Francis A. S. T. Matambalya and Susanna Wolf

Despite the many potential benefits of ICT envisaged in related literature, little empirical evidence exists to show how the diffusion and application of ICT can positively affect economic competition and growth in developing countries. This study, therefore, focuses on the role of ICT in SME performance to ex-

---

10. The adoption of ICT has the potential to raise awareness of general technological developments. Most of the entrepreneurs participating in the survey for this study who used the worldwide web claimed to use it to obtain information on technologies in their area of business.

TABLE 4.5 Basic economic and social indicators for Kenya and Tanzania, 2000 and 2002

	Tanzania		Kenya	
Indicator	2000	2002	2000	2002
Population (millions)	33.7	35.2	30.1	31.3
GDP per capita, PPP (US$)	192	207	328	322
GDP growth (percent per year since 1990)	3.0	3.5	1.7	1.6
Industry value-added (percent of GDP)	16.0	16.3	19.0	19.0
Industry value-added (percentage growth per year since 1990)	3.1	4.0	1.5	1.4
Trade in goods (percent of GDP)	24.2	27.3	46.7	43.6
Annual growth of exports (goods and services since 1990)	9.4	8.5	1.6	2.1
Net primary school enrollment (percent)	49.8	54.4[a]	68.2	69.9[a]
Net secondary school enrollment (percent)	4.8	na	23.1	24.0[a]

SOURCE: World Bank (2004).

NOTES: GDP indicates gross domestic product; na, that data were not available; PPP, purchasing power parity.

[a]2001 data.

amine how micro-level competitiveness is influenced by ICT, taking into account other influencing factors. Hence, the analysis incorporates the influence of the overall resources, in terms of factor inputs like labor, physical capital, and raw materials. In looking at two East African countries, Kenya and Tanzania, the analysis focuses on a particularly marginalized region in terms of world markets. Other specific characteristics of East Africa's SMEs—such as their small size, the comparatively short time they have been operating, their human capital stock and profile, and their levels of investments in new technologies—are included in the analysis.

East African Economies and SMEs

As stated, East Africa is a marginalized region in terms of economic production and world trade. Nevertheless, there are remarkable differences between the two countries studied (Table 4.5). Whereas Kenya is relatively more developed—having twice the per capita GDP of Tanzania, a higher percentage of industry value-added in GDP, and a higher school enrolment rate (especially at the secondary level)—Tanzania is the more dynamic country, with higher annual GDP growth, industry value-added, and exports.

The three sectors chosen for the empirical analysis in this study—food processing, tourism, and textile production—differ in importance to the two countries. In Kenya, food products account for the highest share in manufacturing

TABLE 4.6 The manufacturing sector in Kenya and Tanzania, 1995

Indicator	Kenya	Tanzania
Total value-added (million US$), 1997	814	119
Food products (percent)	32	11
Textiles and apparel (percent)	7	19
Employment (thousands), 1995	199	157
Value-added per worker, 1995	4,025	767
Average wage (including benefits), 1995	1,251	238

SOURCES: World Bank (2004) and United Nations (1997, 2003).

value-added, at 32 percent in 1995, while textiles were the largest manufacturing sector in Tanzania that year, at 19 percent of value-added. Value-added per worker was only US$767 in Tanzania compared with US$4,025 in Kenya, and despite Tanzania's larger population, employment in manufacturing was also lower than in Kenya. Tourism is an important sector for both countries, although more so for Tanzania. International tourism totaled US$739 million in Tanzania in 2000 and US$730 million in 2002, compared with only US$276 and US$297 million, respectively, for Kenya (Table 4.6).[11]

SMEs dominate Tanzania's economy,[12] not unlike the overwhelming majority of developing economies. SMEs provide employment for more than 33 percent of the employed manufacturing workforce in Kenya and 32 percent in Tanzania (Beck, Demirgüç-Kunt, and Levine 2003). SMEs also account for a significant share of manufacturing GDP.

The dominance of SMEs in developing economies results from a variety of factors. In particular, poor infrastructure creates isolated markets and limited demand, best served through small-scale local production. Hence the majority of small-scale producers are located in rural areas, absorbing workers when seasonal agricultural employment is unavailable. Manufacturing demand is largely focused on simple items that can be produced efficiently in cottage industries using minimal technologies (Liedholm and Mead 1987; Tybout 2000). However, features unique to the business environment in developing countries threaten the success of SMEs. Among these are limited access to manufactured inputs (especially high-quality imported goods), low-quality infrastructure

---

11. In relative terms, Tanzania's tourism industry, measured in gross international sales, represented 57 percent of total exports in 2000 and 47 percent in 2002, whereas Kenya's tourism industry represented 10 and 9 percent shares for the same years, respectively (World Bank 2004).

12. In dynamic terms, the influence of SMEs is underscored by several additional facts. SMEs utilize local resources and exert little pressure on limited foreign currency reserves; they provide a flexible and skilled production base; they facilitate access to new markets; and they are crucial to rural areas (Mead and Liedholm 1998). SMEs also face severe competitive disadvantages because, on average, they are less efficient, less productive, and their products are of lower quality.

(including crime prevention and legal systems), and highly volatile macro-economic conditions and prices. Low levels of human capital (particularly workers with low secondary education and lack of technical skill), limit the range of goods that can be produced and the ability of SMEs to absorb new technologies (Tybout 2000). The sample enterprises for this study cited negative factors like unfavorable tax and business start-up regulations, difficulties in terms of business financing and corruption, lack of reliable product markets, and inflation as major obstacles to doing business (Matambalya and Wolf 2001).

The Data

The data used in this study were collected from 150 SMEs in both Kenya and Tanzania (300 total), distributed equally across the food processing, textile, and tourism sectors.[13] The data were collected between November 1999 and May 2000. Sample enterprises were randomly selected from the countries' major commercial corridors, based on two key considerations: their economic significance and their ability to proxy for developing-country SMEs.[14] In Tanzania, of the 144 enterprises that had consistently plausible data, 29 used no ICT, 13 used external telephone services, and the remainder invested at various levels in at least one technology. Thirty-nine enterprises only used fixed line telephones, and an additional 26 enterprises also used cellular phones. Five enterprises also had fax machines but did not use PC-based communication technologies, while less than one-third of the sample enterprises (45) used the Internet and email. For Kenya, the picture is somewhat different than expected based on the country's better overall infrastructure and higher development level. However, 37 of the 151 sample enterprises used no ICT at all, and 18 enterprises used external telephone services only. The majority of the enterprises that subscribed to telephone services only used fixed line telephones, and only for communication; a higher number of enterprises (25) used fax machines in Kenya than in Tanzania, however.

In Tanzania 56.5 percent of the sample enterprises invested less than US$200 per year in ICT facilities like telephones, fax machines, and computers. This places a high number of enterprises below critical mass in terms of ICT investments (although it should be noted that starting from such a low investment base, the purchase of a single cellular phone could result in a comparatively

---

13. Thus, the weight of sectors in the sample is not proportional to their relevance for the Kenyan and Tanzanian economies. This should be borne in mind in the interpretation of the regression results.

14. The selected commercial corridors are the lake zone, the coastal zone, and the Arusha region in Tanzania and the coastal zone and lake zone in Kenya, thus including rural and urban enterprises. As the quality of the answers in the questionnaire varies, the number of observations is not the same for all areas. For financial data, in particular, the number of observations was reduced because of missing values and implausible answers.

TABLE 4.7 Enterprise characteristics by country and sector

Characteristics	Kenya			Tanzania		
	Food	Textile	Tourism	Food	Textile	Tourism
Number of employees	24.3	8.7	18.7	14.1	9.1	12.0
Average years of staff schooling	11.0	10.6	12.0	9.1	9.6	11.5
Age of enterprise	10.0	10.7	11.3	6.2	7.8	8.2
ICT investment per employee (US$)	49.7	431.4	432.8	53.1	43.9	401.7
Percent of exporting firms	24.5	17.3	74.0	20.7	25.5	89.7
Percent of firms in capital	63.3	59.6	80.0	41.4	51.1	38.5

SOURCE: Calculated by authors from primary survey data (1999–2000).

high ICT investment share). This is one explanation as to why Tanzanian enterprises invest a higher percentage in ICT on average. The limited resources of the enterprises and the high costs of procuring and using ICT seem to be the major factors that hinder ICT diffusion. This explanation was given by 91 percent of the enterprises that did not use computer-dependent ICT. Nonpossession of computers was attributed to the high costs of hardware and software (80 percent) and the high labor costs of computer-skilled employees (62 percent). In addition, close to 72 percent of the sample enterprises did not see the value of computer-dependent ICT. This could manifest from limited business skills, or a product market in which lower order sources of competitiveness, like cheap labor, still dominate (Matambalya 2003). Notably, in both countries, the workforce in enterprises that do not use ICT or that only use the telephone have fewer years of schooling; such enterprises are generally less export oriented and also more labor intensive than the enterprises that use more advanced forms of ICT.

These differences can be explained in part by sector characteristics (Table 4.7). For example, average years of schooling are highest in the tourism sector in both countries, and this corresponds to the use of more advanced ICT and greater export orientation. Tourism enterprises are also older on average, while enterprises in the food processing sector are larger. This stems from the different production structure in the food processing industry, whereby a greater minimum capacity is required to achieve productivity.

Skill levels were also shown to be relevant in the survey. Education, for example, improves the quality of human resources and increases enterprises' ability to adopt advanced technologies, including ICT. Further, more highly educated staff increase the ability of enterprises to deal with disequilibria, such as changing factor and product prices (Shultz 1975; Weir 1999). Cognitive skills also enhance the ability of entrepreneurs to access and use productivity-enhancing knowledge, and to adopt more positive attitudes toward modernization and risk-taking (Weir 1999).

The Impact of ICT on SME Performance in East Africa

Diffusion of ICT in East Africa is low by international standards. Comparisons with Sub-Saharan African averages emphasize this reality. In Tanzania, before 2000, the intensity of fixed line and cellular telephones was about one-third of the comparable intensity for Sub-Saharan Africa. Rates were somewhat better in Kenya for fixed line telephones, but the situation was worse for cellular phones. Both countries have improved their access to ICT more recently, mainly through the development of cellular networks. Fixed line service remains low in both countries, however. Waiting times for fixed line phones are by far the longest in Kenya compared with the rest of East Africa, increasing from 5.6 to 8.1 years between 1997 and 2000, and to over 10 years in 2002. Lack of fixed line infrastructure also means that cellular phones can actually be more reliable than fixed line telephones (Table 4.8).

Fixed line business telephone tariffs are relatively low. In Kenya the connection and monthly subscription costs were US$30 and US$3.3 in 2000, respectively, and US$29 and US$5.6 in 2002, respectively; in Tanzania the costs were a little higher, at US$48 for connection and US$4.1 for subscription in 2000, and US$41 for connection and US$3.6 for subscription in 2002. This compares with average European rates of US$117 for connection and US$9.7 for monthly subscription in 2000, and US$96 for connection and US$10.5 for monthly subscription in 2002.

In East Africa, privatization of ICT infrastructure remains limited. Competition exists in Kenya in the cellular phone and Internet markets, but the state-owned fixed line service operator, Telkom Kenya, has not been privatized. An independent regulator was established in 1999, giving Telkom Kenya exclusivity within Nairobi until 2004, although three companies were granted Regional Telecommunication Operator (RTO) licenses in 2000 to introduce competition outside of Nairobi. In addition, two cellular telephone licenses were issued to Safaricom (a semi-public subsidiary of Telkom) and Kencell Communications Ltd. (a private company). Coverage has consequently improved substantially since 2001 and the cellular network now covers most of the major towns in Kenya. In Tanzania the situation is similar, although the fixed line service provider, the Tanzania Telecommunications Company Ltd. (TCCL), was privatized in 2000.[15] The sector is regulated by an independent regulator, the Tanzania Communications Commission (TCC), which was established in 1994. TCCL also provides cellular and paging services, but the cellular phone market is fully competitive. The fixed line monopoly negatively affected service for both voice telephony and the Internet in Tanzania, although cyber cafes, which are also used by businesses, are prevalent.

---

15. Competition has yet to be realized, however. TCCL still operates a monopoly on the mainland, while there is a duopoly in Zanzibar.

TABLE 4.8 Diffusion and costs of selected ICT in East Africa, 2000 and 2002

Indicator	Kenya 2000	Kenya 2002	Tanzania 2000	Tanzania 2002	Sub-Saharan Africa 2000	Sub-Saharan Africa 2002
Fixed lines per 100 inhabitants	1.1	1.0	0.5	0.5	1.4	1.5
Waiting list for fixed lines (thousands)	134.1	134.0[a]	14.4	8.0	na	3,406.5[a]
Waiting time for fixed lines (years)	8.1	>10	1.3	2.0	6.0	5.0[b]
Average cost of a three-minute local call (US$)	0.1	0.1	0.1	0.1	0.1	0.1
Average cost of a three-minute call to the United States (US$)	7.4	5.8[a]	8.2[c]	5.3	5.2	3.6
Cellular phones per 100 inhabitants	0.4	4.2	0.6	2.0	0.5	1.6
Fax machines per 100 inhabitants	0.1	na	0.1	na	na	na
Personal computers per 100 inhabitants	0.5	0.6	0.3	0.4	1.0	1.2
Total number of Internet hosts	1,621	2,963	602	1,731	na	243,171[b]
Internet users per 100 inhabitants	0.3	1.3	0.1	0.2	0.9	1.6

SOURCES: World Bank (2004) and ITU (2002, 2004).

NOTE: na indicates that data were not available.

[a]2001 data.

[b]Data include all Africa.

[c]1999 data.

FIGURE 4.2 Use of ICT in Kenyan small and medium-sized enterprises, 1990–2000

Firms using ICT (percent)

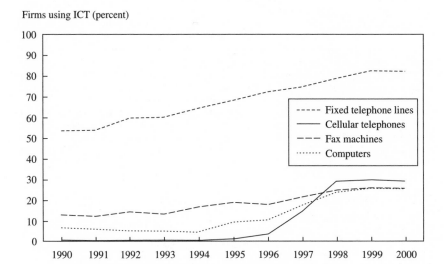

SOURCE: Calculated by authors from a primary survey (1999–2000).
NOTE: The number of observations is 151.

The study sample indicates that ICT use by SMEs increased during 1990–2000 in both Kenya and Tanzania. As of 2000, fixed line telephone use was still lower in Tanzania than in Kenya, in line with overall teledensity. The share of firms using cellular phones was rising in both countries, and had already outgrown fax machine use in Tanzanian businesses, despite the late (1994) introduction of cellular networks. Computers remain a relatively expensive investment for most SMEs; as of 2000 their use was slightly higher in Kenya than in Tanzania and increasing slowly (Figures 4.2 and 4.3).

How might improved access to ICT affect the performance of SMEs in Kenya and Tanzania? As discussed in the previous case study, flexibility is considered a major source of competitive advantage for SMEs over larger enterprises. The use of ICT could enhance flexibility by creating faster, more reliable communication channels. Yet larger enterprises can benefit from this same opportunity, in turn gaining their own competitive advantage.[16] In general, compared with larger enterprises, SMEs rely much more on informal information systems. Owner/operators are generally limited in their personal resources (in terms of time, knowledge, and skills) so the Internet offers significant opportunities

---

16. See Brynjolfsson and Hitt (2000a) for a discussion of the interrelationship between information technology and organization.

FIGURE 4.3 Use of ICT in Tanzanian small and medium-sized enterprises, 1990–2000

Firms using ICT (percent)

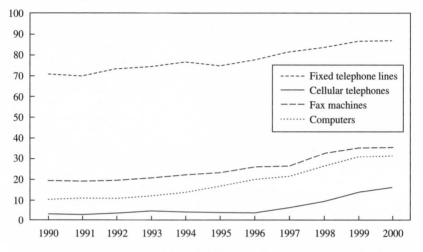

SOURCE: Calculated by authors from a primary survey (1999–2000).
NOTE: The number of observations is 144.

when it comes to sourcing information and communicating with trading partners and customers (Mueller-Falcke 2002). Nevertheless, other infrastructure still needs to be in place, such as transport for the delivery of goods and a reliable banking system for the transmission of payments. With the use of ICT, transaction costs could be lowered, in turn reducing the economies of scale associated with exporting. This could enable SMEs to expand beyond local markets, both nationally and internationally. On the other hand, reduced costs could open the local rural markets traditionally served by SMEs to competition from larger enterprises. This increased competition could force local SMEs to become more productive if they are to survive.

As was established in the previous case study, few studies have analyzed the effect of ICT on small enterprises in developing countries, in large part because of data problems. The survey conducted for this study elicited information on the owner/operators' perception of the benefits of ICT. Those enterprises that used different forms of ICT rated their effects most positively (Figure 4.4). Computer applications are perceived to considerably increase management efficiency and competitiveness by 88 and 76 percent of users, respectively. The majority of enterprises considered cellular phones to be the most significant

FIGURE 4.4 Perceived effects of ICT

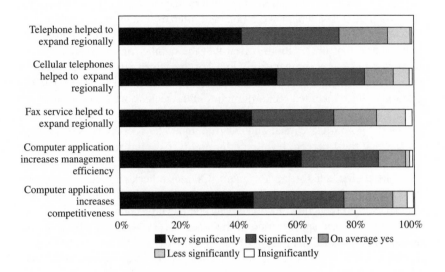

SOURCE: Calculated by authors from a primary survey (1999/2000).

contributor to regional market expansion, followed by fixed telephones and fax machines.[17]

Results

The increased use of ICT in enterprises observed in our sample (Figures 4.3 and 4.4) leads to a substitution of other forms of capital and labor for ICT equipment and may generate substantial returns for enterprises that invest in ICT and restructure their organizations. However, this does not necessarily imply that TFP will increase.[18]

To test for this we follow the methodology described in Appendix 4A, and construct a simple model to measure the impact of ICT on output, including the independent variables non-ICT capital (K), ICT capital (ICT), labor (L), other production inputs (I), investment in ICT (ICT), and dummies for the use of different communication technologies like the telephone, fax machine, and Internet.

---

17. These data only include enterprises that use specified technologies, so they may be biased.

18. In fact, in industrial countries, the growth of TFP associated with technical change actually declined in parallel with the increased use of ICT in the last decades of the 20th century (Jorgenson and Stiroh 1999).

The estimation of the modified production function (Equation [2] of Appendix 4A) allows examination of the determinants of TFP. The results of the regression analysis, which were obtained after excluding three outliers, are shown in Table 4.9.[19] A regression on the pooled data set was run to utilize the larger number of observations, given that the number of observations in the Kenyan data set was comparatively low. For this larger data set, two specifications of the regression equation were used. As productivity usually varies across sectors, we also included sector dummies in the regression. In most cases, the correlation coefficients between the independent variables are relatively low; however, for non-ICT capital and material input, the coefficient is 0.703 (significance at the 1 percent level) and for non-ICT capital and ICT capital it is 0.652.

The coefficients for labor, capital (ICT plus other), and other production inputs sum to almost one for all regressions, implying that the assumption of a Cobb–Douglas production function is plausible, and no economies of scale exist.[20]

After the basic specification of the model (A) (where only the basic production function of Equation (2) of Appendix 4A is estimated, controlling for sectors and country), different variables that might affect productivity were added. The investment in ICT has a negative sign in all the regressions, but the coefficients are never statistically significant. This observation can be explained by the relatively long time-span needed to make full use of ICT because of the need to train employees and restructure the enterprise. Because computer-literate personnel are scarce in both countries and enterprises have to train employees, it is not surprising that productivity falls with investment in more expensive ICT. There is also some evidence that returns to investment in ICT only accrue after a certain threshold is reached (Matambalya 2003). In addition, because ICT in East Africa is more expensive than in developed countries, returns to investment are lower.

However, when analyzing the impact of access to ICT approximated through the use of fax machines, a significant positive correlation with productivity for both countries in all regressions where it is included (B, D, and E) was found.[21] This is consistent with Brynjolfsson and Hitt (1995), who identify a positive effect of information technology on productivity. These results were consolidated even further in a more recent study by Brynjolfsson and Hitt (2000b), which again underscores the importance of IT for productivity growth.

---

19. The outliers differed by more than three standard deviations.

20. This finding confirms the enterprise studies on Ghana by Söderbom and Teal (2001), which also found no scale economies.

21. Because most of the SMEs use several types of ICT concurrently, not all types of ICT were able to be included within a single regression; hence ICT access was approximated by fax use, which captured most of the variance of the other ICT variables (fixed line telephones, cellular phones, and PCs).

TABLE 4.9 Estimation of a production function

Variable	A		B		C		D		E	
	Coeff.	t-stat.	Coeff.	t-stat.	Coeff.	t-stat.	Coeff.	t-stat.	Coeff.	t-stat.
Constant	4.065	7.125**	4.706	8.071**	4.116	7.147**	4.717	7.858**	4.762	7.521**
ln I	0.534	8.628**	0.512	8.509**	0.536	8.639**	0.513	8.409**	0.516	8.378**
ln K	0.111	2.064*	0.041	0.735*	0.103	1.906*	0.042	0.738	0.037	0.627
ln ICT	0.007	0.227	-0.048	-1.336	-0.017	-0.478	-0.059	-1.585	-0.058	-1.514
ln L	0.234	1.392	0.341	2.064*	0.239	1.421	0.328	1.961*	0.308	1.716*
Fax use			0.494	3.401**			0.446	2.866**	0.495	2.917**
Exp					0.008	2.122*	0.005	1.463	0.005	1.290
Interaction terms:										
Kenya * fax use									-0.150	-0.372
Kenya * ln L									0.083	0.230
Kenya * ln ICT									-0.057	-0.259
Textiles	-0.076	-0.406	-0.071	-0.392	-0.113	-0.596	-0.099	-0.539	-0.089	-0.480
Tourism	0.527	2.324*	0.228	0.967	0.207	0.742	0.021	0.074	0.046	0.157
Kenya	-2.637	-5.414**	-3.350	-6.496**	-2.683	-5.498**	-3.321	-6.313**	-3.449	-3.583**
No. of observations	160		160		160		157		157	
Adjusted R^2	0.880		0.887		0.874		0.884		0.882	

SOURCE: Calculated by authors from primary survey data (1999–2000).

NOTES: *Indicates significance at the 10 percent level; **indicates significance at the 5 percent level.

The mechanisms and direction of causality, however, are not clearly established because firms that perform well may purchase additional ICT with their profits. Therefore, as in their case, we cannot infer causality between firm performance and ICT use, only positive associations.

In all regressions, the country dummy had a significant negative coefficient, meaning that Kenyan enterprises are less productive than Tanzanian ones. This seems inconsistent with Kenya's more advanced development level, yet its less dynamic, adverse political environment may have had a negative impact on productivity. In specification C, we introduced a market extension index (exp) in the regression to capture the firms' coverage of regional as well as export markets for fax use. This index also has a significant impact on productivity, which is in line with other findings showing that higher competition in foreign markets forces enterprises to increase productivity. However, if fax use and market extensions are simultaneously entered into the regression, only fax use is significant (market extension becomes insignificant). This may be because fax use is also a determinant of export orientation, given that only firms with modern communications technologies are able to market their products internationally. In specification E, we combined determinants of productivity with the Kenyan dummy to determine whether they have different effects in the two countries. The effects of investment in ICT, fax use, or labor did not differ significantly between Kenya and Tanzania.

The results of the regressions are fairly robust with respect to the variables included. However, a number of variables that were expected to affect productivity were not significant and, hence, were excluded from the regressions. Among these were the age of the enterprise and the skill intensity of the labor force (measured by average years of schooling). Age usually affects productivity because it is correlated with the experience of the owner/operator, and therefore proxies for human capital (Biggs and Srivastava 1996; Söderbom and Teal 2000). As the use of ICT is already associated with higher quality human capital, the effects of age and skills could be captured by the ICT variables. On the other hand, older enterprises tend to use older technologies, so the two effects could cancel each other out.

Conclusion

Analysis of the data on SMEs in Kenya and Tanzania indicates that ICT has a positive impact on TFP. While no significant relationship between ICT investment and productivity was found, this only implies that ICT investment is no more productive than any other investment in the short term. Based on the analysis in the study, and reports by others, a positive effect of ICT is assumed to occur once a certain threshold is met. Furthermore, given that only the use of the fax machine had significant impact on productivity, the effect depends on the appropriateness of the technology rather than on the total investment. As was discussed in the previous case study, it is possible that the lack of a discernable effect from the use of ICT may simply reflect the time-lag before investments in these technologies begin to payoff. In addition, the sole focus on productivity may be too narrow, and ICT may exert its influence through improved product quality and service, and expanded networks.

Most African countries have ICT development plans and even e-commerce programs in place (or they plan to develop them). The donor community is also enthusiastic about the role of ICT in development, especially because it facilitates increased interaction by otherwise excluded societal groups. Nevertheless, as our empirical results and other considerations show, the use of ICT is at best one factor among many that improves firm performance. Therefore, ICT should not be regarded in isolation. Access to credit, managerial and other skills, infrastructure, and the legal system are at least as important as information and ICT. These factors should include not only general improvements to infrastructure but also specific improvements in the quality and accessibility of ICT.

In terms of human capital, secondary schooling should be complemented with vocational training about ICT skills (Matambalya 2003). Improved communication networks could facilitate cooperation among SMEs in terms of sharing best practice, general know-how, and management capabilities. This is especially so because economies of scale do not appear to be relevant to the three sectors involved, indicating significant potential for ICT to increase potential economies of scale. Through an improved network, SMEs could, for example, reduce the costs of imported inputs to enhance their competitiveness.

One important aspect of access to ICT is the high cost of devices and services in many African countries. ICT sector liberalization and privatization will be an important step in ensuring competition, thereby increasing ICT use across societal groups. Special priority should be given to telecommunications infrastructure, which is still generally lacking in rural and remote areas of developing countries (see Torero 2000 and Chapter 3 of this volume). To increase access to relevant information, ICT intermediaries, such as nonprofit organizations and SME associations, could play a key role by adding value to their existing services. Based on their existing awareness of the information needs of small enterprises, such organizations could facilitate the formation of networks to disseminate information about best practice, market price at different locations, source of supply of inputs, and so on. Dissemination of relevant government information about regulations and support programs—through government Web sites, for example—is another important factor. In addition to saving time, publicly accessible information could increase transparency and reduce obstacles to business operation.

The Impact of Telecommunications on Rural Enterprises:
The Case of Rural Laos
Arjun S. Bedi and Gi-Soon Song

Unlike some of the case studies in this chapter, which consider the impact of more advanced ICT, this study focuses on the effect of access to fixed-line telephony on the economic performance of firms in rural Laos.[22] While telephony is the most basic form of ICT, the state of rural telecommunications infrastructure in Laos makes the prospect of universal access an important factor in the development of rural enterprises. This case study profiles the patterns of telecommunications access, intensity of use, and expenditure among the sample firms, providing a sense of telecommunications diffusion in rural Laos and an idea of the information needs of firms. It also provides an overview of the benefits associated with access to basic telephony. In addition to this qualitative analysis, a quantitative analysis of the link between economic performance of firms and access to basic telephony is presented. For background information on Laos and the development of its telecommunications sector, see the introduction to the Laos case study in Chapter 3.

The Rural Telecommunications Project

As was discussed in the Laos case study in Chapter 3, the Government of Laos embarked on a plan to promote rural telecommunications, prompted by regional imbalances in telecommunications service (as well as other economic and security considerations). With the financial support of the German Development Bank (KFW), the Rural Telecommunications (Rurtel) project was launched in 1992 (see ZEF 2001 and Chapter 3 of this volume for more details). The facilities installed under the project have been heavily used by rural residents, yielding revenues much higher than were projected in the feasibility study undertaken for the project. Yet exactly how the Rurtel project influences behavior in rural Laos is not well known. The purpose of this study is to fill that gap, thereby obtaining a better understanding of the contribution of telecommunications services to rural welfare, specifically in terms of the effects of access to telephony on rural firms in Laos.[23]

The Data

Between May and September 2000, a survey of households and firms was carried out in six sites in rural Laos. These sites were widely spread across the country, and about 20 firms were randomly selected and surveyed from each site. The survey was designed to evaluate various aspects of the Rurtel project, so information was gathered on a variety of dimensions including firm performance (sales, expenditure on intermediate inputs, and profits), characteristics of the firms (such as number of employees), and characteristics of the owner of

---

22. About 80 percent of the population resides in rural areas; hence many of the small and medium firms are rural. The sample was drawn from six sites in rural Laos and collected information on firms' engaged in trading, manufacturing, construction, and services.

23. The impact assessment study was commissioned by the German Development Bank (KFW), and the results reported in this case study form part of the overall report to KFW. For more details of the impact assessment, see ZEF (2001).

TABLE 4.10 Descriptive statistics of surveyed firms, 2000

Variable	Mean	Standard deviation
Years in operation	6.83	3.14
Sales per month (US$)	7,850	25,557
Current value of assets (US$)[a]	41,498	124,932
Intermediate expenditure per month (US$)[b]	4,466	9,604
Value-added per month (US$)	1,090	2,598
Value-added per employee per month (US$)	173	213
Assets per employee (US$)	4,601	7,923
Number of employees	8.33	23.8
Years of education of owner/operator	7.52	2.59
Years of experience of owner/operator	8.52	5.46
Owner/operator previously a government employee (1/0)	0.429	0.497
Number of observations	121	

SOURCE: Compiled by authors from primary survey data (2000).

[a]Excludes value of telecommunications-related investments.

[b]Excludes expenditure on telecommunications.

the firm (such as education and experience). Since the main aim of the survey was to identify the effect of access to telecommunications on firm performance, detailed information was collected on telecommunications expenditure, intensity, and patterns of use, as well as on the information needs of the firms.

Table 4.10 provides key descriptive statistics for the sample firms. The surveyed firms were drawn from three broad sectors: trading (72 percent), manufacturing and construction (32 percent), and services (33 percent). About 37 percent of the firms were engaged in more than one sector (hence sector shares do not sum to 100 percent). Almost all the firms were privately owned (118 out of 121). The average firm in the sample had been operating for about 7 years and no firm has been in existence for more than 15 years. The average firm was also quite small, employing about 8 workers (although this figure is a little misleading because the distribution of employees was skewed). The median was about two workers per firm, and 83 percent of the firms employed fewer than 10 workers. Average monthly sales were about $8,000, although once again the distribution was skewed, such that the median monthly sales were around $1,300. Since most of the sample firms were engaged in trading activities, expenditure on intermediate inputs was quite high, and the value-added per employee was about $173 per month. In most cases the survey respondents were the owners of the firms. On average, firm owner/operators had about 7.5 years of education and about 8.5 years of management experience; a substantial proportion (43 percent) were previously employed as government employees. This large proportion may reflect the effects of the new economic mechanism (see the Laos case study in Chapter 3). Under this program, civil service retrenchments occurred during 1988–91.

Results

Table 4.11 provides an overview of telephone access, use, and related variables among the surveyed rural firms in Laos. In terms of access, 41 firms (34 percent) had a fixed line telephone installed at their premises and 55 firms (45 percent) used the telephone regularly but did not subscribe. Most of these user-nonsubscribers had access to public calling facilities within 2 kilometers of their businesses. The remaining firms did not use telephones. Among users, services were used quite intensively. The average firm placed about three calls per day and spent about US$44 per month on telecommunications. About 62 percent of these calls fell into the domestic long-distance category. In terms of calling patterns, most users placed and received calls to gather information on prices and availability of inputs, or on the output market.

In terms of benefits, respondents pointed out that compared with other methods, telecommunications provided faster access to information, reduced costs, and saved time. Further clues about the usefulness of telecommunications were provided in responses to questions concerning telecommunications needs and willingness-to-pay. Almost all the nonsubscribers (92.5 percent) indicated their desire to subscribe to fixed line telephone services. Further, about 89 percent of the nonsubscribers indicated their willingness to pay the current installation costs (US$100) and monthly fixed charges (US$1.3). Using willingness-to-pay as a signal of service usefulness, at a minimum, the monetary benefits associated with telecommunications access were equal to the costs of becoming a subscriber. Overall, the patterns reported in Table 4.11 suggest that the telephone was accepted as a useful business tool by the majority of surveyed firms in rural Laos. These patterns, combined with the willingness to pay for telephone subscription, lend support to the idea that firms derive considerable benefits from access to telecommunications services.

Telecommunications and Economic Performance. While the previous section supports the idea that firms derive benefits from access to ICT, the following discussion directly explores the effects of telecommunications access on economic performance. Ideally, our analysis would be able to identify a causal relationship between access to telecommunications and indicators of business performance. This is not possible based on available cross-section data because it is likely that better-performing firms may simply use more telecommunications services as opposed to performing better because of them. It is also quite possible that firms with better economic outcomes are more likely to use telecommunications and that access to telecommunications further enhances their performance.

Regardless (although not ideal), it is possible to use cross-section data to evaluate whether differences in access to telecommunications services across

TABLE 4.11 A profile of telecommunications use by firms in rural Laos, 2000

1.	Telephone access	
	• 41 (34%) Subscribers	
	• 55 (45%) Nonsubscriber users	
	• 25 (21%) Non-users	
2.	Use of telecommunication services	
	• 96 (79%) Fixed line telephony	
	• 28 (23%) Fixed line telephony and fax	
	• 4 (3.3%) Fixed line, fax, and cellular telephony	
3.	Duration of access	80 percent for at least 3 years
4.	Cost of installation	$204.8 (186.8)[a]
5a.	Monthly expenditure on telecommunications	$44.5 (114.5)[a]
5b.	Expenditure as a percentage of total Expenditure	1.83 (4.57)[a]
6.	Intensity of use	
	Average no. of local calls	24.3 (39)[a]
	Average no. of long-distance calls	53 (69)[a]
	Average no. of international calls	9.2 (25)[a]
6a.	Telecom needs	
	• 74 (92.5%) of 80 nonsubscribers/non-users indicate desire for subscription.	
6b.	Willingness to pay	
	• 66 (89%) of 80 nonsubscribers/non-users indicate willingness to pay current installation costs and monthly fixed fee.	
7.	Benefits of telecommunications	
	• Lower monetary and time costs as compared to alternative methods, allows immediate feedback.	
8.	Information needs	
	• 102 (84%) mentioned input price and availability as rather or very important.	
	• 95 (79%) mentioned information related to output market as rather or very important.	
	• Information related to the labor market/government policies were not rated as important.	
9.	Telephone calling patterns	
	• 74 (77%) of 96 users call suppliers/buyers most frequently.	
	• For 53 (74%) of 72 users suppliers/buyers are the most frequent callers.	
10.	Obstacles faced by enterprises	
	• 69 (63%) of 110 respondents mentioned lack of infrastructure as the main business obstacle.	
	• 30 (43%) of these mentioned lack of roads as the primary drawback.	
	• 18 (26%) mentioned poor telecommunication services.	
	• 12 (17%) mentioned lack of electricity.	

SOURCE: Compiled by authors from primary survey data (2000).
[a]Standard deviations.

TABLE 4.12 Selected descriptive statistics, conditional on telephone access

Variable	Telephone subscriber (1)	Telephone user— nonsubscriber (2)	Non-user (3)
Log sales per month[a]	8.650	7.243	6.488
	(1.514)	(1.260)	(0.896)
		4.534[b]	*2.6243*[c]
Log value added per month per employee	5.188	4.664	4.347
	(0.773)	(0.911)	(1.081)
		2.682	*1.443*
Capital per employee	8,965	2,720	1,759
	(12,166)	(2,625)	(2,638)
		3.699	*1.5154*
Number of employees	18.65	3.36	2.32
	(39.1)	(2.08)	(1.67)
		0.7423	*3.0522*
Years of education—owner	8.14	7.76	5.96
	(2.56)	(2.42)	(2.50)
		0.3542	*2.484*
Years of experience—owner	9.39	8.96	6.12
	(6.41)	(5.46)	(2.43)
		2.907	*2.199*
Number of observations	41	55	25

SOURCE: Compiled by authors from primary survey data (2000).

NOTES: The dependent variable is output (ln). Standard deviation is shown in parentheses; *t*-statistics are shown in italics.

[a]Financial variables are reported in U.S. dollars.

[b]Test for differences between means are reported in columns 1 and 2.

[c]Test for differences between means are reported in columns 2 and 3.

firms is associated with variations in economic performance. Before turning to our estimates, consider the descriptive statistics presented in Table 4.12. These statistics are conditional on telephone access and clearly display that, compared with nonsubscribers, firms with fixed line telephone services on-site employ about six times as many workers, have substantially higher sales and value-added per worker, and have three to four times more (capital) assets per employee than nonsubscribing firms. Differences in variables between firms that use telephones but do have services on-site (nonsubscribers) and firms that are non-users are not statistically significant. While it is possible that access to telephony is responsible for some of the differences between subscribing and nonsubscribing firms, the magnitude of the differences suggests that firms with better economic performance (higher capital per employee) are also more likely to be telephone subscribers.

Assessing Impact Using Production Functions. Following the methodology described in Appendix 4A, we estimate the impact of ICT on sales using Equation (2), as a short-run Cobb–Douglas production function. In this equation, we incorporate Q as the firm's monthly sales, K for capital assets, I_E for expenditure on all intermediate inputs. Finally, ICT is decomposed in T_K for telecommunications-related capital expenditure and T_E for telecommunications-related expenditure.

All the variables are measured in terms of monetary units. Results based on this specification are presented in column 1 of Table 4.13. The coefficients reveal that a 10 percent increase in assets (in expenditure on intermediate inputs) is associated with an output increase of about 3.5 percent. The coefficients on telecommunications-related capital and current expenditure variables are small and statistically insignificant. The previous specification may suffer from several weaknesses, as explained in Appendix 4A, so we complement the analysis by measuring the impact of ICT on performance indicators, specifically the firm's value-added per employee (VA/L).

Estimates of several regression variants of Equation (6) are presented in Table 4.13, columns 2–5. The first specification reported in column 2 includes only the two indicator variables. This specification yields the same information as the descriptive statistics in Table 4.12, that is, there is a strong, positive, and statistically significant correlation between subscriber firms and value-added per worker. Column 3 reports the results of a specification that includes three variables to control for the potential endogeneity between subscriber firms and value-added per worker. Although it remains statistically significant at conventional levels, the inclusion of these variables leads to a sharp reduction in the coefficient on the telecommunications subscriber variable (a drop from 0.841 to 0.577).

The results also show that the education and experience of an owner/operator are positively associated with the economic performance of a firm. The marginal effect associated with schooling is 7 percent and, with experience, about 3 percent. The previous employment status of the owner has no bearing on economic performance. So far the results suggest that access to telecommunications has a fairly large and discernible effect on value-added per worker. However, this may be misleading because we have yet to control for the capital endowment of firms. Estimates in column 4 examine the effect of telecommunications access, controlling for capital per employee. There is a remarkable change in these results. A comparison of columns 2 and 4 shows that the coefficient on telecommunications services falls from 0.841 to 0.064 and is no longer statistically significant. Column 5 presents results based on the complete specification displayed in Equation (6). These estimates reveal the same story as the results in column 4. There is no statistically significant impact of telecommunications access on our measure of economic performance. In fact the sign on these variables is now negative. Column 6 presents results

TABLE 4.13 The effect of telecommunications investment, expenditure, and access on economic performance

Variable	ln sales (1)	ln (VA/L) (2)	ln (VA/L) (3)	ln (VA/L) (4)	ln (VA/L) (5)	ln (VA/L) (6)
Constant	0.559	4.347	3.765	0.867	0.643	0.452
	2.03	*23.3*	*11.92*	*1.90*	*1.35*	*0.89*
ln assets	0.352					
	8.81					
ln telecom investment	0.0025					
	0.38					
ln intermediate inputs	0.537					
	14.4					
ln telecom inputs	0.043					
	1.26					
ln (assets/employee)				0.508	0.485	0.502
				8.04	*7.68*	*6.57*
Telephone subscriber		0.841	0.577	0.064	−0.077	0.268
		3.41	*2.22*	*0.30*	*−0.35*	*0.48*
Telephone nonsubscriber		0.317	0.112	0.053	−0.071	0.091
		1.39	*0.48*	*0.29*	*−0.38*	*0.27*
Years of education—owner			0.070		0.046	0.034
			1.98		*1.65*	*1.08*
Years of experience—owner			0.032		0.021	0.017
			1.90		*1.55*	*1.24*
Owner previously			−0.071		−0.056	−0.003
government employee			*−0.39*		*−0.39*	*−0.02*
Generalized residual						−0.129
						−0.62
Number of observations	106	105	105	105	105	103
Adjusted R^2	0.93	0.091	0.133	0.441	0.453	0.482

SOURCE: Specified and calculated by authors from primary survey data (2000).

NOTES: The dependent variable is output (ln); *t*-statistics are shown in italics.

based on a formal procedure to correct for the potential endogeneity between telecommunications access and economic performance.

This procedure is similar to a Heckman-type two-stage model (see Vella 1993 for details on the procedure). In the first step, we estimate an ordered Probit model for telecommunications access. A generalized residual calculated on the basis of these first-step results is included in Equation (6) to control for endogeneity. The coefficient on the generalized residual is statistically insignificant, indicating that selection into subscriber status is not based on unobserved characteristics but depends mainly on observed characteristics. Accordingly, the estimates based on this two-stage approach do not overturn the conclusions reached earlier.

The results in columns 2–6 show that inclusion of the capital endowment of a firm in the regression specifications leads to the sharpest changes in the results. Inclusion of these variables leads to a complete dissipation of the telecommunications access effect. The reduction in the access effect indicates that firms with a larger capital base are more likely to be subscribers, and that, at least on the basis of these cross-section data, there is no separate and identifiable effect of telecommunications access on economic performance.

Assessing Impact Using Matching Methods. It is possible that differences in economic performance emanate primarily from subscription to telephone services. We follow the method of matched comparisons, described in Appendix 4A, to assess the impact of ICT on firm performance. Estimates displayed in Table 4.14 present the results of an investigation that relies on a two-part classification of telecommunications access. The first panel presents the observed means and differences in means for subscribers and nonsubscribers. As may be expected there is a large and statistically significant difference in these

TABLE 4.14 Telephone subscribers and differences in average value-added per employee

	Subscriber (treatment)		Nonsubscriber (control)
1. Observed mean	5.188		4.560
	(0.773)		(0.974)
Differences		0.628	
		(0.194)	
		3.226	
2. OLS estimates		−0.0226	
Coefficient on subscriber		*0.168*	
3. Kernel matching—mean	5.188		5.168
	(0.12)		(0.014)
Differences		0.0201	
		0.120	
4. Nearest neighbour	5.188		5.117
Matching—mean	(0.773)		(0.689)
Differences		0.0716	
		0.272	

SOURCE: Specified and calculated by authors from primary survey data (2000).

NOTES: The results reported are based on 32 subscribing firms and 73 nonsubscribing firms. The number of matched control observations used to calculate the nearest-neighbor estimates is 14. Standard errors for the kernel matching estimates are based on 50 bootstrap replications. Standard deviations are shown in parentheses; *t*-statistics are shown in italics. OLS indicates ordinary least squares.

means. Panel 2 presents the coefficient on telephone subscribers from a regression specification that includes capital per employee and the vector of X variables. The effect of being a telephone subscriber on value-added is not statistically significant, and the sign is in fact negative. Thus, similar to earlier estimates, there is no discernible effect of telecommunications access once the capital endowment of a firm is included in the model.

Our prior investigation suggests that access to telecommunications depends on observed characteristics, firms in our sample operate in similar environments, and data on their operations were gathered using the same questionnaire. These points suggest that conditions for applying matching methods are met, so the results should be credible in the current context. Among several matching methods that may be used to create suitable control groups (Heckman, Ichimura, and Todd 1997), results based on kernel matching and nearest-neighbor matching methods are presented in panels 3 and 4 of Table 4.14. Both results reveal a similar pattern. There is no discernible difference between the mean value-added for treatment and control groups. Once again, the pattern of results indicates that telecommunications access does not influence the economic performance of firms.

Conclusion

The majority of firms surveyed for this study used telecommunications services quite intensively in their business operations. About 80 percent of the firms were fixed telephone subscribers, reporting usage of almost 90 calls per month as of 2000. Based on interest in subscription and willingness-to-pay, their unmet demand for telephone subscription appeared to be substantial. About 90 percent of the households/firms that were not telephone subscribers expressed their willingness to pay the current telephone installation fee and fixed monthly charge for telephone services.

Despite these patterns of adoption and usage, formal analysis does not support the argument that access to telecommunications services enhances economic performance in firms. Regardless of the measure of economic performance (sales or value-added per worker) or the methodology, no impact on economic performance was detected through the use of telecommunications. Explanations for these results are the same as those provided in the previous two case studies in this chapter. First, data-related reasons may be relevant, such as measurement errors in the independent variables. Second, given that most firms had had telecommunications services for at least three years, any competitive advantage may have already been competed away, in which case cross-section data would not detect an impact. Third, teledensity in Laos was very low (0.75 in 2000), and it is likely that access to telecommunications services only begins to exert a discernible impact on economic performance once a minimum density has been reached (see Röller and Waverman 2001 and Chapter 2 of this volume). Fourth, while access to telecommunications services enhances information flows, conversion of this information into discernible economic effects requires the presence of supporting and complementary infrastructure, such as roads (Canning and Bennathan 2000; Van de Walle 2000). It is possible that the poor road and transport system in rural Laos impedes the effect of improved communications. Finally, it may be that access to telecommunications does not exert a quantitative impact but rather a qualitative impact, which is not captured by the indicators used in this study.

Regardless of the reasons for the lack of impact, the analysis in this study reveals that telecommunications have been widely adopted by firms in rural Laos. Firms call frequently and use telecommunications as a primary means of gathering information on input and output markets. Despite the absence of a discernible impact on sales/value-added per worker, there appears to be a substantial effective demand for telephone services. Using this demand as a measure of the usefulness of telecommunications service, it is clear that the majority of firms in Laos view access to telecommunications as an essential business tool.

ICT and Export Performance: The Case of Garment Manufacturing Enterprises in India
Kaushalesh Lal

In recent years, outward-looking policies in many developing countries have played a crucial role in their social and industrial development. Comparative advantages based on natural resource endowments have been replaced by the "acquired advantage" (Helleiner 1995). Many developing countries have been able to acquire or strengthen their comparative advantage by adopting new technologies and developing the skills to use them effectively (Noland 1997). The role of technology and skill in influencing international trade has been emphasized, particularly in terms of the importance of technological differences (Harrigan 1995; Moreno 1997). Moreno (1997) found that technology had a significant effect on the evolution of Spanish industrial exports, suggesting that nonprice factors such as product quality and differentiation exert a significant influence on international competitiveness. A partial survey of literature by Bedi (1999) on the role of ICT in economic development suggests numerous benefits from its adoption, including increased employment and productivity, consumer surplus, and improved product quality.

Recognizing the contribution of ICT to the operations and performance of firms, this case study focuses on the impact of ICT on international trade. The effect of ICT adoption on export performance is explored with reference to garment manufacturing SMEs in India. Linkages in the adoption of ICT in SMEs and large firms are also considered. See Appendix 4C for a presentation of the theoretical framework devised for this case study, along with the major hypothesis tested.

The Data

Data for the study were drawn from 74 garment-manufacturing firms covering two-thirds of all garment-manufacturing firms in Okhla, Delhi (randomly chosen from a directory published by the Okhla Entrepreneurs Association). Although garment manufacturing occurs in four separate areas of India, the pattern of ICT adoption is deemed to be the same in all; this was confirmed by numerous firms in the study sample that had operations in more than one area. Hence, the sample is considered to be representative of garment-manufacturing firms in India. Several qualitative and quantitative variables, such as intensity of ICT adoption, profit margins, skill intensity, wage rates, quality of raw materials, and entrepreneurial abilities, were needed for the analysis. A semi-structured questionnaire was prepared to collect historical, financial, employment, and technological data from the sample firms. Data on performance and international orientation as well as qualitative data on the entrepreneurial abilities of the firms' managing directors were also collected.

Entrepreneurial abilities were viewed in terms of the importance the managing director assigned to flexibility in product design, international competitiveness, delivery schedule, and fabric-saving advantage of IT.[24] The managing director's opinions regarding these variables were expected to play a significant role in influencing the export performance of sample firms. The fabric-saving advantage was considered to be crucial for price-competitiveness, whereas other variables augmented the nonprice competitiveness of firms. The cost of fabric accounts for roughly 50 percent of the total manufacturing cost of a garment. It was found by Hoffman and Rush (1988) that IT tools used for cutting the fabric could save up to 10 percent of the fabric cost.

For the purpose of analyzing the export performance, firms were classified based on their market preferences. Firms that operated in domestic markets were classified as domestic-market-oriented units (DMOUs); firms that operated solely in export markets were classified as export-oriented units (EOUs); and firms that operated in both markets were classified as domestic-market and export-oriented units (DMEOUs). At the time of the survey, garment-manufacturing firms in India had mainly adopted ICT in the design and preassembly stages of the manufacturing process. The specific technologies in use were

1. integrated management information systems (IMIS);
2. computer-aided design (CAD) integrated with marker maker systems (MMS);
3. CAD integrated with high-resolution scanners, used for embroidery; and

---

24. Fabric-saving in the sense that computerized cutting maximizes fabric use.

4. Internet and email, used to obtain information and communicate with suppliers and foreign buyers.

Aside from quantitative data, we also collected qualitative data to assess the impact of entrepreneurship on the performance of firms. The qualitative variables include the academic qualification of managing directors, the importance assigned by managing directors to flexibility in designing garments, the fabric-saving advantage of IT, product quality, proximity of raw material suppliers, international competition, market networks, and delivery schedule. Opinions on these variables were measured on a three-point scale, on the basis that the variable (1) was not important, (2) was important, and (3) was very important. With regard to the qualifications of managing directors, those with education below the postgraduate level were assigned the lowest rank, 1. Managing directors with postgraduate degrees were given the next higher rank, 2; and those with bachelors degrees in accounting, engineering, and law, for example, or masters degrees in business administration were assigned the highest rank, 3.

Results

A simple analysis of the data collected indicated that, at the time of the survey, firms were using ICT tools mainly at the preassembly stage for design, grading, and marker making. CAD systems manufactured by Gerber Garment Technology (GGT), a United States–based company, were very popular in India. Fourteen sample firms were using the GGT system; however, a few sample firms were using simple CAD systems. Firms that manufactured garments with embroidery were using an IT-based system that consisted of a very-high-resolution CAD system integrated with a scanner. Many of the sample firms were using an integrated management information system (IMIS) for office automation. Five sample firms were not using ICT, even for office automation.

Firms were also using email and Internet facilities to obtain the latest market trends and to download the designs provided by the foreign buyers. The Government of India had encouraged access to the Internet by providing such facilities at nominal cost. It was found to be very useful for smaller firms that could not afford email and Internet access at their plant premises. Internet facilities in Delhi were provided by the Apparel Export Promotion Council, and in Tiruppur by National Informatics Centre. Firms were categorized in three groups depending on the intensity of ICT use. Firms that were not using ICT (even for office automation) were given the lowest rank, 1, and are identified as non-IT firms. Firms that were using IT in nonproduction activities only were assigned the next higher rank, 2, and are identified as IT-n firms. Firms that were using IT tools in production as well as nonproduction activities were assigned the highest rank, 3, and are identified as IT-p firms.

The managing directors of several firms stated that they also had a plant at Tiruppur, Mumbai, and Bangalore and that the pattern of ICT adoption did not

TABLE 4.15 Correlation matrix

Variable	EXP_INT	IT_DUMMY	WRATE	FLEX	RAWMAT	IT_INV
EXP_INT	1.00					
IT_DUMMY	0.455284					
WRATE	0.261437	0.202945				
FLEX	0.355836	0.395481	0.088134			
RAWMAT	0.265657	−0.07146	−0.11125	0.166582		
IT_INV	0.594707	0.721605	0.236995	0.471776	0.05729	1.00

SOURCE: Specified and calculated by authors from primary survey data (2000).

differ significantly among garment manufacturing clusters in India. Therefore, sample firms may be treated as representative of Indian garment manufacturing firms.

Impacts of ICT on Performance. Following the methodology proposed in Appendix 4A for measuring the impact of ICT on performance when the dependant variable is a ratio, we construct a model to assess the impact of independent variables on export intensity. Following several existing studies (Hughes 1986; Aitken, Hanson, and Harrison 1997; Moreno 1997), we estimate the impact of the IT adoption level (IT_DUMMY), the monthly wages paid (WRATE), the ratio of raw material expenditure to sales turnover (RAWMAT), and the design flexibility (FLEX) on export intensity (EXP_INT), measured as the ratio of exports to total sales turnover.

The correlation matrix of all the variables is presented in Table 4.15, the results of the estimation using Tobit are presented in Table 4.16, and the results of a third estimation replacing the IT_DUMMY with investment in ICT are presented in Table 4.17.

The intensity of ICT adoption was shown to play a significant role in the export performance of the sample firms (see Table 4.16). Wakelin (1997) found that export performance is determined by firm- and industry-specific characteristics. The arguments neither dispute the factor intensity theory nor challenge the theory of comparative or competitive advantage. Nevertheless, technological

TABLE 4.16 Maximum likelihood estimated with Tobit model (IT_DUMMY)

Variable	Coefficient	T-ratio	Significance	Variable label
IT_DUMMY	0.80268	4.062	0.00005	Level of IT adoption
RAWMAT	1.48140	2.559	0.01051	Quality of raw material
FLEX	0.60270	2.510	0.01207	Flexibility in design
WRATE	0.64418	2.371	0.01773	Wages per month
		Log-likelihood: 60.70238		

SOURCE: Specified and calculated by authors from primary survey data (2000).

TABLE 4.17 Maximum likelihood estimated with Tobit model (investment in ICT)

Variable	Coefficient	T-ratio	Significance	Variable label
IT_INVESTMENT	0.07745	1.727	0.08415	IT Investment
RAWMAT	1.34760	2.103	0.03549	Quality of raw material
FLEX	0.58923	2.128	0.03337	Flexibility in design
WRATE	0.59078	1.918	0.05516	Wages per month
		Log-likelihood: 66.95676		

SOURCE: Specified and calculated by authors from primary survey data (2000).

innovation and adoption have been widely used to explain variations in export performance. In science-based sectors, for example, innovative capacity is highly important, whereas in labor-intensive industries, such as clothing and foot-wear, technologies are the crucial factor (Freeman 1982; Pavitt 1984; Hirsch and Bijaoui 1985; Dosi, Pavitt, and Soete 1990; Abd-el-Rahman 1991). Considering the labor-intensive nature of the garment industry, the findings of this study are consistent with existing literature that explains differential trade performance in terms of technological capacity.

The results show that the EOU expenditure on raw materials was higher than DMOU expenditure, implying better quality raw materials and consequently better quality products overall (Keesing and Wolf 1981; Hoffman and Rush 1988). Product quality generally affects export performance (Cohen 1975). For example, a foreign buyer in the garment industry might insist on the use of a particular fabric or raw material not manufactured in India, requiring the EOU to use imported materials. This is an issue that a firm in the domestic market would not encounter. NEDO (1971) and Keesing and Wolf (1981) predicted that the garment manufacturing industry may experience a shift from developed to developing countries because of the abundant unskilled labor available in developing countries—although the quality of the fabric may also play a role. These arguments are supported by the findings of this study.

The impact of wage differences on export performance has been analyzed by several scholars, leading to the conclusion that export-oriented firms pay higher wages than other firms (Wakelin 1997). Bernard and Jensen (1997), who included U.S. apparel-manufacturing firms in their sample, obtained the same results. Findings are also similar in the case of Indian garment-manufacturing firms. Wage differences can be attributed to the unique skill of the designers, pattern-makers, and graders employed, most of whom inherited the profession along with the necessary levels of skill and creativity. As a result, these individuals command high salaries, and, understandably, EOUs cannot afford to lose them. In addition, although garment manufacturing firms in India rarely use IT in the assembly of garments, they do employ highly skilled and efficient tailors to ensure quality. For these reasons, EOUs must pay higher wages to their employees.

The results also show that the managing directors of EOUs considered flexibility in garment design to be very important. This is not surprising, given that design trends in international markets change far more rapidly than those in the domestic market. The significant contribution of CAD in increasing flexibility in product design has been reported by many scholars (Faulkner 1980; Hoffman and Rush 1988; Lal 1996). Patternmakers and graders can easily modify patterns for garments on their computers using a CAD system, and new patterns can be sized and reproduced with a minimum of computer keystrokes. Similarly, patterns are graded with the use of a mechanized plotter that traces the pattern onto mounted paper rather than through a costly and methodical process of manually tracing cardboard templates. EOUs could not survive using such manual methods.

ICT Adoption: The Linkages between Large Firms and SMEs. The intensity of ICT adoption is significantly higher in export-oriented firms compared with those operating in domestic markets. The positive relationship between the size of a firm's operation and its export intensity suggests that large firms have adopted more advanced ICT. This does not reveal, however, whether the adoption of ICT by large firms is linked to the intensity of adoption of ICT in smaller firms, nor does it demonstrate the effect of ICT on employment in a labor-intensive industry like garment manufacturing. To explore these two issues, two firms were selected from the top five garment-exporting firms in India since 1991. A detailed technological profile and performance of these firms follows.

Gokaldas Images. At the time of the survey for this study, Gokaldas Images was one of the top three garment-manufacturing firms in India, having maintained the number two position for several years. Both the corporate office and 18 manufacturing plants were located in Bangalore, and performance had consistently improved since the firm's establishment in 1972. The firm had used CAD/CAM (computer-aided design and manufacture) since 1995, and a local area network (LAN) had been installed in the corporate office in 1997, along with email access. All the manufacturing plants were connected via an intranet using an integrated services digital network (ISDN). The firm adopted the latest garment-manufacturing technology as it became available. A general sewing data (GSD) system had been imported from the United Kingdom in 1999 and installed and integrated into the firm's intranet—a strategy that was deemed highly useful in planning and monitoring manufacturing activities among the various plants.

The firm had recently implemented a form of enterprise resource planning (ERP) software, STAGE, which had been exclusively developed in India for export-oriented garment-manufacturing firms. The firm's management believed that the electronic procurement and electronic data interchange (EDI) modules of STAGE software were likely to have a significant impact on the firm's operations. The Internet was used to interact with foreign buyers and other business partners. Despite severe competition in international markets, especially from China, the firm had been able to improve its performance. The compound annual growth rate (CAGR) of sales turnover has been 19.56 percent since 1994/95, while employment has increased at 10.49 percent per year over the same period. Sales turnover was Rs. 1,506.97 million in 2000/01 (US$32.6 million). The firm's management believed that survival in international markets very likely depended on the use of the latest technologies; they did not report any adverse impact on the firm through the adoption of new ICT.

The firm did report, however, that the adoption of ICT in nonmanufacturing activities had created pressures in obtaining appropriate raw materials and accessories from their suppliers, so the firm had arranged to have email and Internet facilities installed in the supplier's premises to improve the coordination of activities. Subcontracting is very common in the garment-manufacturing industry in India, and a number of small firms provide specialized services to large export firms. Although the intensity of ICT adoption by small firms is comparatively low, this firm had influenced its supplier to adopt ICT.

Sonal Garments. This multiplant firm began operations in 1976. As of 2000/01, it had manufacturing plants in Bangalore, New Delhi, Salem, and Tiruppur. The firm's corporate office, located in Mumbai, was fully computerized, including a LAN, but the manufacturing plants were not linked via an intranet. Business activities were being coordinated through the Internet, and the firm had a Web site. The firm used remote login technology to interact with foreign buyers. The firm's electronic business technology consisted of the LAN, the Internet, a CAD/CAM system, and the company Web site. The management of the firm admitted that pressure from buyers had been the driving force in the adoption of the new technologies. The firm used the Internet effectively to search for new buyers and submit bids for new contracts. Management believed that these technologies had made a visible contribution to the firm's performance. Sales turnover was Rs. 1,088.35 million in 2000/01 (US$23.5 million), having grown at 8.41 percent per year since 1994/95; the CAGR of employment was 4.45 percent per year over the same period.

Management claimed that, in addition to contributing to product design and employee productivity, the adoption of remote login technologies had reduced transaction costs by around 30–40 percent. The company had not been able to link its manufacturing plants because of their geographic distribution; doing so would require an investment in telecommunications at a magnitude that was unlikely to be economically viable. Like all the sample firms, Sonal did not perceive any negative impact on either the firm or its workforce from the adoption of ICT. Sonal had also engaged several small subcontracting firms to supply raw materials and accessories. Unlike the situation with Gokaldas, Sonal's suppliers were located in different cities, so email and Internet access were considered imperative to daily operations. Sonal's management did not consider that they had compelled their suppliers to adopt these technologies, but rather that the majority of subcontractors had made the decision themselves. Activities related to the purchase of raw materials were centrally monitored through the firm's corporate office, an efficiency that would not have been possible had the subcontractors not adopted the necessary ICT.

Conclusion

Results of the analysis in this case study show that the intensity of ICT adoption is the most significant variable influencing export performance of firms. Export-oriented garment-manufacturing firms appeared to have adopted more advanced ICT to meet international standards for product quality and design flexibility. Other important variables influencing firms' export performance were expenditure on raw materials (used as a proxy for product quality) and wage rates. The importance that managing directors assigned to flexibility in product design was also significant. These results are consistent with earlier studies (Soete 1987; Hoffman and Rush 1988; Bernard and Jensen 1997).

The case studies on two of the top five garment-exporting firms suggest that the benefits of ICT adoption can be better harnessed when business partners (suppliers and buyers) also adopt relevant technologies. Based on these results, in order to remain competitive in international markets, Indian garment-manufacturing firms should adopt the latest ICT available. As of 2000/01, 74 percent of exports were in countries where India had a quota (as established under a multifiber arrangement [MFA] in 1974; WTO 1996). The MFA set quotas for different categories of apparel and textile imports to the United States and European Union with the result that these markets were reserved for Indian products. This protection has been phased out, however, and ceased as of January 1, 2005, in accordance with negotiations under the Agreement on Textiles and Clothing at the Uruguay Round of the WTO. Consequently, the importance of appropriate IT-based production systems has increased, making stronger adoption and use of ICT a valuable step in enhancing competitiveness.

Appendix 4A: Overview of Methodology

Several methods can be used to examine the interaction between ICT and firm performance. All methods have the same objective, but they measure performance differently: through the impact on sales, specified firm performance indicators, and performance ratios, and through the use of matching methods to measure changes in performance.

Measuring the Impact of ICT on Sales

Well-established literature uses the canonical Cobb–Douglas production function to examine the effect of ICT-related inputs on firm output (sales).[25] While this approach may be criticized for ignoring the potential endogeneity be-

---

25. See, for example, Brynjolfsson and Hitt (1996) for a review and a recent application, relying mainly on data from the United States.

tween some of the input variables and output, it permits comparisons and serves as a useful starting point for further investigation. Accordingly, a short-run Cobb–Douglas production function is first estimated. This production function is as close as possible to the type of specifications that have been used to evaluate the links between firm performance and ICT (Brynjolfsson and Hitt 2000b; Söderling 2000; Söderbom and Teal 2001),[26] that is, we estimate the equation:

$$Q_i = \varepsilon^{\beta_0} \prod_{j=1}^{n} X_j^{\beta_j}. \tag{1}$$

This equation expresses the production level (Q) as a function of all the different inputs (X) that intervene in the production process. Taking logarithms, this equation can be easily estimated as follows:

$$\ln(Q_i) = \beta_0 + \beta_1 \ln(L_i) + \beta_2 \ln(K_i) + \beta_3 \ln(ICT_i) + \ldots + \mu_i. \tag{2}$$

Since we are interested in the impact of investment in ICT on productivity, we divide capital into ICT capital (ICT) and other capital (K). A shorter function specification would only include L, for the firm's labor force, K for its capital assets, ICT for its level of ICT, plus a random disturbance (μ). The βs are the coefficients to be estimated, representing production input elasticities (the percentage change in the production level resulting from a percentage change of an input).[27] Similar results can be obtained through more complex models including additional production inputs or the disaggregated inputs, such as the separation of total labor into skilled and unskilled categories. Finally, for Cobb–Douglas production functions to be satisfied (and the results correct), all βs must sum to one, representing a constant return of scale function.

Measuring the Impact of ICT on Performance Indicators

As mentioned earlier, specification (1) can suffer from several drawbacks. First, it ignores the potential endogeneity between expenditures on variable inputs and output. Second, although the specification does control for current expenditure it would be interesting to account for firm size (differences in the number of employees per firm). Finally, a performance indicator could well be a more appropriate measure of economic performance than sales turnover. Using value-added as a more appropriate measure of economic performance than sales, a short-run Cobb–Douglas function can be defined as follows:

$$VA = AK^\alpha L^\gamma, \tag{3}$$

where VA is value-added (output less intermediate expenditure), A represents the level of technology (ICT), K stands for the capital assets, and L is the

---

26. The Cobb–Douglas functional form is assumed for simplicy and to address the scarcity of information.

27. The coefficient of interest in this case is β_3.

number of employees. This equation can easily be estimated by dividing Equation (3) by L and taking logs:

$$\ln(VA/L) = \ln A + \alpha \ln(K/L) + (\alpha + \gamma - 1)\ln L. \tag{4}$$

If the production function exhibits constant returns to scale (a Cobb–Douglas assumption), the coefficient on $\ln L$ will be zero. Consequently, Equation (4) may be rewritten as[28]

$$\ln(VA/L) = \ln A + \alpha \ln(K/L), \tag{5}$$

where $\ln A$ represents ICT and is a function of observed variables, such as access to telecommunications services (ATS), and unobserved variables are represented by a random error term, μ. With these adjustments Equation (5) may be rewritten as

$$\ln(VA/L) = \beta_0 + \beta_1 ATS + \alpha \ln(K/L) + \mu. \tag{6}$$

While Equation (6) is an improvement over Equation (1), it still suffers from a potential endogeneity problem. The state of telecommunications access of individual firms and value-added may be jointly determined. One strategy to tackle this problem is to include variables that are likely to influence access to telecommunications services in Equation (6). If access to telecommunications services depends only on observed variables, then their inclusion in Equation (6) should reduce any endogeneity problems. The augmented specification may be represented as

$$\ln(VA/L) = \beta_0 + \beta_1 ATS + \beta_2 X + \alpha \ln(K/L) + \mu, \tag{7}$$

where X is a vector of the three additional variables.

Measuring the Impact of ICT on Performance When the Dependent Variable Is a Ratio

Similar to the first estimation presented in this appendix, a model for the effect of an n set of variables on firm performance can be described as follows:

$$Y_i = \beta_0 + \sum_1^n \beta_i \ln(X_i) + \mu_i. \tag{8}$$

where Y represents a performance indicator calculated as a ratio of exports to total sales turnover, and X represents all variables that have an effect on performance, such as level of IT adoption. The main difference between this specification and the one above is that the dependant variable only takes values between

---

28. Specifications that include log-labor consistently show that the coefficient on this variable is not different from zero. This finding supports the hypothesis of constant returns to scale. Accordingly, we rewrite Equation (3) excluding the log-labor term.

1 and 0. It is therefore necessary to apply a censored regression model to obtain the correct outcomes (a Tobit model).

Measuring Impact Using Matching Methods

An alternative approach that may be used to estimate the effect of ICT on firm performance uses matching methods. So far, we have treated telecommunications access as a three-state variable (that is, no access, access, and level of IT adoption), but it is possible that differences in economic performance emanate mainly from whether or not a firm is a telephone subscriber. If this is the case, it would be appropriate to treat telecommunications access as a two-state variable and to divide firms into those with telephone subscriptions and those without.

Hence, the approach is to compare the average value-added per employee of firms (as an instrument for a possible outcome of access to IT) with telecommunications access (the treatment group) to that of firms without telecommunications access (the control group). This approach works well if selection into treatment and control groups depends mainly on observed characteristics and the distribution of unobserved attributes is the same across treatment and control groups (for details see Rosenbaum and Rubin 1985 and Heckman, Ichimura, and Todd 1997). There are two additional conditions that help to ensure consistent comparisons: information on treatment and control groups should be gathered using the same questionnaire, and the two groups operate in a common environment.

Appendix 4B: Supplementary Tables, the Case of Small-Scale Industry in India

See tables on pages 218, 220–226.

Appendix 4C: Methodology and Theoretical Framework: The Case of Garment Manufacturing in India

It is argued that the export performance of firms is significantly influenced by internal and external factors. These factors induce changes in production processes that result in efficient utilization of inputs and improvements in product quality. Since EOUs are expected to use high-quality raw materials to compete in world markets, the unit isoquants of EOUs and DMOUs are likely to be different. We first theoretically discuss the impact of internal and external factors on isocost and isoquant curves of garment-manufacturing firms. External factors are the tariff structures of buyer countries, the MFA quota, and technological profile of firms in competing countries. A strong technological profile of competing firms—that is, the use of latest technologies—is likely to compel Indian firms to adopt similar tools. Therefore, the degree of adoption of ICT is viewed

TABLE 4B.1 Basic statistics

Statistic	Labor productivity, 1998/99 (US$)	Growth of labor productivity, 1997/98–1998/99 (percent)	Net profit margin, 1998/99 (percentage of turnover)	Growth of net profit 1996/97–1998/99 (percent)	Average monthly wage in administration and management, 1998/99 (US$)	Percentage of graduates in management and administration, 1998/99	Annual turnover, 1998/99 (US$)	Growth of annual turnover, 1996/97–1998/99 (percent)
Number of observations	251	231	244	204	259	249	260	229
Mean	8,787	9.2	6.9	–2.2	90.8	68.7	257,111	13.4
Median	5,942	3.9	7.3	0.0	83.2	80.0	118,850	5.0
Standard deviation	9,929	36.7	15.5	14.7	36.7	36.0	514,170	83.4
Minimum	354	–60.0	–166.7	–173.3	32.1	0.0	2,481	–94.0
Maximum	81,497	213.0	40.0	30.0	237.7	100.0	5,704,778	1,100.0

SOURCE: Compiled by author from primary survey data (1999).

as an external factor. The impact of tariffs and MFA quotas will be the same on all firms. Hence, these factors are not included in the model. Internal factors are basically the production factor intensities and prices, the quality of raw materials, and export subsidies. Being the same for all firms, export subsidies are also not included in the model. The model concentrates mainly on the impact of intensity of ICT adoption, the quality of raw materials, and the abundant unskilled labor on the export performance of firms.

Intensity of ICT Adoption

The technological evolution occurring in this industry over time has created tremendous pressure on Indian firms to adopt new technologies. The technological development in the world market mainly affects export-oriented firms. Garment-exporting firms are compelled to adopt new technologies to remain competitive in global markets. Figure 4C.1 presents the unit isoquant curves of EOUs and DMOUs in *H-L* space, where skilled labor/human capital is *H;* and unskilled labor, *L*. Unit isoquant curves of EOUs are shown by IQ_{xi} (i = 1,2), whereas IQ_d is the unit isoquant curve of DMOUs. The unit isocost lines are indicated by IC_j (j = 1,2).

If r and w are payments for skilled and unskilled workers, then the unit isocost line can be written as

$$1 = rH + wL \text{ or } H = 1/r - (w/r)L.$$

If factor intensities do not change, and assuming a price equal to the marginal cost and constant returns, the tangential unit isocost line will represent the equilibrium.

As can be seen in Figure 4C.1, the line joining points 1 and 2 is the unit isocost line at initial equilibrium. In terms of export-oriented firms, suppose that EOUs adopt ICT tools that both improve quality and increase the productivity of labor. The resulting unit isoquant curve of these firms shifts inward. The new isoquant curve of EOUs is shown by IQ_{x2}. This results in a reduction of unskilled labor in export-oriented units. The new equilibrium is attained at points 3 and 4. Therefore, as the result of ICT adoption, the slope of the new unit isocost, IC_2, decreases. Export-oriented units may improve or retain their share in the export market due to lower production costs and better quality products. However, the impact on DMOUs is akin to that of an increased supply of unskilled workers. This is because the reduction in demand of unskilled labor by EOUs leads to an excess supply of unskilled workers. Mathematically, this can be represented as follows:

$$|(-w/r)| > |(-w'/r')| \Leftrightarrow w/r > w'/r',$$

where w' and r' are the costs of one unskilled and skilled worker, respectively, in new equilibrium. Since $w' < w$ and $r' > r$, the gap between factor prices increases.

TABLE 4B.2 Comparison of mean ranks

Type of technology	Status/ adoption time	Labor productivity, 1998/99 (US$)	Growth of labor productivity, 1997/98– 1998/99 (percent)	Net profit margin, 1998/99 (percent of turnover)
Comparisons between user and non-user groups				
Fax machine	Non-use/use	102/144**	122/112	109/117
Pager	Non-use/use	119/140**	117/113	112/115
Cellular phone	Non-use/use	111/155**	119/109	109/121
Computer	Non-use/use	109/136**	125/111	109/116
Email	Non-use/use	115/147**	118/113	115/111
Comparisons between user groups according to time of adoption				
Fax machine	Until 1992/1993–96/1997	64/66/59	55/56/66	72/57/71*
Pager	1994–95/1996–97/1998	54/44/38	47/43/33	51/45/36
Cellular phone	1995/1996–97/1998	45/47/43	45/43/38	51/44/46
Email	1995–96/1997/1998	50/55/35**	33/37/37	42/41/41
Comparison between usage levels				
Telephone		79	93	85
+ Fax (office use)		84	125	103
+ Fax machine		99	102	102
+ Computer		110	95	103
+ Email		121**	88	

SOURCE: Calculated by authors from primary survey data (1999).

NOTES: *Indicates significance at the 10 percent level; **indicates significance at the 5 percent level.

Intensity of Unskilled Labor

Isocost and isoquant curves of EOUs and MDOUs are depicted in Figure 4C.2. IQ_x is the unit isoquant of EOUs, and IQ_{dj} ($j = 1,2$) represents the isoquant of MDOUs. IC_k ($k = 1,2$) represents the two different unit isocost lines. IC_1 represents the initial equilibrium.

The availability of excess unskilled labor reduces the price of L, that is, w. Consequently, there is an outward shift of the unit isoquant curve of DMOUs. The new equilibrium is represented by isocost line IC_2. The new unit isocost is traced by joining points 1 and 3. As shown in Figure 4C.2, IC_2 is flatter than IC_1. Consequently, the relative factor price (unskilled labor) is lower in the new equilibrium. We may conclude, therefore, that the abundance of unskilled labor leads to substantial wage differences between the two types of firms. The net effect is the greater disparity in wages and a significantly different level of ICT adoption in EOUs and DMOUs. While describing the theoretical framework,

Growth of net profit from 1996/97 to 1998/99 (percentage points)	Average monthly wage in administration and management, 1998/99 (US$)	Percentage of graduates in management and administration, 1998/99	Annual turnover, 1998/99 (US$)	Growth of annual turnover, 1996/97– 1998/99 (percent)
95/108	121/136	121/128	86/162**	102/124**
90/126**	127/135	125/125	114/164**	103/139**
94/118	124/140*	120/134	108/170**	102/138**
93/107**	122/134	118/128	90/151**	102/122**
101/105	123/144**	125/125	114/162**	111/122
55/50/68	72/72/66	56/66/71	67/74/57	58/59/69
43/36/39	44/49/45	42/45/51	49/47/43	41/42/43
37/32/41	64/44/55	49/48/44	69/47/47	50/45/40
34/35/36	43/45/41	45/49/37	54/55/37**	34/44/37
72	92	105	53	79
78	112	73	69	80
90	108	113	100	101
92	109	108	128	106
89	119	106	137**	102**

we assume that the growth of demand of ready-made garments is less than the growth of unskilled labor in the economy:

$$\frac{\partial L}{\partial t}\left(\frac{1}{L_b}\right) \geq \frac{\partial D}{\partial t}\left(\frac{1}{D_b}\right),$$

where L_b and D_b denote the amount of unskilled labor available and the total demand for garments in the base year, respectively.

The theoretical framework discussed above considers the role of adoption of ICT, the quality of raw materials, and the wage difference in export performance. However, the model assumes that other variables, such as firm size and entrepreneurship, remain constant. In the empirical analysis, these variables have also been included.

Hypotheses

Based on the theoretical framework previously described the following hypotheses are formulated.

TABLE 4B.3 Test statistics for independence of user and non-user sample

Type of technology	Parametric and nonparametric tests	Labor productivity, 1998/99 (Rs.)	Growth of labor productivity, 1997/98– 1998/99 (percent)	Net profit/loss as a share of turnover, 1998/99 (percent)
Fax	Mann-Whitney U	5,169	5,934	5,753
machine	Wilcoxon W	10,947	14,979	10,031
	z	−4.457	−1.128	−0.854
	Asymp. sig. (two-tailed)	0.000***	0.259	0.393
Pager	Mann-Whitney U	5,811	5,723	5,691
	Wilcoxon W	20,176	8,726	16,422
	z	−2.072	−0.431	−0.318
	Asymp. sig. (two-tailed)	0.038**	0.666	0.751
Cellular	Mann-Whitney U	4,563	5,479	5,358
telephone	Wilcoxon W	18,258	8,639	15,369
	z	−4.638	−1.091	−1.335
	Asymp. sig. (two-tailed)	0.000***	0.275	0.182
Computer	Mann-Whitney U	5,668	5,383	5,214
	Wilcoxon W	9,673	16,558	7,842
	z	−2.801	−1.494	−0.722
	Asymp. sig. (two-tailed)	0.005***	0.135	0.470
Email	Mann-Whitney U	5,323	5,666	5,613
	Wilcoxon W	19,018	8,669	8,773
	z	−3.246	−0.549	−0.414
	Asymp. sig. (two-tailed)	0.001***	0.583	0.679

SOURCE: Calculated by authors from primary survey data (1999).
NOTES: *Indicates significance at the 10 percent level; **indicates significance at the 5 percent level; ***indicates significance at the 1 percent level. Rs. indicates rupees.

Degree of IT Adoption (IT_LEVEL). Two estimates of this variable have been considered in the analysis. One is the investment in ICT; the other is an ICT intensity dummy. The dummy variable is defined as

$$IT\_DUMMY = \begin{cases} 1 & \text{for IT-p firms} \\ 0 & \text{otherwise} \end{cases}.$$

The model discussed in the theoretical framework in Appendix 4B showed that the adoption of more advanced ICT tools results in an inward shift of the isoquant curve of export-oriented firms. This in turn enables the firms to remain globally competitive and improve or retain their market share in international markets. The effect of technological progress on international trade has long been incorporated into trade models (Posner 1961; Hufbauer 1966; Krugman

Change in profit margin, 1996/97–1998/99 (percentage points)	Average monthly wage for employees in administration and management (Rs.)	Share of graduates in management and administration (percent)	Log turnover, 1998/99	Turnover growth, 1996/97–1998/99 (percent)
4,409	7,059	7,052	3,436	5,078
7,895	12,312	12,305	9,214	9,449
−1.487	−1.618	−0.842	−7.962	−2.532
0.137	0.106	0.400	0.000***	0.011**
3,058	7,190	6,986	4,646	3,989
11,836	21,386	10,727	19,697	15,617
−4.225	−0.793	−0.046	−5.034	−3.936
0.000***	0.428	0.963	0.000***	0.000***
3,612	6,861	6,306	4,088	4,082
12,657	19,902	19,347	18,116	15,257
−2.706	−1.768	−1.514	−6.330	−3.931
0.007***	0.077*	0.130	0.000***	0.000***
3,974	6,812	6,380	4,032	4,886
6,252	10,817	9,950	8,037	8,126
−1.563	−1.322	−1.082	−6.221	−2.249
0.118	0.186	0.279	0.000***	0.025**
4,626	6,252	7,004	4,853	5,367
13,272	20,958	10,745	19,388	16,542
−0.388	−2.239	−0.011	−4.850	−1.241
0.698	0.025**	0.991	0.000***	0.215

1979; and Dosi, Pavitt, and Soete 1990). Technology variables included in factor proportion trade models have generally been considered very important in influencing trade patterns. However, scholars have considered different indicators of technology. Stem and Maskus (1981) used the ratio of research and development (R&D) expenditure to value-added as a proxy of the technology variable; Soete (1981) used the number of patents; whereas Wakelin (1997) considered the number of the firm's innovations as an indicator of the level of advanced technology used. All three studies, however, found technology to be very important in explaining the export performance of firms. In view of the theoretical and empirical evidence, we hypothesize that the degree of ICT adoption is likely to influence the export performance of firms.

Wage Rate (WRATE). The theoretical model suggests that wage rates are likely to be significantly different between EOUs and DMOUs due to the different skill levels required. Bernard and Jensen (1997) and Francois and Nelson (1998) show that export-oriented firms pay higher wages than others to attract

TABLE 4B.4 Kruskal–Wallis test for independence of user groups with different time of adoption

Type of technology	Kruskal–Wallis test	Labor productivity, 1998/99 (Rs.)	Growth of labor productivity, 1997/98–1998/99 (percent)	Net profit/loss as a share of turnover, 1998/99 (percent)
Fax	Chi^2	0.927	2.088	4.850
	df	2	2	2
	Significance	0.629	0.352	0.088*
Pager	Chi^2	3.823	3.586	3.127
	df	2	2	2
	Significance	0.148	0.166	0.209
Cellular telephone	Chi^2	0.373	0.983	0.320
	df	2	2	2
	Significance	0.830	0.612	0.852
Email	Chi^2	10.675	0.211	0.024
	df	2	2	2
	Significance	0.005***	0.900	0.988

SOURCE: Calculated by authors from primary survey data (1999).

NOTES: *Indicates significance at the 10 percent level; ***indicates significance at the 10 percent level. Rs. indicates rupees.

more highly skilled workers. These authors argue that trade is linked with shifts in wage rates. Bernard and Jensen (1997) found that the wage gap played a significant role for trade in U.S. manufacturing firms. In the Indian context, and particularly in the garment-manufacturing sector, a wage gap is likely to have a bearing on export performance. The creativity of designers' input makes a visible difference in the final product, so EOUs employ designers and graders with the highest levels of creative skill and pay them more than their peers in DMOUs. The high turnover of staff with creative skills is another reason for higher wages in EOUs. Hence, a close relationship is expected to exist between wages and firm export intensity.

Quality of Raw Material (RAWMAT). A recent study on export behavior of Mexican manufacturing firms by Aitken, Hanson, and Harrison (1997) found that the cost of raw materials was a significant influencing factor in the decision by firms of whether or not to export. Moreover, our theoretical framework is based on the assumption that EOUs and DMOUs use raw materials of differing quality. It was noticed in surveying firms that it was the buyers who determined the quality of the raw materials. Foreign buyers in the global market decided on the quality of the fabric used, whereas in domestic markets the (low-

Change in profit margin, 1996/97– 1998/99 (percentage points)	Average monthly wage for employees in administration and management (Rs.)	Percentage of graduates in management and administration	Log turnover, 1998/99	Turnover growth, 1996/97– 1998/99 (percent)
4.311	0.705	2.657	4.591	2.087
2	2	2	2	2
0.116	0.703	0.265	0.101	0.352
1.505	0.663	1.131	0.576	0.048
2	2	2	2	2
0.471	0.718	0.568	0.750	0.976
2.802	4.488	0.948	2.491	1.002
2	2	2	2	2
0.246	0.106	0.622	0.288	0.606
0.076	0.360	4.273	9.490	1.418
2	2	2	2	2
0.963	0.835	0.118	0.009***	0.492

and high-income) preferences of the entrepreneur determined the type and quality of raw materials used. In addition to fabric quality, foreign buyers often insisted on specific imported accessories (such as buttons and threads). Differences in the quality of raw materials substantially affect the cost of production, so the isoquant curves of EOUs and DMOUs also differ significantly. Therefore, as discussed theoretically, a positive relationship is hypothesized between export intensity and expenditure on raw materials.

Education Levels (EDU_LEVEL). This variable was measured as the ratio of workers with diplomas or degrees to the total number of workers employed by a firm. This category included employees with degrees in accounting and business administration (among others) and diplomas from an institute of fashion technology. A substantial amount of literature deals with employee qualifications and firm performance (Prais 1981; Bernard and Jensen 1997). Studies found that export-oriented firms employ more highly qualified workers. It is therefore expected that employee education levels will be an important influence on the export performance of firms.

Labor Productivity (LABPROD). During the survey it was found that many firms were involved in subcontracting; hence labor productivity was calculated as the ratio of value-added to total employment. A recent study by Robert and Wright (1998) found that the U.K. manufacturing sector was successfully competing with developing countries by increasing its overall productivity, and that

TABLE 4B.5 Kruskal–Wallis test for independence of ICT usage levels

Kruskal–Wallis test	Labor productivity, 1998/99 (Rs.)	Growth of labor productivity, 1997/98– 1998/99 (percent)	Net profit/loss as a share of turnover, 1998/99 (percent)	Change in profit margin, 1996/97– 1998/99 (percentage points)	Average monthly wage for employees in administration and management (Rs.)	Percentage of graduates in management and administration	Log turnover, 1998/99	Turnover growth, 1996/97– 1998/99 (percent)
Chi²	16.265	6.701	4.994	3.871	5.337	6.236	64.888	7.901
df	4	4	4	4	4	4	4	4
Significance	0.003***	0.153	0.288	0.424	0.254	0.182	0.000***	0.095***

SOURCE: Calculated by authors from primary survey data (1999).

NOTES: ***Indicates significance at the 1 percent level. Rs. indicates rupees.

FIGURE 4C.1 Exports, ICT, and wages

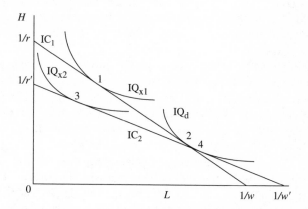

NOTE: H indicates skilled labor (human capital); L, unskilled labor (human capital); r and w, payments for skilled and unskilled workers, respectively; $IQ_{xi(i=1,2)}$ and IQ_d, unit isoquant curves for export-oriented units (EOUs) and domestic-market- and export-oriented units (DMEOUs), respectively; and $IC_{j(j=1,2)}$, the two unit isocost lines.

FIGURE 4C.2 Exports, factor intensity, and wages

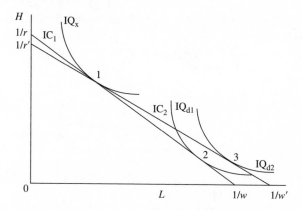

NOTE: H indicates skilled labor (human capital); L, unskilled labor (human capital); r and w, payments for skilled and unskilled workers, respectively; IQ_x and $IQ_{dj(j=1,2)}$, unit isoquant curves for export-oriented units (EOUs) and domestic-market-oriented units (DMOUs), respectively; and $IC_{k(k=1,2)}$, the two unit isocost lines.

developing-country firms needed to do the same to maintain their share of international markets. The study suggested that the main source of productivity gains would come from the use of new technologies. Wakelin (1997) found that labor productivity was positively correlated with exports. Export-oriented firms are therefore expected to be more productive.

Size (SIZE). Sales turnover was used as a proxy for firm size in export-related studies; however, sales turnover would not be representative of size in this study because many of the sample firms subcontracted activities. Therefore, the number of employees was chosen as a proxy for firm size. Several scholars (Hughes 1986; Lall 1986; Willmore 1992; Kumar and Siddharthan 1994; Wakelin 1997) have studied the export–size relationship, reporting mixed findings. Hughes (1986) finds a significant linear relationship between size and export performance, whereas Willmore (1992), Kumar and Siddharthan (1994), and Wakelin (1997) find an inverted U-shaped relationship. Kumar and Siddharthan (1994) argue that the emergence of an inverted U-shaped relationship could be attributed to an oligopoly among large firms in the domestic market. SMEs dominate in the low-technology garment-manufacturing industry in India, however, so a linear relationship is hypothesized between size and export performance for this study.

Opinion Variables (OPINIONS). Entrepreneurial abilities were also considered to be important factors that could influence the export performance of firms. Managing directors' ratings of the importance of the fabric-saving advantage of IT, flexibility in product design, international competition, and delivery schedule were considered as proxies for entrepreneurship. Hoffman and Rush (1988) also find these variables to be very important in the international trade of garments. Hence we hypothesize that entrepreneurial attitude may influence the export performance of firms.

References

Abd-el-Rahman, K. 1991. Firms' competitive and national comparative advantages as joint determinants of trade composition. *Weltwirtschaftliches Archiv* 127 (1): 83–98.

Aitken, B., G. H. Hanson, and A. E. Harrison. 1997. Spillovers, foreign investment, and export behavior. *Journal of International Economics* 43: 103–132.

Ascutia, R. C. 2002. Global crunch drives IT outsource boom. <ph.jobstreet.com/career/jobs123/ind2.htm>.

Avgerou, C. 2000. Information systems: What sort of science is it? *OMEGA International Journal of Management Science* 28: 567–579.

Bala Subrahmanya, M. H. 1998. Shifts in India's small industry policy. *Small Enterprise Development* 9: 35–45.

Beck, T., A. Demirgüç-Kunt, and R. Levine. 2003. Small and medium enterprises, growth, and poverty: Cross-country evidence. Policy Research Working Paper 3178. Washington, D.C.: World Bank.

Bedi, Arjun S. 1999. The role of information and communication technologies in economic development: A partial survey. Discussion Paper No. 7. Bonn: ZEF.

Bernard, A. B., and B. Jensen. 1997. Exports, skill upgrading, and the wage gap. *Journal of International Economics* 42: 3–31.

Bhatttacharjee, S., and S. Bhattacharya. 2000. Global supply chains: New models to enhance value through IT-enabled systems. In *World markets series business briefing on global electronic commerce.* Organized by the Committee for Trade, Industry and Enterprise Development, United Nations Economic Commission for Europe <www.wmrc.com/businessbriefing/pdf/ euroifpmm2001/reference/92.pdf>.

Biggs, T., and P. Srivastava. 1996. *Structural aspects of manufacturing in Sub-Saharan Africa.* Africa Technical Department Series, Discussion Paper No. 346. Washington, D.C.: World Bank.

Blili, S., and L. Raymond. 1993. Information technology—Threats and opportunities for small- and medium-sized enterprises. *International Journal of Information Management* 13: 439–448.

Brynjolfsson, E. 1993. The productivity paradox of information technology. *Communications of the ACM* 36 (12): 67–77.

Brynjolfsson, E., and L. Hitt. 1995. Information technology as a factor of production: The role of differences among firms in economics of innovation and new technology. *Economics of Innovation and New Technology* 3 (3–4): 183–199.

———. 1996. Paradox lost? Firm-level evidence on the returns to information systems spending. *Management Science* 42 (4): 541–558.

———. 2000a. Beyond computation: Information technology, organizational transformation, and business performance. *Journal of Economic Perspectives* 14 (4): 23–48.

———. 2000b. *Computing productivity: Firm level efficiency.* MIT Sloan School of Management/University of Pennsylvania.

Brynsolfsson, E., and S. Yang. 1996. Information technology and productivity: A review of the literature. *Advances in Computers* 43: 179–214.

Canning, D., and E. Bennathan. 2000. The social rate of return on infrastructure investments. Policy Research Working Paper 2390. Washington, D.C.: World Bank.

Cohen, B. 1975. *Multinational firms and Asian exports.* New Haven, Conn., U.S.A.: Yale University Press.

Dos Santos, B., and L. Sussman. 2000. Improving the return on IT investment. *International Journal of Information Management* 20: 429–440.

Dosi, G., K. Pavitt, and L. Soete. 1990. *The economics of technical change and international trade.* London: Harvester Wheatsheaf.

Faulkner, H. W. 1980. *The apparel industry's self-revival.* Boston: Applied Technology Management.

Francois, J. F., and D. Nelson. 1998. Trade, technology, and wages: General equilibrium mechanics. *The Economic Journal* 108: 1,483–1,499.

Freeman, C. 1982. *The economics of industrial innovation.* London: Frances Pinter.

Gillis, M., D. H. Perkins, M. Romer, and D. R. Snodgrass. 1996. *Economics of development,* 4th ed. New York: W. W. Norton.

Government of India. 2001. *Economic survey 2000/2001.* New Delhi.

Hallberg, K. 2000. A market-oriented strategy for small- and medium-scale enterprise. IFC Discussion Paper No. 40. Washington, D.C.: World Bank.

Haltiwanger, J. 1999. Job creation and destruction: Cyclical dynamics. In *Entrepreneurship, small- and medium-sized enterprises and the macroeconomy,* eds. Z. Acs, B. Carlsson, and C. Karlsson. New York: Cambridge University Press.

Harrigan, J. 1995. Technology, factor supplies and international specialization: Testing the neo-classical model. University of Pittsburgh, June. Mimeo.

Heckman, J., H. Ichimura, and P. Todd. 1997. Matching as an econometric evaluation estimator: evidence from evaluating a job training programme. *Review of Economic Studies* 64 (4): 605–654.

Helleiner, G. K., ed. 1995. *Manufacturing for exports in the developing world: Problems and possibilities.* London: Routledge.

Hirsch, S., and I. Bijaoui. 1985. R&D intensity and export performance: A micro view. *Weltwirtschaftliches Archiv* 121: 138–151.

Hitt, L. H. 1999. Information technology and firm boundaries: Evidence from panel data. *Information System Research* 20 (2): 121–142.

Hitt, L. H., and E. Brynjolfsson. 1996. Productivity, profit and consumer welfare: Three different measures of information technology's value. *MIS Quarterly* (June).

Hoffman, K., and H. Rush. 1988. *Micro-electronics and clothing: The impact of technical change on a global industry.* New York and London: Praeger.

Hufbauer, G. C. 1966. *Synthetic material and the theory of international trade.* London: Gerald Duckworth.

Hughes, K. 1986. *Exports and technology.* London and New York: Cambridge University Press.

IDC-India. 1999. Internet subscribers in India to Reach 530,000 by March 2000, says IDC. <www.idcindia.com/Pressrel/19Nov99.html>.

IFC (International Finance Corporation). 2000. *Paths out of poverty: The role of private enterprise in developing countries.* International Finance Corporation, Washington, D.C. Also available at <www.ifc.org/publications/paths_out_of_poverty.pdf>.

————. 2001. *Review of small business activities.* Washington, D.C.: International Finance Corporation.

ITU. 2001. *World telecommunication indicators 2000/2001.* Geneva.

————. 2002. *World telecommunication indicators 2002.* Geneva.

————. 2004. *World telecommunication indicators 2004.* Geneva.

Jorgenson, D. W., and K. Stiroh. 1999. Information technology and growth. *American Economic Review* 89 (2): 109–115.

Karshenas, M., and P. Stoneman. 1993. Rank, stock, order, and epidemic effects in the diffusion of new process technologies: An empirical model. *Rand Journal of Economics* 24: 503–528.

Keesing, D. R., and M. Wolf. 1981. Questions on international trade in textiles and clothing. *The World Economy* 4 (March): 79–101.

Krueger, A. B. 1993. How computers have changed the wage structure: Evidence from microdata, 1984–1989. *Quarterly Journal of Economics* 108 (1): 33–60.

Krugman, P. 1979. A model of innovation, technology transfer, and the world distribution of income. *Journal of Political Economy* 87: 253–266.

Kumar, N., and N. S. Siddharthan. 1994. Technology, firm size, and export behavior in developing countries: The case of Indian enterprises. *The Journal of Development Studies* 31 (2): 289–309.

Lal, K. 1999a. Determinants of the adoption of information technology: A case study of electrical and electronic goods manufacturing firms in India. *Research Policy* 28: 667–680.

———. 1999b. Information technology and exports: A case study of Indian garments manufacturing enterprises. Discussion Papers on Development Policy No. 15. Bonn: ZEF.

Lall, S. 1986. Technological development and export performance in LDCs: Leading engineering and chemical firms in India. *Weltwirtschaftliches Archiv* 122: 80–91.

Lefebvre, É., and L. A. Lefebvre. 1996. *Information and telecommunication technologies: The impact of their adoption on small and medium-sized enterprises.* Ottawa: International Development Research Centre (IDRC).

Liedholm, C., and D. Mead. 1987. Small-scale industries in developing countries: Empirical evidence and policy implications. International Development Paper 9. Agricultural Economics Department, Michigan State University.

Lybaert, N. 1998): The information use in a SME: Its importance and some elements of influence. *Small Business Economics* 10: 171–191.

Matambalya, F. 2003. Information and communication technologies (ICT) for Africa's economic development. In *African economic development,* ed. E. Nnadozie. Boston: Academic Press.

Matambalya, F., and S. Wolf. 2001. The role of ICT for the performance of SMEs in East Africa: Empirical evidence from Kenya and Tanzania. Discussion Paper No. 42. Bonn: ZEF.

Mead, D., and C. Liedholm. 1998. The dynamics of micro and small enterprises in developing countries. *World Development* 26: 61–74.

Moreno, L. 1997. The determinants of Spanish industrial exports to the European Union. *Applied Economics* 29: 723–732.

Mueller-Falcke, D. 2002. Use and impact of information and communication technologies in developing countries' small business: Evidence from Indian small-scale industry. Development Economics and Policy Series No. 27. Frankfurt: Peter Lang.

NASSCOM (National Association of IT Software and Service Industry). 2001. Internet and E-commerce scenario in India. <www.nasscom.org/template/inetec.htm>.

Nassimbeni, G. 2001. Technology, innovation capacity, and the export attitude of small manufacturing firms: A logit/Tobit model. *Research Policy* 30 (2): 245–262.

NEDO (National Economic Development Organization). 1971. *Technology and garment industry.* London.

Noland, M. 1997. Has Asian export performance been unique? *Journal of International Economics* 43: 79–101.

Pavitt, K. 1984. Sectoral patterns of technological change: Towards a taxonomy and a theory. *Research Policy* 13: 343–373.

Piore, M. J., and C. F. Sabel. 1984. *The second industrial divide: Possibilities for prosperity.* New York: Basic Books..

Porter, M. E., and V. E. Millar. 1985. How information gives you competitive advantage. *Havard Business Review* (July–August): 149–160.

Posner, M. V. 1961. International trade and technical change. *Oxford Economic Papers* 13: 11–37.

Prais, S. J. 1981. Vocational qualifications of the labor force in Britain and Germany. *National Institute of Economic Review* 98 (November): 47–59.

Read, R. B. 2002. Riding the outsourcing wave. <www.callcentermagazine.com/article/CCM20020729S0004>.

Robert, C. H., and P. W. Wright. 1998. Trade with low-wage economies, employment, and productivity in U.K. manufacturing. *The Economic Journal* 108: 1,500–1,510.

Rogers, E. M. 1995. *Diffusion of innovation,* 4th ed. New York: Free Press.

Röller, L.-H., and L. Waverman. 2001. Telecommunications infrastructure and economic growth: A simultaneous approach. *American Economic Review* 91 (4): 909–923.

Romijn, H. 1998. Technology support for small industries in developing countries: From "supply-push" to "eightfold-C." Queen Elizabeth House (QEH) Working Paper Series No. 21. University of Oxford, U.K.

Rosenbaum, P., and D. Rubin. 1985. Constructing a control group using multivariate matched sampling methods that incorporate the propensity score. *American Statistician* 39: 35–39.

Shultz, T. 1975. The value of ability to deal with equilibria. *Journal of Economic Literature* 13: 827–896.

Snodgrass, D., and T. Biggs. 1996. *Industrialization and the small firm: Patterns and policies.* Stockton, Calif., U.S.A.: International Center for Economic Growth.

Söderbom, M., and F. Teal. 2000. Skills, investment, and exports from manufacturing firms in Africa. *Journal of Development Studies* 37 (2): 13–43.

———. 2001. Firm size and human capital as determinants of productivity and earnings: New evidence from manufacturing firms in Ghana. Paper presented at the Annual Conference 2001 of the ESRC Development Economics Study Group, Nottingham.

Söderling, L. 2000. Dynamics of export performance, productivity and real effective exchange rate in manufacturing: The case of Cameroon. *Journal of African Economies* 9 (4): 411–429.

Soete, L. 1981. A general test of technological gap theory. *Weltwirtschaftliches Archiv* 117: 638–659.

———. 1987. The impact of technological innovation on international trade pattern: The evidence reconsidered. *Research Policy* 16: 101–130.

Solow, R. 1987. "We'd better watch out." *New York Times Book Review,* July 12, p. 36.

Stem, R., and K. Maskus. 1981. Determinants of the structure of U.S. foreign trade 1958–76. *Journal of International Economics* 11: 207–224.

Stoneman, P., and M. J. Kwon. 1996. Technology adoption and firm profitability. *The Economic Journal* 106:952–962.

Tam, K. Y. 1998. The impact of information technology investments on firm performance and evaluation: Evidence from newly industrialized economies. *Information System Research* 9: 85–98.

Torero, M. 2000. *The access and welfare impacts of telecommunications technology in Peru.* Discussion Papers on Development Policy No. 27. Bonn: ZEF.

Tybout, J. 1998. Manufacturing firms in developing countries: How well do they do and why? World Bank Policy Research Paper No. 1965. Washington, D.C.: World Bank.

———. 2000. Manufacturing firms in developing countries: How well do they do, and why? *Journal of Economic Literature* 38 (1): 11–44.

UNDP (United Nations Development Programme). 2002. Human development report 2002: Deepening democracy in a fragmented world. Available at <www.undp.org/hdr2002>.

United Nations. 1997. *African statistical yearbook 1996.* New York.

———. 2003. *African statistical yearbook* 2003. New York.

Van de Walle, D. 2000. Are returns to investment lower for the poor? Human and Physical Capital Interactions in Rural Vietnam. Policy Research Working Paper 2425. Washington, D.C.: World Bank.

Vella, F. 1993. A simple estimator for simultaneous models with censored endogenous regressors. *International Economic Review* 34 (2): 441–457.

Wakelin, K. 1997. *Trade and innovation: Theory and evidence.* Cheltenham, U.K., and Northampton, U.S.A.: Edward Elgar.

Weir, S. (1999). *The effects of education on farmer productivity in rural ethiopia.* Working Papers Series 99-7. Oxford: CSAE.

Willmore, L. 1992. Transnationals and foreign trade: Evidence from Brazil. *Journal of Development Studies* 28 (2): 314–335.

World Bank. 1998. *World development report 1998/99—Knowledge for development.* Washington, D.C.

———. 2004. World development indicators, GDN Web page, Washington, D.C.

WTO (World Trade Organization). 1996. *Annual report.* Geneva.

ZEF. 2001. Impact assessment of a telecommunications project in rural areas of the Lao People's Democratic Republic. Project Report. Bonn.

5 Impacts of ICT on Low-Income Rural Households

MAXIMO TORERO AND JOACHIM VON BRAUN

Globally, 1.2 billion people live in extreme poverty—75 percent of them in rural areas, and despite continuous migration and rapid urbanization, this proportion will remain around 50 percent by 2035 (IFAD 2001). Hence, no poverty alleviation program can be successful without addressing rural poverty. The term "rural penalty" has been used to describe the source of rural poverty, with distance being the primary factor (Hudson 1992). In an increasingly integrated and interdependent world, distance means time and money. The farther a community is located from an economic center, the less it benefits from mainstream economic growth. Developing-country governments seldom have sufficient physical and financial resources to provide infrastructure and social services to rural areas, and when they do, the financial returns to such investments are low. As a result, rural residents in developing countries lack access to basic needs like water, food, education, healthcare, sanitation, and security.

Information is an indispensable ingredient in decisionmaking for the livelihood of households (as has been discussed elsewhere in this volume). Information problems tend to be serious in the rural areas of developing countries, again because of distance and lack of resources and infrastructure. The traditional "personal" methods of information sharing have been eroded, while their modern equivalents have yet to be established (Geertz 1978; World Bank 1998). ICT is thought to hold unprecedented opportunities for rural households. Potential gains include economic benefits through

- time and cost savings;
- more and better information, leading to better decisions;
- greater efficiency, productivity, and diversity;
- lower input costs;
- higher output prices; and
- expanded market reach.

There are also potential social benefits through

- more efficient social service provision;
- enhanced informal social safety nets;
- decentralization and integration of subnational regions; and
- empowerment of rural communities (Song and Bertolini 2002).

Despite these potential benefits, the development of ICT in rural areas has not been a priority because primary infrastructure and social services—such as roads, electricity, education and health services—are in such demand. For investment in rural ICT to be fully justified, its benefits need to be clearly demonstrated. The impact of ICT on rural households and income distribution is of particular interest for poverty reduction (both in absolute and in relative terms). Nevertheless, establishing a causal link between ICT and rural livelihood is not easy. Studies are scarce and of limited methodological and geographic scope.

This chapter continues with our analysis of the benefits of ICT, and presents case studies that focus on different aspects of household-level ICT access and use in rural areas of Bangladesh, China, Ghana, Laos, and Peru (Figure 5.1). For background details on these five countries, see the preamble to the case studies in Chapter 3.

FIGURE 5.1 Conceptual framework: Area of analysis dealt with in Chapter 5

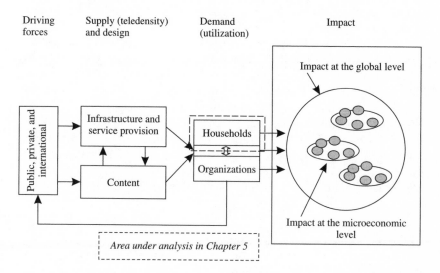

Country Studies of Different Experiences

In focusing on the impact of ICT on rural households, particularly the poor, a natural first step is to explore the determinants of access—that is, the salient characteristics of users. ICT was once regarded as a household luxury. While this is certainly not the case today, concerns remain about the ability of poor households to gain access to ICT. In the case of public access, the incidence of use by rural households is substantial in all five of the study countries, ranging from 33 percent in Laos to 69 percent in Peru. Applying qualitative and quantitative approaches, the five studies identify the main determinants of access to telephone services as income (expenditure), income source (occupation), education level, and distance to telephone facilities or a main road (as shown in the China case).

In all cases, age appears to be irrelevant in the decision of whether or not to use a telephone. Being female appears to be negatively correlated with telephone use in the Bangladesh, Ghana, and Laos cases, while the Ghana case also identifies, education, income, and distance to telephone services as the significant determinants. The general trend shows that access to telephone services depends on income, occupation, and education levels, though most of the studies report that demand for telephone services is not the exclusive domain of the well-educated, high-income segments of the population. For example, the sizable rise in telephone use in segments of the population with elementary education compared with those without (shown in the China and Ghana cases) illustrates that the education threshold for telephone use is quite low. Results from the Laos case study indicate that the prevalence of information available via the telephone is another important factor in the demand for household service. Further, demand for telephone services increases with service availability (as is discussed in Chapter 3). In Laos, user rates increased from 8 to 38 percent once telephone services became available in the community, and in Peru the perceived benefits of the telephone were higher among people in villages with telephone access than among villages without it.

While the potential of ICT to facilitate social development is acknowledged and supported by emerging evidence, the analyses in this chapter focus on the economics of the "welfare effect" of ICT, under the general assumption that monetary welfare improvements eventually bring about nonmonetary welfare improvements. Hence, the case studies use income or expenditure as the measure of welfare.[1] The prevalent indicator of the welfare effect of ICT is con-

---

1. The cases on China and Laos in this chapter provide anecdotal evidence of some of the noneconomic benefits perceived by users. For the potential impact of ICT on social services, particularly in terms of healthcare, see Chapter 6.

sumer surplus, calculated from willingness-to-pay—that is, the difference between the maximum consumers are willing to pay and what they effectively pay (Saunders, Warford, and Wellenius 1994). Using compensating variation (see Appendix 5A for details), the cases of Bangladesh and Peru attempt to measure the welfare effect of telephone use compared with available alternatives, such as visiting in person, sending a messenger, or sending letters. While the resulting benefits vary depending on which method of communication the telephone replaces, both cases indicate that the compensated variation is substantial (particularly when the alternative method of communication is traveling), and that the welfare effect does not vary much across income quartiles. This last observation shows that the reduced direct and indirect costs of telephone access (compared with alternative methods of communication) would benefit the rural population generally and the rural poor in particular. In addition, the compensated variation shows that the rural population would be willing to pay more than the current costs of telephone service. This implies that rural telecommunications could be provided sustainably with minimal subsidies.

Caveats accompany this conclusion, however. First, compensated variation may overestimate the rural residents' willingness-to-pay—especially when it comes to traveling, which is measured in terms of time. With unemployment and underemployment prevalent in rural areas, people may value time spent traveling differently; the time spent may also involve other activities. Second, the rationalization of rural telephone tariffs based on the willingness-to-pay may exclude the poorest segments of the population because income is a major determinant of access. Nonetheless, distance and the costs incurred through distance seem to be prohibitive factors for rural households when it comes to using and gaining benefits from telephone services. Consequently, universal access criteria should be reviewed, taking the relationship between telephone access and travel into consideration.

In addition to compensating variation, the cases of China and Laos in this chapter attempt to identify and measure the effect of telephone services on the economic performance of households. Using three-year panel data and regression analyses, the study on China explores the impact of telephone service subscription on household annual income and household businesses (other than agricultural businesses). Most telephone subscription variables show a positive impact on the growth rate of annual income, though it cannot be determined as significant, and the analysis shows different results across provinces. No significant relationship was identified between telephone services and household businesses. In addition to the usual problems related to measurement and omitted variables, this lack of evidence seems to relate to the type of access analyzed, meaning that the mere presence of a residential telephone is an insufficient proxy for telephone use (telephones are also available in public facilities). Moreover, because telephone services can be particularly limited in the rural areas of developing countries, service subscription does not reflect pure demand, distorting the analysis.

The Laos case explores the impact of telephone use through regression and matching methods, to take into account the suspected problem of endogeneity in establishing a causal relationship between ICT use and household benefits. With one-year cross-section data, all applied methods indicate a positive and significant effect stemming from access to telephone services. Although the diagnostics involved indicate no significant bias due to unobserved characteristics, it is possible that missing variables have led to the result of an unexpectedly large impact. In an attempt to verify the impact, a panel data analysis was undertaken, finding a positive but insignificant impact from the availability of telephone services. Nevertheless, the results suggest that a large share of changes in consumption can be attributed to the use of telephone services. Time lags, lack of critical mass in service provision, and unobserved characteristics may be factors in the results for both the China and Laos cases.

Synthesis

Results from the case studies indicate several policy implications. First, the welfare effect of telephone use in rural households is verified by the benefits perceived by users, the high demand for service, the substantial consumer surplus associated with telephone use, and results from formal econometric analyses. In particular, since public facilities are widely used and people are willing to pay more than the existing service charge, universal access through publicly accessible facilities should be promoted. Moreover, such services could be provided in rural areas with little need for subsidization. As previously mentioned, however, access for the poorest groups in society would need to be assured, given that in these areas service will not be commercially viable, and subsidies may be justified to extend services beyond the market. Emerging evidence of increasing income disparity between telephone users and non-users in developing countries suggests the need for strategies to support and promote the use of telephony by the rural poor.

It is widely believed that the impact of advanced ICT would be greater than the impact of telephony because of the diverse forms of information involved and the significant network and content externalities. This could be both true and false depending on the context. In rural areas, where overall education and income levels are much lower than in urban areas and infrastructure is poor, the introduction of advanced ICT could result in wasted resources. Telephone services do not require specialized skills and are comparatively inexpensive. This is the lesson of rural telecommunications. Any advanced forms of ICT introduced in rural areas should be easy to use and economical, and provide current and locally relevant content. One example is the Simputer, a portable alternative to personal computers.[2] Attempts to introduce ICT in rural areas without addressing the problems caused by poverty and rural isolation will be compromised.

Our case studies illuminate several interesting issues relating to ICT adoption by rural households. At the same time, they shed light on issues requiring further investigation. For example, observations over a longer period would be required before it would be possible to establish any direct causal relationship or confirm the occurrence of socioeconomic effects. Such observations would have to track both qualitative and quantitative changes in household performance, that is, changes in health and educational performance as well as in the provision of social services (see Chapter 6).

The China case looks at the impact of ICT on changing economic activity in rural households and resulting institutional change, such as the development of new markets. For example, Chowdhury (2002) explores the impact of telephone services on the marketing behavior of rural households. While it was observed that the number of intermediaries in transactions decreased with improved communications and the availability of information, it was also apparent that the sophistication of technology required intermediaries to assist rural inhabitants to access information. This happens in many pilot projects; however, the impact of information intermediaries is unknown. While more micro-level evidence is needed to determine the impact of ICT on markets in varied contexts, a mezzo-model, including the microeconomics of household marketing decisions, would give new insights into the impact of ICT on markets.

While communication with family and friends is reported to represent a large share of telephone usage, little is known about the real purpose of personal communication. For rural households, a close relationship with family and friends is a valuable asset, and we assume the ensuing information exchange is productive. This, however, needs more formal investigation. The impact of ICT on informal networks is of particular interest, because ICT may foster or drain informal networks by providing better communications and more channels of information reaching beyond personal groups. This requires an in-depth assessment of information needs and flows within and between rural communities.

After examining the case studies and available literature, it is fair to say that ICT has a positive impact on rural households, notwithstanding the supply and demand constraints that make it difficult for rural populations to benefit.

---

2. Developed by a group of Indian scientists and engineers, the Simputer is a cheap (9,000 rupees or about US$190) hand-held, networked device that uses open-source software. It provides voice technologies for the illiterate and smartcards for device sharing, is sturdy and simple to use, translates English into local languages, and plays contents aloud.

We can increase that positive impact by making ICT more accessible in rural areas, adapting new technologies to the rural setting (such as Simputer), and through the innovative use of old technologies, such as information services provided by telephone.

The Impact of Public Telephones in Rural Areas: The Case of Peru
Virgilio Galdo and Maximo Torero

Poverty and uneven income distribution persist across Latin America. Vast segments of the population are isolated in rural areas, subsisting on agriculture. The process of privatizing state-owned enterprises (SOEs) in the 1980s and 1990s led to improvements in the quality of infrastructure and freed state resources for more pressing needs. In addition, service coverage in the reformed sectors increased substantially, and the introduction of market mechanisms and incentives facilitated private investment, ultimately increasing service efficiency. A large service gap still remained (and remains) in most countries, however, particularly in rural areas, where the inherent high costs and associated risks of service provision make private-sector participation unprofitable. The Fund for Investment in Telecommunications (FITEL) was created in 1994 to address this service gap in Peru (see the case study of Peru in Chapter 3 for details). The primary objective of the fund was to promote private telecommunications investment in rural and remote areas to achieve universal service access. The longer-term goal was overcoming the isolation of distance through the provision of access to electronic information and communications, thereby promoting social and economic development.

The purpose of this case study is to identify the direct financial gains to rural households in southern Peru resulting from access to public telephones. To do this, we estimate the compensating variation associated with the reduced costs of telephone use compared with other methods of communication, and we examine the distribution of these welfare gains across different income groups. (See Appendix 5A for details of the methodology used in this case study.)

The Benefits of Access to Public Phones in Rural Peru

The rural areas considered under the FITEL project were villages with fewer than 3,000 inhabitants and either fewer than 100 clustered houses or more than 100 scattered houses. This concept, which was new at the time, was followed by various countries throughout the region (Figure 5.2). To maximize the benefits to the general population, public telephones were installed in 4,430 rural villages (Figure 5.3).

In 2003, total teledensity was still very low in rural Peru despite the FITEL program. Only five rural departments (the local-level administrative unit) had at least one public phone per 500 inhabitants as of 2003, which corresponds to teledensity of 0.2 compared with a national average of about 13. About 70,000

FIGURE 5.2 Public telephones in selected Latin American countries, 1998–2000

Number of public telephones

Public rural telephones

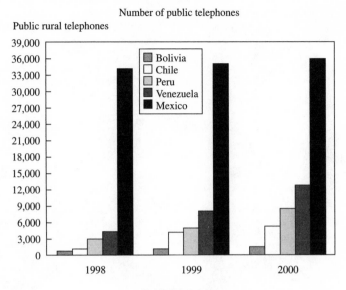

Public teledensity
(telephones per 1,000 inhabitants)

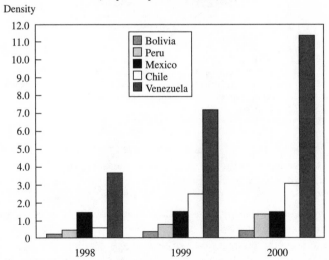

SOURCES: Compiled by authors using data from OSPITEL's Fund for Investment in Telecommunications (FITEL); the Telecommunications Development Fund (SUBTEL); the Federal Telecommunications Commission (COFTEL); the National Telecommunications Commission (CONATEL); and the Telecommunications Superintendency (SITTEL).

FIGURE 5.3 Public telephones in rural towns in Peru under OSPITEL's Fund for Investment in Telecommunications, 1998–2003

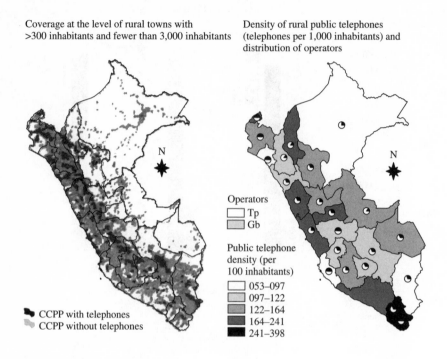

Coverage at the level of rural towns with >300 inhabitants and fewer than 3,000 inhabitants

Density of rural public telephones (telephones per 1,000 inhabitants) and distribution of operators

Operators
☐ Tp
▨ Gb

Public telephone density (per 100 inhabitants)
☐ 053–097
☐ 097–122
▨ 122–164
▨ 164–241
■ 241–398

🐦 CCPP with telephones
🐦 CCPP without telephones

SOURCE: OSIPTEL (2004).
NOTE: The figure indicates the number of rural towns with more than 300 and less than 3,000 inhabitants where there is a public phone operated by *Telefónica del Perú* or other operators including Telerep and C&G Telecom/Avantec. Gilat to Home was out of service as of 2003.

rural villages that met FITEL's criteria remained without access to telecommunications services, so further expansion was necessary. Meeting the goal of one public phone per 500 inhabitants would still require the installation of an additional 4,500 public rural telephones. Table 5.1 provides a regional breakdown of rural communications projects under FITEL as of 2003. Table 5.2 shows details of coverage by department.

More recently, competition and technology developments have reduced the costs associated with network development, making expansion of telecommunications coverage in the rural areas of Peru more feasible. Private enterprises were able to find creative ways of expanding services, given the reduced costs associated with satellite communications (VSAT). In the mid-1990s, installing a satellite telephone would have cost US$60,000, whereas, as of 2002, it cost between US$2,000 and US$4,000. It is also true that market conditions have

TABLE 5.1 Program of rural communication projects in Peru, 2003

Project/region	Number of rural villages	Number of direct beneficiaries	Number of indirect beneficiaries
Northern frontier region	193	58,872	85,650
Northern region	938	519,957	499,114
Southern region	534	135,917	249,468
South central region	1,029	303,260	528,734
Northern jungle region	374	141,621	187,424
North central region	582	317,648	363,682
Orient central region	780	259,668	343,930
Total	4,430	1,736,943	2,258,002

SOURCE: OSPITEL (2004).

NOTE: The concession for the northern frontier region was won by Village Telecom; concessions for the southern, south central, and northern jungle regions were won by Telerep; and concessions for the northern, north central, and west central regions were won by C&G Telecom/Avantec.

changed. By the early 2000s, it had become feasible for companies to initiate projects serving as few as 200–500 residents or involving monthly income of US$100–200 per line. Hence rural access to telecommunications has improved.

To identify the impact of telecommunications services on rural livelihoods, the Group for the Analysis of Development (GRADE) and the Center for Development Research (ZEF) conducted a comprehensive survey in four rural departments in southern Peru in 2000. A representative sample of 1,000 households was chosen based on telephone and road access and population size. The results indicated an increase in the use of public phones in rural areas. More than 70 percent of the sample households reported using public phones even when their village did not have one.[3] There were significant differences, however, based on the availability of public phones, the village's poverty level, the average travel time to the nearest public phone, and the perceived (direct and indirect) costs of using a public phone (Table 5.3).

Sample households attribute significant benefits to public telephone access; among these are the ability to communicate faster, avoid travel, and save money and time (Figure 5.4). Households reported substantial savings through the use of public phones as a substitute for personal visits, letters, or similar time-consuming methods of communication (Figure 5.4).[4]

---

3. When a rural village had no public phone, the nearest public phone in another village was used.

4. International experience shows encouraging results. In Bangladesh, for example, research shows that the use of rural public telephones results in a ratio of benefits (savings) to costs of between 2.2 and 7.8 depending on the distance involved (ITU 1998).

TABLE 5.2 Public telephone coverage in rural Peru by department, 2003

Department	Population (1,000s)	Rural population (1,000s)	Rural villages	Covered rural villages	Public telephones operated by *Telefónica del Perú*	Public rural telephones under other operators	Total public rural telephones	Public rural telephones per 100 inhabitants
Amazonas	336.7	217.1	2,331	269	86	401	487	22.4
Ancash	955.0	407.0	5,958	386	204	579	783	19.2
Apurimac	382.0	248.0	3,600	269	93	201	294	11.9
Arequipa	916.8	130.9	3,536	178	93	146	239	18.3
Ayacucho	492.5	255.7	4,232	328	100	252	352	13.8
Cajamarca	1,259.8	948.7	5,730	739	206	910	1,116	11.8
Cusco	1,028.8	557.0	6,873	463	244	371	615	11.0
Huancavelica	385.2	284.6	4,366	253	89	216	305	10.7
Huanuco	654.5	401.7	6,781	376	123	435	558	13.9
Ica	565.7	93.5	1,389	55	47	44	91	9.7
Junin	1,035.8	357.6	3,335	285	190	245	435	12.2
La Libertad	1,270.3	399.9	3,308	264	157	289	446	11.2
Lambayeque	920.8	211.2	1,167	121	97	89	186	8.8
Lima	6,386.3	207.5	4,209	191	116	294	410	19.8
Loreto	687.3	288.9	1,896	238	65	211	276	9.6
Madre de Dios	67.0	286.6	384	35	16	31	47	16.4
Moquegua	128.7	22.1	729	58	28	59	87	39.3
Pasco	226.3	92.9	1,508	146	71	144	215	23.1
Piura	1,388.3	411.5	2,141	386	246	327	573	13.9
Puno	1,079.8	656.6	9,433	460	204	341	545	8.3
San Martin	522.4	216.4	2,199	252	110	199	309	14.3
Tacna	218.4	22.4	379	33	44	37	81	36.2
Tumbes	155.5	18.6	130	37	17	28	45	24.1
Ucayali	314.8	110.0	749	84	19	139	158	14.4

SOURCE: OSIPTEL (2003).

TABLE 5.3 Use of public phone services in rural Peru, 2000

Category	Public phone use (percent)	Average time to reach the nearest public phone (hours)	Direct monthly expenditure on public phone use (Peruvian new soles)	Indirect monthly expenditure on public phone use (Peruvian new soles)	Ratio of indirect to direct expenditure (percent)
Expenditure group					
First quartile	88.8	0.50	15.80	2.09	13.2
Second quartile	83.2	0.91	8.41	1.61	19.1
Third quartile	68.4	0.98	5.04	1.22	24.2
Fourth quartile	65.2	1.13	2.48	0.43	17.2
Village access					
Public phone	70.3	1.65	7.10	3.04	42.8
No public phone	82.6	0.11	8.45	0.05	0.6
Economic level					
Poor	69.0	1.01	4.53	0.86	19.1
Nonpoor	86.8	0.71	13.01	2.02	15.5

SOURCE: Calculated by authors from primary survey data (2000).

NOTE: Households were classified as poor and nonpoor based on Peru's definition of the poverty line.

FIGURE 5.4 Perceived benefits of public phones by rural users in Peru, 2000

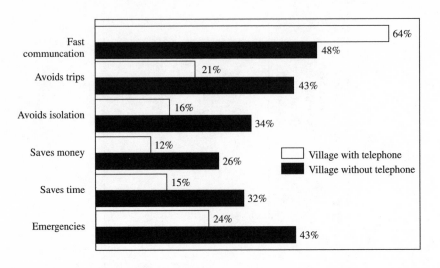

SOURCE: Calculated by authors from primary survey data (2000).

Understandably, households with higher incomes made more telephone calls (Table 5.4). For example, households in the lowest income quartile make 1.71 average calls per month, while those in the highest income quartile make 3.99 average calls per month. On the basis of these calls alone, the direct and indirect costs of alternative communication services would be 2 to 3.5 times higher overall, and more for households in the poorest quartiles.

Measuring Compensating Variation of Telephone Use

Analysis of the survey data presented in the previous section suggests that rural households value the speed and economy of public phone use over alternative methods of communication. The data further suggest that households can make substantial savings through the use of public telephone services. In order to fully capture the benefits to consumers resulting from the use of public phones (that is, the consumer surplus) compensating variation was estimated using the methodology described in Appendix 5A. Details of the estimations and statistical results are provided in Appendix 5B. The results are discussed below.

Determinants of Rural Public Phone Use. A positive correlation was shown to exist in all three of the estimation specifications between the head of household's education level and the use of public telephones. Further (and once again under all three specifications), households exclusively undertaking an economic activity in one room of their house had a higher probability of using public

FIGURE 5.5 Alternative methods of communication to public phones in rural Peru, 2000

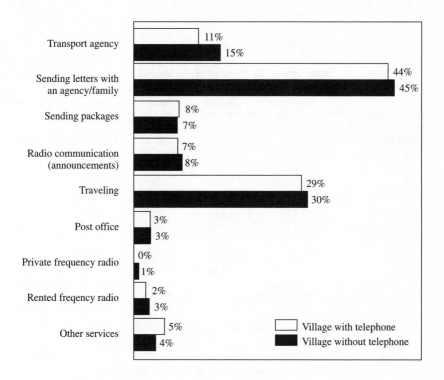

SOURCE: Calculated by authors from primary survey data (2000).

phones. Age was not shown to be a significant factor in public phone use, though there was a negative correlation between the maternal native language and the probability of using public phones. Understandably, villages with a public phone were more likely to use the service based on the comparatively lower indirect costs of use (such as traveling costs and traveling time). There were also positive and statistically significant correlations among the variables representing the perceived benefits of public phone use. Households in which public phone use was perceived to increase the speed of communication, reduce travel, reduce isolation, and provide monetary savings (compared with alternative communication methods) were more likely to use the service. The issue of time savings was less significant, probably because the impact of time savings was captured through the speed-of-communication variable.

Welfare Benefits. The benefits of using public phones in rural areas depend on which method of communication the telephone replaces. If the combined

TABLE 5.4 Household expenditure, calling patterns, and expenditure on public phone calls and alternative communication methods in rural Peru, 2000

Category	Average monthly household expenditure on public phone calls (Peruvian new soles)	Average number of calls per month[a]	Share of local calls[b] (percent)	Share of domestic long-distance calls[c] (percent)	Average number of call minutes per month
Expenditure group					
First quartile	1,269	3.99	45.5	54.5	20.2
Second quartile	648	2.63	44.2	55.8	13.4
Third quartile	491	2.00	43.9	56.1	9.1
Fourth quartile	313	1.71	33.2	66.8	6.0
Village access					
Public phone	741	3.04	46.8	53.2	15.5
No public phone	620	2.14	39.3	60.7	13.3
Economic level					
Poor	427	1.87	38.9	61.1	9.91
Not poor	1,036	3.52	46.5	53.5	17.7

SOURCE: Calculated by authors from primary survey data (2000).

[a]Includes outgoing calls only.

[b]Includes outgoing calls to another village within the district, to the district capital, and to the department capital.

[c]Includes outgoing calls to another department.

[d]Includes the indirect costs of making public phone calls, such as transportation.

[e]Includes the average cost of the alternative method of communications reportedly used by the household.

[f]Calculated based on the householder's hourly wage and the number of hours required for the reported alternative method of communication.

direct and indirect costs of phone use are lower than the equivalent costs of the alternative communication method, the user benefits. The "welfare neutral" payment is the amount of money the household is willing to pay in order not to have to use the alternative method of communication. This is known as the compensating variation. The concept can also be understood as the amount of money needed to compensate the household for using alternative communication methods so that its welfare remains constant. Microeconomic theory states that if the amount of compensation is larger than the marginal cost of using a public phone, then policies oriented toward expanding service coverage improve welfare. On the other hand, if the amount of compensation is smaller than the marginal cost of using a public phone, then such policies do not improve house-

Share of local minutes (percent)	Share of domestic long-distance minutes (percent)	Direct expenditure on public phone calls (Peruvian new soles)	Indirect expenditure on public phone calls[d] (Peruvian new soles)	Direct expenditure in alternative communications services[e] (Peruvian new soles)	Value of time spent using alternative service[f] (Peruvian new soles)
47.3	52.7	15.80	2.09	28.12	8.65
46.3	53.7	8.41	1.61	14.78	5.87
44.6	55.4	5.04	1.22	11.73	4.43
33.6	66.4	2.48	0.43	6.31	4.00
48.2	51.8	8.45	0.05	18.32	7.36
40.2	59.8	7.10	3.04	15.91	6.10
39.4	60.6	4.53	0.86	11.35	4.67
48.2	51.8	13.01	2.02	25.15	8.19

hold welfare (Deaton and Mullbauer 1980; Hausman 1981; Varian 1992; Mas-Colell, Whinston, and Green 1995).

As expected, when the alternative method of communication involves traveling, compensation—that is, the benefit of using public phones—is higher (Appendix 5B, Table 5B.2). Compensation is also high for sending letters via mail because not all rural villages have post offices, so sending letters generally involves travel to a post office or hiring a messenger. As observed by Gertler and Glewwe (1989), compensating variation does not vary substantially among expenditure groups, although households belonging to the highest income quartile are less willing to pay. This seems counterintuitive, since the highest quartile has a higher probability of access to telephones and, therefore, should have a higher willingness-to-pay. Poorer households, however, are more sensitive to the potential cost savings. Hence, the marginal effect of a relative reduction in the cost of public phone services in rural areas is much greater among poorer households. Moving down through the expenditure groups, the results show that the net effect of reduced prices is an increase in households' willingness-to-pay. It should be noted that the welfare calculation only includes the direct benefits of access to and use of rural public phone services. The approximation may underestimate household welfare because it does not include indirect benefits, such as social integration, improved market performance, the impact on prices, and so on.

TABLE 5.5 Subsidies per operator in rural Peru, 1998–2000

Villages with service	Total assigned subsidy (US$)	Assigned subsidy per village (US$)	Assigned subsidy per inhabitant (US$)	Assigned subsidy per telephone (US$)
Village Telecom	1,661,537	8,609	11.5	7,801
Telerep	10,990,888	5,674	7.1	5,216
C&G Telecom/Avantec/ Gilat to Home	27,854,610	12,111	12.1	7,594
Total	40,507,035	9,144	10.1	6,765

SOURCE: OSPITEL (2004).

In addition, the subsidy paid to the service operator under the FITEL project is relatively low, but it is not the lowest among similar projects (Table 5.5).[5] This may imply the need for further research to establish the reasons for the higher subsidy level and ways in which a more effective distribution of the funds could be implemented.

In evaluating rural telecommunications projects involving subsidy programs, Serra (2000) and Wellenius (1997) show that beneficiaries tend not to be the poorest villages. Our study, however, indicates that compensating variation is higher among the poorer rural villages, and that smaller rural villages have higher aggregate compensating variation relative to larger rural villages (Figure 5.6). Nevertheless, the more developed rural villages tend to be the ones able to meet the minimum demand requirements to ensure that services are self-sustaining and still enable the poorer villages (where services are not self-sustaining) to gain access to phones within walking distance.

Conclusion

Rural households in southern Peru receive a number of direct and indirect benefits from the use of public telephones. Our results indicate that, for the general rural population, the direct and indirect costs of other forms of communication are 2–3.5 times higher than the costs of using public phones. The savings accruing from public phone use are even higher for poorer households. Our estimates of compensating variation also indicate that the willingness-to-pay within rural households in Peru is sufficient to ensure the sustainability of telecommunications projects and to further expand rural coverage. It is clear, therefore, that access to public phones in the rural areas of Peru improves welfare, and that policymakers should support universal access. The high willingness-to-pay

---

5. Chilean experience reports an average of US$3,380 per telephone. See Serra (2000) for details.

FIGURE 5.6 Aggregated compensating variation by population in rural Peru, 2000

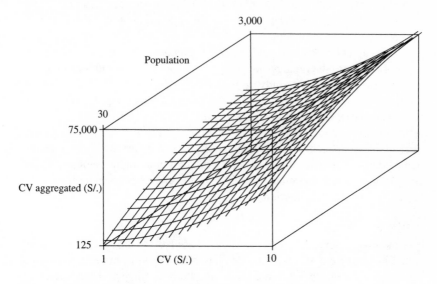

NOTE: 2.5 calls per household were assumed. S/. indicates Peruvian new soles.

for access also implies that subsidy schemes could achieve high impact at relatively low cost. Since some poor villages were shown to be willing to pay the marginal cost of service, subsidies in those areas should be reduced, releasing funds for additional subsidies in poorer villages where the willingness-to-pay is small but demand is sufficient to ensure service sustainability.

The Benefits of Rural Telecommunications: The Case of Laos
Gi-Soon Song and Arjun S. Bedi

Prompted by urban–rural imbalances in the provision of telecommunications services, along with other economic and security considerations, the rural telecommunications (Rurtel) project was launched in Laos in 1992, funded by the German Development Bank (for details of the project, along with country-specific background information, see the Laos case study in Chapter 3).[6] By the end of 2000, three phases of the project had been completed, and 41 of 128 rural district capitals had access to telecommunications. In terms of revenue, the rural network was performing far better than originally anticipated; projections

---

6. See also ZEF (2001) and Song (2003).

suggested annual revenues of US$370 per line, while actual revenues as of 1999 were three times higher, at around US$1,000 per line. These substantially higher revenues reflect the wide usage of services by rural residents and the significant underestimation of rural demand.

The gap between actual and expected revenues calls for a more thorough investigation into the linkages between household welfare and telecommunications access. This case study aims to fill this gap. First, the incidence and intensity of telecommunications use is examined, including the key characteristics of users. This enables identification of the extent and distribution of telecommunications adoption across various education and income groups. Second, the benefits of telecommunications access are assessed using qualitative evidence gathered through a survey of rural household members. This is complemented with quantitative analysis of the effects of telecommunications use on household consumption.

The Data

The analysis presented in this case study is based on the cross-section data collected in 2000 from 100 households randomly chosen from each of six rural sites (see the data section in the Laos case study in Chapter 4 for further details). In addition, of these 600-odd households, 200 were chosen from two sites to be interviewed both before and after the implementation of the Rurtel project for the purpose of forming a control group. Of these 200 households, 190 were successfully interviewed in both 2000 and 2001, allowing the construction of a short panel data set.

Since the main aim of the survey was to evaluate various aspects of the Rurtel project, in addition to standard information, such as household size, age, education, occupation, consumption, and housing characteristics, detailed information on telecommunications expenditure, calling patterns, purpose of calls, and household information needs were collected. This information provided a richer picture of the linkages between telecommunications services and household welfare.

While the data are unique in some aspects, they also suffer from some drawbacks. Because the Rurtel project focuses on district capitals (as service hubs), the surveys were also conducted in the capitals, where households are likely to be comparatively more prosperous than those in other rural areas. To assess the extent of these economic differences, data from the two case study surveys were compared with data for the same districts from the 1997/98 Laos Expenditure and Consumption Survey (LECS).[7] There are sharp differences in the sample

---

7. The National Laos Expenditure and Consumption Survey was carried out between March 1997 and February 1998 and included 8,882 households selected from 450 villages across the country.

means for all characteristics except the number of cattle. Case study data indicate that household heads are more educated, agricultural land endowments are higher, and annual per capita consumption is higher. Hence the case study data are not representative of rural Laos as a whole, and results should be interpreted with this difference in mind. Details of the statistical comparisons between the surveys are provided in Appendix 5C.

Telecommunications Use at the Household Level in Rural Laos

As was discussed in Chapter 3, most of the available lines installed under the Rurtel project are assigned to businesses and local government offices, leaving only a small proportion for private users and one or two for public use. Hence, users typically accessed telephones at public facilities (about 38 percent), at offices of local administrative bodies, or at their neighbors' houses. Most users (79 percent) walked or rode bicycles/motorcycles up to 3 kilometers to access a telephone. Accordingly, less than 10 percent of respondents reported making any payments for transportation resulting from telephone use. In many cases, users made their phone calls while traveling for a number of reasons, thus, reducing the opportunity cost of time associated with the calls. Although these figures are based on users, they suggest that the costs of travel and time are not major constraints in the use of telephones. About 33 percent of the sample (606 households) made regular use of telephones and hence were classified as "telecommunications users." On average a user household made three local and six long-distance calls per month. Average expenditure on telecommunications was about \$3.05, which represented 3 percent of monthly cash expenditure.[8]

Linkages between Household Characteristics and Telecommunications Use. Based on our sample, a positive relationship existed between literacy, formal education, and telecommunications use (Table 5.6). User rates were about 39 percent among the literate and only about 3 percent among the illiterate (Figure 5.7). A strong positive relationship also existed between the amount of schooling (in years) and telecommunications use. Usage rates increased from 4 percent for the illiterate to about 66 percent for those with tertiary education. A nonlinear relationship was found to exist between telecommunications use and age (Figure 5.8). Usage growth rates gradually declined from the highest rate, up to around age 30, becoming negative from about age 43.

Usage rates also differ across occupations (Table 5.6). As may be expected, individuals in occupations that require a higher level of education (professionals, technicians, and managers) reported usage rates of between 66 and 79 percent. However, usage rates for workers in less-skilled elementary occupations (59 percent) and the handicraft sector (30 percent) were also substantial. The

---

8. Among paying users, the average monthly expenditure on telecommunications was about US\$5, which is 6.6 percent of cash expenditure.

TABLE 5.6 Selected statistics on households and telecommunications use in rural Laos, 2000

	Total	Users	Non-users
1. Sample incidence of use		33 percent	
2. Frequency of calls		Three local and six long-distance calls per month	
3. Average expenditure		US$3.05	
4. Telecommunications expenditure as a share of total cash expenditure		3.0 percent	
5. Literacy		Incidence of use	
Literate		39 percent	
Illiterate		3 percent	
6. Occupation			
Professional and manager		66 percent	
Technician and associate professional		79 percent	
Service worker		71 percent	
Operation and assembly[a]		75 percent	
Elementary occupation[b]		59 percent	
Handicraft worker		30 percent	
Agriculture and fishery		12 percent	
7. Income source			
Single income source		20 percent	
More than one income source		52 percent	
8. Main information and communication need	29 percent	25 percent	31 percent
Maintaining contact with social network	15 percent	38 percent	4 percent
Government policies and administration	10 percent	24 percent	3 percent
Prices/availability of nonagricultural products	26 percent	6 percent	35 percent
Agricultural markets			

9. Main purpose of last call made and received
   Well-being of friends and relatives .... 58 percent
   Acquiring information on government policies .... 18 percent
   Arrangement of money, product, or labor transfers ...... 5 percent
   Prices/availability of inputs/output .... 11 percent
10. Source of information for non-users
    Personal contact .... 65 percent
    Mass media .... 6 percent
    Other telecommunications .... 1 percent
    No response .... 27 percent
11. Reasons for not using telecommunications service
    Not very useful .... 86 percent
    Too costly .... 4 percent
    Not available/too far away .... 8 percent
    Do not know how to use .... 2 percent

SOURCE: Primary survey data (2000).

[a]Mainly drivers for public transportation.

[b]Unskilled workers in retail business and construction.

FIGURE 5.7 Telecommunications use and education in rural Laos, 2000

Probability of telephone use

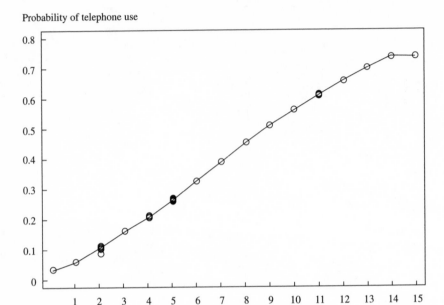

Years of education, household head

SOURCE: Primary survey data (2000).

lowest rates were found among households involved primarily in agriculture and fisheries (12 percent). While agriculture is the main rural industry, about 42 percent of all households engaged in multiple industries and relied on more than one source of income. These households were more likely to use the telephone. Usage rates were about 52 percent among households with more than one income source and only 20 percent among those with a single income source.

It is very likely that higher overall consumption causes higher telephone use, which in turn may lead to even higher consumption. The purpose of this analysis is not to determine causality but rather to examine how telephone usage rates differ across consumption groups (Figure 5.9). Predictably, telephone use increases with consumption, although at a decreasing growth rate. In the highest quintile, usage rates were about 50 percent or more; in the second-lowest quintile they ranged between 17 and 20 percent; and in the lowest quintile they ranged between 4 and 17 percent. Interestingly, usage was not restricted to the highest income quintiles.

Household Information Needs. About 29 percent of all households reported that information about their families and friends was their main information

FIGURE 5.8 Telecommunications use and age in rural Laos, 2000

Probability of telephone use

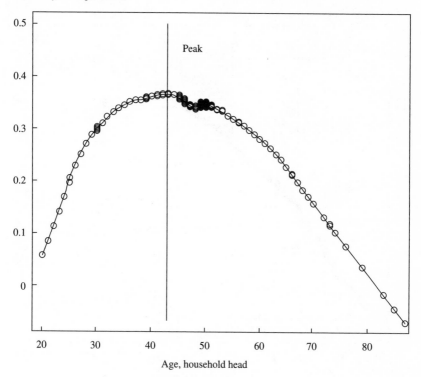

Age, household head

SOURCE: Primary survey data (2000).

requirement. This was followed by the need for information on agricultural markets (26 percent), information on government policy and government administration (15 percent), and information on nonagricultural products. In terms of the different types of information sought by telephone users and non-users, a large proportion of users sought information on government policy and government administration, while most non-users sought information on agricultural markets. Hence the difference in information needs between users and non-users related to their economic activities. Users tended to require information on government administration and on prices and availability of non-agricultural products, while non-users showed more interest in information related to agricultural inputs and outputs.

When asked about the type of information exchanged during their most recent phone calls, about 58 percent of respondents reported having had

FIGURE 5.9 Telecommunications use and total cash consumption in rural Laos, 2000

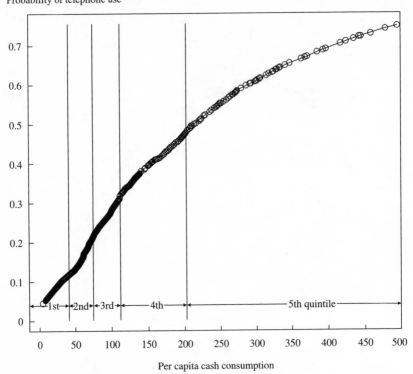

Probability of telephone use

Per capita cash consumption

SOURCE: Primary survey data (2000).

conversations with family, friends, or relatives, inquiring about their well-being. About 18 percent of respondents communicated about government policy and government administrative issues, about 5 percent inquired about monetary issues or product transfers, and about 11 percent sought information on inputs or outputs.

In terms of non-users, there are two key questions: what channels of information and communication do they use, and why do they not use the telephone? Survey responses show that the majority of non-users (65 percent) relied on personal contact for the information they needed (meaning they either went to the information source in person or asked someone who had been to the information source). Given that reliability and easy access were the two most important criteria for choosing communication methods, it would appear that non-users regard information obtained this way to be more reliable and more accessible. Of the non-users, 86 percent indicated that they did not use the telephone because they did not see any need to. The most important information to non-users was the well-being of their family and friends, and agricultural inputs; so it is possible that (a) family and friends live close by and were not yet connected to a telephone network, and (b) non-users may not have contacts outside their community for information on agricultural inputs. Interestingly, the cost of using the telephone appears to be only a minor inhibiting factor in telephone use. Only 4 percent of non-users indicated that cost was an issue in their choice not to use the telephone.

Benefits Perceived by Users

The sample households also provided information on perceived benefits of telephone access and use. Business and community leaders were included along with the sample households.[9]

More Efficient Administration. Local governors usually used the telephone to contact provincial and central governments. Among the benefits of access to telephone services, they reported faster and interactive communication, which contributed to efficiency in the day-to-day operations of the local government. Governors also mentioned that the telephone enabled them to learn from the experiences of other district governments when they faced problems. Officials also pointed out the invaluable benefit of the telephone in times of emergency and disaster.

Prior to the Rurtel project, local governments relied on shortwave radio communication, letters, or face-to-face communication. It is likely that the telephone provides significant time and cost savings over these alternatives. Telephone use appears to promote bottom-up as well as top-down communication among different levels of government, which is expected to improve the management of decentralized operations and assist the government's effort to integrate regions into the national socioeconomic development plan.

Increasing Efficiency in Economic Activities. As mentioned earlier, rural households in Laos engage in a variety of economic activities. Households and firms that were engaged in trading activities pointed out that they saved time and money by using the telephone to place orders and seek cheaper prices from suppliers. Similarly, suppliers noted their increased ability to contact retailers and check regional demand. Calls to and from suppliers constituted the most frequent use of telephones by sample firms, many of which were household-based.

Respondents also mentioned the effects of telephone access on farming practices and profits. Several community leaders attributed potential increases

---

9. Details on the community leader interviews are available in Song (2003).

in agricultural productivity and trade with other regions to fast and easy telecommunications. According to respondents, information on new methods and new crops was transferred locally and from neighboring countries. Respondents from Songkhon mentioned that information on market prices, made available via the telephone, had allowed them to obtain better prices for their watermelons. The increased access to information enabled them to obtain a better bargain with middle men or to sell directly to city markets rather than via an intermediate agent.

Social Networks. Using the telephone to keep in touch with family and friends was the most commonly reported benefit of telephone access. About 58 percent of users reported that their last telephone conversation was with a family member. While these calls were placed mainly to inquire about the personal well-being of relatives, respondents indicated that such calls also involved economic concerns, such as the transfer of money, produce, labor, information on input and output markets, employment opportunities, and technology.

Several respondents receive remittances from family living abroad. Prior to the Rurtel system it was not uncommon for people to cross the Mekong River (into Thailand) to use telephones to arrange product and monetary transfers. The availability of the telephone has facilitated such arrangements, however. Using the telephone to arrange seasonal labor, such as in the planting and harvesting seasons, is also common among families. Being able to arrange quick transfers of cash, labor, and products is important to ensuring the smooth workings of daily life, ultimately helping to ensure constant and sustainable livelihoods and constant consumption. Respondents frequently reported the importance of telecommunications in facilitating and sustaining their social networks.

Gold Prices and Exchange Rates. The mass media is not highly developed in Laos. Print media is sparse, and in rural areas the lack of roads makes newspaper delivery difficult. Electronic media is more widely accessible, but household access to radio and television is limited. JTEC (2001) estimates that 15 percent of households have a radio receiver and 7 percent a television set. In such circumstances it is difficult for rural households to access beneficial information.

Several respondents mentioned the importance of knowing the prevailing exchange rate for the Laotian currency, the kip. This information was commonly needed by households and businesses involved in buying and selling products from neighboring countries, but it was also needed by other households. The dollar is widely accepted in Laos, and knowledge of the prevailing exchange rate ensures that households receive fair prices. Respondents also mentioned their need to know the price of gold. Because of high inflation and seasonal variations in household income, it is common for rural households to buy gold in the harvest season and sell it when they need cash. Jewelers often act as banks in local financial markets, and, before the availability of telephones, rural residents were dependent on the information they provided, which was often out of date and unevenly distributed. With publicly accessible telephones,

TABLE 5.7 Descriptive statistics of telecommunications users in rural Laos, 2000

Variable	User (1)	Non-user (2)	*t*-test[a] (3)
Annual per capita consumption (US$ in 2000 prices)	278.61 (226.94)	151.03 (131.87)	8.350
Annual per capita cash consumption (US$ in 2000 prices)	230.08 (184.68)	97.55 (115.74)	10.560
Household size	5.90 (2.30)	6.00 (2.40)	0.530
Age of household head	43.30 (10.30)	44.30 (13.00)	0.955
Years of schooling—household head	9.10 (3.70)	4.40 (3.80)	14.500
Agricultural land (acres)	1.56 (2.30)	1.70 (1.90)	0.530
Number of cattle	1.31 (2.72)	2.45 (4.14)	3.520
Income source, agriculture only (percent)	21.50 (41.10)	61.50 (48.70)	10.010
More than one source of income	65.50 (47.60)	30.20 (46.00)	8.750
Household head participates in the labor market (percent)	97.00 (17.10)	93.30 (17.10)	2.350
Number of working members in the household	2.46 (1.21)	2.71 (1.21)	1.860
Sample size	200	406	

SOURCE: Primary survey data (2000).

NOTE: Standard deviations are shown in parentheses.

[a]Differences in sample means.

rural residents can acquire information on exchange rates and gold prices in urban markets directly.

Impact of Telecommunications Services on Rural Households

Assessing Impact Using Consumption Functions and Matching Methods. A quantitative analysis of the impact of telecommunications on rural households confirms sharp differences between user and non-user households (Table 5.7). Annual per capita consumption among user households was about 1.7 times higher than non-user households; heads of user households had completed about nine years of education compared with only four years for non-user household heads; non-user households were more likely to work in the agricultural sector; and non-user households owned more cattle and represented the larger share of households involved solely in agriculture.

The aim of this analysis is to control for all observed and unobserved factors that may determine consumption and isolate that part of the consumption gap between user and non-user households that may be attributed to telecommunications use. We estimated the impact of telecommunications on consumption using (a) ordinary least squares (OLS), (b) a maximum likelihood with treatment-effects model (MLE), and (c) matching methods using data from 2000 (see Appendix 5A for details of the methodologies used).

To identify the effect of telecommunications use, the specification includes control variables that may determine consumption or be correlated with telecommunications users. The variables are gender, age, education of the household head, land, livestock, income source, and whether a household has a shop. These last two variables were included to control for diversity of income sources. The specification also includes sets of variables to control for (a) housing characteristics, such as access to electricity and water, type of construction, and presence of a toilet; (b) household ownership of consumer durables, such as televisions, cars, motorcycles; and (c) a set of regional controls.

The results from OLS and MLE of treatment effects model show that none of the personal characteristics of the household head have significant bearing on either total or cash consumption (Table 5.8). Similarly, landholdings and the number of cattle owned have statistically insignificant effects on per capita consumption. Households that derived their livelihood from agriculture alone consumed $35–51 less than households with diverse sources of income; and households that owned a shop reported consumption of about $66–68 more than households that did not.

The total yearly per capita consumption of telecommunications users is $27 higher than the consumption of non-users (Table 5.8, column 1). Cash consumption is slightly higher (about $32). However, only the effect of telecommunications use on cash consumption is statistically significant at conventional levels. Given that the observed consumption gap between users and non-users is about $127 for total consumption and $132 for cash consumption, the variables included in the OLS equation seem to be quite successful in controlling for observed differences in the consumption levels of users and non-users. Nevertheless, it is important to examine whether unobserved characteristics are influencing the differences in consumption.

The coefficient on the generalized residual (the term that controls for the potential correlation) is negative, indicating that unobserved factors that determine telecommunications use are negatively correlated with unobserved factors that determine consumption (Table 5.8). In such cases, OLS would underestimate the effect of telecommunications. Accordingly, the MLE estimates are substantially larger than the OLS estimates (Table 5.8). Although the effects of telecommunications use are larger, the coefficient on the generalized residual for both specifications (and for a variety of other specifications) is not statistically significant. It is likely that we are unable to detect the effects of unobserved

TABLE 5.8 The effect of telecommunications use on consumption in rural Laos, 2000

Variable	Total consumption OLS (1)	Cash consumption OLS (2)	Total consumption MLE (3)	Cash consumption MLE (4)
Telecommunications user	27.440	31.670	99.410	81.290
	1.450	*1.970*	*1.900*	*1.060*
Gender of household head	−33.320	−35.330	−42.260	−40.920
	−1.150	*−1.360*	*−1.530*	*−1.620*
Age of household head	−0.196	0.021	−0.116	0.093
	−0.260	*0.040*	*−0.150*	*0.140*
Years of schooling of household head	0.694	1.289	−1.007	0.118
	0.370	*0.800*	*−0.490*	*0.050*
Agricultural land (acres)	7.612	2.797	6.384	1.848
	1.170	*0.500*	*0.960*	*0.310*
Number of cattle	0.239	0.109	0.874	0.584
	0.150	*0.070*	*0.530*	*0.400*
Income source, agriculture only (percent)	−47.120	−35.030	−51.120	−37.960
	−2.640	*−2.260*	*−2.730*	*−2.170*
Household has a shop	68.510	68.370	66.380	67.260
	2.990	*3.690*	*2.950*	*3.650*
Generalized residual	—	—	−44.890	−31.050
			−1.540	*−0.684*
R^2	0.264	0.310	—	—
Log-likelihood	—	—	−3,735.590	−3,806.130
Number of observations	555	581	555	581

SOURCE: Primary survey data (2000).

NOTES: OLS indicates ordinary lease squares; MLE indicates maximum likelihood with treatment-effects model; *t*-statistics are shown in italic. Standard errors are heteroskedasticity consistent. Other regressors include (a) a set of variables to control for housing characteristics, such as access to electricity, water, presence of a toilet, and type of construction material; (b) a set of variables that captures the presence of durable goods, such as ownership of television sets, cars, and motorcycles; and (c) a set of variables indicating province of residence. Three variables—household ownership of an ox cart, plow, and tractor—are included in the telecommunications user equation to aid identification of the generalized residual.

variables on consumption because of lack of suitable identifying variables. Taken literally, this indicates that unobserved factors do not play a significant role in determining telecommunications use.[10]

---

10. The parametric selection model estimated here relies on the assumption of joint normality of the error terms in consumption and adoption equations. It is well known that these parametric treatment-effect models are sensitive to this assumption, as well as to the specification of the telecommunications use equation and the specification of the consumption equation. We experimented with several specifications of both equations. There was substantial variation in the size and

An alternative approach to estimating the effect of telecommunications use is matching methods. This approach is based on comparing the average per capita consumption between households that are telecommunications users (the treatment group) with a group of households that are not users (the control group). Households in the two groups should be as similar as possible in all other observed characteristics. (See Appendix 5A for further details on matching methods.) Results reported in the previous section suggest that telecommunications use depends on observed variables and that unobserved characteristics are not significant. This being the case, and given that the sample households answered the same questionnaire and operate in a similar environment, the results of estimation using matching methods should be credible.

Our data set contains 200 user and 406 non-user households. This non-user group was used as a hypothetical control group. The outcome variables of interest are annual per capita total and cash consumption of households, and the treatment is telephone use. As discussed earlier, the observed characteristics of user and non-user groups are quite different. The potential comparison group, therefore, may be quite small. Dehejia and Wahba (1998) show that even with small treatment and control groups, matching methods can provide accurate estimates of the treatment impact.

A Logit model was used to estimate the probability of a household being a telecommunications user, and three different matching methods were used to create suitable control groups.[11] Results based on nearest-neighbor matching, five nearest-neighbors matching, and kernel matching are presented in Table 5.9. Treatment effects based on nearest-neighbor matching range from US$56 to $61 and are statistically significant at about the 10 percent level, while effects based on kernel matching are larger and range between US$74 and $85 and are statistically significant at conventional levels. The magnitude of the effect is considerably larger than the OLS estimates, lying between the treatment effects estimated using OLS and MLE. The size of these mean treatment effects is quite large, ranging between 22 and 32 percent of per capita total and cash consumption. It appears that telecommunications use is responsible for 48–66 percent of observed differences in total consumption and 42–59 percent of the observed differences in cash consumption.

Despite evidence that unobserved factors do not significantly affect household consumption, the size of the effect associated with telecommunications use raises doubts as to whether this is indeed true. It seems likely that the large

---

the statistical significance of the effect of telecommunications use, but in all cases the coefficient on the generalized residual was statically insignificant.

11. The use of a Probit model to estimate the probability of a household being a telecommunications user, and to subsequently generate control groups, did not lead to sharp differences in the estimated treatment effects.

TABLE 5.9 Mean treatment effect of telephone use on household consumption in rural Laos

Matching method	Per capita total consumption (1)	Per capita cash consumption (2)
Nearest neighbor matching	$61	$56
	1.85[a]	*1.75*
	(22 percent)[b]	(24 percent)
Five nearest neighbor matching	$50	$51
	2.23	*2.61*
	(18 percent)	(22 percent)
Kernel-based matching	$85	$74
	3.40	*3.08*
	(31 percent)	(32 percent)

SOURCE: Estimated by authors from primary survey data (2000, 2001).

NOTE: *t*-statistics are shown in italics.

[a]Standard errors are based on 100 bootstrap replications.

[b]Treatment effect as a percentage of average per capita total and cash consumption.

effect of telecommunications use estimated using propensity score matching has been contaminated by some missing observed or unobserved variables.

Panel Data Estimates. So far we have used cross-sectional variation to identify the effect of telecommunications use on per capita household consumption. The availability of information on the same households over time allows us to use an alternative approach. Rather than relying on traditional parametric approaches to correct for the potential correlation between the error terms in consumption and adoption equations, the data can be differenced to remove the effect of unobserved characteristics that do not vary over time. These differenced data can then be used to estimate the extent to which temporal changes in consumption may be explained by temporal changes in the incidence of telecommunications use. (Once again, details of the methodology are provided in Appendix 5A.)

Using the first difference model, we attempted to identify the impact of changes in telephone user status on the changes in consumption levels between 2000 and 2001 (Table 5.10). These estimates allow us to gauge the extent to which changes in consumption during this time period may be attributed to changes in access to telecommunications. Given the short span of time between the two surveys (7–9 months) and the limited variation in the independent variables, it is not surprising that almost all the coefficients were not precisely estimated. Nevertheless, the signs on the coefficients do provide some clues as to the factors that influence changes in consumption. Although statistically

TABLE 5.10 The effect of telecommunications use on panel-data estimates of consumption for rural Laos

Variable	Change in total consumption (1)	Change in cash consumption (2)
Telecommunications use	17.210	14.280
	0.990	*1.120*
Household size	−14.670	−7.630
	−2.070	*−1.440*
Agricultural land	−4.390	−2.690
	−0.710	*−0.590*
Number of cattle	3.890	2.230
	0.910	*0.700*
More than one source of income	20.510	7.040
	1.320	*0.620*
Household head participates in the labor market	−52.000	−19.660
	−1.550	*−0.770*
Number of workers in the household	0.611	7.940
	0.070	*1.200*
R^2	0.110	0.076
Number of observations	161	174

SOURCE: Estimated by the authors based on primary survey data (2000, 2001).

NOTE: *t*-statistics are shown in italics. All variables are in first differences.

insignificant at conventional levels, the coefficient on the differenced telecommunications use variable is positive for both consumption measures and suggests that access to telecommunications is potentially responsible for a large proportion of the changes in consumption during this time period. The magnitude of the coefficient indicates that a change (from non-user to user status) in the differenced telecommunications use variable is responsible for a shift in consumption from US$14 to $17. Real consumption shows a modest decline over this period, and the positive coefficient on telecommunications use suggests that access to telecommunications contributes to reducing this decline.

Conclusion

This case study set out to investigate the links between rural household welfare and access to telecommunications. It emerged that the average telecommunications user was more highly educated, more likely to work in skill-intensive occupations, and consumed more per capita compared with the average non-user. Nevertheless, usage rates were also substantial among low-income households and among workers in jobs requiring less skill. Users and non-users were also shown to have different needs for information, and it is possible that the telephone is less useful to the information needs of non-users. The direct and indirect costs of accessing the telephone appeared to play a minor role in the choice not to use the telephone. Sample households used the telephone to build and maintain social networks; to access information on government policy and administrative issues; to acquire information on gold prices and exchange rates; and to arrange product, money, and labor transfers. By far the most important benefit associated with access to the telephone was maintaining contact with family and friends.

A number of different methods were used to quantitively estimate the effect of telephone use on household consumption with inconclusive results, probably due to missing variables. However, high revenues, speedy adoption of the telephone after its introduction, and anecdotal evidence strongly suggest that users derive substantial benefits from access to telephone services. Finally, our investigation concludes that achieving higher rates of telephone use and increasing the usefulness of the Rurtel network require not only the availability of the technology but also access to credible sources of information that meet the needs of agricultural households.

Implications of Access to Public Telephones:
The Case of Rural Bangladesh
Shyamal K. Chowdhury

This study measures the welfare implications of public telephones in rural areas in Bangladesh through the measurement of Hicksian compensating variation (see Appendix 5A for details). There are both economic and development rationales for providing telecommunications access, as has been discussed elsewhere in this volume. Access to telecommunications may be explicitly rationed by direct costs such as tariffs, or implicitly rationed by indirect costs, such as the cost of transport and the opportunity cost of time.

In the case of Bangladesh, households living in rural areas were not explicitly rationed through high and differential tariffs. Due to the regulatory nature of the telecommunications industry, however, the direct costs of public phone use did not vary between rural and urban areas based on the cost of provision, or between poor and rich households based on their ability to pay. Despite the absence of variation in the direct costs of use, rural households in Bangladesh were rationed by the indirect costs of telephone use. Households that are willing to pay the tariff as well as transport and opportunity costs of their time could travel to the nearest publicly accessible telephone. However, if a household were willing to pay the tariff but not the transport and opportunity costs it would effectively be excluded from access to telecommunications services.

The distance, one-way travel time, and associated transport costs to the nearest public telephone, along with the usage rate in the rural areas of Bangladesh are shown in Table 5.11. As expected, rural household usage depends on

TABLE 5.11 Distance, travel time, and transport costs to the nearest public telephone, and usage rate in rural Bangladesh

Distance or time to nearest phone	Share of sample in category (percent)	Usage rate (percent)
One-way travel time		
Within the village[a]	15.8	64.4
Within 30 minutes	45.0	26.6
Within one hour	27.8	21.5
More than one hour	11.2	18.8
One-way distance		
Less than 2 kilometers	27.1	51.9
2 to < 5 kilometers	33.5	15.8
5 to < 10 kilometers	22.5	32.8
10 kilometers or more	16.9	20.8
One-way transport cost		
No transport cost	21.5	47.5
Up to Tk. 10	50.7	27.1
>Tk. 10 to Tk. 20	16.9	31.3
>Tk. 20	10.9	9.7
Total	100	30.3

SOURCE: Primary survey data (2001).

NOTE: Usage rate is the percentage of households with access to a phone within the specific distance and who use it.

[a] Zero or negligible distance.

nontariff costs, such as transport and travel time, among other factors; the longer the travel time, the lower the usage rate. In addition, one-way distance to the nearest public telephone and usage rate, and one-way transport cost to the nearest telephone and usage rate also show a similar trend. This implies that, given the tariff rates and other factors, the higher the nontariff cost to the nearest telephone, the lower the usage. This also suggests that the reduction in nontariff costs of public telephone use may increase a household's telephone use.

Since 1996, the rural telecommunications market in Bangladesh has been competitive. However, service access has remained very low. Rural fixed line teledensity was only 0.039 in 1998 (Table 5.12). In an attempt to address this issue, the Grameen Bank and Grameen Phone initiated a joint project called the village payphone (VPP) program (for further background details, see the Bangladesh case study in Chapter 3).

The objective of this case study is to evaluate access and use of telephones by rural households, and the welfare implications of such use. The findings of the study are based on a primary survey that was carried out in Bangladesh in 2001.

TABLE 5.12 Access to telecommunications in rural areas under different regimes

Indicators	State monopoly 1989	Private monopoly 1995	Competition[a] 1998
Share of rural area	10.5%	8.9%	8.9%
Rural fixed line teledensity	0.031	0.036	0.039
Urban fixed line teledensity	1.175	1.640	1.735

SOURCE: BBS, various years.

NOTES: The share of rural area indicates the total number of fixed lines in rural areas relative to the total number of fixed lines in Bangladesh; rural/urban teledensity is the number of fixed lines per 100 rural/urban inhabitants.

[a]In Bangladesh, the authority introduced competition in the cellular telephone market in 1996. However, rural fixed telephony has remained under private monopoly.

Telephone Users and Expenditure, and Reasons for Use

In the past, the implicit rationing of telephone services, as discussed above, kept rural telephone use at a very low level. However, though the change in availability has resulted in increased usage, the majority of rural households now use public telephones.

Who Are the Users of Telephones in Rural Areas of Bangladesh? Surveyed households were categorized as either telephone users or non-users (Table 5.13). Among the sample households, more than 30 percent had at least one or more members who used public telephones. However, usage varies. It appears that the availability of public telephones within villages affects overall telephone use. Among sample households, usage is higher in villages with telephones compared with villages without telephones. This finding remains constant across similar income groups (that is, poor households, nonpoor households, and total households). This observation supports the argument that nontariff (that is, indirect) costs play an important role in the decision to use telephones and a reduction in nontariff costs may increase use by both poor and nonpoor households.

With users and usage identified, it is important to quantify rural household expenditure on public telephones. For this, users were arranged into four expenditure groups based on income quartiles, two categories based on the type of village, and two categories based on poverty status (Table 5.14). Telephone usage is positively correlated with income. While only around 11 percent of the lowest income quartile use public telephones, more than 59 percent of the highest income quartile use them. It is important to note, however, that household demand for public telephones is not met in the lowest income quartile. More than 14 percent of poor households that live below the national poverty line use public telephones. It appears that there is a positive correlation between income and expenditure on public telephones. This implies that both poor and wealthy

TABLE 5.13 Who uses the telephone?

	Total	With telephone			Without telephone		
		Total	Poor	Nonpoor	Total	Poor	Nonpoor
Number of households	284.0	141.0	56.0	85.0	143.0	42.0	101.0
Yes (percent)	30.3	36.2	17.9	48.2	24.5	9.5	30.7
No (percent)	69.7	63.8	82.1	51.8	75.5	90.5	69.3

SOURCE: Primary survey data (2001).

NOTE: The classification of poor/nonpoor is based on national poverty line. The survey is representative of five districts: Dhaka, Bogra, Comilla, Feni, and Tangail.

households use public telephone services, and that consumption increases with income.

Households in villages with public telephones have higher usage rates compared with households in villages without public telephones (Table 5.14). One of the main reasons for this is the substantial indirect costs of accessing services (in terms of travel and time) for households in villages without a public phone. The indirect costs of telephone use for households in villages with a public phone represent 10 percent of the total cost of use; for households in villages without a public phone, that amount increases to more than 41 percent. For this reason, the expansion of public phones in rural areas benefits not only the village where the phone is located but also nearby villages that benefit from reduced indirect costs associated with telephone access.

However, though some of the households in rural Bangladesh use public telephones, others do not. It is important to investigate the available alternatives to public telephone use and reasons behind the choice (Figure 5.10). Households were categorized based on whether or not their village has a public telephone. Three main alternative methods of communication were reported by sample households: sending a person, sending a letter through the public postal system, and traveling to the nearest available public telephone. Other means mentioned included use of courier services and fax machines. For both types of households, sending a person was considered the most acceptable alternative form of communication.

The average number of telephone calls made by rural households varies from 0.5 to 6.9 per month depending on income (Table 5.15). Households in the lowest income quartile do not make any local or international calls, meaning they only make domestic long-distance calls. Though migration of unskilled workers from rural areas in Bangladesh to East Asia and the Middle East is a visible phenomenon, poor households rarely migrate, a characteristic reflected in their calling patterns. The call structure also indicates that poor households may substitute local calls with personal visits, but they make long-distance calls when it is economically beneficial for them to do so.

TABLE 5.14 Use of public telephones, associated travel time, and direct and indirect telecommunications expenditure in Bangladesh

Category	Public telephone use	Average travel time to the nearest public phone (minutes)	Direct monthly expenditure on public telephones (tariffs)	Indirect monthly expenditure on public telephones (traveling time converted to agricultural wage rate)	Ratio of indirect to direct expenditure
Expenditure group					
First quartile	59.2	41.06	255.57	136.67	53.5
Second quartile	29.6	39.65	159.87	29.10	18.2
Third quartile	21.1	35.56	54.60	11.82	21.7
Fourth quartile	11.3	30.49	27.46	2.50	9.1
Type of village					
With public telephone	36.2	13.62	144.85	15.94	11.0
Without public telephone	24.5	59.44	221.22	157.18	71.0
Poverty status					
Poor	14.3	31.73	55.75	11.95	21.4
Nonpoor	38.7	39.30	199.30	87.38	43.8

SOURCE: Primary survey data (2001).

FIGURE 5.10 Alternatives to the use of public telephones in rural Bangladesh

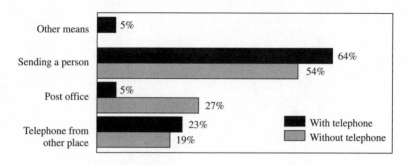

SOURCE: Primary survey data (2001).

Expenditure on public telephones varied among sample households from Tk. 27.4 for the lowest income quartile (less than 1 percent of household income), to Tk. 255.5 for the highest income quartile (over 1 percent of household income). Not surprisingly, poor households as a whole spend a slightly higher proportion of their income on public telephone use than nonpoor house-

TABLE 5.15 Total household expenditure, calling patterns, expenditures on public phone calls, and the costs of alternative methods of communication in rural Bangladesh, 2001

Category	Household's average monthly expenditure (Tk)	Household's average number of calls per month (minutes)	Average number of local calls per month
Expenditure group			
First quartile	18,373.35	6.95	0.34
Second quartile	6,263.79	5.33	0.42
Third quartile	4,194.89	2.67	0.46
Fourth quartile	3,159.38	0.50	0.00
Type of village			
With public telephone	10,555.31	4.16	0.38
Without public telephone	12,945.65	6.74	0.29
Poverty status			
Poor	3,282.92	2.29	0.30
Nonpoor	13,131.36	5.78	0.36

SOURCE: Primary survey data (2001).

NOTE: The exchange rate at the time of the survey was US$1 to Tk. 56.

holds. Households from villages without public telephones also spend a higher proportion of their income on public telephone use compared with households in villages with public telephones.

The direct cost of alternatives to public telephone use represents more than 6 percent of household income in the lowest income quartile and less than 1 percent of household income of the highest income quartile. In terms of poverty status, the direct cost of alternative forms of communication represents more than 2 percent of household income for poor households and more than 1 percent of household income for the nonpoor households. The total (direct and indirect) costs of alternative communication methods represent eight times the cost of public telephone use for households in the lowest income quartile and around twice the expenditure of public telephone use for the households classified as poor. This shows an important inequality among poor households. The comparative costs of the alternative methods of communications are one of the reasons why rural households, regardless of income group, choose to use public telephones rather than available alternative forms of communication.

Why Do the Households Use Public Telephones? Households in rural areas of Bangladesh use public telephones both for economic and personal reasons. Sample households provided information on the primary reasons why calls were made and the most important information gained through their conversations

Average number of international calls per month	Direct monthly expenditure on public telephones (Tk)	Total monthly expenditure on public telephones (Tk)	Direct costs of alternative methods of communications (Tk)	Total costs of alternative methods of communications (Tk)
0.19	255.57	392.24	141.68	833.21
0.19	159.87	188.97	190.54	613.62
0.07	54.60	66.42	38.57	74.29
0.00	27.46	29.96	200.00	240.00
0.20	144.85	160.79	81.76	719.13
0.09	221.22	378.40	211.67	546.43
0.07	55.75	67.70	70.00	122.00
0.17	199.30	286.68	149.73	703.10

FIGURE 5.11 Primary reasons for making public telephone calls, and type of information received, in rural Bangladesh, 2001

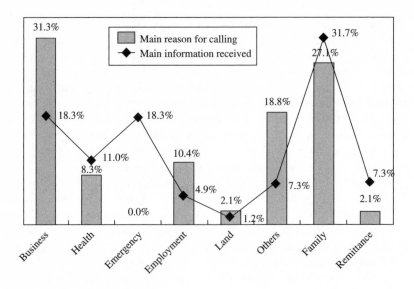

SOURCE: Primary survey data (2001).

(Figure 5.11). About one-third of telephone calls related to business issues, including searching for market information and prices and making business transactions. The next most common reason for telephone use was contact with family and friends. While some of these calls would be social, family and friends form an important economic network in Bangladesh, so a proportion of these calls would also be business related. The third reason given for making telephone calls was for gathering information about employment opportunities, both within and beyond Bangladesh. Other important reasons for calling included health and medical issues. Notably, there was a mismatch between the main reason given for calling and the main type of information received through calls. The mismatch may result from nonavailability of the required information or biased survey responses, or both.

It is interesting to look at the difference in the reasons for making phone calls and the type of information received between households in villages with a public telephone and those in villages without a public telephone (Table 5.16). While, in villages with a public telephone, the main reason for making calls was to contact family and friends, only 25 percent of households in villages without a public phone called family and friends. Conversely, around 25 percent of the in-

TABLE 5.16 Main reason for calling and type of information received in rural Bangladesh, 2001

	Main reason for calling		Type of information received	
Category	Village with telephone	Village without telephone	Village with telephone	Village without telephone
Business issue	14.0	21.9	24.0	34.8
Communication with doctors	14.0	6.3	4.0	13.0
Emergency news	6.0	37.5	0.0	0.0
Employment opportunity	6.0	3.1	16.0	4.3
Family/friends	36.0	25.0	28.0	26.1
Land transaction	2.0	—	4.0	—
Poultry, dairy	—	—	4.0	—
Remittance	12.0	—	4.0	—
Social reasons	4.0	3.1	—	—
Others	6.0	3.1	16.0	21.7
Total	100	100	100	100

SOURCE: Primary survey data (2001).

formation received by the households in villages with a public phone is business related, while business-related information represents around 39 percent of the information received by households in villages without a public phone.

More than 67 percent of information received by households in the lowest income quartile related to family and friends (Table 5.17). It is interesting to observe that the role of family and friends decreases as income increases. This observation supports the view that when access to markets is limited and

TABLE 5.17 Type of information received through phone calls based on income quartiles in rural Bangladesh, 2001

	Income quartiles				
Category	First quartile	Second quartile	Third quartile	Fourth quartile	Total
Business issue	29.3	5.6	6.7	12.5	17.1
Family and friends	26.8	22.2	40.0	62.5	31.7
Health	14.6	5.6	13.3	—	11.0
Emergency news	12.2	33.3	20.0	12.5	18.3
Remittance	7.3	5.6	6.7	—	7.3
Employment opportunities	2.4	11.1	—	12.5	4.9
Land transactions	—	5.6	—	—	1.2
Others	7.3	5.6	13.3	—	8.5

SOURCE: Primary survey data (2001).

imperfect, family and friends play an important role in information sharing. Not surprisingly, households in the lower income quartiles do not receive any information on remittances or land transactions. Similarly, they do not receive any health-related information.

What Is the Welfare Gain from Public Telephone Use? As previously discussed, access to public telephones for rural households is implicitly rationed by travel time and transport costs. Under a regulated tariff structure that takes care of the direct costs, one way to increase access is by reducing the indirect costs through the expansion of services (that is, by providing a public telephone in each village). The recent VPP program in Bangladesh has increased household access to public telephones in rural areas. To evaluate the direct welfare benefits of the project, we estimated compensating variation.

Whether households benefit from increased access to a public telephone depends on whether the gain in welfare from having a telephone nearby is higher than the direct and indirect costs of using it. Compensating variation is the maximum amount of money that households are willing to pay for telephone services, while maintaining constant welfare. The estimation of compensating variation involves two stages: first, parameter estimation, and second, the calculation of compensating variation. Compensating variation was measured for four different alternatives following Small and Rosen (1981). (See Appendix 5A for details of the methodology used and Appendix 5D for details of the estimations and the statistical results.)

In the case of Bangladesh, four means of communication reported by households were considered possible alternatives to telephone use: using a telephone elsewhere (for instance, traveling to the nearest town), sending a letter from the nearest post office, traveling to the recipient or sending a person there, and a combination of traveling and making a call from other places. As a result, alternatives to telephone use vary by household. However, for each telephone call there is only one alternative.

Compensating variation was estimated for four methods of communication other than the public telephone. The estimated compensating variation is the benefit to households of using public telephones over the available alternative methods of communication. Compensating variation varies across different income groups and among different alternative communication methods (Table 5.18). To facilitate comparison, local prices were converted to U.S. dollars based on the prevailing nominal exchange rate at the time of the survey.

The estimated compensating variation shows that for all income groups the rural telephone project improves welfare by comparison with the alternative methods of communication. In particular, public telephone use directly contributes to rural household welfare. In the case of Bangladesh, though the lowest income quartile does not receive greater benefits than the higher income quartile, the absolute welfare gain from the use of a public telephone is higher for this group than for other groups.

TABLE 5.18 Estimated compensating variation for alternative communication methods to the use of public telephones in rural Bangladesh

	Quartile of expenditure			
Method of communication	First quartile	Second quartile	Third quartile	Fourth quartile
Alternative forms of communication	Compensating variation per call (US$)			
Telephone from other place	0.15	0.21	0.20	0.20
Sending letter (post office)	0.11	0.14	0.13	0.13
Travel	0.65	0.84	0.78	0.81
Other	1.19	1.59	1.44	1.56
Cost of public telephone use	Direct and indirect costs per call (US$)			
	0.98	0.54	0.76	0.88

SOURCE: Primary survey data (2001).
NOTE: The exchange rate is US$1 = Tk. 56.

Conclusion

Based on the calculations of compensating variations undertaken for this case study, Bangladesh's rural telephony project, the VPP program, enhances welfare for the rural community across all four income quartiles. In some cases, it also enhances distributional equity. Rural households living below the national poverty line spend a higher proportion of their income on public telephone use than do households living above the poverty line. This implies that a reduction in both the tariff and nontariff costs of public phone use can increase rural household welfare in absolute and relative terms. Because poor households spend comparatively more on alternatives to public telephone use, their savings from the increased availability of public telephones in rural areas are substantial.

Farmers, Incomes, and the Use of Telephones: The Case of Rural China
Wensheng Wang

Given rapid political, economic, and social change, China's information and telecommunications sector grew at annual rates of 30–50 percent during 1990–2003 as mentioned in Chapter 3. By the end of 1999, China had the second-largest public telephone network and the largest cellular phone market in the world. It is extremely important to recognize the social and economic impact of ICT in rural China because more than half the population resides in rural areas. Theoretically, the introduction of sufficient ICT services in rural areas should stimulate social and economic development and an improved standard of living. Balit, Calvelo Rios, and Masias (1996) point out that the least expensive input for rural development is knowledge and information, essential for bringing about social and economic change.

FIGURE 5.12 Location of sample provinces in China

To obtain a comprehensive understanding of the effects of ICT in rural China, an empirical study was conducted on Chinese farm households, using a household survey, by the Fixed Sites Rural Survey (FSRS) office.[12] To simplify the analysis, three provinces were selected for study (Figure 5.12). These three provinces cover 15 percent of China's total land area and 22 percent of the to- tal population (Table 5.19). The data set includes 2,200 households and covers a three-year period, 1995–97. Jiangsu is located in the eastern coastal area and borders Shanghai. The distinctive feature of Shandong province is a peninsula that faces the Yellow Sea and the Bo Sea, providing an advantageous location for international trade with South Korea and Japan. The province of Sichuan is

---

12. The office resides with the Ministry of Agriculture's research Center for Rural Economy and covers the whole of rural China (31 provinces and autonomous regions, excluding Taiwan), which encompasses about 20,000 farm households in the survey.

TABLE 5.19 Area, population density, and per capita gross domestic product by province in China, 1997

Province	Land area (1,000 km²)	Population (millions)	Population density (people per km²)	GDP per capita (yuan)
Jiangsu	102.6	71.48	697	9,344
Shandong	156.7	87.85	560	7,569
Sichuan	485.0	84.30	192	3,938
National total	9,600.0	1,236.26	129	6,048

SOURCE: SSB (1998).

NOTE: 1 Yuan ≅ US$0.12 in 1997.

a land-locked basin located in China's central west. Sichuan is isolated by surrounding mountains that significantly limit its economic and social exchange with other regions.

This case study focuses on the economic impact of access to telephones by farm households and tries to determine whether there is a positive relationship between telephone adoption and improved income status. The study also investigates the socioeconomic characteristics of households that are likely to use the telephone.

The Potential of Telephone Use for Rural Development

In China, subsistence farmers don't need to interact significantly with people beyond their own families. Yet in raising output above the subsistence level, communication is important. Despite low levels of ICT in rural China, studies have shown that ICT, including the telephone and Internet, have positive impacts on farm households in terms of industrial patterns, market expansion, sale and supply channels, and education and healthcare. For example, duck farmers in the Hubei province now sell their ducks directly to customers through a telephone order system (Ke and Zhang 1999). With access to telephones, the potential exists to eliminate intermediaries who do not add value to products. For example, Haikou village, in the suburbs of the city of Wuhan, is well known for producing balsam pears. Although farmers had bumper harvests for years prior to installing telephones, they did not profit from them because local intermediaries had forced prices down. After the installation of telephones in 1998, farmers were able to contact vegetable dealers in their neighboring province and sell their products at much higher prices. This experience led to the installation of 41 telephones in this village within two months (Ke and Zhang 1999).

ICT can also be an economical means of investing in human capital in rural China. The use of ICT in education programs has provided rural residents with previously unimagined opportunities. Telecommunications can facilitate education for both children and adults at low cost. Agricultural universities and research institutes have become pioneers in providing Internet-based education for farmers. The Capital Farmer Network (www.capitalfamer.net) is a popular Web site that specializes in agricultural technology and provides free online seminars to farmers on new agricultural techniques. Lack of Internet infrastructure, however, means that few farmers benefit from these services. Medicine is another field benefiting from telecommunications. In the mountain areas of Yunnan province, village doctors use cellular phones to consult experts at provincial capital hospitals several hundreds of miles away. Similarly, patient records can be transmitted via the Internet.

ICT can have even more wide-ranging effects for farm households. For example, ICT can provide access to timely information on natural disasters and environmental hazards, and, by facilitating links with government authorities, it can improve the security of rural communities and make governments more effective and more transparent, especially in remote areas.

Characteristics of Telephone Subscribers

The extent to which telephones have penetrated rural households can be viewed in two ways—spatially and socioeconomically. Spatially, telephone penetration varies among and within provinces. Penetration is high in the plains of the east and hills of the central region and relatively low in mountain areas of the west, particularly where economic development is low. As of 1997, of the three sample provinces, 14.3 percent of farm households had a telephone, and teledensity ranged from 22.6 percent in Jiangsu province to 0.7 percent in Sichuan province. The socioeconomic characteristics associated with telephone use include annual household income, sources of household business income, grain sales, farm size, and the education level of the household head.

There is a positive relationship between telephone subscription and annual household income, and between telephone subscription and annual per capita household income. Household income is significantly lower in households without a telephone. It seems that telephone subscription correlates with a per capita income within the range of about 2,000–3,000 yuan (Figure 5.13). Analysis of the survey data suggests varied results when it comes to additional sources of business income as a determinant of telephone subscription. Farm size seems not to be relevant. Households where the head was 31–50 years old had higher telephone density than those with either younger or older household heads. Similarly, households where the head was more educated were more likely to have a telephone.

The Determinants of the Decision to Subscribe to Telephone Services

To measure the influence of socioeconomic factors on telephone subscription in the sample farm households, the relationship between the various socioeconomic factors and the household choice of whether or not to subscribe to telephone services were quantified through a Logit regression. Details of the

FIGURE 5.13 Net per capita income of telephone subscribers in China, 1995–97

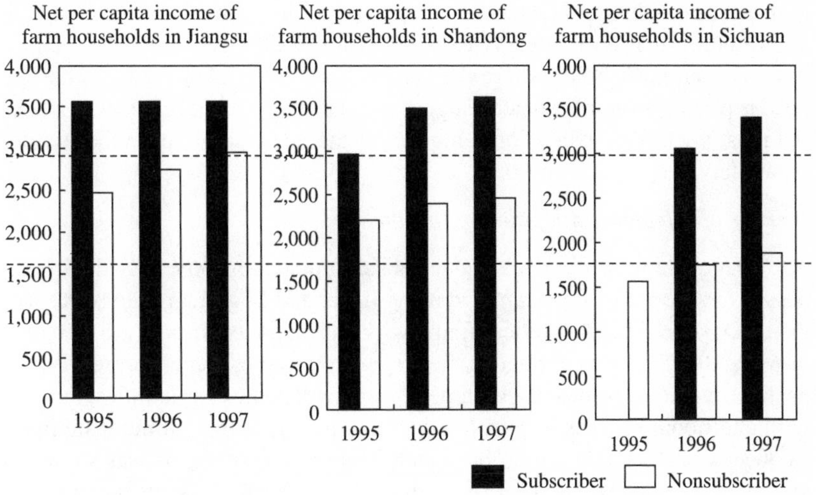

SOURCE: Primary survey data (1995–97).

methodology used are provided in Appendix 5A, while statistical results are provided in Appendix 5E.

The model results show that there is a significant positive relationship between telephone subscription and the variables of net annual income, value of productive fixed assets, number of household members with a professional title, and educational level of head of household. Distance to a main road from villages, however, is negatively correlated with telephone subscription. The probability of telephone subscription increases over time in all three sample provinces. For additional sources of business income, the analysis shows that households conducting additional agricultural business activities had a higher probability of subscribing to telephone services than households conducting additional nonagricultural business activities. Households reporting "mainly agricultural and other" business activities were most likely to be telephone subscribers, whereas households reporting "other" business activities were much less likely to subscribe. This result, contrary to what other case studies have shown (that households undertaking nonagricultural activities were more likely to use telephones), may be caused by the large absolute number of households conducting mainly agricultural and other business activities, despite the relatively low level of telephone density.

The household survey classified farm household heads by education level: illiterate, primary school education, secondary school education, and university education or above. Results are consistent with most existing studies of household demand for telephone subscription: the higher the level of education, the higher the probability of telephone subscription. Although (also consistent with other studies such as the Ghana case study in this chapter), the large gap in adoption between households where the head is illiterate and households were the head is primary-school educated suggests that primary school education makes the most significant educational impact on the decision to subscribe to telephone services.

Impacts of Telephone Adoption on Income

The relationships between telephone subscription and income growth or business diversification were examined using linear and Logit regressions, respectively. Details of the theoretical framework and statistical results are provided in Appendix 5E. As mentioned earlier, even though subsistence farmers do not need to interact significantly with persons outside their own families, farmers with additional sources of business income may need to communicate more frequently with people within or outside their communities, as was shown in previous case studies. Therefore the hypothesis we try to test is whether the shift from agricultural to nonagricultural businesses (as a proxy for major household welfare) is related to telephone subscription. Thus, we constructed a Logit model to explain the shift by farm households from primarily agricultural businesses to nonagricultural types of businesses with variables including province, additional business income sources, geographic features of the village where the farm is located, number of family members with professional titles, distance from village to a main road, fixed productive assets, net annual household income, and telephone subscription.

The estimation results, consistent with our previous results, indicate that there is no significant relationship between telephone subscription and shifts in the kinds of additional businesses conducted by farm households. This may mean that telephone use influences business efficiency but not the transition of other types of businesses in the short term. Alternatively, telephone subscription may not cause changes in the kinds of additional businesses operated by farm households; rather, the change in the business may create a need for a telephone.

Conclusion

The analysis for this case study shows that the primary determinants of telephone subscription for farm households in China are net annual income, educational level of household head, number of household members with a professional title, and additional sources of business income. In particular, the demand for telephone services in farm households largely depends on net income. Primary education plays an important role in the decision to subscribe to telephone services; if the head of household has a professional title, the household is highly likely to have a telephone.

There are also positive relationships between telephone subscription and income growth, although some of the effects of these factors are not statistically significant. Changes in sources of additional business income do not appear to be correlated with telephone subscription. This may either mean that telephone subscription does not cause changes in the economic activities of farm households or that a shift in types of businesses operated by farm households may lead to the need for a telephone. Further, access to a telephone may improve business efficiency rather than causing a change in the type of business conducted by the household in the short term.

The analysis provides economic insights about the characteristics of rural telecommunications demand China. For example, the per capita income threshold for telephone subscription (approximately 2,000 and 3,000 yuan) is indicative of the potential rural telecommunications market and may have implications for telecommunications policy.

The Effects of Public Telephone Services: The Case of Rural Ghana
Romeo Bertolini

This case study explores household characteristics associated with the use of public telephones in rural Ghana, focusing on who uses public telephone services in rural areas, what determines use, and how the intensity of use relates to household characteristics. To identify the direction, magnitude, and significance of influencing variables on the decision to use public telephone services, in terms of both use and intensity, a concept developed by Mitchell (1978) and modified by Torero (2000) was applied (details of the methodology are provided in Appendix 5A). Households make decisions when using telephone services. The first decision is to access the telephone, depending on whether their benefits from use exceed the cost (for example, the transportation and time cost of going to the telecenter). Once the decision to use the phone is made, the next decision is how much they will use it (that is, their intensity of use). In this case study, the first decision is modeled using a dichotomic Logit model and the second using a Tobit model (given that the intensity of use is only relevant for those households that use to the telephone, not for all of them; details of the conceptual framework and statistical results are provided in Appendix 5F).

Survey Design and Data

Telecommunications services in rural areas of low-income countries are usually provided in the form of public phone booths or telecommunications centers (telecenters). Individual access is scarce and mainly subject to infrastructural constraints, meaning lack of telephone lines and switching capacity (Bertolini et al. 2000). Bearing this in mind, locations were chosen where public telephone access was available and where the predominant economic activities included agriculture, rural industry and services, and trade in agricultural products

(Republic of Ghana 1995). The town of Akatsi in the Akatsi District of southern Volta was selected, along with Agbedrafor and Gefia, 1 and 5 kilometers from Akatsi, respectively. These two additional communities were chosen, respectively, to be within and outside the universal access area, defined as the area from which public telephone services could be reached within 30-minute walking distance.

Within the Akatsi District, 20 fixed lines were available in the district capital (Akatsi) through an exchange located in the regional capital (Ho). Seven of these 20 lines were publicly accessible. Despite long waiting lists, indicating significant unmet demand, lack of infrastructure prevented expansion of the network, leaving 88,000 district inhabitants sharing 20 fixed telephone lines—though inhabitants in the western boundaries can also access telephones outside the district. Regardless, teledensity is extremely low in rural Ghana (Bertolini et al. 2000).

In a first round of interviews, 410 sample households were assessed based on whether or not they used public telephone or facsimile services. The results showed that 48 percent of all screened households (197) were regular users. A more detailed household questionnaire was then applied randomly to a subset of households to assess the main socioeconomic features of the two groups and reasons for telecommunications use. Ultimately, 170 detailed household surveys could be used in the data analysis.

As mentioned earlier, household expenditure reflects the intensity of telecommunications use. Households were asked how much they spent on telecommunications over the previous month. Average expenditure of Ghanian cedis (ϕ) 21,882.5 was also compared with overall household expenditure (Table 5.20).[13] This comparison led to the conclusion that telephone services accounted for approximately 5 percent of the sample households' overall expenditure.

Determinants of Telephone Use

Table 5F.1 present two alternative estimations of the reasons why household access public telephones services. The first specification uses a measure of income constructed from the survey, while the second includes as an explanatory variable a self-assessment of the economic status reported by the household relative to other households of the same village. Households with male heads have a higher probability of accessing public telephone services in both specifications as do those with younger heads, although this second variable is only statistically significant in the first specification.

Similarly, and as shown in all the previous case studies, the higher the education, the higher the probability that a rural household will access a public telephone. Although, as our measure of income improves, the marginal effects

---

13. The exchange rate in April 1999 was cedis 1,000 = US$0.37.

TABLE 5.20 Household expenditure on telephone services in rural Ghana, 1999

Expenditure	Number of observations	Minimum	Maximum	Mean	Standard deviation
Monthly expenditure on household telecommunication services (cedis)	120	0	400,000	21,882.50	41,299.70
Expenditure on telecommunications services as a share of overall expenditure (percent)	120	0	25.5	5.1	4.5

SOURCE: Primary survey data (1999).

NOTE: The exchange rate in April 1999 was cedis 1,000 = US$0.37.

of higher levels of education are absorbed. This can clearly be seen by comparing the results of the first and the second specifications. In the first specification, income has a positive and significant impact on access, but in terms of education only access to primary education is significant. In the second specification, however, where our measure of income is a relative comparison with other village households (and hence captures fewer income differentials), all the levels of education are significant and positive, and the self-assessment of economic status is either significant or, in the case of the poorer households, significant and negative. This shows that differences in education levels reflect the effects of education on income when these effects measured in aggregate.

This clearly implies an important correlation between income and education, creating a problem for our specification. Nevertheless, we decided that the income variables in the first specification incorporate other useful explanatory variables, such as entrepreneurship and other income activities, so there were additional benefits to including these variables. When the income variable is excluded, all education variables are significant and positive, as expected. Finally, and as is the case in other studies, the results show that primary school education has the strongest educational influence on telecommunications use. Finally, the impact of location on the likelihood of telecommunications use was estimated using dummy variables for Agbedrafor and Gefia. The results showed no significant impact for Agbedra and were mixed for Gefia, but they confirmed that increased distance from the household location to telecommunications services in Akatsi had a negative impact on telecommunications use.

Determinants of the Intensity of Use

Explanations for the intensity of telephone use among households are similar to the explanations for use. Similarly, households with male heads, younger heads, more educated family members are the ones that use the telephone more frequently. Moreover, gender, education, and income seem to be the most important variables determining intensity of telephone use. Specifically, in the case of income the results showed that intensity of household telephone use is extremely sensitive to income increases.[14] An increase of 10 percent in household income results in a doubling of household expenditure on telephone use. Similarly, a reduction in 10 percent in household income implies a fall of over 20 percent in household expenditure on telephone use. There are two possible explanations to this result. On one hand, it has been shown in the literature that the lower the penetration of telephones, the higher the own price elasticity of the households (see, for example, Torero, Schroth, and Pascó-Font 2003); therefore, given that the area of study is characterized by a very low telephone penetration and we are not controlling for the price of the telephone call, this could be captured in the high income elasticity identified.[15] A second explanation is that rural households are more sensitive to income shocks than wealthier urban households, hence they will immediately adjust the consumption of goods not necessary for subsistence under negative income shocks.

The size of the household, although positive, is only significant in the second specification, so the hypothesis that the more household members the greater the household's telephone use intensity can only be accepted with reservation.

The index that reflects the degree of participation of the household in community-based organizations is positive, although not statistically significant in either of our specifications. This result could imply that issues discussed and analyzed at the community level mainly refer to local issues so there is not necessarily a significant benefit from obtaining additional information through the use of the telephone. This result requires further research to try to differentiate the type of community-based organizations with respect to their requirements of information outside specific local issues.

In terms of household location, the results of the Tobit equation support the results obtained in the accessibility models. Gefia seems not only to have less access to public telephones but also lower use intensity, which could be a reflection of lower household income or be related to a restricted supply.

Conclusion

The analyses undertaken for this case study confirm a set of characteristics that increase the likelihood of rural household telecommunications use and intensity in rural Ghana. The first set of characteristics relate to the household head,

---

14. It is important to mention that the relationship was not determined to be causal, however; telephone access could actually be responsible for the higher household income.

15. We cannot control for the price of a telephone call because the survey was implemented at one point in time, hence there is insufficient price variation to capture price elasticity.

whereby households with male heads and heads with at least a primary school education are more likely to use public telephones intensely. Household income also has a strong positive impact on household telecommunications use and intensity of use.

Specific variables that were included in the Tobit model estimations—income source, participation in community-based organizations, and household size—did not generate the expected results. This is particularly true for household participation in community-based organizations and the primary source of household income. Interestingly, it seems that both the likelihood and intensity of service use do not necessarily increase with increased wealth or education.

The location of the household is also not as important as anticipated. Within the regression exercise, a statistical difference in use and intensity of use by inhabitants of Akatsi and Agbedrafor could not be shown. The expense and time required to travel to Akatsi to access telecommunications services reduces both use and intensity of use by households located in Gefia, though the effect was not as significant as expected, at least for results from the Probit model.

Appendix 5A: Overview of Methodology

When trying to understand household demand for telephone services, the basic model followed in this chapter initially assumes that a single consumer has constant marginal utility of income (meaning the additional amount of satisfaction received from an additional unit of consumption is constant) and a separable utility function (that is, the relationship between the marginal utility generated by the consumption of telephone calls and the marginal utility of the consumption of other goods is irrelevant, and therefore both utilities can be added), for telephone calls q and other goods x (Mitchell 1978):

$$U(x, q) = x + V(q). \tag{1}$$

The consumer maximizes utility in Equation (1) subject to his or her budget constraints:

$$y = x + \partial(L + pq), \tag{2}$$

where y is income measured in x units, L is the fixed monthly charge for telephone service, and p is the vector of prices of local and long-distance calls. The parameter is $\delta = 1$ if the consumer obtains telephone access, and $\delta = 0$ if the consumer does not.

As mentioned in Mitchell (1978), we can recast the optimization problem as one of maximizing the differences between the utility of telephone access and its cost, the difference being the net economic gain of having a telephone:

$$\underset{\partial, q}{\text{Max}}\, [V(q) - \partial(L + pq)]. \tag{3}$$

In this way, the demand for access or connection is stated as

$$\partial = 1 \quad \text{if} \quad R(p) \geq L,$$
$$\;\; = 0 \quad \text{if} \quad R(p) < L \tag{4}$$

where the consumer's reservation price or surplus $(R(p))$, is given by

$$R(p) = \max_p [V(q) - pq]. \tag{5}$$

Econometrically, the access is measured using a qualitative variables model. Specifically, each household realizes a cost–benefit analysis of having or not having access to a telephone, comparing the consumer surplus $R(p)$ with the cost of access, L. This variable, z^*, cannot be observed, but it can be expressed as

$$z^* = \partial'x + \varepsilon \tag{6}$$

where ε is normally distributed with mean zero and variance 1. Given that we only observe households with or without access to a telephone, the observation is

$$z = 0 \quad \text{if} \quad z^* \geq 0$$
$$z = 1 \quad \text{if} \quad z^* > 0, \tag{7}$$

with symmetry, the probability of $z = 1$ is

$$\text{Prob}[z^* > 0] = \text{Prob}[\varepsilon < \partial'x].$$
$$= \Phi(\partial'x) \tag{8}$$

The next step is to measure impact of the telephone based on access and intensity of use. The main problem in identifying impact is the difficulty of disentangling the extent to which the telephone use and rural household consumption may be linked in a cause–effect relationship. We use both traditional and relatively new methods to control for simultaneity between telecommunications use and consumption, and then attempt to identify the effect of telecommunications on household consumption. The availability of panel data, while short, also increases our ability to address the issue of endogeneity.

Consumer surplus, the most frequently used method of measuring the welfare effect of ICT, is described below through the use of compensating variation techniques; consumption functions and matching techniques, the quantitative tools used in case studies in this chapter, are presented thereafter.

Measuring Compensating Variation

In order to measure the consumer surplus more formally, we calculate compensating variation adopting the methodology proposed by Gertler and Glewwe (1989) for the case of education. We use the central elements of the Gertler and Glewwe model, but add a new price. It is assumed that rural households have a utility function that depends on the consumption of other goods and services and of the access to the public telecommunications in the rural areas. Both goods have a cost, so the household must choose an optimal combination given its budget constraints. The price of using a public telephone in rural areas includes the direct cost (the call fee) and the indirect costs (transport cost, time of trip, and so on). Rural households compare the utility of using a public phone with the utility of not using one, and if the utility of use is higher, they will choose to use the service. Formally, this decision can be expressed as U_a, and the expected utility is then expressed as

$$U_a = U_a(C_a, A), \tag{9}$$

where A is the access to the public phone and C_a is the feasible consumption after the direct and indirect costs of access are taken into account. On the other hand, if the household chooses not to use the public phone, the utility function can be expressed as

$$U_{na} = U_{na}(C_{na}), \tag{10}$$

where C_{na} is possible consumption, discounting the cost of using an alternative means of communication, such as traveling, sending a letter, and so on. Therefore, rural households will access public phones if $U_a > U_{na}$, given their budget constraints:

$$C_a + P_a = C_{na} + P_{na} = Y, \tag{11}$$

where P_a is the direct and indirect cost of accessing a public telephone, P_{na} is the cost of the alternative means of communication, and Y is the disposable household income.

A linear specification of the conditional utility function is not possible because the family income, among other variables, can influence the decision of whether to use the phone. If this specification were used, it would mean that the decision rule $U_a - U_{na}$ would not depend on the income. Therefore, following Gelter and Glewwe (1988), a semiquadratic specification is used that combines a linear specification of access to a public phone with a quadratic equation representing net consumption:[16]

$$U_a = \alpha_0 A + \alpha_1(Y - P_a) + \alpha_2(Y - P_a)^2 + \varepsilon_a. \tag{12}$$

The utility of using alternative communication methods can be written as

$$U_{na} = \alpha_1(Y - P_{na}) + \alpha_2(Y - P_{na})^2 + \varepsilon_{na}$$
$$U_{na} = V_{na} + \varepsilon_{na}. \tag{13}$$

The identification of the parameters of Equations (12) and (13) is guaranteed as long as the indirect costs of accessing a public phone or alternative form of communication vary among households.

---

16. A semiquadratic specification is preferred to ensure that the difference $U_a - U_{na}$ depends on income. This does not occur if a linear specification is used.

It is also possible to assume that the utility obtained through the use of the public phone by each household depends on the motivation for use, the specific characteristics of each household, the characteristics of the household members, the expected benefits, the quality of the service, the communication needs, and so on. All these variables can be represented in vector X. Therefore, the equation can be specified as $\alpha_0 A = \beta X + \varepsilon_a$, with the following modifications to Equation (12):

$$U_a = \beta'X + \alpha_1(Y - P_a) + \alpha_2(Y - P_a)^2 + \varepsilon_a + \xi_a \qquad (13)$$
$$U_a = V_a + \tau_a.$$

According to the model of random utility,[17] the demand for public phone service is the probability that U_a is greater than U_{na}. The following equalities can be expressed:

$$\Pr ob[A] = \Pr ob[U_a > U_{na}]$$
$$\Pr ob[A] = \Pr ob[V_a + \tau_a > V_{na} + \varepsilon_{na}] \qquad (14)$$
$$\Pr ob[A] = \Pr ob[V_a - V_{na} + \upsilon > 0].$$

Then, assuming that n distributes as a logistic function, the probability of access to public phone services can be expressed as

$$\Pr ob[A] = \frac{1}{1 + e^{(V_{na} - V_a)}}. \qquad (15)$$

The Logit estimation of Equation (15) permits the calculation of the household disposition to pay for the telephone service rather than an alternative form of communication (see Maddala 1983; McFadden 1984). This disposition to pay is calculated as a compensated variation. In this way, an estimation of the benefit obtained by a rural household for the use of a public phone is obtained. The compensated variation of a Logit model can be expressed as

$$VC = (1/\lambda)[\ln[\exp(V_{na}) + \exp(V_n)] - \ln[\exp(V_{na}') + \exp(V_a')]\}, \qquad (16)$$

where V_i and V_i' are functions evaluated for the alternative form of communication or different distances to the nearest public telephone.

Assessing Impact Using Consumption Functions

Rather than concentrating on the individual household consumer surplus, the main objective of this methodology is to identify whether a difference exists in the consumption of user versus non-user households. Therefore, the aim is to control for all other observed and unobserved factors that may determine consumption, and isolate the consumption gap between user and non-user house-

---

17. See in Greene (2000) for an explanation of a random linear utility model and Train (1993) for an explanation of a random nonlinear utility model.

holds that may be attributed to the use of a public telephone. To clarify this discussion and outline the estimation methodology, consider the following two-equation system:

$$C_i = X_i \beta + \delta T_i + \varepsilon_i \text{ and} \tag{17}$$

$$T_i = Z_i \gamma + u_i, \tag{18}$$

where C_i is per capita total or cash consumption for household I; X_i and Z_i are, respectively, vectors of variables that potentially influence consumption and the probability of being a telephone user; T_i indicates whether a household is a telephone user or not; β, δ, and γ are coefficients to be estimated; and ε_i and u_i are assumed to be $N(0, \sigma_\varepsilon^2)$ and $N(0, \sigma_u^2)$, respectively. A potential strategy is to rely on ordinary least squares (OLS) to estimate Equation (17) and obtain estimates of the coefficient on T_i. The estimated coefficient on the telephone use indicator may be interpreted as a public phone use (treatment) effect. While straightforward, this strategy may be flawed. The simultaneity problem arises as unobserved factors that determine telephone use may be correlated with unobserved factors that determine consumption. In such a situation T_i and ε_i will be correlated. If they are positively (or negatively) correlated, then estimates that do not account for this correlation will overestimate (or underestimate) the effect of telephone use on consumption. While incorrect or inconsistent estimates of the use effect are a possibility, there are circumstances under which OLS will yield consistent estimates. If X contains all the variables that may influence the probability of a household using a telephone and the error terms in Equations (17) and (18) are uncorrelated (conditional on X), then OLS estimates of Equation (17) will yield consistent estimates of the use effect.

Therefore our estimates should control for the possibility that the use status of households depends on unobserved characteristics. This procedure is an extension of the Heckman selection model and is often called the treatment-effects model in the literature (see Vella 1993, for example). The idea is to create and include an additional variable in Equation (17). This additional variable (generalized residual) controls for the potential correlation between the two error terms. The estimation of Equation (17) with the inclusion of this additional variable should lead to consistent estimates.

Assessing Impact Using Matching Methods

An alternative approach to estimating the effect of telephone use is to rely on matching methods. This approach is based on comparing average per capita consumption between user households (the treatment group) and non-user households (the control group) ensuring that the two groups are as similar as possible in terms of their observed characteristics. In practice, each household in the treatment group is matched to a household in the control group on the basis of similarities in their probability of using telephone services. This approach to evaluation works well if selection into treatment and control groups depends on observed characteristics and the distribution of unobserved characteristics is the same across both groups (for details see Rosenbaum and Rubin 1983; Heckman, Ichimura, and Todd 1997). Other conditions to ensure consistent comparisons are for information on the treatment and control groups to be gathered using the same questionnaire and for the two groups to come from the same economic environment.

Inferences about the impact of access to telephone services on an individual household involve speculation about how the household would have responded had it (or at least its members) not obtained telephone access. The simplest of such models is

$$y_i = \alpha_j + \gamma d_j + \varepsilon_j, \tag{19a}$$

where j is the index for both the control group ($j = 0$) and the treatment group ($j = 1$); d_j is 1 if the household has access to a telephone and zero if it does not; and γ is the impact of the treatment effect of access to a telephone. In this sense the no-treatment counterfactual is assumed to obey an additive model, while the treatment effect is constant:

$$y_{0j} = \alpha_j + \varepsilon_j; E[y_{0j}] = \alpha_j \tag{19b}$$

$$y_{1j} - y_{0j} = \gamma. \tag{19c}$$

Equation (19b), stating that changes in household welfare in the treatment group (expressed either as the household's expenditure or its income) only stem from the use of public phones, is required for identification of causality. If the additive model is conditional on covariates X, then identification will be based on

$$E[y_{0j} | X] = \alpha_j(X) \text{ and} \tag{20a}$$

$$E[y_{1j} - y_{0j} | X] \equiv \gamma(X). \tag{20b}$$

To estimate the hypothetical difference in the impact variables for households that use public phones compared with the households that do not, we follow the Roy–Rubin model.[18] If we define a binary assignment indicator, D, indicating whether an individual unit participated in the program, the treatment effect of each individual unit is then defined as the difference between its potential outcomes:

$$\Delta = Y^T - Y^C, \tag{21}$$

where Y is the change in the impact variable and the supra indices refer to the treatment group (T) and the control group (C). Since there is no opportunity to

---

18. The original ideas can be found in Roy (1951) and Rosenbaum and Rubin (1983). For further discussion of these approaches, see Hujer and Wellner (2000) and Lechner (2000).

estimate individual gains with confidence without observing Y^T and Y^C for the same individual unit simultaneously, we must concentrate on the average population gains from treatment, or the average treatment effect on the treated:

$$E[\Delta \mid D = 1] = E(Y^T \mid D = 1) - E(Y^C \mid D = 1). \tag{22}$$

Then, if the following condition holds:

$$E(Y^C \mid D = 1) = E(Y^C \mid D = 0), \tag{23}$$

we can use nonparticipants as an adequate control group. If, in addition to the treatment and outcome, we also observe a background variable (or vector of variables) X_i, and we believe that the treatment depends on the potential outcomes only through X_i, we can state the unconfoundedness[19] condition formally as

$$E(Y^C \mid D = 1, X_i = x) = E(Y^C \mid D = 0, X_i = x). \tag{24}$$

As mentioned previously, in nonexperimental data, access to a telephone would generally not be independent of potential outcomes because the decision to obtain access to the telephone is likely to be correlated, for example, with the local level of income or with unobserved village characteristics related to its overall income level. However, because public telephones were assigned in our case study data in a quasi-experimental fashion, independent of household income, and because the outcomes of interest are impacts over welfare of access to telephones, unconfoundedness is likely to be conditional on characteristics of the household observed.

Appendix 5B: Statistical Results, the Case of Peru

Probabilities relating to rural household access to public phones were first estimated using a Logit model. Table 5B.1 reports the results of this analysis, based on three different specifications, along with the parameters and marginal effects. The first model incorporates the variables of consumption and squared consumption and the characteristics of the head of the household (age, education, native language, economic activity). The second model incorporates a control variable—the type of village in which the household is located. Finally, the third model incorporates additional control variables—household perceptions of the possible benefits of public phone use. In addition, a variable measuring household composition (the number of household members) was also included.

The coefficients of the variables net consumption and squared net consumption are statistically significant in the three specifications. Therefore, utility

---

19. Unconfoundedness is a stronger causality criterion condition implying lack of causal biased of the conditional expected values $E(Y \mid X = x)$. Unconfoundedness holds in randomized experiments, but it may hold in nonrandomized experiments, as well.

TABLE 5B.1 Determinants of the use of rural public phones in Peru, Logit model

Variables	Model 1		Model 2		Model 3	
	Parameters	Marginal effect	Parameters	Marginal effect	Parameters	Marginal effect
Consumption (× 10^{-2})	0.1144***	0.0172***	0.1036***	0.0156***	0.10140***	0.0148***
	(0.0328)	(0.0046)	(0.0323)	(0.0046)	(0.0347)	(0.0047)
Squared consumption (× 10^{-4})	-0.0018***	-0.0003***	-0.0016***	-0.0002***	-0.00154***	-0.0002***
	(0.0005)	(0.0001)	(0.0005)	(0.0001)	(0.0005)	(0.0001)
Years of education of the head of the family	0.1359***	0.0198***	0.1300***	0.0188***	0.12944***	0.0178***
	(0.0260)	(0.0036)	(0.0265)	(0.0037)	(0.0279)	(0.0037)
Exclusive room for economic activity (Yes = 1, No = 0)	0.8257***	0.1080***	0.7651***	0.1003***	0.76060***	0.0959***
	(0.2383)	(0.0446)	(0.2401)	(0.0445)	(0.2437)	(0.0262)
Age of the head of the family	0.0304	0.0043	0.0322	0.0046	0.02585	0.0032
	(0.0356)	(0.0054)	(0.0356)	(0.0054)	(0.0389)	(0.0056)
Squared age of the head of the family	-0.0003	-0.0001	-0.0004	-0.0001	-0.00033	-0.0000
	(0.0004)	(0.0001)	(0.0004)	(0.0001)	(0.0004)	(0.0001)
Native language (Yes = 1, No = 0)	-0.7351***	-0.1024***	-0.7386***	-0.1026***	-0.66932***	-0.0898***
	(0.2333)	(0.0491)	(0.2355)	(0.0490)	(0.2411)	(0.0278)
Use of communication services (number of activities)			0.0207	0.0030	0.02769*	0.0040*
			(0.0166)	(0.0024)	(0.0167)	(0.0024)
Rural village with public telephone (Yes = 1, No = 0)			0.4014***	0.0651***	0.43518***	0.0699***
			(0.1695)	(0.0376)	(0.1764)	(0.0260)
Household composition (number of members)					-0.01615	-0.0020
					(0.0466)	(0.0067)
Assigned benefits to the use of public telephones Increases speed of communication (Yes = 1, No = 0)					0.51609***	0.0771***
					(0.1952)	(0.0293)

Reduces travel (Yes = 1, No = 0)		0.66407***	0.0870***
		(0.2344)	(0.0263)
Reduces isolation (Yes = 1, No = 0)		1.01903***	0.1133***
		(0.3261)	(0.0269)
Provides monetary savings (Yes = 1, No = 0)		0.55879*	0.0695*
		(0.3269)	(0.0344)
Provides time savings (Yes = 1, No = 0)		0.07738	0.0029
		(0.3042)	(0.0408)
Constant	−0.3902	−0.6942	−1.13186
	(0.9176)	(0.9190)	(0.9536)
Number of observations	991	990	987
Log-likelihood	−452.4	−448.2	−434.7
Wald chi²	121.02	133.47	148.6
Prob > chi²	0.000	0.000	0.000
Pseudo R²	0.141	0.148	0.171
Hit rate	0.769	0.776	0.784

SOURCE: Estimated by authors.

NOTES: Standard errors are shown in parentheses. *Indicates significance at the 90 percent level; ***indicates significance at the 99 percent level.

TABLE 5B.2 Compensating variation for the use of alternative methods of communication in rural Peru

Communication method	Expenditure group			
	First quartile	Second quartile	Third quartile	Fourth quartile
Alternative communications methods	Compensated variation[a] per phone call (Peruvian new soles)			
Sending a letter (post office)	5.83	6.31	6.52	6.81
Sending a letter (transport agency)	4.89	5.10	5.29	5.48
Radio	4.91	5.13	5.35	5.65
Traveling	7.00	8.52	9.27	9.82
	Direct and indirect costs per phone call (Peruvian new soles)			
Rural public phone use	4.48	3.81	3.13	2.91

SOURCE: Calculated by the authors from primary survey data (2000).
[a]Following Small and Rosen (1981).

is nonlinear in consumption. It is worth mentioning that the direct and indirect costs of public phone use (P_a in the model) are entered into the regression through such variables. The variability of this price makes it possible to identify the coefficients of the model. Next, we analyzed the welfare effect of public phone use compared with available alternatives by calculating compensating variation from the results of the Logit model estimations (Table 5B.2). Once again, calculations were made for four expenditure groups. The costs of alternative communication methods are included, along with the time commitment required for each. In all cases, the estimated compensating variation is greater than the cost of using public phones, which confirms the increased welfare to the rural population. This result is consistent with Bayes, von Braun, and Akhter (1999) for a similar project in the rural areas of Bangladesh. It is also consistent with the results observed in Cannok (2001) for Peru.

Appendix 5C: Detailed Data Comparison, the Case of Laos

Table 5C.1 compares descriptive statistics from the 2000 primary survey with selected statistics from the 1997/98 LECS. Table 5C.2 presents selected descriptive statistics for the two primary data sets used in this case study. The first column in Table 5C.2 contains information on the complete data set collected in 2000. The mean per capita annual consumption was $192 (including an imputed monetary value for a household's own consumption), while per capita cash consumption was somewhat lower, at about $140. On average, the household consisted of 6 members, 2.63 of whom were working; the household head

TABLE 5C.1 A comparison of descriptive statistics for rural Laos, 1997/98 and 2000

Variable	ZEF (2000) Mean	LECS (1997/98) Mean	Mean difference[a]
Household size	6.0	6.4	−0.4037
	(2.4)	(2.5)	*−3.6860*
Age of household head	44.0	42.4	1.6100
	(12.2)	(12.6)	*2.8390*
Years of education of household head	6.0	4.1	1.8838
	(4.4)	(3.7)	*9.7300*
Agricultural land (acres)	1.6	0.8	0.8738
	(2.0)	(1.2)	*10.0810*
Number of cattle	2.1	1.9	0.1615
	(3.8)	(4.0)	*0.8970*
Annual per capita consumption	192.64	102.14	90.0000
(US$ in 2000 prices)	(178.96)	(100.27)	*11.4740*
Sample size	606	2,441	

SOURCE: Laos Expenditure Consumption Survey (LECS 1997/98) and primary survey data (2000).

NOTES: Standard deviations are shown in parentheses, *t*-statistics are shown in italic. Data are based on a subset of LECS data.

[a]*t*-test for equality of means.

was about 44 years old and had completed primary school; and the household had about 1.6 acres of land and 2 head of cattle. An interesting feature is that 42 percent of the households had more than one source of income. Employment activities were quite diverse. While some household members worked on farms, others carried out trading activities or ran small businesses. Typically, households with diverse income sources had higher consumption levels than households with only one source of income.

Descriptive statistics for 190 households surveyed in 2000 and 2001 (the control group) are shown in columns 2 and 3 of Table 5C.2. Real consumption changed very little during the year, and all other changes in variables were minor.[20] This is not surprising considering the short time span between the two surveys.

In terms of the incidence of telecommunications use, for the full survey sample the rate was about 33 percent. For the sample subset, the incidence of

---

20. We were unable to find inflation figures for the period 2000–01, hence rates for 1999–2000 (about 10.6 percent) were used to deflate the consumption figures. It is possible that the actual inflation rate was lower because it was reported that inflation has been stable since 2000. In that case we may have underestimated real consumption.

TABLE 5C.2 Selected descriptive statistics from the 2000 and 2001 household surveys

Variable	Full sample 2000 (1)	Households in Bounnua and Phukun 2000 (2)	Households in Bounnua and Phukun 2001 (3)
Annual per capita consumption (US$ in 2000 prices)	192.64 (178.96)	131.21 (79.55)	129.87 (89.29)
Annual per capita cash consumption	141.35 (155.19)	79.21 (59.59)	75.09 (69.75)
Incidence of telephone use (percent)	33.00 (47.06)	7.80 (27.00)	37.80 (48.60)
Household size	6.00 (2.40)	6.05 (2.46)	6.08 (2.53)
Age of household head	44.00 (12.20)	43.40 (13.59)	44.40 (13.24)
Years of schooling- household head	6.00 (4.40)	3.47 (2.51)	4.65 (3.90)
Agricultural land (acres)	1.63 (2.04)	1.43 (0.99)	1.41 (1.12)
Number of cattle	2.10 (3.80)	2.01 (2.65)	2.32 (2.93)
Income source, agriculture only (percent)	48.30 (50.00)	64.70 (47.90)	63.70 (48.20)
More than one source of income	41.90 (49.30)	30.50 (46.10)	33.60 (47.30)
Household head participates in the labor market (percent)	94.50 (22.70)	92.60 (26.10)	97.80 (14.40)
Number of household members working	2.63 (1.21)	2.55 (1.12)	2.73 (1.18)
Sample size	606	190	190

SOURCE: Primary survey data (2000, 2001).

NOTE: Standard deviations are shown in parentheses.

telecommunications use increases from 7.8 percent in 2000 to 37.8 percent in 2001, clearly indicating the implementation of the Rurtel project and households' prompt adoption of the newly available technologies.

Appendix 5D: Statistical Results, the Case of Rural Bangladesh

Table 5D.1 presents summary statistics on user status; annual household expenditure; education, occupation, age, and gender of household head; and size

TABLE 5D.1 Summary statistics, the case of rural Bangladesh

Variable	Minimum	Maximum	Mean	Standard deviation
User status	0	1	0.30	0.46
Expenditure, yearly total (Tk.)	6,300	1,055,000	81,496.29	98,190.45
Education, household head[a]	0	1	0.84	0.38
Occupation[b]	0	1	0.54	0.50
Age, household head	15	85	46.57	12.747
Household size	2	10	5.38	1.74
Settlement with telephone (yes = 1)	0	1	0.49	0.50
Gender, household head (male = 1)	0	1	0.94	0.23

SOURCE: Primary survey data (2001).

NOTE: The 2001 exchange rate for Bangladesh was US$1 to Tk. 56.

[a]Literate–illiterate dummy, where illiterate = 0.

[b]Agriculture–nonagriculture dummy, where agriculture = 1.

of household; along with a village public telephone access dummy. Among the covariates included in the estimation, household expenditure is measured in local currencies; age is measured in years; and user-status, occupation, and gender are dummy variables.

For the purposes of the estimation (and to calculate compensating variation), both the direct and indirect costs of public telephone use were taken into account. The direct cost of telephone use includes the total cost of each telephone call made, two-way transport costs to the nearest public telephone, and the opportunity cost of time of the return journey, converted to the prevailing wage rate. For the determinants of telephone use, a Logit model was estimated based on three different specifications that are assumed to capture the stability of estimated coefficients. Table 5D.2 presents the Logit coefficients, while Table 5D.3 presents the standardized Logit coefficients. The estimated coefficients remained stable and consistent across all three specifications.

The individual coefficients, the coefficients of consumption, and the coefficients of consumption squared are significant at the 1 percent level, implying that the marginal utility gain from consumption (net of telephone expenditure) diminishes relative to the gain from the consumption of telecommunications services. Direct and indirect costs of telephone use are incorporated into the consumption variables, and it is the variation in prices that is significant. The coefficient of a village dummy that expresses whether a village has a public telephone or not is significant and positive, implying that the availability of a telephone at a minimum distance significantly increases telephone consumption. Other significant covariates are the education and occupation of the head of household. Literate household heads are more likely to be telephone users,

TABLE 5D.2 Determinants of telephone use in rural Bangladesh (Logit coefficients)

Covariates	Model 1	Model 2	Model 3
Consumption ($\times 10^{-2}$)	0.021	0.02	0.02
	(0.004)***	(0.004)***	(0.004)***
Consumption squared ($\times 10^{-4}$)	-1.92×10^{-5}	-1.58×10^{-5}	-1.78×10^{-5}
	(5.79×10^{-6})***	(6.09×10^{-6})***	(6.21×10^{-6})***
Household characteristics			
Education of head of		1.6185	1.6556
household		(0.6631)***	(0.6601)**
Occupation of head of		−0.6333	−0.7062
household		(0.3173)**	(0.3228)**
Age of head of household		0.0067	−0.0397
		(0.0748)	(0.0793)
Age of head of household		0.00001	0.0004
squared		(0.0007)	(0.0008)
Size of household		0.1014	0.1019
		(0.0961)	(0.0986)
Sex of head of household		−1.4678	−1.4249
(male = 1)		(0.6306)**	(0.6458)**
Village has a public telephone			0.8831
(yes = 1)			(0.3250)***
Constant	−2.1075	−2.555	−1.9209
	(0.2593)***	(1.9713)	(2.0237)
Log-likelihood	−145.95	−136.69	−132.84
Number of observations	280	280	280
LR chi^2	46.72	65.25	72.95
Probability > chi^2	0.0000	0.0000	0.0000
Pseudo R^2	0.1380	0.1927	0.2154

SOURCE: Primary survey data (2001).

NOTES: Standard errors are shown in parentheses. **Indicates significance at the 5 percent level; ***indicates significance at the 1 percent level. LR indicates likelihood ratio.

as are nonagricultural households. In addition, female household heads are more likely to use a telephone than their male counterparts.

Appendix 5E: Statistical Results, the Case of Rural China

Determinants of the Decision to Subscribe to Telephone Services

The sample population consists of approximately 6,000 farm households in the three selected provinces for the period 1995–97. In the model specification, telephone subscription is defined as a binary dependent variable (to subscribe or not to subscribe). The following independent variables are selected and used

TABLE 5D.3 Determinants of telephone use in rural Bangladesh (standardized Logit coefficients)

Covariates	Model 1	Model 2	Model 3
Consumption ($\times 10^{-2}$)	0.00416	0.00318	0.00341
	(0.001)***	(0.001)***	(0.001)***
Consumption squared ($\times 10^{-4}$)	-3.86×10^{-6}	-2.96×10^{-6}	-3.29×10^{-6}
	(0.0)***	(0.0)***	(0.0)**
Household characteristics			
Education of head of		0.2235	0.2236273
household		(0.0581)***	(0.05645)**
Occupation of head of		−0.1198	−0.1321879
household		(0.06)**	(0.0607)**
Age of head of household		0.0012	−0.0073519
		(0.014)	(0.01468)
Age of household head		2.46×10^{-6}	.0000786
squared		(0.00014)	(0.00014)
Size of household		0.01899	0.0188562
		(0.01795)	(0.01821)
Sex of head of household		−0.3362	−0.3244714
(male = 1)		(0.151)**	(0.15588)**
Village has a public telephone			0.1633277
(1)			
(0.05956)***			
Log-likelihood	−145.95	−136.69	−132.84
Number of observations	280	280	280
LR chi^2	46.72	65.25	72.95
Probability > chi^2	0.0000	0.0000	0.0000
Pseudo R^2	0.1380	0.1927	0.2154
Predicted probability	0.2486	0.2496	0.2452

SOURCE: Primary survey data (2001).

NOTES: Standard errors are shown in parentheses. **Indicates significance at the 5 percent level; ***indicates significance at the 1 percent level. LP indicates likelihood ratio.

in the telephone subscription Logit model: net annual income, value of productive fixed assets, education level of household head, number of household members with a professional title, additional sources of business income, geographic features of the village, distance of village to a main road, province, and timeframe. Table 5E.1 presents the resulting coefficients from the Logit model.

Impacts of Telephone Adoption on Income

Estimation methods were employed to examine changes in the value of the dependent variables during 1995–97 by holding independent variables constant for the base year 1995 (with the exception of variables related to telephone subscription). Panel data analysis was required to record changes in economic

TABLE 5E.1 The determinants of the decision to subscribe to telephone services in rural China, 1995–97 (Logit model)

Variable	B	Standard error	Significance
Year			
1995			0.0000
1996	0.6852	0.1343	0.0000
1997	0.8346	0.1309	0.0000
Province			
Jiangsu			0.0000
Shandong	−0.5038	0.1215	0.0000
Sichuan	−5.8801	0.4772	0.0000
Sideline business type			
Agricultural			0.0000
Mainly agricultural	0.3645	0.1226	0.0029
Mainly nonagricultural	0.3119	0.1917	0.1038
Nonagricultural	−0.9702	0.2596	0.0002
Other	−1.7211	0.3135	0.0000
Education level			
Illiterate			0.0000
Primary	1.1075	0.4167	0.0079
Secondary	1.6535	0.4098	0.0001
High or above	2.2805	0.4187	0.0000
Geographic feature			
Plain			0.0000
Hill and plain	2.7820	0.1225	0.0000
Mountain	−1.5993	1.0129	0.1144
Distance to road (> 1 km)	−1.2940	0.1696	0.0000
Professional title	1.0939	0.1372	0.0000
Fixed productive assets	2.11×10^{-5}	6.397×10^{-6}	0.0009
Ln (net income)	1.2068	0.1207	0.0000
Constant	−14.6000	1.2343	0.0000
−2 log likelihood	2,521.9590		
Goodness of fit	34,046.3580		
Nagelkerke R^2	0.496		

SOURCE: Calculated by author from primary survey data (1995–97).

factors such as growth of annual net income and changes in additional sources of business income. However, due to annual household changes, only about 40 percent of the sample households satisfied the panel data conditions over the three years. Despite the large number of omitted households, a significant number of households remained to be included in the analysis and no systematic bias seems to be present, though the sample may be less representative of farm households in the selected provinces and in rural China more generally.

To focus on the dynamic impact of telephone subscription on the income of farm households over the three years, three variables related to telephone subscription were introduced into the model: weighted telephone subscription for 1996 and new telephone subscription for 1997. The weighted telephone subscription is defined as the sum of telephone subscription for the three years, reflecting the duration of household subscription (using an advantage avoids any bias caused by telephone disconnection).

In the estimation, the dependent variable is the average growth rate of annual net household income per capita during 1995–97. In addition to the three telephone variables, the following independent variables for the base year 1995 were also included: net per capita income, additional sources of business income, education level of household head, geographic features of the household village, and distance from village to a main road. To avoid variance across the provinces, the model was run separately with data from each province. However, due to the small number of telephone subscriptions in Sichuan province, the analysis results for Sichuan were statistically unreliable; hence, the analysis only includes results for Jiangsu and Shandong.

The duration of telephone subscriptions and the addition of new subscriptions in 1997 have positive correlations with the growth rate of annual net income per capita in Jiangsu, though these relationships are not statistically significant (Table 5E.2). One of the possible reasons for this result could be that in the household survey, public telephone access was not taken into account. Another reason could be the allocation of administrative regions for telephone service, which resulted in high phone tariffs and low rates of telephone use. In Jiangsu

TABLE 5E.2 Impact of telephone subscription on changes in net farm household income in Jiangsu

Independent variables	Coefficient	t-value	Significance
Constant	1.885	7.163	0.000
Telephone weighted (1995–97)	6.221×10^{-3}	0.282	0.778
New telephone in 1996	-6.488×10^{-2}	−0.767	0.444
New telephone in 1997	2.028×10^{-2}	0.224	0.823
ln (net income per capita in 1995)	−0.520	−6.941	0.000
Sideline business types			
Mainly agricultural	-6.321×10^{-2}	−1.321	0.187
Education level			
Secondary or above	-2.056×10^{-2}	−0.663	0.508
Village in plain and hilly areas	-4.019×10^{-3}	−0.071	0.943
Number of observations: 360			
F-stat.: 8.141			
R: 0.373; R^2: 0.139			

SOURCE: Primary survey data (1995–97).

TABLE 5E.3 Impact of telephone subscription on changes in net farm household income in Shandong

Variables	Coefficient	*t*-value	Significance
Constant	1.814	6.426	0.000
Telephone weighted (1995–97)	3.920×10^{-2}	2.362	0.019
New telephone in 1996	3.236×10^{-2}	0.718	0.473
New telephone in 1997	3.937×10^{-2}	0.735	0.463
ln (net income per capita in 1995)	−0.543	−6.342	0.000
Sideline business types			
Mainly agricultural	-5.381×10^{-3}	−0.145	0.885
Education level			
Secondary or above	4.624×10^{-2}	1.470	0.143
Village in plain areas			
Village in plain and hilly areas	0.116	2.414	0.017
Distance to a main road >1 km	2.397×10^{-3}	0.060	0.952

Number of observations: 219
F-stat.: 6.115
R: 0.435; R^2: 0.189

source: Primary survey data (1995–97).

province, although some farm households have telephones, they rarely use them because calls beyond the village are charged at the domestic long-distance rate. The third reason may be that telephone subscription reflects only potential telephone use rather than actual use or the reason for the use. In addition, local officials in some regions have reportedly forced farmers to subscribe to telephone services for the sake of the appearance of local development, regardless of economic rationality. In addition, new telephone subscriptions in 1996 and 1997 are not significantly correlated with growth of net per capita income.

The duration of telephone subscriptions, and new telephone subscriptions in 1996 and 1997 have positive relationships with the growth of annual net income per capita in Shandong (Table 5E.3). Although the problems mentioned above for Jiangsu may also occur in Shandong, the effect of the duration of telephone subscription is statistically significant at the 5 percent level. As with Jiangsu, new telephones do not have a statistically significant impact on the growth of net income per capita.

Comparison of the effects of the duration of telephone subscription between the two provinces may suggest that the measurable significance of the impact of telephone subscription relates to the level of local economic development. As a local economy develops, the purpose of telephone adoption for farm households may change from productive usage to consumption usage, such as from business use to daily use. The result of the analysis shows that the duration of telephone subscription for farm households in Jiangsu did not significantly relate to the household's income growth. In contrast, in Shandong, where the level of economic development was lower, the duration of telephone subscription demonstrated a statistically significant relationship with growth of household income.

Appendix 5F: Conceptual Framework and Statistical Results, the Case of Rural Ghana

Based on the conceptual framework, determinants of telephone use must be identified. It is assumed that telephone use is determined by human and financial resource factors.[21] Related variables include age, sex, and educational attainment of the household head (EDUC); economic status and main source of household income; number of household members (nohhmem); and the degree of household participation within community-based organizations (part_hh). Specification was carried out separately, relating the variables to the hypotheses tested by the regression analyses.

Estimating Use

To estimate whether households use public telephone services, a model was specified as follows:

$$Y_{use} = f(\text{Sex, Age, Education, Income, Location}). \qquad (25)$$

The results tested the following hypotheses:

1. It is hypothesized that when the household head is female, use of public telephone services is less likely than when the household head is male. Despite the image that Ghanaian women are heavily involved in business and trade, it is assumed that women are disadvantaged when it comes to telephone usage. Also, other surveys have shown that, "in general, women tend to use [public calling offices] significantly less often than men in most developing countries. . . . This reflects sociocultural restrictions as well as the lower average level of education and employment common among women in most countries" (Saunders, Warford, and Wellenius 1994, 248).
2. Similarly, the older the respondent the less likely that he or she will use public telephones. It is expected that telephone using households will have a younger household head than non-using households.

---

21. For the analysis, cultural factors and natural conditions were omitted. This is based on the assumption of homogeneity within the limited range of the survey area.

3. It is assumed that respondents with higher levels of education will be more likely to use telephone services.
4. Income measures are expect to have a high positive impact on the likelihood of household telecommunications use. Household income and wealth are represented by two measures: the logarithmic form of household expenditure over the previous month is regarded as a proxy for household monetary income (lnhhinc), while a discrete variable reflects the self-assessed economic status within the community. Households assign themselves one of three values: poorer than average, about average, or wealthier than average (Weinberger 2000). This assessment acknowledges that wealth may not be appropriately expressed in monetary terms but also includes other measures such as land and cattle holdings.
5. The likelihood of household telecommunications use is expected to decline as communities change and, thus, with the distance to Akatsi where the services are available. This should be particularly so for households in Gefia, given the longer distance and increased time required to reach telecommunications services in Akatsi.

Estimating the Intensity of Use

In the second step, the effect of the defined determinants on telephone use intensity was estimated, requiring the following modifications:

1. The household head being female was assumed to have a negative effect on telephone use intensity, measured as overall household expenditure on telecommunications. Thus, in addition to being less likely to use telecommunications, households headed by females are also expected to use telecommunications less intensely.
2. The age of the household head is expected to be negatively correlated with the intensity of telecommunications use, meaning that the older the household head, the less the household will access telecommunications services.
3. Intensity of telecommunications use is expected to increase with education level of the household head.
4. Higher income is expected to result in a higher consumption and consequently in higher telecommunications use. In addition, usage becomes more intense with increased economic activity.
5. In terms of household characteristics that exclusively influence telecommunications use intensity, households involved in agriculture are expected to use telecommunications less than households involved in other economic activities. The high degree of subsistence farming in the district results in limited need for business-related information exchange.
6. The number of members in the household needs to be considered. It is assumed that the higher the number of household members the higher the intensity of telephone use.

TABLE 5F.1 Results of the Probit estimation, rural Ghana

Telecommunications service use (*Y*use)	With household income		With self-assessed wealth status	
	dF/dx	Robust standard error	*dF/dx*	Robust standard error
Sex of respondent	0.2424003***	0.0873132	0.261563***	0.086028
Age of respondent	−0.005116*	0.0026775	−0.0039914	0.0028877
Primary education achieved (edu_prim)	0.2050924**	0.0976226	0.2160738**	0.0962428
Secondary education achieved (edu_seco)	0.1473076	0.1003003	0.1940599*	0.0855625
Post-secondary education achieved (edu_post)	0.1717017	0.0894068	0.2039191*	0.0863314
Household income (lnhhinc)	0.2087056***	0.0631221	na	na
Self-assessed economic status richer than average (richer_a)	na	na	0.1074597	0.1345818
Self-assessed economic status poorer than average (poorer_a)	na	na	−0.2063459**	0.101627
Agbedrafor (dumagbe)	0.0612721	0.0980511	−0.0112843	0.0962819
Gefia (dumgef)	−0.1552482	0.1192659	−0.2349069**	0.1236071
Pseudo R^2	0.3304		0.3054	

SOURCE: Primary survey data (1999).

NOTES: *Indicates significance at the 10 percent level; **indicates significance at the 5 percent level; and ***indicates significance at the 1 percent level. Pseudo $R^2 = 0.3304$. na indicates that data were not available.

7. It is assumed that the higher the household involvement in community-based organizations and groups, the higher the intensity of telephone use.

8. It is expected that the intensity of telecommunications use will decline across the different communities. This decline is assumed to be for households in Gefia given the time and expense required to reach telecommunications services in Akatsi.

Building on these assumptions, the model was revised as follows:

$$Y_{intensity} = f(\text{Sex, Age, Education, Income, Household Members,} \\ \text{Main Source of Income, Participation, Community}). \quad (26)$$

Determinants of Telephone Use and Intensity of Use

The estimation results for telephone use and intensity of telephone use are presented in Tables 5F.1 and 5F.2, respectively.

TABLE 5F.2 Results of the Tobit estimation, rural Ghana

Expenditure on the services during the month before the interview (Y lntcexp)	With household income		With self-assessed wealth status	
	Coefficient	Standard error	Coefficient	Standard error
Sex of respondent	2.861864***	0.8887017	3.35302***	0.9060806
Age of respondent	−0.058514**	0.0285072	−0.0356433	0.0293543
Primary education achieved (edu_prim)	3.579792***	1.262319	3.652683***	1.291089
Secondary education achieved (edu_seco)	2.784674*	1.54874	3.583043**	1.567375
Post-secondary education achieved (edu_post)	2.993444*	1.647255	3.853434**	1.643787
Main source of household income from agric. (incs_agr)	−0.4660754	0.9794701	−0.8048257	1.011193
Main source of household income from gov. (incs_gov)	1.193293	1.262673	0.400474	1.289544
Main source of household income from other (incs_oth)	−1.807188	1.741143	−2.395335	1.773378
Household income (lnhhinc)	2.277078***	0.6237518	na	na
Self-assessed economic status richer than average (richer_a)	na	na	1.989797	1.293691
Self-assessed economic status poorer than average (poorer_a)	na	na	−2.272576**	1.00606
Number of household members (nohhmem)	0.1885548	0.1245833	0.2338107*	0.1258232
Degree of participation in community-based organizations (part_hh)	0.3917128	0.5348763	0.2862266	0.5451377
Agbedrafor (dumagbe)	0.1597895	1.024162	−0.7668153	0.9864155
Gefia (dumgef)	−2.378048**	1.174898	−3.243002***	1.154301
_cons	−22.52781	7.984212	5.460053	2.467585
Goodness of fit	Number of observations = 157 LR chi^{i2}(13) = 100.03 Prob > chi^2 = 0.00 Log-likelihood = −353.60 Pseudo R^2 = 0.1239		Number of observations = 157 LR chi^{i2}(14) = 95.35 Prob > chi^2 = 0.00 Log-likelihood = −355.94 Pseudo R^2 = 0.1181	

SOURCE: Primary survey data (1999).

NOTES: *Indicates significance at the 10 percent level; **indicates significance at the 5 percent level; and ***indicates significance at the 1 percent level. na indicates that data were not available.

References

Balit, S., M. Calvelo Rios, and L. Masias. 1996. *Communication for development for Latin America: A regional experience.* Rome: FAO.

Bayes, A., J. von Braun, and R. Akhter. 1999. Village pay phones and poverty reduction: Insights from a Grameen Bank initiative in Bangladesh. Discussion Papers on Development Policy 8. Center for Development Research. Bonn: ZEF.

Bertolini R., A. Anyimadu, P. Asem, and O. Sakyi-Dawson. 2000. Telecommunication services in Ghana—A sector overview and case studies from the Southern Volta Region. In *Neue Medien und Öffentlichkeiten—Politische Kommunikation in Asien, Afrika und Lateinamerika,* Band 2, S. Bruene, ed. Hamburg: Deutsches Überseeinstitut.

Cannock, G. 2001. Telecom subsidies: Output-based contracts for rural services in Peru. *Private Sector* No. 234. Washington, D.C.: World Bank.

Chowdhury, S. K. 2002. *Institutional and welfare aspects of the provision and use of information and communication technologies in rural areas of Bangladesh and Peru.* Frankfurt: Peter Lang.

Deaton, A., and J. Muellbauer. 1980. An almost ideal demand system. *American Economic Review* 70: 312–326.

Dehejia, R. H., and S. Wahba. 1998. Propensity score matching methods for nonexperimental causal studies. Working Paper No. 6829. Cambridge, Mass., U.S.A.: National Bureau of Economic Research.

Geertz, C. 1978. The bazaar economy: Information and search in peasant marketing. *American Economic Review* 68: 28–32.

Gertler, P., and P. Glewwe. 1989. The willingness to pay for education in developing countries: Evidence from rural Peru. LSMS Working Paper No. 54. Washington, D.C.: World Bank.

Greene, W. H. 2000. *Econometric analysis.* 4th ed. Upper Saddle River, N.J., U.S.A.: Prentice-Hall.

Hausman, J. 1981. Exact consumer's surplus and dead-weight loss. *American Economic Review* 71: 662–676.

Heckman, J., H. Ichimira, and P. Todd. 1997. Matching as an econometric evaluation estimator: Evidence from evaluating a job training program. *Review of Economic Studies* 64: 605–654.

Hudson, H. 1992. Telecommunications policies for rural development. Research Paper No. 30. Center for International Research on Communication and Information Technology Policy. University of San Francisco.

Hujer, R., and M. Wellner. 2000. The effects of public sector sponsored training on individual employment performance in East Germany. Discussion Paper No. 141. IZA Bonn: Forschungsinstitut zur Zukunft der Arbeit (IZA).

IFAD. 2001. *Rural poverty report 2001: The challenge of ending rural poverty.* New York: Oxford University Press.

ITU. 1998. *African telecommunication indicators (ATI) 1998.* Geneva.

JTEC. 2001. *Study report on rehabilitation and expansion of TV/radio broadcasting networks in Lao People's Democratic Republic.* Vientiane, Laos: Japan Telecommunications Engineering and Consulting Service.

Ke, B., and X. Zhang 1999. *The development of ICT and its impacts on rural economy in China*. Beijing: RCRE.

Lechner, M. 2000. An evaluation of public sector sponsored continuous vocational training programs in East Germany. *Journal of Human Resources,* Spring: 347–375.

Maddala, G. S. 1983. *Limited-dependent and qualitative variables in econometrics.* New York: Cambridge University Press.

Mas-Colell, A., M. D. Whinston, and J. R. Green. 1995. *Microeconomic theory.* New York: Oxford University Press.

McFadden, D. 1984. Econometric analysis of qualitative response models. In *Handbook of econometrics,* vol. 2, Z. Griliches and M. Intrilligator, eds. Amsterdam: Elsevier.

Mitchell, B. M. 1978. Optimal pricing of local telephone service. *American Economic Review* 68: 517–537.

OSIPTEL (Oganísmo Supervisor de Inversión Privada en Telecomunicaciones). 2004. Compendio de Estadísticas del Sector de Telecomunicaciones en Perú 1994–2003. Estudios en Telecomunicaciones No. 17. Lima: OSIPTEL.

Republic of Ghana. 1995. *Ghana—Vision 2020.* Presidential Report to Parliament on Coordinated Programme of Economic and Social Development. Accra: Government of Ghana.

Rosenbaum, P. R., and D. B. Rubin. 1983. The central role of the propensity score in observational studies for causal effects. *Biometrika* 70 (1): 41–55.

———. 2004. *Compendio de estadísticas del sector de telecomunicaciones en Perú 1994–2003.* Estudios en Telecomunicaciones No. 17. Lima: Osiptel.

Roy, A. D. 1951. Some thoughts on the distribution of earnings. *Oxford Economic Papers* 3: 135–146.

Saunders, R. J., J. J. Warford, and B. Wellenius. 1994. *Telecommunications and economic development.* Baltimore: Johns Hopkins University Press.

Serra, P. 2000. Subsidies in Chilean utilities. Universidad de Chile. Mimeo.

Small, K. A., and H. S. Rosen. 1981. Applied welfare economics with discrete classic models. *Econometrica* 49 (1): 105–130.

Song, G. 2003. *The impact of information and communication technologies on rural households: A holistic approach applied to the case of Lao People's Democratic Republic.* Frankfurt: Peter Lang.

Song, G., and R. Bertolini. 2002. Information and communication technologies (ICTs) for rural development: An example from rural Laos. *Landnutzung und Landentwicklung* 43 (2): 64–70.

SSB (State Statistical Bureau). 1998. *China statistical yearbook 1998.* Beijing.

Torero, M. 2000. The access and welfare impacts of telecommunications technology in Peru. Discussion Papers on Development Policy 27. Center for Development Research. Bonn: ZEF.

Torero, M., E. Schroth, and A. Pascó-Font. 2003. The impact of telecommunications privatization in Peru on the welfare of urban consumers. *Economia* 4 (1): 99–122.

Train, K. 1993. *Qualitative choice analysis.* Cambridge, Mass., U.S.A.: MIT Press.

Varian, H. 1992. *Microeconomic analysis.* New York: W. W. Norton.

Vella, F. 1993. A simple estimator for simultaneous models with censored endogenous regressors. *International Economic Review* 34: 441–457.

Weinberger, K. 2000. *Women's participation: An economic analysis in rural Chad and Pakistan.* Frankfurt: Peter Lang.

Wellenius, B. 1997. Extending telecommunications service to rural areas—The Chilean experience. *Private Sector* No. 105. Washington, D.C.: World Bank.

World Bank. 1998. *World development report 1998–1999: Knowledge for development.* Washington, D.C.: World Bank.

ZEF. 2001. Impact assessment of a telecommunications project in rural areas of the Lao People's Democratic Republic. Project Report to KfW. Bonn.

6 ICT for Pro-Poor Provision of Public Goods and Services: A Focus on Health

MAJA MICEVSKA

A primary responsibility of government is the provision of public goods and services. Governments at the central and local levels typically provide a wide range of services including defense, education, health, transportation, and basic infrastructure like power, water, and waste disposal. Consensus is emerging that the provision of such primary services is fundamental to development, even where the primary goal is economic growth (Deaton 2001). Further, the 2004 *World Development Report* recognized that health and literacy are fundamental to liberation from poverty (World Bank 2003). In turn, the successful provision of healthcare and education depends (among other things) on effective service delivery, informed household decisions, and the integration of technological change. In light of the broad public service needs of developing countries, focus on the role of information and communication technologies (ICT) in development policy has been criticized. However, this argument overlooks the reality that ICT—when wisely applied—can facilitate improved public service provision, reduce social and economic inequalities, and support sustainable wealth creation. Hence, this chapter investigates how ICT affects the provision of public goods and services in developing countries, focusing on potential complementarities that significantly increase the economic returns to ICT infrastructure investment.

ICT infrastructure investment is positively correlated with the provision of public goods and services. However, as has been shown in this book, this does not imply a causal relationship.[1] Public goods provision is affected by many factors, and it is possible that ICT is actually a proxy for other variables, such as income. Policymakers require a clear picture of these dynamics, but few studies to date have concentrated on the effect of ICT investment on the provision of public goods and services (Corrigan and Joyce 2000; McMahon and Bruce 2002). This chapter attempts to offer new insights into the issue.

---

1. See the section "Quantitative Evidence of the Effect of ICT on Health: Cross-Country Analysis" for evidence of the positive correlation between increased teledensity (number of telephone lines per 100 inhabitants) and improved public health as a proxy for better provision of public health services.

Innovative Use of ICT for Public Service Provision

The United Nations' Millennium Declaration stipulated that health, education, and environmental sustainability were development imperatives. These are also areas where ICT can make a significant contribution.

Healthcare

An anecdote describes a South African chief who was asked what he would want for his village if he could choose among a telephone line, a school, and a clinic. He replied, "The telephone line, so that I can lobby ministers in the capital about the school and the clinic." This captures the central message of this chapter: if applied properly, ICT can function as an enabling tool to empower poor people and provide effective, pro-poor provision of public goods and services.

The potential role of ICT in public health promotion is clear. The World Health Organization (WHO) claims that 40 percent of health-related outcomes stem from exchange of information.[2] Hence, ICT can play a critical role in the control of epidemics and contagious diseases. But on a more basic level, ICT enables health professionals to access critical information resources, share information on relevant health issues, access medical and public health publications, and communicate with each other effectively about their patients. ICT also has the potential to enable the public to obtain information about health issues and publicly available healthcare services. Across the developing world, medical information is being electronically transmitted in what has been dubbed "telemedicine" to improve access to specialized health services by both patients and providers. Technologies range from traditional and radio telephony to complex interactive video consultations and robotic surgery. A current focus is the remote linking of doctors to enable consultations, training, and guidance, ultimately improving the quality of care in rural areas.

HealthNet is a telecommunications network that links healthcare workers around the world via email.[3] More than 10,000 healthcare members use the system to access medical and shared reporting databases, consultation and referral schedules, epidemic alerts, medical libraries, and email. Many physicians in developing countries rely on HealthNet as their sole source of information on the treatment of HIV/AIDS and tropical diseases and on essential drugs, pediatric care, and public health promotion. Other AIDS-related treatment initiatives include the ProCAARE discussion forum (www.procaare.org) and the WorldSpace Foundation (WSF)–Africare HIV/AIDS initiative (www.worldspace .org), which aims to provide lifesaving information about preventative and treatment measures for Africa.

---

2. This was repeatedly mentioned at their Web site (www.who.int/en/).

3. HealthNet is provided by a nonprofit organization, SatelLife, with the assistance of local and international partners (see www.healthnet.org).

Education

Assessing the cost-effectiveness of ICT in education is difficult because of lack of meaningful data, variation in ICT implementation, and difficulties both in drawing general conclusions from specific programs and in assessing qualitative educational differences. It has also been argued that—despite the potential of ICT in developing countries—care should be taken to avoid the loss of skilled labor through brain drain and "virtual" brain drain, as in the case of local workers employed by foreign companies. For instance, it has been estimated that approximately 25 percent of ICT-skilled workers leave South Africa in search of better employment opportunities and remuneration each year (DOI 2001).

Many universities provide educational programs via the Internet and virtual classrooms, video and audio lectures, and correspondence instruction. This results in savings to students, who pay as much as 80 percent less than those attending universities in person. Students can also obtain higher education at their own pace while working to support their families. A typical example is the African Virtual University, a network of universities that have joined with the World Bank in bringing courses in computer science and business management to African students and professionals (www.avu.org). This is achieved through a combination of lectures telecast by satellite and training materials accessed via the Internet.

There are also projects that are developing networks for the purpose of recycling computer equipment and donating it to schools in developing countries.[4] As a result, computers are increasingly being integrated into school curriculums, and people living in rural areas are learning to use computers and carry out equipment maintenance. Such programs have the potential to make a valuable although not sufficient enough contribution toward bridging the rural–urban divide and decreasing the marginalization of rural communities.

Sustainable Development

ICT can contribute to sustainable development through environmental information sharing among researchers, government agencies, and nongovernmental organizations (NGOs). One of the areas that ICT is being applied to is climate change. The main applications are in improving environmental awareness, capacity building, and related research. The UN Framework Convention on Climate Change (UNFCCC) Web site contains information on the environment in the context of global initiatives such as the Kyoto Protocol (www.unfccc.org). In addition, UNFCCC provides training materials for capacity building in least developed countries. Distance education is being used to enhance the capacity of developing-country policymakers to address climate change issues and ap-

---

4. See, for example, www.geocities.com/sohclara.

ply ICT toward that objective. The Climate Change Network mailing list is an Internet-based mailing list that provides up-to-date data on climate change issues and conferences (www.ccn.org). This facilitates awareness of the relevant issues and participation in activities related to climate change.

E-Law is an Internet-based NGO that facilitates the development and practice of environmental law in keeping with the public interest (www.elaw.org). National and local environmental advocates use the E-Law network to exchange legal, scientific, and technical information, along with precedents and strategies in support of environmental preservation. Lobby groups, such as Eco-News, have also made use of the Internet in addressing environmental issues (www.econews.org).

Quantitative Evidence of the Effect of ICT on Health: Cross-Country Analysis

The preceding discussion, while indicative of the positive impact of ICT, is based on anecdotal evidence only. Relying on such evidence to justify ICT investment, however, can lead to poorly designed strategies and haphazard program implementation that overlook national and local conditions. Hence, rigorous quantitative analysis is called for. While the role of ICT in the provision of public health services has important implications in developing countries, particularly for poor people, research to date has largely focused on developed countries, mainly because of the availability of adequate data (particularly panel data). In the following analysis, empirical evidence from developing and transition countries for the period 1980–2000 is used to examine the possible impact of ICT development on public health promotion as a proxy for the provision of public health services.[5]

Data and Correlations

Data include general health and economic variables and country characteristics from the 2002 World Development Indicators database (World Bank 2002), such as life expectancy at birth; infant and child mortality rates (birth to one and birth to five years old, respectively); physicians and hospital beds per 1,000 people; real GDP per capita; population; adult and female illiteracy rates; immunization for diphtheria, tetanus, and pertussis vaccine (DPT) and measles; urban population share; poverty headcount; and the Gini index.[6] Data on a

---

5. The number of countries included in the analysis is based on data availability.

6. The Gini index is a summary measure of the extent to which the actual distribution of income or consumption expenditure (or a related variable) differs from a hypothetical distribution in which each person receives an identical share.

TABLE 6.1 Variable description and summary statistics, developing and transition economies, 1980–2000

Variable	Number of observations	Mean	Standard deviation	Minimum	Maximum
Annual growth rate of life expectancy at birth, 1980–2000	142	0.31	0.54	−1.98	1.56
Annual growth rate of child mortality, birth to five years old, 1980–2000	105	−2.98	1.98	−7.07	1.23
Annual growth rate of fixed line teledensity, 1980–2000	141	6.81	3.84	−4.48	21.70
Annual growth rate of GDP per capita in constant 1995 US$, 1980–2000	109	0.48	2.16	−7.27	8.29
Annual growth rate of adult illiteracy, 1980–2000	118	−3.05	1.44	−8.04	−0.24
Annual growth rate of immunization for diphtheria, tetanus, and pertussis, 1980–2000	86	7.41	8.53	−2.04	61.85
Annual growth rate of urban population, 1980–2000	146	1.38	1.23	−1.10	6.20
Poverty headcount as share of population, most up-to-date data per country	71	35.62	16.93	4.60	68.00

SOURCES: Calculated by author based on World Bank (2002) and ITU (2002).

NOTES: Annual growth is calculated as a compounded growth rate. Where data for 1980 and 2000 were not available, observations ranging from 1981–82 and 1998–99, respectively, were used. GDP indicates gross domestic product.

number of telecommunications development indicators from the International Telecommunications Union (ITU 2002) were also incorporated, including absolute numbers of fixed telephone lines, fixed line teledensity (the number of lines per 100 inhabitants), subscriber waiting lists for fixed lines, estimated number of Internet users, income from telephone services, and investments in telecommunications.

The primary variables used in the analysis are presented in Table 6.1, along with summary statistics for developing and transition countries. The annual growth rate for life expectancy at birth during 1980–2000 was 0.31 percent, and

FIGURE 6.1 Public health and telecommunications infrastructure, developing and transition economies, 1980–2000

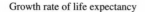

Growth rate of life expectancy

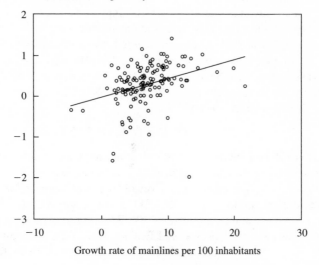

Growth rate of mainlines per 100 inhabitants

SOURCES: Calculated by author based on World Bank (2002) and ITU (2002).
NOTES: R-squared equals 0.11; the number of observations is 138.

the annual growth rate for fixed lines was 6.81 percent.[7] Overall, improved life expectancy is positively associated with increased numbers of fixed lines, resulting in a correlation of 0.34. Figure 6.1 shows the relationship for 138 developing and transition countries. A univariate, linear cross-country regression of the growth rate of fixed lines explains about 11 percent of the growth rate variance for life expectancy.[8] Nevertheless, the possibility of a spurious correlation exists because country-specific telephony improvements may in fact be linked with other health-promoting measures like income, investment in human capital, and health expenditure. Efforts were made to control for the effects of all these factors.

---

7. Countries with negative growth rates for life expectancy are Belarus, Botswana, Burundi, Central African Republic, Congo Democratic Republic, Côte d'Ivoire, Iraq, Kazakhstan, Kenya, Lesotho, Liberia, Malawi, Mozambique, Namibia, Russia, Rwanda, South Africa, Swaziland, Tanzania, Uganda, Ukraine, Zambia, and Zimbabwe. The only countries with negative growth rates for fixed lines are Congo Democratic Republic and Liberia.

8. The use of mortality rates instead of life expectancy in the regression yields similar results.

An Econometric Model of Telecommunication Investment,
Aggregate Health, and Wealth

Life expectancy and child mortality rates are the dependent variables in this analysis.[9] This is justifiable on the basis that improved access to good quality public services is a key influence on health outcomes (Musgrove 1996; Gupta, Verhoeven, and Erwin 1999). It should be noted, however, that these particular dependent variables make the interpretation of coefficients somewhat problematic because they may be directly affected by factors other than the delivery of public health services. The following equation evaluates the potential impact of ICT on aggregate health:

$$\text{HEALTH}_i = f(\text{TELECOM}_i, \text{GDP}_i, Z_i), \tag{1}$$

where HEALTH_i is a social indicator reflecting improved health status for a country i, which is a function of increased telecommunications infrastructure (TELECOM_i), GDP_i per capita, and a vector of socioeconomic variables Z_i. Two indicators are used to gauge HEALTH_i: annual growth rate of life expectancy at birth and annual growth rate of child mortality. The annual growth rate of fixed line teledensity proxies TELECOM_i, while GDP_i per capita is measured in constant 1995 U.S. dollars. The regressions also include the following set of control variables:

- *Annual growth rate of adult illiteracy.* Many studies show a strong inverse relationship between adult or female illiteracy and public health status (Schultz 1993 for example).
- *Annual growth rate of immunization.* Evidence shows that increased coverage of immunization in children has a positive impact on health status (Hojman 1996); hence, the share of children immunized for DPT by the age of one year is used as a control variable.
- *Poverty headcount index.*[10] As noted by Deaton (2001), if a rich country has a lot of poor people it will have low average health relative to its per capita income. Data limitations prevent the inclusion of the average growth rate of the poverty headcount index, so the most up-to-date values were included instead.

---

9. Limited analyses using the number of hospital beds and the number of physicians per 1,000 people as dependent variables were also undertaken; more extensive use of these variables was constrained by the scarcity of data.

10. The poverty headcount index is highly correlated with regional dummies, especially with the dummy variable for Africa. Since the number of observations is relatively small, and the focus of this study is cross-country variations in life expectancy and child mortality rates, the poverty headcount index was included in the regressions (without regard to geography) rather than regional dummies.

- *Annual growth rate of urbanization.* Schultz (1993) finds that mortality is higher in rural, low-income, agricultural households, suggesting that increased urbanization is associated with improved health.

Equation (1) is estimated in a linear form using ordinary least squares (OLS) and two-stage least squares (2SLS) regressions. The 2SLS technique is primarily used to address the problem of reverse causality. In addition, 2SLS regressions address potential measurement errors on variables. The number of observations in the regressions varies depending on the availability of data for the variables used. The number of observations for the 2SLS specifications is relatively low.[11]

The results of regressions for the period 1980–2000 using annual growth rates of life expectancy and child mortality as dependent variables are reported in Table 6.2. On average, the explanatory variables account for about 40 percent of the cross-country variation in the rates of life expectancy and child mortality. In all the regressions, the coefficient on the growth of fixed lines carries the expected sign and is statistically significant at the 5 percent level. In contrast, the growth of real GDP per capita is statistically insignificant.

The regression results show that other control variables, such as immunization and urbanization, are important in explaining variances in public health indicators. In line with the empirical literature on determinants of health status, increases in immunization rates have a positive and significant effect on life expectancy. On the other hand, increased urbanization has a negative impact on public health status. On face value, this may appear contradictory, given that urbanization increases access to public health services; however, it also exerts negative forces such as stress, pollution, and congestion (with more rapid spread of infectious disease). Thus the effect of urbanization depends on the net impact of these factors.

These results are potentially alarming, considering that demographers expect world population to increase by nearly two billion people between 2000 and 2030, almost all of them in cities in Africa, Asia, and Latin America (Sheehan 2002). Two conclusions can be drawn from the results shown in Table 6.2. First, despite the lack of data on some control variables, the regressions explain a significant part of the cross-country variation in both public health indicators. Second, telecommunications investment may be associated with improved health status.

Quantitative Evidence of the Effect of ICT on Health: A Microeconomic Approach

Knowledge of which public goods and services are most likely to improve welfare outcomes is limited. In much of the developing world, institutions are weak,

---

11. See Appendix 6A, Tables 1 and 2 for lists of the countries included in the regressions.

TABLE 6.2 ICT and health in developing countries, 1980–2000

Variable	Annual growth rate of life expectancy		Annual growth rate of child mortality rate	
	OLS	2SLS	OLS	2SLS
Annual growth rate of fixed line teledensity	0.081**	0.090**	−0.203**	−0.202**
	(0.039)	(0.042)	(0.083)	(0.082)
Annual growth rate of GDP per capita in	−0.066	−0.081	0.245	0.276
constant 1995 US$	(0.062)	(0.066)	(0.105)	(0.174)
Annual growth rate of adult illiteracy	0.088	0.075	−0.242	−0.293
	(0.057)	(0.051)	(0.203)	(0.209)
Annual growth rate of immunization for	0.037***	0.034**	−0.070	−0.078
diphtheria, tetanus, and pertussis	(0.012)	(0.014)	(0.046)	(0.053)
Annual growth rate of urban population	−0.265***	−0.262**	0.978***	1.139**
	(0.104)	(0.122)	(0.256)	(0.284)*
Poverty headcount as a share of population,	0.002	0.007	0.006	0.014
most up-to-date data per country	(0.007)	(0.007)	(0.019)	(0.018)
Constant	0.042	−0.124	−3.571**	−4.250***
	(0.391)	(0.380)	(1.310)	(1.383)
Adjusted R^2	0.379	0.367	0.417	0.411
Number of observations	40	35	37	33

SOURCES: Calculated by author based on World Bank (2002) and ITU (2002).

NOTES: Growth rates were calculated as compound annual growth rates. White's heteroskedasticity-consistent standard errors are shown in parentheses. The instruments used in the 2SLS regressions were annual growth rates of fixed line teledensity, GDP per capita squared, female illiteracy, population, and dummy variables for African countries and the Gini index. *Indicates significance at the 10 percent level, **indicates significance at the 5 percent level, and ***indicates significance at the 1 percent level. GDP indicates gross domestic product; OLS, ordinary least squares; 2SLS, two-stage least squares.

corruption is rampant, and, frequently, laws are not enforced. In this context, it is difficult to focus on optimal expenditure allocations for schools, hospitals, road maintenance, and so on. Yet, the provision of public goods has serious implications for poor people.[12] Unfortunately, we do not have a great deal of local-level data; hence, collecting micro-level data is a research priority.

Micro-level studies can include more real-world factors in analysis than can macro-level studies, as well as providing valuable insights that are often masked in aggregated data analysis. Household surveys from three emerging market economies—Bangladesh, Laos, and Peru—were used in the analysis

---

12. Many local public goods are site-specific, and it is possible to exclude some individuals from their use for various social reasons. Thus, local public goods do not always conform to the standard public goods definition.

that follows.[13] In addition to telecommunications data, the surveys collected information on the health expenditures and socioeconomic characteristics of the sample households. These data offer a unique opportunity to test hypotheses linking ICT to demand for public health services in different ways. The main goal of the empirical analysis is to obtain a consistent estimate of β_1 in the context of the following model:

$$INFO_{ij} = \beta^0 + \beta_1 \, HEALTH\_EXP_{ij} + \gamma X_{ij} + \varepsilon_{ij}, \tag{2}$$

where INFO is an indicator of telephone usage to obtain health-related information or household demand for this type of information, HEALTH_EXP is the share of household expenditure on medical expenses as a proxy for household demand for health services and medication, X is a vector of all other variables that influence INFO, ε_{ij} are error terms assumed to be independently and identically distributed over i and j with mean zero, and the subscripts i and j refer to households and provinces, respectively.

Medical and Telecommunications Expenditures

Medical and telecommunications expenditures are relevant for ICT-related development strategies because they are important in explaining the use of the telephone to obtain information on medical care or household demand for health-related information. Because results are similar using data from all three countries, only the results for the Laos surveys are presented.[14] Appendix 6A, Tables 6A.3–5 present data on the distribution of the medical and telecommunications expenditure by expenditure quintile per household head for all three countries.

Figures 6.2a and 6.2b show medical and telecommunications expenditure shares as a function of the logarithm of total household expenditure per head, a measure of overall household living standards. The figures are calculated using a nonparametric regression. The share of medical care expenditure remains relatively uniform for households in the lower and middle expenditure quintiles but declines for the wealthiest households. This is consistent with empirical studies showing low-income elasticity of demand for medical services (for example, Andersen and Benham 1970). Figure 6.2b shows contrasting results for the share of telecommunications expenditure, whereby shares are lower for the

---

13. For detailed information on these surveys, see the relevant case studies in Chapter 3.

14. It should be noted, however, that the survey results are not directly comparable among the three countries because of differences in the formulation of questions on health and telephone expenditures. For instance, the relatively low health expenditure share in Peru compared with comparable expenditure in Bangladesh and Laos results from a different definition of health expenditures; for Peru, the respondents were only asked for expenditures related to diseases, accidents, or consultations with medical personnel (see Appendix 6A, Tables 6A.3–5).

FIGURE 6.2a Medical expenditure shares, all households, in Laos

Share of telecommunication expenditure
in total expenditure (percent)

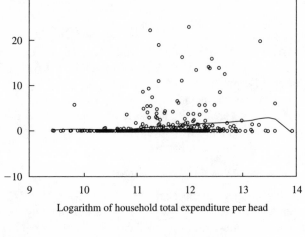

Logarithm of household total expenditure per head

FIGURE 6.2b Telecommunications expenditure shares, all households, in Laos

Share of telecommunication expenditure
in total expenditure (percent)

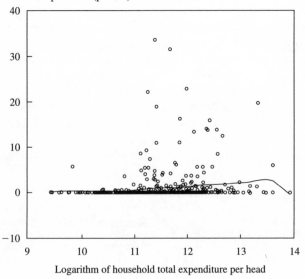

Logarithm of household total expenditure per head

SOURCES: Primary survey data (2000).

poorer households and increase significantly for wealthier households. Hence telecommunications services are a luxury item for rural households in Laos.

To illustrate further, Figures 6.3a and 6.3b show the results of a comparable nonparametric regression on medical and telecommunications expenditure shares, but this time only for households that subscribe to telephone services. Once again, the share of medical expenditure is higher among poorer households. Overall, the share of medical expenditure for households that use telephone services is lower than the share for all households, which is to be expected because, on average, wealthier households are more likely to use the telephone. The distribution of telecommunications expenditure is more variable. Omitting the outliers at both ends of Figure 6.3b, the share of telecommunications expenditure appears to increase for the lower expenditure quintiles and then gradually decrease for the wealthier households. As expected, the share of telecommunications expenditure for households that use the telephone is significantly higher than the share for all households.

The analysis above is suggestive only. The curves in Figures 6.2a and 6.2b make no attempt to control for other factors, such as education, health status, or telecommunications service provision, that are likely to be positively correlated with both overall household expenditure and the outcome, so that the effects of expenditure are almost certainly overstated. Nevertheless, the figures illustrate that, on average, poorer households spend a higher proportion of their income on health-related expenses than wealthier households, while wealthier households, on average, spend a higher proportion of their income on telephone services.

In the analysis that follows, health and telephone expenditure shares are used as measures of the relative importance of medical and telephone services to households, respectively. The main question is whether households for which medical services are relatively more important are more likely either to use the telephone to obtain health-related information or to have higher demand for this type of information.

Evidence from Bangladesh

Bangladesh was selected for inclusion as a case study because of the uniqueness of its innovative village payphone (VPP) program, whereby telecommunications infrastructure has been expanded through village-based leasing of cellular phones to members of a local microfinance entity.[15] In this section, the effects of expanded telecommunications infrastructure on the provision of health services information are assessed. The survey on telephone use asked respondents to provide examples of how the telephone saved their household

---

15. See the Bangladesh case study in Chapter 3 of this volume and Bayes, von Braun, and Rasheda (1999) for more information.

FIGURE 6.3a Medical expenditure shares, households using telephone services, in Laos

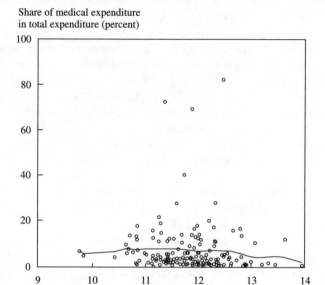

Share of medical expenditure
in total expenditure (percent)

Logarithm of household total expenditure per head

FIGURE 6.3b Telecommunications expenditure shares, households using telephone services, in Laos

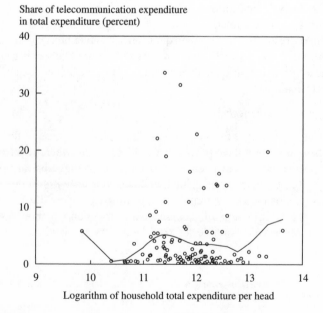

Share of telecommunication expenditure
in total expenditure (percent)

Logarithm of household total expenditure per head

SOURCES: Primary survey data (2000).

valuable time; of the households that used telephone services, 36 percent identified health-related and emergency calls in their responses.[16] This variable was chosen as a proxy for telephone use to obtain faster information on health services.

To account for the sample's selection bias, Heckman's (1979) two-step estimation procedure was adopted. In the first stage, the total sample of 284 randomly selected households was used in a Probit equation to estimate the probability that telephone subscription depends on a number of individual and household characteristics. As expected, the variables that have a positive and significant effect on the probability of a household subscribing to telephone services include the household head being literate, household expenditure per equivalent person,[17] land owned, and value of nonland fixed assets (Table 6.3).

In the second stage, regression analysis was undertaken on the determinants of telephone use to save time in obtaining health information for 86 households that used telephone services. The independent variables used in the second-stage Probit regression were health and telephone expenditure shares, a dummy variable for the presence of a child under five years old or an adult over 70 years old, and a variable for food security measured as the number of months per year that household members were well fed. As expected, the share of health expenditure —a measure of the relative importance of public health services for households— is positively and significantly correlated with the use of the telephone to save time in obtaining health information.[18] This supports the proposition that ICT can significantly contribute to delivering timely information on health services to households for which this type of information is most important.

Evidence from Peru

During the 1990s, economic trends in Peru, as in most emerging market economies, varied across income groups. Wealthy segments of the population benefited from demand for skills and education, while poorer segments benefited from increased public expenditure (Graham and Kane 1998; World Bank 1999). At the same time, the telecommunications market in Peru underwent a period of fundamental change (see the case studies on Peru in Chapters 3 and 5 of this volume, along with Torero 2000). The survey of households in Peru gathered data on the types of information the households needed most. Information on

---

16. Other responses included calls related to business and finance, contacting relatives and friends, land transactions, remittances, livestock and poultry, and obtaining information on markets (such as prices) and on employment opportunities.

17. To account for economies of size, expenditure was calculated per equivalent person using a single-parameter equivalence of 0.5. The model was also re-estimated using household expenditure per head, resulting in an estimated coefficient that remained significant and carried the predicted signs.

18. The coefficient on food security is also positive, though only marginally significant.

TABLE 6.3 Heckit estimation for Bangladesh

Variable	Telephone user	Time saved accessing health information
Age of household head	0.001	
	(0.007)	
Household head works in agriculture	−0.275	
	(0.199)	
Household head is literate	1.124***	
	(0.352)	
Household head is male	−0.619*	
	(0.373)	
Household expenditure per equivalent person[a]	0.011***	
	(0.003)	
Land owned[a]	0.001***	
	(0.000)	
Non-land fixed assets[a]	0.002**	
	(0.001)	
Health expenditure share[b]		0.969***
		(0.179)
Telephone expenditure share[b]		−0.036
		(0.179)
Household includes child under five years old or adult older than 70 years old		41.301
		(40.310)
Food security		18.370*
		(9.390)
Λ		−22.688
		(40.513)
Constant	−1.570**	−240.761**
Adjusted pseudo R^2	0.253	
Number of observations	284	86

SOURCE: Primary survey data (2001).

NOTES: Values in parentheses are standard errors corrected for sample selection bias using Heckman two-step estimation procedure. Coefficients for five district dummies are not shown to conserve space. *Indicates significance at the 10 percent level, **indicates significance at the 5 percent level, and ***indicates significance at the 1 percent level.

[a]Data were cleaned to remove implausible outliers that exceeded the mean by more than five standard deviations.

[b]Estimates were multiplied by 1,000.

healthcare was perceived to be very important by 78 percent of the sample households. This variable was used in the following analysis as a measure of the demand for faster and more reliable health-related information.

As in the case of Bangladesh, household health expenditure shares have a positive and significant effect on the dependent variable, in this case the prob-

TABLE 6.4 Probit regression results for Peru

Dependent variable: 1 if health info is considered very important, 0 otherwise	
Health expenditure share	0.042***
	(0.015)
Household expenditure per equivalent person[a]	0.016*
	(0.009)
Access to safe hygiene	−0.078
	(0.122)
Age of household head	−0.006
	(0.004)
Household head is literate	−0.258
	(0.251)
Household head is male	−0.550**
	(0.214)
Household includes child under five years old or adult over 70 years old	0.122
	(0.103)
Constant	1.843***
McFadden R^2	0.039
Number of observations	985

SOURCE: Primary survey data (2000).

NOTES: Huber/White's heteroskedasticity-consistent standard errors are shown in parentheses. Data were cleaned to remove outliers that exceeded the mean by more than five standard deviations. Coefficients for three regional dummies are not shown to conserve space. *Indicates significance at the 10 percent level; **indicates significance at the 5 percent level; ***indicates significance at the 1 percent level.

[a]Estimates are multiplied by 1,000.

ability of valuing health information as very important (Table 6.4). The coefficient on household expenditure per equivalent person carries a positive, though only marginally significant, sign. Access to safe hygiene does not seem to be significantly correlated with the probability of higher demand for information on healthcare, while the household head being male has a negative and statistically significant effect.

Evidence from Laos

The surveys conducted in Bangladesh and Peru offer good quality micro-level data to estimate the primary determinants of household demand for health-related information. In both cases, the regression analysis showed that health expenditure shares play a significant role in determining the demand for information on health services. Taking the analysis a step further, the Laos survey data is used to investigate the determinants of actual demand for medical and telecommunications infrastructure.

Government expenditure totaled nearly 25 percent of GDP in Laos in 1998 (Bourdet 2000). Although this was low by international standards, it represented a relative increase from equivalent expenditure in the early 1990s. For example, expenditure on education increased from 3 to 8 percent during 1985–95, and expenditure on healthcare increased from 0.4 to 5 percent during 1989–95 (World Bank 1997). It is not clear, however, to what extent these increases where allocated to—or benefited—poor provinces. A related issue is the potential impact of the intensification of residential telephony on demand for information on public goods and services by the rural poor over this period.

Measuring the dynamic effects of ICT requires the availability of panel data (meaning data from both before and after the adoption of ICT). Such data are generally scarce for developing countries, but the Laos survey contains panel data for 60 households.[19] The share of telephone calls relating to information on health issues or medical emergencies increased from 7.7 percent prior to the availability of telephone services to 15 percent after telephone access was obtained.

The Laos survey also elicited information on the infrastructure deemed to be most needed by households, and responses were used as a proxy for household demand for public goods and services.[20] Moreover, the availability of panel data made it possible to determine how this demand changed with the adoption of telephone services. In 2000, only 9 of the 200 sample households chose telecommunications as the most-needed form of public infrastructure, while 43 stipulated the need for a hospital. When these 200 households were re-interviewed in 2001—during which time the number of telephone subscribers increased from 16 to 76—only 25 households indicated a hospital as the most-needed form of infrastructure, while the number of households that chose telecommunications increased significantly to 44. To gauge the importance of these shifts, household structure was analyzed (Table 6.5). The panel is divided into households with and households without subscriptions to telephone services. The rows indicate the original household status in 2000, while the columns show the change in status by 2001.

The matrixes show substantial household mobility, with telecommunications infrastructure having the greatest significance for those households that obtained access to telephone services during the period between the two surveys. Of the households that viewed telecommunications as the most-important form of infrastructure, 52 percent were actually new telephone subscribers. Sur-

---

19. The survey was first conducted in 2000 and included 606 households. In 2001, 200 households were interviewed again. While in 2000 only 16 of the 200 households had access to telephone services, by 2001 this number had increased to 76.

20. In addition to telecommunications and hospitals, the possible responses were schools, safe water, irrigation, agricultural research, agricultural extension services, electricity, road access, and public transportation.

TABLE 6.5 Transition matrix for most-needed infrastructure, Laos

Choice of infrastructure	Telephone service status in 2001		
	No access	Access	Total
a. Choice of telecommunications as the most-needed form of infrastructure			
Telephone service status in 2000			
No access	36.37	52.27	88.64
Access	0.00	11.36	11.36
Total	36.37	63.63	100.00
b. Choice of a hospital as the most-needed form of infrastructure			
Telephone service status in 2000			
No access	76.00	12.00	88.00
Access	0.00	12.00	12.00
Total	76.00	24.00	100.00

SOURCE: Primary survey data (2000, 2001).

prisingly, telecommunications was also important to households that remained without telephone service subscription. A possible explanation for this is that with increased access to telecommunications services in their communities these households had come to recognize the benefits of access.[21]

To illustrate this issue further, the demand for telecommunications infrastructure was regressed on other relevant variables (Table 6.6). In addition to household transition from non-users to users of telephone services, other positive and significant factors affecting the demand for telephone access were the existence of hospital in the community, the years of education of the household head, the amount of farm land owned, and the land occupied by the house. In contrast to the results on changing household perceptions of the need for telecommunications, the need for a hospital was greatest among households that remained without telephone services (Table 6.5b). A striking 76 percent of these households determined that the most-needed form of infrastructure was a hospital. The marked asymmetry between households with and households without access to telephone services can be attributed to the poorer status, on average, of households without access and the accompanying higher proportion of their income allocated to health-related expenses (Appendix 6A, Tables 6A.3–5).

---

21. For more on this concept (known as reference norms) see Easterlin's (1974) pioneering work on the changing nature of norms and aspirations, and Hirschman's (1973) tunnel effect hypothesis.

TABLE 6.6 Probit regression results for Laos

Dependent variable: 1 if telephone is the most wanted infrastructure, 0 otherwise	
Transition from non-user to user of telephone services	0.414*
	(0.249)
Household was a telephone user in both periods	0.223
	(0.378)
Community has a hospital	0.556**
	(0.275)
Age of household head	−0.007
	(0.009)
Years of education of household head	0.090***
	(0.032)
Farm land owned	0.159*
	(0.087)
Land occupied by house	0.008**
	(0.003)
Constant	−2.418***
McFadden R^2	0.186
Number of observations	200

SOURCE: Primary survey data (2000, 2001).

NOTES: Huber/White's heteroskedasticity-consistent standard errors are shown in parentheses. *Indicates significance at the 10 percent level; **indicates significance at the 5 percent level; ***indicates significance at the 1 percent level.

Conclusion

The results of the empirical analysis conducted for this chapter—particularly at household level—clearly reflect that ICT offers great opportunities in the delivery of information on health services, especially in remote areas and for households with the greatest need for this type of information. Nevertheless, despite the vast opportunities, adoption of ICT in developing countries remains problematic in terms of the risk that large segments of the population will remain marginalized. This situation has prompted calls for targeted interventions to complement the role of the market as an engine of technological advancement and economic development (UNDP 2001). However, there are several concerns as to the relevance and impact of ICT-based interventions. These include lack of quantitative analyses of the impact and the cost efficiency of ICT in many areas, including the provision of public goods and services. As a result, best practices in these areas are largely anecdotal, causing a need for more rigorous studies to ensure that ICT-based interventions are both justified and properly applied.

The analysis in this chapter is effectively a call for further country-specific, multidisciplinary research on the role of ICT for pro-poor provision of public goods and services. Principal issues to be investigated include (a) balancing ICT capacity building with economic and employment opportunities to counter brain drain; (b) balancing technological change and the preservation of cultural heritage, given that technology transfer inevitably encompasses cultural differences; (c) how ICT can be used to empower poor people and poor communities and underpin the growth of democracy; and (d) how ICT equates with sustainable development, thereby offering opportunities across different sectors, generating positive externalities.

Appendix 6A: Supplementary Tables

TABLE 6A.1 Countries included in the life expectancy regressions

Argentina	Ghana*	Malawi	Paraguay*
Bangladesh*	Guyana*	Mauritania	Peru*
Brazil*	Honduras*	Mauritius	Philippines*
Burundi*	Hungary*	Mongolia	Rwanda*
Chile*	India*	Morocco*	Sri Lanka*
Colombia*	Indonesia*	Nepal*	Swaziland*
Costa Rica*	Jamaica*	Nicaragua*	Thailand*
Dominican Republic*	Jordan*	Niger*	Trinidad and Tobago*
Ecuador*	Lesotho*	Pakistan*	Uganda*
Egypt*	Madagascar*	Panama*	Zimbabwe*

SOURCE: Primary survey data (2000).

NOTE: *Indicates that the country is also included in the 2SLS regression.

TABLE 6A.2 Countries included in the child mortality regressions

Argentina	Guyana*	Mauritania*	Philippines*
Bangladesh*	Honduras*	Mauritius	Sri Lanka*
Burundi*	Hungary*	Morocco*	Swaziland*
Chile*	India*	Nepal*	Thailand*
Colombia*	Indonesia*	Nicaragua*	Trinidad and Tobago*
Costa Rica*	Jamaica*	Niger*	Uganda*
Dominican Republic*	Jordan*	Pakistan*	Zimbabwe*
Ecuador*	Lesotho	Panama*	
Egypt*	Madagascar*	Paraguay*	
Ghana*	Malawi	Peru*	

SOURCE: Primary survey data (2000).

NOTE: *Indicates that the country is also included in the 2SLS regression.

TABLE 6A.3 Distribution of monthly medical and telecommunications expenditure by quintile per head, Laos

Quintile of total expenditure per head	All households				Households that use the telephone			
	Total expenditure per head (kips)	Share of medical expenditure (percent)	Share of telecom expenditure (percent)	Share of households (percent)	Total expenditure per head (kips)	Share of medical expenditure (percent)	Share of telecom expenditure (percent)	Share of households (percent)
I	70,568	7.89	0.61	68.73	101,534	7.05	2.77	61.67
II	174,585	6.16	1.31	24.91	223,340	5.79	2.43	29.44
III	302,628	10.53	2.11	4.00	396,134	4.91	0.61	6.11
IV	419,179	2.48	0.51	1.45	596,278	0.91	7.53	1.67
V	572,195	1.08	4.57	0.91	767,250	6.53	3.00	1.11
Total	122,008	7.40	0.88	100.00	171,045	6.44	2.62	100.00

SOURCE: Primary survey data (2000).

NOTES: The total number of households for which data on total expenditure were available is 550 (excluding five observations for which the value of total expenditure exceeded the mean by more than five standard deviations). The number of households that used telephone services for which data on total expenditure were available is 180 (excluding one observation for which the value of total expenditure exceeded the mean by five standard deviations).

TABLE 6A.4 Distribution of yearly medical and telecommunications expenditure by expenditure quintile per head, Bangladesh

Expenditure quintile per head	All households				Households that use the telephone			
	Total expenditure per head (taka)	Share of medical expenditure (percent)	Share of telecom expenditure (percent)	Share of households (percent)	Total expenditure per head (taka)	Share of medical expenditure (percent)	Share of telecom expenditure (percent)	Share of households (percent)
I	9,216	5.17	0.87	75.71	14,907	6.23	4.68	74.41
II	25,900	5.60	3.73	18.93	39,604	1.52	1.84	16.28
III	42,550	8.66	1.68	2.14	76,997	0.57	0.63	5.81
IV	61,838	1.34	3.28	1.79	119,000	0.70	0.00	1.16
V	84,300	1.55	0.15	1.43	137,501	4.38	5.27	2.33
Total	15,101	5.21	1.46	100.00	26,599	5.03	3.94	100.00

SOURCE: Primary survey data (2000).

NOTES: The total number of households for which data on total expenditure were available is 280 (excluding four observations for which the value of total expenditure exceeded the mean by more than five standard deviations). The number of households that used telephone services for which data on total expenditure were available is 86.

TABLE 6A.5 Distribution of yearly medical and telecommunications expenditure by quintile per head, Peru

Expenditure quintile per head	All households				Households that use the telephone			
	Total expenditure per head (nuevos soles)	Share of medical expenditure (percent)	Share of telecom expenditure (percent)	Share of households (percent)	Total expenditure per head (nuevos soles)	Share of medical expenditure (percent)	Share of telecom expenditure (percent)	Share of households (percent)
I	2,045	0.77	0.73	83.45	2,269	0.77	0.91	82.79
II	7,515	1.22	0.49	11.91	8,310	2.00	0.44	12.34
III	13,028	2.83	0.34	2.83	14,257	1.06	0.34	2.74
IV	19,036	1.30	0.36	1.21	20,465	0.13	0.63	1.50
V	24,206	0.03	0.73	0.61	27,060	0.04	0.12	0.62
Total	3,347	0.89	0.69	100.00	3,770	0.91	0.83	100.00

SOURCE: Primary survey (1999).

NOTES: The total number of households for which data on total expenditure were available is 991 (excluding eight observations for which the value of total expenditure exceeded the mean by more than five standard deviations). The number of households that used telephone services for which data on total expenditure were available is 802 (excluding five observations for which the value of total expenditure exceeded the mean by more than five standard deviations).

References

Andersen, R., and L. Brenham. 1970. Factors affecting the relationship between family income and medical care consumption. In *Empirical studies in health economics,* H. Klarman, ed. Baltimore: Johns Hopkins University Press.

Bayes, A., J. von Braun, and R. Akhter. 1999. Village pay phones and poverty reduction: Insights from a Grameen Bank initiative in Bangladesh. ZEF Discussion Papers on Development Policy No. 8. Bonn: Center for Development Research.

Bourdet, Y. 2000. *The economic transformation in Laos: From socialism to ASEAN integration.* Cheltenham, UK: Edward Elgar.

Corrigan, P., and P. Joyce. 2000. Reconnecting to the public. *Urban Studies* 37 (10): 1771–1779.

Deaton, A. 2001. Health, inequality, and economic development. CMH Working Paper Series No. WG1:3.

DOI (Digital Opportunity Initiative). 2001. *Creating a development dynamic.* <www .opt-init.org>.

Easterlin, R. A. 1974. Does economic growth improve the human lot? In *Nations and households in economic growth,* P. A. David and M. W. Reder, eds. New York: Academic Press.

Graham, C., and C. Kane. 1998. Opportunistic government or sustaining reform: Electoral trends and public expenditure pattern in Peru, 1990–95. *Latin American Research Review* 33 (1): 71–111.

Gupta, S., M. Verhoeven, and T. Erwin. 1999. Does higher government spending buy better results in education and health care? Working Paper No. 99/21. Washington, D.C.: International Monetary Fund.

Heckman, J. 1979. Sample selection bias as a specification error. *Econometrica* 47: 153–161.

Hirschman, A. O. 1973. Changing tolerance for income inequality in the course of economic development. *Quarterly Journal of Economics* 87 (4): 544–566.

Hojman, D. E. 1996. Economic and other determinants of infant and child mortality in small developing countries: The Case of Central America and the Caribbean. *Applied Economics* 28 (March): 281–290.

ITU (International Telecommunications Union). 2002. *World telecommunication indicators.* Geneva.

McMahon, C., and C. Bruce. 2002. Information literacy needs of local staff in cross-cultural development projects. *Journal of International Development* 14 (1): 113–127.

Musgrove, P. 1996. Public and private roles in health: Theory and financing patterns. Discussion Paper No. 339. Washington, D.C.: World Bank.

Schultz, T. P. 1993. Mortality decline in the low-income world: Causes and consequence. Economic Growth Center Discussion Paper No. 681. New Haven, Conn., U.S.A.: Yale University.

Sheehan, M. O'M. 2002. From Rio to Johannesburg: Urban governance—Thinking globally, acting locally. World Summit Policy Briefs No. 11. Washington, D.C.: Worldwatch Institute.

Torero, M. 2000. The access and welfare impacts of telecommunications technology in Peru. Discussion Papers on Development Policy No. 27. Bonn: Center for Development Research (ZEF).

UNDP. 2001. Human development report. <www.undp.org>. New York.

WHO (World Health Organization). <www.who.int/en/> (accessed 2002).

World Bank. 1997. *LAO PDR Public expenditure review—Improving efficiency and equity in spending priorities.* Report No. 16094-LA. Washington, D.C.

———. 1999. *Poverty and social developments in Peru, 1994–97.* Washington, D.C.

———. 2002. World development indicators 2000. <https://publications.worldbank.org/register/WDI?return%5furl=%2fextop%2fsubscriptions%2fWDI%2f> (accessed December 2002).

———. 2003. *World development report 2004. Making services work for the poor people.* Washington, D.C.: World Bank and Oxford University Press.

7 Conclusions and Implications for Policy and Research

MAXIMO TORERO AND JOACHIM VON BRAUN

The significant spillovers and positive externalities associated with the proliferation of information and communication technologies (ICT) potentially influence all aspects of development through its effects on governance, markets,
media, and public services. Arguably, ICT's most far-reaching development
impact is its role as the virtual backbone of globalization, providing access to
knowledge, finance, labor, and trade. While globalization would have been
possible without the assistance of modern ICT, it would have been far less permanent, and less integrated.

Despite these great potentials, however, the opportunities of the digital age
are not equally accessible, and—as this book has highlighted—poor people
have been left behind. This is not to say that poor constituents are passively for-
going ICT, however. The demand—and at times the struggle—for access by poor
people is accelerating in many countries. Lack of exploitation of the opportunities that ICT holds for the developing world applies to both the public and private sectors, as well as at the community and household levels.

The evolution of ICT-related development policy can best be described as
erratic. It has followed the ups and downs of the political economy, with technological innovation triggering institutional change and policy action. At the
time when ICT opportunities unfolded in the 1970s and 1980s, the need to
create an environment that included developing countries—and especially poor
people and those in remote areas—was not recognized. Official development
cooperation came too late; basic needs (food, health, education) were perhaps
defined too narrowly, neglecting the information needs of the poor; and the public sector shifted its focus from elementary infrastructure, such as electricity
and telecommunications, toward decentralization.

Yet, it is also possible that this delay and neglect in developing countries prevented a repetition of what happened in industrialized countries: misallocation
of funding, early overinvestment in inappropriate ICT, and subsequent melt-
down. Political recognition and action began in the 1990s, as evidenced by the
Okinawa Charter, the Digital Opportunity Task Force of G8 (DOT Force), various United Nations initiatives, and regional and national programs. The challenge

remains, however, to link these broad-based, top-down initiatives with innumer-able small public and private efforts.

Four priority actions were identified by DOT Force as necessary pre-conditions for a development dynamic: (1) fostering policy to ensure regulatory and network readiness; (2) improving connectivity to increase access and lower costs; (3) building human capacity; and (4) encouraging participation in global e-commerce and other e-networks. Moreover, to accomplish these aims, nine points were established under DOT Force's Genoa Plan of Action.[1] Such action largely requires country-level initiatives and, increasingly, public–private part-nerships, including businesses and nongovernmental organizations (NGOs).

We began this book with five critical hypotheses from a clearly skeptical perspective, to challenge the authors and readers and to assess progress made toward realizing the priorities identified in development policy under initiatives like DOT Force. In the following discussion, which at this stage is limited to overarching issues, we revisit these hypotheses, focusing on the findings pre-sented in the previous five chapters.

1. *No clear link exists between ICT growth and economic growth; a key factor may be the lack of a critical mass.* In assessing the potential for ICT to promote economic growth in developing countries, a central question remains to be answered: Has a causal relationship definitely been established, or are other factors involved?

Estimates for 113 countries over a 20-year period show a positive link be-tween telecommunications infrastructure and income as well as between tele-communications infrastructure and GDP. The estimates suggest that a 1 percent increase in the telecommunications penetration rate might be expected to lead to a 0.03 percent increase in GDP. At the same time our models for different country groups revealed a nonlinear effect of telecommunications infrastruc-ture on economic output. The impact was particularly pronounced for lower and higher middle income countries but muted for other country groups. These re-sults imply that telecommunications networks need to reach a critical mass for a discernible impact on economic output to result. In particular, growth effects were found to be strongest in areas with telecommunications penetration rates of 5–15 percent. Above and below this threshold, growth effects were limited. Moreover, given that as of 2000 the average telecommunications penetration rate in low-income countries was below 1 percent, significant network investment

---

1. The action points are "(1) support development of national e-strategies; (2) improve connectivity, increase access, and lower costs; (3) enhance human capacity development, knowl-edge creation and sharing; (4) foster enterprise, jobs and entrepreneurship; (5) strengthen univer-sal participation in global ICT governance; (6) establish a dedicated LDC [less-developed country] initiative for ICT-inclusion; (7) ICT for healthcare and support against disease; (8) support local content and application development; and (9) prioritize the contribution of ICTs in Development Assistance Programs" (DOT Force 2001).

and expansion is needed before ICT can begin to affect growth. Marginal improvements in telecommunications infrastructure are unlikely to yield any discernible growth effects. This implies that other forms of ICT—with even lower levels of penetration in low-income countries—will require even more widespread investment and expansion if ICT-induced growth is to occur.

But can low-income countries, and especially their small- and medium-sized enterprises (SMEs), actually rebound sufficiently from such a slow beginning in terms of ICT investment, infrastructure, adoption, and adaptation? Can the necessary critical mass of ICT be achieved in small business sectors to enable tangible network externalities to unfold, and can network coverage be expanded sufficiently to maximize the net benefits of ICT-enhanced public service delivery? Certainly the relative benefits for developing countries—compared with industrialized countries—are impressive, but so far the absolute benefits of ICT, mainly represented by fixed line phones, remain disappointing. Although technological innovations, such as cellular telephones and wireless broadband access, seem to be playing an important role in building ICT levels globally, strong inequality remains within developing countries, especially between urban and rural areas, where the digital divide continues to widen.

Network externalities are critical to the concept of ICT-induced growth. By its very nature, ICT has the potential to reduce relative inequalities among countries and regions. This can be seen across countries, where levels of inequality differ, where "leapfrogging" sometimes occurs—but sometimes does not, and where the impacts of ICT and its associated network externalities are not yet reaching poor countries, and especially poor areas within countries. These different outcomes are largely determined, along with public action, by institutional arrangements affecting regulation and effective privatization. There is also the question of whether, from the supply side (where both technologies and service provision are concentrated in developed countries), the appropriate technologies are being provided and at affordable cost. Could this be another cause of restricted access in poor countries?

2. Weak institutions block effective use of ICT. This hypothesis has been validated in each of the preceding chapters. ICT cannot be developed without strong institutions that overtly facilitate private investment. Many of the national telecommunications monopolies in developing countries were privatized in the 1980s and 1990s, introducing them to competition.[2] This stimulus, combined

---

2. Privatization and increased competition in telecommunications was further stimulated by commitments negotiated at the Uruguay Round of the General Agreement on Tariffs and Trade (GATT), now administered by the World Trade Organization (WTO). Initially the commitments only affected value-added services, but, as of November 1998, 89 WTO members included basic telecommunications services in their schedules of commitments. The WTO Agreement on Basic Telecommunications Services (ABTS) is a far-reaching multilateral trade agreement requiring signatories to liberalize their telecommunications sectors and adhere to WTO rules. Although significant

with ongoing technological change, prompted the constant development of new services—a shift that was reflected in some developing countries and especially with the exponential increase of cellular telephone penetration in poor countries. But this has not occurred in all countries; in some, the stimulus is taking effect slowly, erratically, and with uncertainty. For example, in some nations (such as Argentina, Chile, Peru, Mozambique, Senegal, and Uganda), the government is facilitating rapid ICT progress through institutional innovations with the help of NGOs and the private sector. In others (such as Cameroon, Congo, North Korea, Ethiopia, and Zimbabwe), the government stands in the way of reform. Within countries, the inequality is even greater, but the lesson for reducing unequal access seems clear: there is a need to differentiate market efficiency gaps from true access gaps (effectively, missing markets), and then for governments to respond with the appropriate set of interventions for each case.[3]

With a market efficiency gap, a difference exists between what markets are achieving under current conditions and what they could achieve were markets working correctly. The first step, and the focus for government in correcting this kind of gap, is to increase service provision by facilitating effective competition through market-oriented policies and regulations that create a level playing field for the private sector and new entrants. The only questions relate to how far the market can reach commercially, and how best to implement and sequence more competitive conditions. Institutions have a crucial role to play here in realizing the potential for market development. This will require strong, autonomous, and capable regulatory agencies that can (a) assure market competition and freedom of business, including technology, choice; (b) provide attractive licenses designed to encourage growth, (c) apply the minimum of regulations necessary, and (d) in particular, promote cost-effective access charges for new entrants (Wellenius and Torero 2004). These types of regulatory institutions are hard to build, especially because local expertise in the area is lacking. Professionals need to be trained in every aspect.

With a true access gap, on the other hand, public intervention in ICT provision is still required for some areas and population groups that would not be served, even under the most optimal, efficient, and liberalized market conditions. Certain people and locations invariably lie beyond market limits; in

---

differences in the commitments of developing and industrialized countries are evident, emerging economies are about five times more likely to have maintained limitations on telecommunications service supplier numbers than industrialized countries, on average, and almost four times more likely to require that particular types of legal entities be established to provide services. Developing economies are also nearly three times more likely to have included additional measures, often involving requirements to use monopoly network facilities (or restrictions on bypassing them), restrictions on the resale of excess capacity of leased circuits, or prohibitions against interconnection with other leased circuits by the suppliers concerned. Limits on foreign equity participation, however, are similar in emerging and industrialized economies.

3. The conceptual framework of the two gaps is developed in Navas, Dymond, and Juntunen (2002).

such cases, service provision requires the mobilization of additional investment—for example, involving public–private (or NGO) partnerships—whereby the government induces service provision through incentives like subsidies. But what are the optimal mechanisms for implementing subsidies to maximize scale economies and production, consumption, and network externalities, while achieving sustainability? In this respect there are three main lessons: (a) bottom-up identification of demand and consumer willingness-to-pay, (b) recognition of the importance of market competition in allocating subsidies, as well as a clear, stable, and credible legal and regulatory environment, and (c) the need for a (sectoral and general business) framework that enables prospective service providers to estimate costs and revenues realistically, and thereby accurately assess their risk (Wellenius and Torero 2004).

3. *ICT has not been adapted to low-income countries and no impact is seen on SMEs.* While adaptation has been slow, the benefits of ICT are now beginning to accrue for SMEs. The SME case studies in this book provide substantial evidence of increased ICT adoption in low-income countries and positive ICT impacts on SME performance. Nevertheless, the need for further data collection over longer time periods is also evident. Such data—and panel data in particular—should focus on SMEs, and on eliminating any doubt as to a causal relationship between the profusion of ICT and economic and social benefits in developing countries and regions. Our results confirm a positive correlation between ICT access and improved SME performance; where panel data were available for analysis, such as for Laos, the relationship seems quite strong.

4. *Household access to ICT remains constrained.* The reduction of the information gap at lower costs is of central importance for the poor. As was shown in Chapter 5, despite restricted rural access, it is fair to say that ICT has an important positive impact on rural households. The welfare effect of rural telephone use is verified by the perceptions of rural users of its benefits, the high demand for service, the substantial consumer surplus associated with telephone use, the willingness to pay for service on the part of rural households, and results from econometric analyses. These positive effects can be expanded by increasing rural service access, adapting new technologies to rural settings, and using existing technologies—such as those provided by telephone—more innovatively.

Some policy problems remain, however, in both SMEs and households. First, most case studies reveal that there is still insufficient competition in telecommunications resulting from lack of private-sector participation because of major regulatory impediments. Consequently, access costs are too high, interconnection between networks is problematic, and infrastructure cannot be shared among operators. Second, a number of potential barriers to the effectiveness of ICT remain. Aside from the provision of facilities and technical support, these include sociocultural factors, which are likely to be important in the success of

ICT interventions for development in terms of adoption and community outcomes. Apart from issues of access and price, barriers to ICT effectiveness fall into three principal categories: barriers involving skill levels, such as in accessing Internet information; barriers involving ICT use for development-related purposes; and barriers related to content relevance. These factors have the potential to influence the rate of adoption and the degree to which available Internet information reaches individuals in the community. Given these barriers, rural ICT expansion may require complementary measures, such as computer and Internet skills training, web pages designed to direct users to locally relevant content, or access that targets specific groups, such as youth, who may experience fewer sociocultural barriers when it comes to ICT use. In many low-income-country contexts, access to telephones is the basis of pro-poor ICT growth because specialized skills are not needed and because telephone access forms a platform for more advanced ICT adoption.

Finally, with respect to the cost barriers, it will be important to learn from existing models; public Internet access, for example, provides efficient, low-cost access to multiple users, both at the SME and household levels. This business model could be modified to suit a dual broadband strategy, promoting both the deployment of wireless broadband networks (for example, through full spectrum licensing for this purpose), and the adoption of voice telephony applications targeted to low-income users (for example, by fully deregulating the voice over Internet protocol [VOIP]).

5. *ICT has yet to play a role in the provision of pro-poor public goods and services.* ICT can be a powerful tool for improving the quality and efficiency of government services, such as health and education, although a clear gap still exists in the use of ICT for the delivery of public goods. The cross-country analysis presented in Chapter 6 indicates that telecommunications investment may well be associated with improved health status. This result is validated by a number of worldwide case studies that show evidence of the potential of ICT to influence health outcomes in rural areas. Prominent applications for health include the creation of "telemedicine" centers, such as those installed in Alto Amazonas, Peru, and Andhra Pradesh, India, offering low-cost medical advice to rural inhabitants via email through hospitals; and those in Sub-Saharan Africa, where health information is provided to remote communities via the Internet. Finally, ICT has been used to design global telecommunications networks, such as HealthNet, which links healthcare workers around the world via email, and related AIDS prevention activities, such as the ProCAARE discussion forum and the WorldSpace Foundation (WSF)–Africare HIV/AIDS initiative.

Successes in the use of ICT for educational purposes also exist, such as the African Virtual University, the distance learning university in India, the development of e-government applications to strengthen the rights and powers of poor people and communities, and the use of the Internet to disseminate information on farming technologies and changing prices to 30,000 villages across six states in India.

These are isolated cases at this stage, however. Poor people are still excluded from many public services, and ICT has not been adapted to the appropriate delivery of pro-poor public goods in general. On the whole, as stated above, ICT is still developed by and marketed in high-income countries, and innovation and adaptation are not occurring in low-income countries because institutions and markets lack the required capacity. Hence a large portion of the population continues to be marginalized and the need remains for innovative ways to provide access to public services using ICT. The strong link perceived to exist between ICT attributes and the Millennium Development Goals (MDGs) reflects this reality.[4] Successfully harnessing the power of ICT could make a substantial contribution to achieving the MDGs, both directly, through the delivery of public services, and indirectly, through the creation of new economic opportunities.

In summary, existing political recognition and development objectives—as evidenced by the Okinawa Charter; the DOT Force; various United Nations initiatives, including the MDGs; and regional and national programs—point in the right direction, but neither the path nor the destination is clear. These initiatives must identify more specific action plans and then closely monitor and evaluate their impact. Currently, most initiatives have action plans implying global subsidies that do not result in clear targeted outputs for poverty reduction. For example, just considering the delivery of public goods and services to address health and promote education implies important actions requiring the coordination of international aid within the institutional framework of each country involved. Targeted subsidies should be generated to create common pool resources for just these two highly important areas, so that costs can be minimized and ICT-related network externalities maximized.

ICT is an opportunity for development, but not a panacea. For the potential benefits of ICT to be realized in developing countries many prerequisites need to be put in place, as identified throughout this book: prompt deregulation, effective competition among service providers, free movement and adoption of technologies, targeted and competitive subsidies to reduce the real access gap,

---

4. The MDGs are (1) reducing the proportion of people living in extreme poverty by half between 1990 and 2015; (2) reducing hunger by half by 2015; (3) enrolling all children in primary school by 2015; (4) making progress toward eliminating gender inequality and empowering women by eliminating gender disparities in primary and secondary school education by 2005; (5) reducing infant and child mortality ratios by three-quarters between 1990 and 2015; (6) providing access to all who need reproductive health services by 2015; (7) and implementing national strategies for sustainable development by 2005 so as to reverse the loss of environmental resources by 2015 (United Nations 2000).

and institutional arrangements to increase the use of ICT in the provision of public goods. Given the diverse potential benefits of ICT, especially in the provision of public goods, subsidies traditionally used for poverty alleviation could be adapted to create incentives for the use of ICT. For example, conditional cash transfer programs,[5] which are largely tied to education or health, could be implemented at the community level to provide Internet access to children where educational and health services are delivered. At the same time, such programs would contribute to the necessary critical mass of ICT previously discussed.

In addition, it is necessary to learn from the positive results on access to cellular telephones in poor countries, as is illustrated by the boom in cellular use in Africa. Competition prompted operators to sell air time in smaller (and hence less expensive) units through a prepaid card system, even though the cost per minute was actually higher. The service offers a viable alternative to poor households whose use is comparatively low and who need greater flexibility in managing their livelihood security.

As mentioned at the beginning of this book, access to information through ICT is not only a question of *connectivity* but also of *capability* to use the new tools and relevant *content* provided in accessible and useful forms. Connectivity has been a priority, as a prerequisite for the other two, but given the speed at which technologies are evolving and assuming they are allowed to move freely—unconstrained by overly restrictive licenses and global patenting—costs could fall significantly, facilitating adoption. Hence, we should not overlook the need for all three "Cs" to progress in tandem.

References

DOT Force (Digital Opportunity Task Force of G8). 2001. DOT Force: Review—The Genoa Plan of Action. <www.ictdevagenda.org/frame.php?dir=07&sd=10&sid=1&id=49> (accessed May 2005).

Navas-Sabater, J., A. Dymond, and N. Juntunen. 2002. Telecommunications & information services for the poor: Toward a strategy for universal access. World Bank Discussion Paper No. 432. Washington, D.C.: World Bank.

Wellenius, B., and M. Torero. 2004. Peru: Marginal-urban and rural telecommunications development. Chapter 5 in OSPITEL telecommunications capacity-building technical assistance project: Report for tasks 1–6, vol. 1. Washington, D.C.: Clifford Chance. <http://rru.worldbank.org/documents/PapersLinks/osiptel.pdf> (accessed 2005).

United Nations. 2000. Millennium development goals. <www.un.org/millenniumgoals> (accessed May 2005).

---

5. Conditional cash transfer programs provide money to poor people on the condition that they invest in their children's human capital, for example, in terms of school attendance or regular use of preventive healthcare services. Such programs are relatively new but are becoming more prevalent.

Glossary of ICT Terminology

Cellular telephone concession	A contract for service assigned by the government (through the relevant administrative body) to telecommunications service providers; concessions are usually awarded through a competitive process.
Fault rate	The number of times a line fails.
Fixed telephone lines	Telephone lines that connect a customer's (government, business, or residential) equipment (telephone set, facsimile machine, or computer) to the public switched telephone network (PSTN) and that have a dedicated port on a telephone exchange. In most countries, fixed (main) lines also include public payphones.
ICT	Information and communications technologies. The application of modern communications and computing technologies to the creation, management, and use of information.
Internet user	A dial-up, leased-line, or broadband (DSL, cable modem, or other broadband) Internet subscriber.
IP	Internet Protocol. IP was originally designed for data networking. The success of IP in becoming a world standard for data networking has led to its adaptation for voice networking.
ISDN	Integrated Services Digital Network. A tele-communications standard for the transmission of digital information over ordinary telephone lines, and the name for the digital telephone network. The network contains channels for digitized speech, data, images, or video signals.

ISP   Internet service provider. An organization with
                        a direct connection to the Internet acting as an
                        intermediary for other users, providing them with
                        an email address and software, access to the
                        worldwide web, and often space on web servers
                        for home pages, web sites, and the like.

LAN   Local area network. A communications system
                        linking computers within a restricted geographic
                        area such as a building or a campus. A LAN also
                        allows computers to share information from a
                        central source.

Leapfrogging   Advanced technologies that allow countries to
  technologies   bypass many, if not most, of the incremental stages
                        of technology development.

Penetration rate   *See* teledensity.

Teledensity
  Cellular teledensity Number of cellular phone subscribers per 100
                        inhabitants.
  Fixed line teledensity Number of fixed telephone lines per 100 inhabitants.
  Internet teledensity Number of Internet users per 100 inhabitants.

USO   Universal service obligation. A common goal as a
                        national communications policy, under which all
                        the inhabitants of a country have access to a tele-
                        phone line, regardless of the cost of providing it.

Universal access   In contrast to universal service obligation, the
                        household-level definition of access prevalent in
                        industrialized countries, a policy of universal
                        access seeks to ensure access at a "reasonable"
                        level, such as at the community level.

VOIP   Voice over Internet protocol. The transmission of
                        voice traffic over IP-based networks.

Contributors

Abdul Bayes (abdulbayes@yahoo.com) is professor of economics and former vice-chancellor of Jahangirnagar University, Bangladesh. In the past, he has worked as a research fellow with the Center for Development Research (ZEF), Bonn, and as a consultant with the International Rice Research Institute (IRRI) in the Philippines. Bayes's research focuses primarily on agriculture and rural development. He is currently collaborating with IFPRI on research related to high-value agriculture.

Arjun S. Bedi (bedi@iss.nl) is an associate professor at the Institute of Social Studies in the Netherlands. His areas of interest are human capital investments and returns, child labor and education, information technology and economic development, and economic reforms and changes in sociocultural practices in India. He has published several articles in international economics and development journals. Before joining the ISS he held positions at the University of Bonn and Columbia University. He holds economics degrees from St. Stephen's College, Delhi University, and Tulane University, New Orleans.

Romeo Bertolini (Romeo.Bertolini@bmz.bund.de) studied economic geography in Germany and the United Kingdom before joining the Department of Economic and Technological Change at the Center for Development Research (ZEF), University of Bonn. Particular foci of his research and consultancy work at ZEF were the digital divide as well as assessment of the use of information and communication technologies at the level of rural households and micro-enterprises in least-developed countries. He then joined the strategy and management department of DETECON GmbH in Bonn, dealing with international consultancies in the field of telecommunications regulation and ICT policy. He currently works for the German Federal Ministry for Economic Cooperation and Development.

Shyamal K. Chowdhury (s.chowdhuru@cgiar.org) has been working on the role institutions and infrastructure play in market development as a member of

IFPRI's Markets, Trade, and Institutions Division. He is currently working on institutional design to rationalize power subsidies in Andhra Pradesh and Punjab in India, on the impact of infrastructure on rural households in Bangladesh, and on vertical arrangements in food value chains in developing countries. Prior to joining IFPRI, he worked for the Global Development Network in Washington, D.C., and the Center for Development Research at Bonn University. A citizen of Bangladesh, he earned a B.Sc. in economics from Jahangirnagar University in Dhaka, an M.A. in economics from Kiel University, and a Ph.D. in agriculture economics from Bonn University.

Virgilio Galdo (virgiliog@iadb.org) worked in the Research Department of the Inter-American Development Bank (IADB) on topics related to privatization, institutions, and labor retrenchment before joining the Office of Evaluation and Oversight (OVE) at the IADB. Previously he was affiliated with Grupo de Análisis para el Desarrollo (GRADE), a nonpartisan think tank based in Lima. He is currently working on topics related to the evaluation of social investment projects. He holds a B.A in economics from the Pontificia Universidad Católica del Perú and is pursuing his Ph.D. studies in economics at Michigan State University.

Kaushalesh Lal (lal@intech.unu.edu) is affiliated with UNU-INTECH. His area of specialization is the diffusion of information and communication technology (ICT) in developing countries. He has published several research papers on the causes and consequences of the adoption of ICT in small and medium-size enterprises. His research interests include the role of institutional, legal, and technological infrastructure in the transformation of business activities into e-business. He is also studying the problems and prospects of open-source software, particularly in developing countries. Before joining UNU-INTECH, Dr. Lal was associate professor at the Institute of Economic Growth, Delhi, India. He obtained his M.Sc. in physics from Kanpur University, his M.Sc. in operations research from the University of Delhi, and his Ph.D. from Erasmus University Rotterdam, The Netherlands.

Francis A. S. T. Matambalya (trisp@fcm.udms.ac.tz) is a professor in the Faculty of Commerce and Management at the University of Dar es Salaam, Tanzania. He is also the lead researcher in the Trade and Integration Studies Programme (TRISP) and a promoter of the professional master of science degree in trade policy management.

Maja Micevska (m.micevska@uni-bonn.de) is a senior fellow at the Center for Development Research (ZEF), University of Bonn, and a senior researcher at the Economic and Social Research Center (ESCE), Cologne and Eisenstadt. She received her Ph.D. in economics from Claremont Graduate University. Her main fields of research are development economics, labor economics, population economics, and information technologies. She has been engaged in several large-scale projects, with particular focus on Central and Eastern European countries.

Dietrich Mueller-Falcke (dietrich.mueller-falcke@telekom.de) worked intensively on ICT for development while at the Center for Development Research (ZEF), University of Bonn, and Detecon, an international telecommunications consultancy. He specialized in the effects of ICTs on small businesses and was engaged in primary research in different countries and regions. Currently he works in the Strategic Financial Planning Department of Deutsche Telekom. He is a trained economist with degrees from the University of Goettingen.

Gi-Soon Song (gisoon.song@undp.org), after receiving her M.A. in international commerce from the Graduate School of International Studies of Korea University, joined the Center for Development Research (ZEF), University of Bonn, as a research fellow. She obtained her Ph.D. from Bonn University. Since joining UNDP Indonesia, she has advised UNDP and partner organizations and managed programs in ICT for development issues.

Maximo Torero (m.torero@cgiar.org) is a research fellow in the Markets, Trade, and Institutions Division of the International Food Policy Research Institute. His research primarily focuses on poverty, inequality, the importance of geography and private/public assets in relation to poverty, and policies aimed at poverty alleviation. His particular expertise is in the ICT sector. His activities in this sector can be divided into three categories: regulation of telephony services; estimation of demand for telecommunications services; and access and use of available information and telecommunications technologies in urban and rural areas. He has collaborated closely with regulatory agencies to develop models on the functioning of the telecommunications industry that support the agency's regulation efforts and simulate demand (residential and commercial) for telecommunication services in order to evaluate the impact of different rate schedules. He holds a Ph.D. in economics from the University of California, Los Angeles.

Joachim von Braun (j.vonbraun@cgiar.org) is the director general of the International Food Policy Research Institute in Washington, D.C. He has worked in developing countries for many years and is known for his work on food security and mitigating and preventing famines. Von Braun has published widely in his various areas of expertise, including food trade and market reforms, the economics of biodiversity and biotechnology in low-income countries, and the relationship of development to governance, information and communications, and employment. Prior to taking up his current role in 2002, he was director of the Center for Development Research (ZEF), University of Bonn, which he helped to found in 1997.

Wensheng Wang (wangwsh@caas.net.cn) is the director of the Network Center for the Chinese Academy of Agricultural Sciences. He studied computer science and applications at the University of Science and Technology of China and Harbin Shipbuilding Engineering College, and agricultural economics at China Agricultural University, before joining the Department of Economic and Technological Change at the Center for Development Research (ZEF), University of Bonn. He received his doctoral degree in agricultural economics from the University of Bonn.

Susanna Wolf (swolf@uneca.org) is a member of the Economic and Social Policy Division of the UN Economic Commission for Africa. She is responsible for writing reports and organizing conferences on various topics, ranging from private sector development and the effects of globalization on employment in Africa to capital flows and current account sustainability. Prior to assuming her current position, she worked for the Center for Development Research (ZEF), University of Bonn, as a research fellow in the Department of Economics and Technological Change. Her research focused on the relationships between the EU and Africa, including aid, trade, and investment, as well as the role of ICT in development and the competitiveness of small and medium-size enterprises. She was an Alexander von Humboldt Fellow in the Department of Agricultural Economics and Agribusiness, University of Ghana, Legon, where she carried out research on private sector development.

Index

Page numbers for entries occurring in figures are followed by an *f;* those for entries occurring in notes, by an *n;* and those for entries occurring in tables, by a *t.*

351